Sacral Grooves, Limbo Gateways

EST. 75 1938
YEARS
THE UNIVERSITY OF GEORGIA PRESS 2013

Sacral Grooves, Limbo Gateways

Travels in
Deep Southern Time,
Circum-Caribbean Space,
Afro-creole Authority

KEITH CARTWRIGHT

THE UNIVERSITY OF GEORGIA PRESS   *Athens and London*

© 2013 by the University of Georgia Press
Athens, Georgia 30602
www.ugapress.org
All rights reserved
Set in Sabon MT Pro and Whitney by Graphic Composition, Inc.
Manufactured by Thomson-Shore
The paper in this book meets the guidelines for
permanence and durability of the Committee on
Production Guidelines for Book Longevity of the
Council on Library Resources.

Printed in the United States of America
17 16 15 14 13 P 5 4 3 2 1

Library of Congress Cataloging-in-Publication Data

Cartwright, Keith, 1960–
    Sacral grooves, limbo gateways : travels in deep Southern time,
Circum-Caribbean space, Afro-creole authority / Keith Cartwright.
        pages cm. — (The new Southern studies)
Includes bibliographical references and index.
ISBN-13: 978-0-8203-4536-9 (hardcover : alkaline paper)
ISBN-10: 0-8203-4536-9 (hardcover : alkaline paper)
ISBN-13: 978-0-8203-4599-4 (paperback : alkaline paper)
ISBN-10: 0-8203-4599-7 (paperback : alkaline paper)
    1. African Americans—Southern States—Social life and customs.
2. Creoles—Southern States—Social life and customs.
3. Blacks—Caribbean Area—Social life and customs.
4. Creoles—Caribbean Area—Social life and customs.
5. Space and time—Social aspects.
6. Authority—Social aspects.
7. Southern States—Social life and customs.
8. Caribbean Area—Social life and customs.
9. American literature—Southern States—History and criticism.
10. Caribbean literature (English)—
History and criticism. I. Title.
E185.86.C327 2013
305.896'073075—dc23   2012041531

British Library Cataloging-in-Publication Data available

Contents

Acknowledgments

Bat has his head on backwards but flies just the same.
—Lukumi proverb

Parts of the introduction will appear in a different version in "To Wash Our Calabashes in the Sea of Ndayaan," in *The American South and the Atlantic World*, edited by Brian Ward, Martyn Bone, and William A. Link (University Press of Florida, 2013), reprinted with permission of the University Press of Florida. Parts of chapter 1 appeared in an earlier version in "Notes Towards a Voodoo Hermeneutics: Soul Rhythms, Marvelous Transitions, and Passages to the Creole Saints in Paule Marshall's *Praisesong for the Widow*," *Southern Quarterly* 41, no. 4 (2003): 127–43, reprinted with permission of *The Southern Quarterly*, © 2003. Parts of chapter 3 appeared in a different version in "Re-creolizing Swing: St Domingue Refugees in the Govi of New Orleans," in *Reinterpreting the Haitian Revolution and Its Cultural Aftershocks*, edited by Martin Munro and Elizabeth Walcott-Hackshaw (University of the West Indies Press, 2006), 102–22; and in "Weave a Circle Round Him Thrice: Komunyakaa's Hoodoo Balancing Act," *Callaloo* 28, no. 3 (2005), 851–63, © 2005 by Charles H. Rowell, revised and reprinted with permission of the Johns Hopkins University Press. Parts of chapter 5 appeared in an earlier version in "'To Walk with the Storm': Oya as the Transformative 'I' of Zora Neale Hurston's Afro-Atlantic Callings," *American Literature* 78, no. 4 (2006): 741–67, © 2006 by Duke University Press, reprinted by permission of Duke University Press. Material from chapter 5 is also set to appear in "'Come and Gaze on a Mystery': Oya as Rain-Bringing 'I' of Zora Neale Hurston's Atlantic Storm Walking," in *Zora Neale Hurston, Haiti, and "Their Eyes Were Watching God*," edited by La Vinia Delois Jennings (Evanston, Ill.: Northwestern University Press, 2013).

For their sharing of experience, I must thank the congregation of Mt. Calvary Baptist Church of Eulonia, Georgia, and the McIntosh County Shouters, the Hog Hammock community of Sapelo Island, Georgia, the people of New

Orleans (and especially the New Orleans hospitality of Eileen Julien, Allison Plyer, and Laura Sampson), Ilé Ocán Oñí (especially Ocán Oñí, Eguin Kolade), elders of the town Jilloor in Senegal, and especially the Diaw family of the village of Guidakhar in Senegal.

For their collegiality, support, and challenges over the years, I thank students and colleagues at Selma University, the College of Coastal Georgia (especially Michael Hannaford and LaVerne Cooper), College of the Bahamas, and Roanoke College (especially Melanie Almeder, Dolores Flores-Silva, and Virginia Stewart). My colleagues who participate in the annual Eastern Caribbean Cultures Conference, organized out of the University of Puerto Rico and UWI Cave Hill, have been invaluable to the vision and completion of this project (especially Candida Gonzalez-Lopez, Marie-Annick Gournet, ChenziRa D. Kahina, and Dannabang Kuwabong), as have the members of the Society for the Study of Southern Literature and the regular attendees of the Southern Intellectual History Circle.

Thanks to the Atlantic Studies Initiative at the University of Michigan, Cambridge University, Emory University, the Faulkner and Yoknapatawpha Conference at the University of Mississippi, Roanoke College's International Cluster, the Southern Intellectual History Circle, and Edward Waters College's Wakaguzi Forum for invitations to share this work.

Abra Nava-Billings, Barbara Ladd, John Lowe, Susan Donaldson, Nicholas Faraclas, Martin Munro, Annette Trefzer, Katie McKee, Michael Collins, Elizabeth Walcott-Hackshaw, and Raquel Gonzalez Rivas have all commented upon, and improved, various parts of this book, as have Timothy Donovan, Michael Wiley, Laura Heffernan, Harry Rothschild, and Clark Lunberry— my colleagues at the University of North Florida. I owe thanks to my past department chairpersons, Bill Slaughter and Sam Kimball, for their steady support of my work.

The University of North Florida has supported the research for this book with conference travel funding, Dean's Council grants, summer research grants, and a sabbatical.

I would like to thank my students at the University of North Florida for dialogue that has helped to improve this book. Among the students who have contributed dynamically to my thinking—whether in graduate seminars, independent studies, conference panels, or conversation outside the reach of professional hailing—I must include Raquel Gonzalez Rivas, Sonia Zamot, Sara Olsen, Ed Turner, Beth Sweet, Andrea Paxton, Allan Marcil, Urshela Atkins, Erin Hoover, Yashira Belliard, Paige Perez, Mudhurie Maharaj, and Fabielle Georges. I am especially grateful for the invocations of Floridian/ Kreyol genius (or *lwa*) that Fabielle Georges gave to this book via the illustrations that accompany each section of chapters.

For her steady patience, gracious professionalism, and real enthusiasm throughout this project, I am indebted (for a second time now) to Nancy Grayson, and I wish her the very best in pursuing new projects of her own in her retirement from the University of Georgia Press. Beth Snead and John Joerschke have kept the production process rolling smoothly. Daniel Simon's open-eyed (*hippikat*) copyediting made a tremendous difference in improving and clarifying this manuscript's presentation and easing its navigation of potentially swamping terrain. I am most thankful, too, for the insights, encouragements, and corrections offered by anonymous readers of this manuscript for the University of Georgia Press.

I must also thank my parents. Joseph Cartwright has shared his richly interrogated set of life experiences, his thoughtful assessments of the fields of southern and Atlantic history, and a humbling generosity of spirit. Pam Callaway Cartwright's steady "certain kind of way" with narrative and possibility—along with her culinary and gardening passions—has imparted its own broughtupsy to the work I do. Finally, I find that my ideas and ritual reconfigurations of reading and experience have long been married to my wife's spirited entries into sacral bush ahead of (and beyond) me. What I know of sacral grooves cannot be separated from the knowledge and travels she has shared with me. And this is true, as well, of what our son, Jesse, has shown me about music. To Maya Oshun, I offer my deepest thanks for a daughter's steady enforcement of the boat-rules on the waters and marshes around our Black Hammock Island home: no professor-pants, no professor-talk.

.

A Note on the Illustrations

All illustrations are by Fabielle M. Georges:

- *Ekose* (Shelled)
- *Zansèt* (Ancestor)
- *Oye Damballah*
- *Tòti* (Turtle)

Sacral Grooves, Limbo Gateways

To Bust Your Shell

. . . somebody got to bust your shell
—Guitar to Milkman in Toni Morrison's *Song of Solomon*

Reborn Again
Orphan Initiations, Motherless Lands

Ya mus dohn wonda wen A tell ya say, "Ya mus be bon gin."
—John 3:7, *New Testament in Gullah, Sea Island Creole*,
   American Bible Society, 2005

I say that this water is what will defeat your deliriums. I say that this water will
extinguish the nuclear fuse you train on the world. I say that this water is the voice
of humanity's future . . .
—René Depestre, *A Rainbow for the Christian West: Vaudou mystery-poem*

"Voodoo," as Hollywood and the humanities have combined to present it,
almost always seems to come from another time, another space, and from
something other than accredited authority. The pin-pricked doll. The zombie.
Frenetic drums in the distance.[1] The National Geographic Society's 2009 *Fast
Facts Book*, for instance, opens a prefatory section on religion titled "What
Is Magical Thinking?" with a striking photograph bearing the caption, "EN-
TRANCED BY THEIR BELIEFS, Haitian women engage in ritual bathing during
a pilgrimage." Readers learn that Haitian religious practice "blends magical
elements of voodoo with Christian traditions."[2] On one side of the blend we
have uppercase "Christian traditions"; on the other lie "magical elements" of
"voodoo." A few pages later a man is depicted making morning ablutions in
the Ganges River—not as an illustration of magical thinking but of ritual in a
venerated world religion. This sets the stage for a timeline of important dates
in the progress of global religion, moving from cave paintings in France to the
lives of Buddha, Christ, and Mohammad, to an endpoint in Martin Luther's
establishment of Protestantism. These facts about the world, coming from
no less an authority than the National Geographic Society, renewed my own
appreciation for that old voodoo economist, Ronald Reagan, and his famous
slip of the tongue at the 1988 Republican National Convention: "Facts are
stupid things." Reagan got this absolutely right. Imagine, for example, if National Geographic's *Fast Facts Book* had used a photograph of a Kansas girl
rising exuberantly from a baptismal font as an illustration of magical thinking. Only a group of others (blended/hybrid others) would do for a *Fast Facts*
illustration of magical thinking: distant streamside voodoo rather than one

of the American heartland's chlorinated baptismal pools. But we are all entranced by belief or ideological consensus in the face of ecological, economic, and spiritual crises sweeping the planet. And most of us know we could use a good cleansing in a river held sacred.

As we face a generalized crisis in the legitimacy of the humanities today, we should recognize that there may be good reason for such a crisis. In this study, I turn to deep southern/Caribbean rites and writings that challenge reader-responders to enter perceived cultural backwaters with a *hippi-kat* (open-eyed) reconsideration of dismissed perspectives and unaccredited gnosis.³ We can start to get our feet wet in nigh-simultaneous swampings of orientation issued by two of the Deep South's most famous novels: William Faulkner's *Absalom, Absalom!* (1936) and Zora Neale Hurston's *Their Eyes Were Watching God* (1937). Writing from the midst of Jim Crow apartheid and in the immediate aftermath of a nineteen-year military occupation of Haiti, both Faulkner and Hurston called readers into initiatory reroutings of knowledge peculiarly registerable in (post)plantation spaces but hardly limited to them. In Faulkner's Yoknapatawpha or Hurston's Okeechobee muck, such baptismal reaffiliations bring characters and readers into ideologically excluded congregations of witness and agency that prove to be not just compatible with modernity but generative of many of its profoundest countercultural forms.

"You would have to be born there," Faulkner's Mississippi-born-and-raised Harvard freshman, Quentin Compson, tells his Canadian roommate Shreve at a moment in *Absalom, Absalom!* when *there* may as likely be immersion in vortices from a suppressed past (where mothers may become fish) as any single plot of Yoknapatawpha soil.⁴ Both the Canadian co-narrator and the co-creating reader of *Absalom, Absalom!* may well get born there in unsettlingly entrancing performances. Hardly national space, not even altogether southern or spatial, this sublime *there* of requisite nativity is a kind of intertidal zone of time/space fluidity: something submerged or abject that we, like Faulkner's Quentin and Shreve, would have to "live and breathe in like air."⁵ *There*—in Quentin's (and increasingly Shreve's) backwater routes of narration via harbors of creolization in Haiti, Martinique, and Louisiana—memory of a broken and reconstructing Deep South finds novel performance authority in a Harvard dorm. Little of this, however, would have been in their curriculum.

Quentin, who has been obsessed not just with his sister's underthings but with his home space's submerged black authority ("Niggers say a drowned man's shadow was watching for him in the water all the time"), finds that there is no moving north of his region's Gulf-bound currents so often named in the language of the dispossessed—Tallahatchie, Bogue Chitto, Suwanee, Mississippi.⁶ Faulkner's readers, along with the Canadian roommate, come to the narratives that precede Quentin's suicidal plunge into the Charles River via a flood-surge of language, pushing us *there* into an initiatory gnosis from below—from what Vodou practitioners call *En-ba-dlo* (beneath the waters), where the spirits reside.[7]

"You got tuh *go* there tuh *know* there," indeed, as Zora Neale Hurston's Florida-set and Haiti-written *Their Eyes Were Watching God* testifies.[8] Her novel also immerses its primary avatar, Janie, in vernacular performance from low spaces, in storm-encounter with "monstropolous" beasts of drowning and dispossession. Hurston's readers have often resisted going there with Janie and Tea Cake Woods and their Bahamian friends into Okeechobee's muck. This fluid space of abjection is what is "radically excluded," according to Julia Kristeva, something that threatens meaning, "disturbs identity," and "does not respect borders."[9] To have to be born *there* (again) is to face an orphaning journey of self-erasure and subsequent reaffiliations of person, kinship, and relation to otherness. In response, therefore, to these Haitian-inscribed hailings of Mississippi and the Florida muck, and coming out of my own circum-Atlantic experience, *Sacral Grooves, Limbo Gateways* undertakes a set of travels or pilgrimages through Gulf and Gulf Stream waters . . . into new (but simultaneously old, long-tested) modes of consciousness.

Currents coursing through American, African American, and Southern Studies have had Americanists looking away from the nation's city on a hill, turning gazes southward—and thankfully southward still, over the waters—to reconsider an aqueous set of relations with the postplantation Caribbean, the other Americas, the Atlantic rim, and the planet at large. As a key review by Jon Smith and an essay by Lizabeth Paravisini-Gebert and Margarite Fernández Olmos have noted, the conceptual channel markers for these transcultural journeys were set out by longtime navigators of the Caribbean.[10] What has emerged—in works as vital to my project as Wilson Harris's *The Womb of Space* (1983), Paul Gilroy's *The Black Atlantic* (1993), Antonio Benítez-Rojo's *The Repeating Island* (1996), Édouard Glissant's *Poetics of Relation* (1997), Wai Chee Dimock's *Through Other Continents* (2006), Valérie Loichot's *Orphan Narratives* (2007), and Monique Allewaert's "Swamp Sublime" (2008)—is an expansion of scale beyond the space of national sovereignty and beyond the periodicities of history, literary or otherwise.[11]

Sacral Grooves, Limbo Gateways focuses on modes of Afro-creole agency shaping the Caribbean's and Deep South's long experience of a heterogeneous and unsettling modernity.[12] Although I do not ground my study in other radically excluded southern perspectives—such as those of the Choctaw or Carib—my attentiveness to the counterclockwise movement of Afro-creole hermeneutic circles has often brought me to rely on the memory guarded by various Muskogee-speaking nations (Creek, Seminole, Choctaw, and Chickasaw) to render this book's perspective. The Deep South's inhabitants share an ongoing relation to what Cherokee writer Jace Weaver has called the "psychic homicide" of Native removal, removals that expanded national investment in the normative violence of the white-supremacist plantation economy.[13] *Sacral Grooves, Limbo Gateways* points to *one* potent set of Afro-creole recognitions and treatments—to spirited countermeasures of time and space, polyrhythmic disembeddings of clock time and chronology, antiphonal loops and tangles of kinship, thickening what Wai Chee Dimock presents as "deep time" or the *longue durée*.[14] Native to a peculiarly homicidal and broken time-space, the children of African slaves in much of the circum-Caribbean grew up speaking a new language of their own invention, practicing new rites of their elders' and their own reassembly, facing new challenges to their humanity. Their African parents named these new people *criollos* (creoles), natives to a truly New World in which they served as culture brokers, guides, translators, go-betweens, pharmacists, and scapegoated others. Blacks in the New World were among the first orphan initiates and self-conscious subjects of a globalizing modernity.

To be born there—inescapably native to a broken time-space—is to retain awareness of the violent and shadow-haunted side of the sacred (registered in the range of meaning in the Latin *sacer*, from "beneficent" to "accursed"), a knowledge repressed in the triumphant sacrality of a Western Christianity intent on transcendence.[15] My title's focus on the "sacral" seeks to remind us of the sacrificial elements of the sacred, to avoid approaching the sacred through an accustomed propriety. Such a reminder is necessary because the sacred in Atlantic creole societies has been maintained in travels not only through violence and death but also through shit. Elders of Afro-Cuban *Regla de Ocha* (*Santería*), for instance, account for the arrival of the tradition's divination nuts and sacred stones in tales of these fundaments being swallowed by initiates in Africa prior to boarding the slave ships. The sacred *fundamentos* had to pass in shit in the stench of the ships if they were to foster godchildren's belief in a new world.[16] Indeed, transatlantic slavery and its afterlives subjected the enslaved to what Orlando Patterson termed "natal alienation" and "social death."[17] But as Paul Gilroy's *The Black Atlantic* has shown, a resilient "counterculture of modernity" emerged out of the most abject chattel slavery, fostering a resocializing "rapport with death" and a calling-responsive "ethics of antiphony" in grooves that recreated Africa's bush-groves of autonomous authority.[18] In the Americas, Africans and creoles tapped worn pathways of performance to reestablish the kind of sacred grove that the Nigerian divination priest Kolawole Ositola described to Margaret Thompson Drewal: "We are reborning ourselves," Ositola asserted of rites he led in his urban *igbodu* or sacred bush.[19]

Whoever would be responsible to the call of the black Atlantic's sacral grooves must come to move and read ever-more flexibly, to pass low, under what Guyanese writer Wilson Harris configures as a "limbo gateway" into cross-cultural community. Harris's conceptualization of the limbo gateway (1970) has drawn attention recently for being a re-creative countermeasure and "a new kind of space . . . not simply an unbroken schedule of miles in a logbook" but an apocalypse-traversing threshold of survival.[20] In the limbo dance, "born, it is said, on the slave ships," Harris finds his chronotope, or time-space figure, of creolization: the spread-eagled test of flexibility by which "the slaves contorted themselves into human spiders."[21]

For Harris, limbo (like Haitian Vodou) activates phantom limbs and pains of Africa and Middle Passage but also fosters a "new corpus of sensibility," "an inter-tribal or cross-cultural community of families."[22] Harris's limbo gateway is nothing less than enslaved peoples' miraculous reassertion of a symbolic and social order from within a plantation system that denied them agency. Carnival limbo, Harris insists, "seeks to re-play a dismemberment of tribes (note again the high stilted legs of some of the performers and the spider-anancy masks of others running close to the ground) and to invoke a curious psychic re-assembly of the parts of the dead god or gods . . . issued from a state of cramp to articulate a new growth" (159). What he terms "the limbo imagination of the folk" (160), treading a "gateway complex between cultures" (165), evinces a powerful "creative phenomenon" that remains denigrated in its sacral and carnivalesque forms (159). In response to enduring psychological censorship, Harris points the Caribbean artist-academic lower, in a "gamble of the soul" to embrace "a risk which identifies . . . with the submerged authority of dispossessed peoples" (166).

Harris's trope of the limbo gateway marks a secret history of Atlantic time and space. This history is secret because plantation censorships forced its countercultural opacity, but "secret" also because Afro-Atlantic cultures have vetted deep knowledge and authority only upon the responsibly initiated. The closest Yoruba equivalent for "religion," the word *awo* (secret or ritual knowledge), signals experience in what is regarded as the "journey" or travels of spectacle performance.[23] In their often opaque rapport with initiatory rebirthings, deaths, and transition, Afro-Atlantic rites utilize chronotopes of time-space travel. Eileen Julien's memoir, *Travels with Mae*, illustrates something of this, for example, in its work of remembering both her mother's and black New Orleans's whole culture of tenaciously restored behaviors. She reveals how even an act as ordinary as the preparation and consumption of gumbo may serve as a limbo gateway: "a kind of communion," "a rite that puts me in touch with myself," "a spiritual experience which makes me understand in some unutterable way the continuity in my life with the lives of women now far away from me, our common history, our uncommon love."[24] Such gumbo hermeneutics require "not only . . . special ingredients but also the right setting, a special feeling. Folks who have eaten it all their lives—or who act like they have" in a communion of learned behaviors and practiced relations.[25] Here, gumbo rites define a community apart from others, but one open to whoever may act with a socially and spiritually limber enough response.

Since "things get mixed up, and the juice kind of swaps around" in a gumbo, as Huck Finn affirms, we find our usual (naïve) subjects, genealogies, individualist notions of self and nation thickened and swapped around in any gumbo/limbo narrative.[26] Just as gumbo starts with a roux base, we commence with the linguistic-performative modalities of the creole basilect, in a relation of linguistic polarity with the metropolitan-leaning (Euro-standard) acrolect. The historically low-prestige variety of speech (or cultural grammar) within a stratified continuum in each of the contact languages known as Atlantic Creoles, the *basilect* provides a sociolinguistic *base* for a bottom-to-top *lection* (variant reading) of circum-Atlantic experience. As Valérie Loichot helps us see, texts from plantation spaces require a "calling-responsive" co-writing from readers if we are to slip beneath the bar of print culture's ideal citizen-subject standards to move, spiderlike and more limberly, along the lowest common ground and thereby "foster" texts otherwise orphaned from their extended family networks.[27] Basilectal forms of agency navigate a "swamp sublime" within which—as Monique Allewaert's reading of William Bartram's *Travels* points out—we not only *can* but probably *must* engage certain plantation texts as swampings of metropolitan subjectivity, rendering new possibilities for inhabitation of terrain where the juices swap around.[28]

Seen from white-supremacist machineries of power, the integral religiosity of the Afro-creole majority was rendered "a hybrid, crude, and undefinable medley of truth and falsehood," as the *Southern Christian Advocate* complained of the "pseudo religion" of black South Carolinians in 1846.[29] In *The Creoles of Louisiana* (1884), George W. Cable similarly dismissed the splendor of Mardi Gras, ridiculing its "makebelieve art, frivolous taste, and short-sighted outlay."[30] And George H. W. Bush chose a most reliable adjective in 1980 for disparaging Ronald Reagan's "trickle-down" tax-cut plan as "voodoo economics." Creole peoples face the constant assertion that they speak no real language, have no real religion, no claim to authority except in movement to the higher ground of acrolectal (Euro-standard) forms. So responding to Afro-Baptist, Vodou, Santería, and jook housings of subalternized agency, I will examine texts and performances from two remaining groves of creole language in the coastal South (the Sea Islands and Louisiana) and from two longtime frontiers of creolizing contact (Florida and an extended Gulf South) to chart deep southern ties to Caribbean rites, writing, and needs to make right. From these moorings, my study embarks upon two currents of Afro-creole agency: (1) reassertions by the enslaved of independent sacred societies; and (2) flexible "limbo" performances in which authors have gone low under the bar of sacred folk forms in texts that lend wider circulation and transformed authority to Atlantic countercultures of modernity. This book thereby addresses what Ifeoma Nwankwo terms "cosmopolitanism from below," and would have us acknowledge such cosmopolitanism not only in its acrolectal movement (toward the metropolitan standard) but also in its basilectal vitality, in what many consider the most backwater cultural forms.[31]

Gulf-Konesans and Authority—Some Conceptual Markers for the Journey

"To dare transition," Wole Soyinka insists, "is the ultimate test of the human spirit."[32] In his classic essay "The Fourth Stage" (1973), Soyinka drew on Yoruba repertoires of Ogun, the *orisha* (deity) of metallurgy's creative/ destructive cycles, to describe how Ogun's musically backed rites have nurtured a transitional rapport with the dead, the unborn, and wild agencies of the bush. For Soyinka, passage through any given "abyss of a-spirituality and cosmic rejection" draws most potently from a "ritual summons, response, and expression [that] is the strange alien sound to which we give the name of music."[33] Soyinka's notions on the role of ritual muse and music in supporting travels of "spiritual re-assemblage" through a "transitional gulf" can help us appreciate African initiatory preparedness to face even the extreme a-spirituality of Middle Passage and chattel slavery.[34] Soyinka's focus has been on Africa itself; however, his ideas about the metallurgic orisha Ogun and his mythic forays into abjection and the sublime apply even more aptly to those of Ogun's devotees who were hauled across the Atlantic to Brazil, Cuba, Haiti, Trinidad, and Louisiana: "Only one who has himself undergone the experience of disintegration, whose spirit has been tested and whose psychic resources laid under stress by the forces most inimical to individual assertion, only he [*sic*] can understand and be the force of fusion between the two contradictions [destruction and creation]."[35]

From American shores of the Atlantic, Édouard Glissant's *Poétique de la relation* (1990, translated as *Poetics of Relation* in 1997) charts a relational rapport with the sublime steeled by this most trying *"chaotic journey."*[36] Glissant reconfigures Soyinka's abyssal "fourth stage" of ritual transition as a traumatic passage through *"le gouffre-matrice"* (the gulf-matrix), the physical crossing that—in the Middle Passage for Glissant—marks a new people in recircuited networks of relation.[37] Glissant does not gloss over the ineffable terrors wrought by slavery's crimes against humanity: "the belly of this boat dissolves you, precipitates you into a nonworld from which you cry out" from within a *"Génératrice"* pregnant with the dead, living, and unborn.[38] If the first stage of passage aboard Glissant's "Open Boat" enacts disorganizations of the self, a second stage acknowledges the Atlantic as a single grave with its "thousand channels" delineated by "scarcely corroded balls and chains" (3, 6). This gulf's gravesite and dread extend into island spaces of arrival since "the most petrifying face of the abyss [*la face la plus médusante du gouffre*] lies ahead" in an impossible futurity—the "panic of the new land," the question of having reached "edges of a nonworld that no ancestor will haunt?" (6–7). From this third Medusa-like gulf avatar ("*avatar du gouffre*"), the ocean reflects petrifying loss; however, the mournings of so many initiates of a thousand African groves catalyze a fourth re-creative stage of relation in a plantation space of nigh-exterminated first inhabitants, unsettled Europeans, indentured Asians, and enslaved Africans. Thus, Glissant positions the creole Caribbean as carrier of an initiate gnosis: "Not just a specific knowledge, appetite, suffering, and delight of one particular people, not only that, but knowledge of the Whole [*la connaissance du Tout*], greater from having been at the abyss and freeing knowledge of Relation [*le savoir de la Relation*] within the Whole" (8). "*Connaissance*" (familiar rapport or know-how), born of forced "*fréquentation*" of the gulf, becomes a below-sea-level plantation "*savoir*" (knowledge) of Relation.[39]

Afro-creole sacred societies have long tended to such knowledge. According to Karen McCarthy Brown, the production and transmission of *konesans* "is one of the goals of Vodou initiation ceremonies."[40] Drawing on her study and experiences of Haitian Vodou, Brown explains, "Konesans is the ability to read people . . . diagnose and name their suffering," and "to heal" them. The experiential power of *konesans* is born of the initiation room's sacred space, a kind of "alchemical oven in which suffering is transformed into knowledge, into experientially rooted priestly power."[41] In response to the traumas of chattel slavery, black Atlantic ritual reassemblies of agency proved crucial to sustaining alternative sets of relation and consciousness. A performative, musically infused "slave sublime" provided the base for what Paul Gilroy calls a black Atlantic "politics of transfiguration" demanding far more than fulfillment of extant legal and scriptural codes. The politics of transfiguration cannot be reduced to print. Hailing its subjects differently, it must get "played, danced, and acted, as well as sung and sung about, because words," Gilroy insists, "will never be enough to communicate its unsayable claims to the truth."[42]

Glissant's "Open Boat," Gilroy's "slave sublime," and Harris's "limbo gateway" share a nondisclosable secret of sea-change. This is not quite the Kantian sublime: the overwhelming encounter with nature, followed by the authoritative self's "reconquered mastery" in a willful turning away that produces an almost orgasmic rush—a "discharge all the more powerful"—for having followed a momentary, little death.[43] Enlightenment aesthetics posits a necessarily detached separation between the subject and object of sublime experience. It is this detachment that produces the masterful taxonomies of Enlightenment reason.[44] Glissant, Gilroy, and Harris, on the other hand, present a black Atlantic sublime that remains porous to otherness, remains corporeal, composite, and calling-responsive.

Although Sanford Budick has insisted that a "cultural sublime" undergirds Western traditions of agency and has long served as an initiatory test of authorship, Europe's transatlantic colonial projects brought new challenges and resources into play. From this perspective, a (trans)cultural sublime might gain importance, for as Budick explains, one of the effects of experiencing engulfment by an overwhelming force is to open up the possibility of alternative response, beyond the accredited repertory.[45] In fact, "the author," as we have come to know him, was re-created out of Europeans' transatlantic "bush" travels. Donald Pease writes that the cultural sanction of medieval *auctores* "remained more or less unquestioned until late in the fifteenth century, with the discovery of a New World whose inhabitants, language, customs and laws, geography, and plant and animal life did not correspond to referents in the *auctores'* books."[46] Losing something of the self in New World encounters, the explorer's survival authorized him as someone whose reportage carried an experience-based authority and even new language (from *hurricane* to *raccoon* and *barbeque*). From Cabeza de Vaca's *La Relación* (1542) to Bartram's *Travels* (1791), we find an authority born of stepping outside the accredited boundaries and of appropriating and becoming captivated by the authority, gods, lands, and bodies of others. Much of the Renaissance found initiation in a transatlantic sublime's reciprocal enculturations. This transformation seems best named, however, not by Western metaphysics but by a new word, *criollo* (creole), its earliest documentation appearing in Joseph Acosta's *Historia natural y moral de las Indias* (1590).[47]

The word "creole" marks a countercultural black authority born of traumas of dislocation unaccredited in Western thinking. Inca Garcilaso de la Vega's early history, *La Florida* (1605), presented *criollo* as a term invented by Africans to acknowledge gulfs of orientation between enslaved African parents (often of differing African nations) and their children born in the Americas.[48] "Creole" thus appears as an articulation of identity subject to the conditions of what Mary Louise Pratt has called "the contact zone": "the space in which people geographically and historically separated come into contact with each other and establish ongoing relations, usually involving conditions of coercion, radical inequality, and intractable conflict."[49] The contact zone is creole space: our space of ongoing social and environmental climate changes.

Afro-Atlantic articulations of New World formations keep gaining currency. Two *PMLA* articles from a 2002 issue spoke, for example, of an "increasing hybridization or creolization of cultures" and of "increasingly creolized conditions of metropolitan life."[50] We are all now having to be born *there*, in trying spaces that call for imaginative and intellectual risk. Carib-bean and postplantation writers, native to the contact zone's historic core, may prove diagnostic in their responses to the challenges of a long-globalizing economy. With Édouard Glissant we may seek to reconstitute an "aesthetics of the earth," a relational "passion for the land where one lives . . . an action we must endlessly risk."[51] Similarly, Wilson Harris turns us along a "limbo gateway" to take up "a risk which identifies . . . with the submerged authority of dispossessed peoples."[52] Glissant's "cross-cultural poetics" and Harris's "cross-cultural imagination" emerge from postplantation spaces where risk *is* a native land.

Part of the risk of authorship born of the contact-zone writing that Pratt terms "autoethnography" lies both in the censorship of its basilectal ground-ing and in the self-fashioning of a literacy insidiously bound up with colonial representations.[53] Modernity and cosmopolitanism have been terms defined by the colonizer. And at the very sweep of time when black god-signs and authors appeared renascent in places like Paris, Harlem, Havana, Port-au-Prince, Rio de Janeiro, and Lagos, both God and the Author were famously declared dead, leaving the professional metropolitan scriptor to adjudicate the play of textuality. For instance, in Roland Barthes's classic essay, "The Death of the Author," Barthes's *écriture* and *jouissance* happen as discharge in a paradoxical zone of contact—the sublime time-space of Western author-ity's loss become gain: "This disconnection occurs, the voice loses its origin, the author enters his own death, writing begins" out of "the destruction of every voice, of every point of origin."[54] In his metropolitan take on aspects of creolization, Barthes adds that "the sense of this phenomenon, however, has varied; in ethnographic societies [*les sociétés ethnographiques*] the responsi-bility for a narrative is never assumed by a person but by a mediator, shaman or relator whose 'performance'—the mastery of the narrative code—may possibly be admired but never his 'genius' [*le 'génie'*]."[55] As Montaigne had done centuries before, Barthes turns to "*les sociétés ethnographiques*" for a certain kind of freedom. But in "The Death of the Author"—along with an openness to being born *there* in self-sacrificial possessions—comes a moment of colonial possession in relation to "ethnographic societies" that exist only in metropolitan writing: those subjects whom ethnographers write, whom "we" know only in textual fabrications. These *sociétés ethnographiques* whose scripted roles provide a make-believe model for losing our own subject(ivity) in performance may—we are told—admire mastery of the code but never a performer's "genius" (*le "génie"*). Barthes, however, got this partly wrong due to inattention to meanings secreted in relation to the word *génie:* its Latin "guardian spirit" imported into Arabic as *djinn* (genie) and admired across much of Africa in the form of bush-spirits of the sublime. These djinn, ori-shas, *lwa*, are the very forces served in ritual performance. It is indeed the genius that is admired even as the possessed person (the "mount" or "horse" of the spirit) may be granted a certain authority for her initiate training in giving momentary disconnect to herself to become mount of a genius. Clearly some peoples' genies (and cultural "horses") have been so discredited as to appear to exist only in ethnographic textual productions. A need for both authorship and guardian genius remains. Nevertheless, Barthes does make a compelling case for the Author, God, and autonomous first-person "I" of the Western tradition being in need of a killing.

"The Death of the [Western] Author" may in the end mark too partial a path. The West African "shaman" and author Malidoma Somé points out that the Western world's ancestors (really its authors) need healing, and asks, "Why is it that the modern world can't deal with its ancestors and endure its past?"[56] Endurance of ancestors put into relation seems the unremitting job of folk like Faulkner's Dilsey, the ex-slave subject (and "mammy") made to stand between the abject and the families she serves. She endures modernity's ancestors and helps initiate the modern text. Faulkner could not be, could not *have been*, without Dilsey.[57] If any of her biological children become authors, we are not told. After all, their public pursuit of authority could well have led to their murder. Maybe Parisians, like Londoners or Bostonians, can afford to kill their authors. Authors do make excellent scapegoats and may be charged with carrying our cultural baggage—the trash or shame we refuse to touch—into a past to which we are no longer responsible. But does death or the author get performed the same way in Parisian circles (or even at the University of Iowa or Mississippi) as in Port-au-Prince or New Orleans or in Zora Neale Hurston's Eatonville? Who are the ancestors and authors of our peculiar modernity? How do we come to serve and endure them, ourselves, each other? A single repeating Afro-Atlantic initiation tale offers pointers and clues.

Kumba's Calabash—Egg-Fetching Travels

On a recent CD titled *Give and Take*, Senegalese music star Youssou N'Dour invokes a tradition of travel as initiatory, educational agency, singing: "Ku dul tukki doo xam fu deck neexe / Booy tukki yaw" (Who doesn't travel can't know where sweetness is / Boy, go travel).[58] A fundament of West African societies has been the "travel" of bush initiation. The traveler undergoes a series of tests, learning to give and take in the wilderness through a journey into foreign terrain. Youssou N'Dour's song to Senegal's contemporary global travelers, along with Malidoma Somé's Dagara elders' advice ("Go and let yourself be swallowed . . . be swallowed into the wilderness"), could well inform a tipping of libations to Ralph Ellison and his *Invisible Man*'s grandfather's directive ("Let em swoller you till they vomit").[59] Indeed, a strategic agency may well arise from allowing oneself to be consumed by the other, by otherness itself—to fetch the secrets of the foreign and put them into play.

Throughout the black Atlantic we find the initiatory wilderness journey preparing the undone/remade seeker for new modes of kinship, knowledge, and power. In one very widespread Afro-Atlantic tale of an orphan's initiation, her bush-travel is enabled by what Bahamians would call her "broughtupsy" or the guiding presence of the dead mother, a presence that enables the orphan's receptivity to fostered reaffiliations.[60] My prior book, *Reading Africa into American Literature*, presented a Louisiana version of such a tale in its entirety, noting the tale's reproduction of Senegambian models.[61] But we should no longer be content with genealogies of African broughtupsy in America. If the tales helped sustain ritual kinships and economies of reciprocity across Atlantic gulfs, then they may teach something about navigating an abyssal modernity. While the tale appears in various places throughout the Americas, let us look to the Senegalese (Wolof) prototype paraphrased below:

The Wolof orphan tale features two girls named Kumba: "Orphan Kumba" and "Kumba-with-a-mother." The father remains alive, but it is a surviving co-wife who is charged with parenting the orphan and her own daughter. The co-wife/foster mother uses orphan Kumba as a virtual slave until the girl comes of age, and then sends Kumba on a journey she is not meant to survive. The orphan must cross the wilderness to wash a dirty calabash in the Sea of Ndayaan (the Atlantic). On her journey through the wilderness the orphan meets a jujube tree that is chopping itself down, and then a skillet doing its own cooking on a fire. In both cases she greets the spectacle with openness and is rewarded— with jujubes (a natural anxiety medicine) and a handful of the skillet's cooked food. Kumba finally encounters a crone in her path: a woman with only one leg, one arm, one eye, one ear, and one finger. Keeping her composure in this encounter, and following the crone's instructions to cook a single bone and pound and boil a single grain of millet, orphan Kumba enjoys a plentiful meal of meat and couscous. Given a pair of needles to defend herself against the bush crone's "children" (wild animals, including Bouki the Hyena), the orphan uses the smallest needle to prick the "children" just enough to move them back into the bush so that she may sleep. Come morning the crone gives Kumba three eggs with instructions for breaking them in the forest on her way home. Orphan Kumba follows the instructions precisely, and bursts the eggs, an act that allows her to arrive back in town with the wealth that crowns her new status, including drummers, armed guards, slaves, gold, and cattle that emerge out of the bursted eggs on the orphan's path back home. The stepmother then responds to the orphan's transformation by sending her own blood-daughter Kumba into the bush. This Kumba's journey turns deadly because the girl cannot "give and take" in the spirit realm, can't abandon preconceptions of normalcy, ridicules all she sees, tortures the crone's animal children mercilessly, does not follow directions, and is devoured by the beasts that emerge from the eggs she receives. Of the failed traveler, the tale says simply that vultures fed on her entrails and cried out, high over the girls' home: "Here is the heart of the little girl who set out for the wilderness by the Sea of Ndayaan."[62]

The orphan—seen by her stepmother as a competitor with the stepmother's own children for goods, marriage, and inheritances—fulfills what is meant to be an infanticidal task: the washing of a dirty calabash spoon in the Atlantic. Here we must recall the dangers of the coast during the Atlantic slave trade. Orphan Kumba, however, totes her dead mother's broughtupsy with her: a fear-overcoming ritual respect that helps the orphan navigate potentially murderous wilderness and maintain composure in her encounter with the disfigured crone/djinn/orisha known throughout the black Atlantic as the herbalist of initiatory transformation.[63]

Although Senegal is not my study's focal point, nor are the Atlantic's African or European shores, African initiatory grounding aids our examination of Afro-creole reassemblies of agency in American plantation societies. In the Islamicized world of modern Senegal, Wolof people have abandoned the kind of bush schooling that Kumba's tale describes. Nevertheless, Kumba's initiation tale has flourished as a narrative of restored behavior in this oldest black Atlantic contact zone. Kumba is not only a common Wolof female name but one that bears quintessentially ethnic or local "country marks."[64] For instance, of the four Senegalese "communes" of early French colonial assimilation (St. Louis, Gorée Island, Dakar, and Rufisque), three remain guarded by Atlantic or river-mouth siren-genies named Kumba: Maam Kumba Bang of the old French capital and slave depot of St. Louis, Maam Kumba Kastel of the slave depot of Gorée Island, and Maam Kumba Lambay of Rufisque.[65] Kumba appears to be both the orphan traveler *and* the initiate djinn/genius of a Wolof sublime. Her contact-zone locations may be Muslim or Christian or secular but are always aflow with another, sedimented agency.

So what do we make of the task of washing a dirty calabash in the Atlantic? At the risk of conflating West African traditions, which, after all, converged on the Atlantic's American shorelines, we can turn to Yoruba calabash washings. Yoruba Ifa priest Kolawole Ositola regularly initiates boys whose lives have yet to find their ritual container, but he also discusses the practice of initiating men who have found their lives "shattered and scattered like a broken calabash."[66] Margaret Thompson Drewal explains that as fruit and container, the calabash is a womb-symbol of women's birthing power, and since life's secret is held by women, it is calabash and earthenware containers that guard ritual fundaments from the uninitiated gaze.[67] It is generally women too—or men who have become woman in initiation (Yoruba possession priests are "brides" of the spirits) who serve as vessels becoming momentary mount or "'horse of the god' (esin orisa)."[68] The story of Kumba washing her dirty (menses-stained) calabash in the Atlantic serves not simply to pressure girls into conformity with models of female submission as Christiane Owusu-Sarpong remarks of a similar Ghanaian orphan initiation tale.[69] Far more than this, these tales chart a path into all initiation, modeling open-eyed responses to the wildest realities in preparation for marriage to the spirit. We are all invited to become Kumba. As Deleuze and Guattari put it, "all becomings begin with and pass through becoming-woman. It is the key to all the other becomings."[70]

How account for the wounded bush-genie and her imposed tasks? In Nigeria and in the Yoruba diaspora of the Americas, the one-eyed, one-armed, one-legged forest spirit is Osain, guardian of the herbal medicines indispensable to initiations. The tale cultivates respect for the mentor's guidance through disfiguring frequentation of the sublime. Just as Yoruba possession priests, male and female, are made ritual "brides" or iyawo of the orisha (whether the orisha are male or female), Kumba's tale insists that initiation calls for a becoming-woman in preparation for marriage to the spirit. Something of this comes across in a Wolof tale of two bush-schooled brothers as the orphan boy accepts each of Kumba's tasks from the one-legged/armed/eyed "queen of the djinn," including the dry bone to be boiled and the single grain to be pounded and cooked for the initiation meal.[71] In these tales we often face the dark side of the sacral "genie"—her transfiguration as the organ-devouring vulture who picks the bones and eats the hearts of failed initiates. What we come to intuit is that the two Kumbas are one, that the dark side of this experience belongs to them both, and that the only way the orphan emerges transfigured is through acceptance of her own death and rebirth in an evisceration of the raw ego in sacred bush.

It can hardly be surprising to see Kumba's allegory of bush encounter repeatedly narrated in a New World plantation system on the other side of an abyssal Atlantic (from the Bahamas to St. Kitts, South Carolina, Grenada, St. Vincent, St. Lucia, Dominica, Guadeloupe, Haiti, Louisiana, and Florida): a world in which humanity is orphaned, kinship is in need of rerouting, and internal authority—even the language to speak it—is a dangerous invention.[72] In meeting her stunningly disfigured spiritual parent in the bush, the orphan accepts one promise demanded of her according to Senegambian and Louisiana creole variants: "You must promise me not to laugh at anything which you will see."[73] No matter the marvels she encounters, the seeker greets the unfamiliar with open-eyed respect. No presumptive questions. No slack-jawed wonderment. No spilling of secrets. Orphan Kumba offers a model of flexibility as a stranger in the sacred's strange land. Her shadow sister's egg-botching inability to give and take in foreign/otherly space is perhaps an even more urgent cautionary model.

Swallowed by wilderness, Orphan Kumba manages to assemble what Deleuze and Guattari call the Body without Organs (BwO): "The BwO is the egg," and "[t]he egg is the BwO . . . you always carry it with you."[74] As Deleuze and Guattari ascertain from readings of Dogon ethnography: "If it [the BwO/egg] is tied to childhood, it is not in the sense that the adult regresses to the child and the child to the Mother, but in the sense that the child, like the Dogon twin who takes a piece of the placenta with him, tears from the organic form of the Mother an intense and destratified matter that on the contrary constitutes his or her perpetual break with the past, his or her present experience, experimentation."[75] Kumba's tale indeed fosters a certain radical openness (not without discernment): a knowing not to impose domestic assumptions of normalcy on the contact encounter. This radical openness lies at the heart of creole genius. It is Kumba's dead mother's broughtupsy—the egg or piece of placental motherland Kumba caries with her—that keeps opening her to life-affirming potentiality in the face of abjection, periodic bleeding, and loss.

Swallowed by Zion—Cumba's Crossings

So what do we gain by washing our calabashes in the sea of Ndayaan? In journeys along shores too often seen as nigh-absolute boundaries, we may begin to recognize that the Africans whose social personalities were eviscerated and swallowed by colonial plantation systems did not enter the belly of that beast unprepared to consume New World materials themselves. Kumba's egg-fetching undoing and redoing in initiatory wilderness steeled her for passage through unspeakable trauma and encouraged her to foster others' social and psychic reincorporation. Most often renamed by whoever held title to her, Kumba still reemerged on other Atlantic shorelines, bringing her narrative of initiation with her. In North America, Kumba's Wolof and Mande sisters, children, and cousins arrived regularly in the plantation ports of Charleston and Savannah around which the anglo-creole language of Gullah or Geechee became a majority language. Surprisingly little, however, remains of her initiatory tale there. One of Joel Chandler Harris's Georgia tales introduces us to an "old Affiky ooman, 'e call 'im name Coomba," who finds her desires stoked by "one snake-nes' fill wit' aig."[76] After Coomba breakfasts on the snake's eggs, she faces the snake's reciprocating threat: "You is bin 'stroy me chillum. Tek keer you' own; tek keer you' own."[77] Coomba must then guard her own daughter by relying on a call-and-response secret password song. With the child opening the door only in response to Mother Coomba's song, the snake sets out to master every nuance of Coomba's performance. Eventually, of course, the snake offers an adequate "crossover" performance and swallows the child whole. Coomba tracks the slow-moving snake and beheads it to cut her girl free—and alive—from its belly. In the end she has commandeered the snake's eggs while protecting her own . . . even as her daughter has been swallowed by a bush-serpent from whom she reemerges.

Kumba guarded her eggs well, for her namesakes appear throughout the Sea Island cultures of South Carolina and Georgia. A Savannah woman proudly wrote of her body servant Koomba Johnson's beauty and fashion sense.[78] Lorenzo Turner's *Africanisms in the Gullah Dialect* (1949) recorded the name of "Kumba" in twentieth-century use on the Georgia coast.[79] A runaway Cumba was captured in South Carolina in 1770.[80] And in 1792 a South Carolinian planter of color inherited Cumbah from his slave-trading white father.[81] Kumba's initiation tale, however, let itself be swallowed by lowcountry narratives of Cinderella. One Gullah remnant appears in a text written (circa 1922) by Ada Bryan, a student at Edding's Point School in St. Helena, South Carolina.[82] Ada Bryan presents us with an unnamed orphan girl so mistreated by her stepmother and natural father that she flees to the river to cry, meets a mermaid there (a Maam Kumba Bang–type water spirit), who takes the girl underwater with a password song, feeds the girl, and brings her back to the surface again. A spying stepsister discovers the secret alliance, and the orphan soon finds her whole stepfamily gathered by the river, botching the password song miserably. When the disgusted orphan finally sings the song herself, the mermaid surfaces only to be shot and killed by the father, leaving the orphan to drown herself in sorrow. Unusually abbreviated with its violent mystery-killing ending, this narrative penned from the classroom bespeaks the damage done to Gullah/Geechee vision by an orphaning mode of metropolitan-designed schooling still in place in postplantation classrooms.

Although the initiating mermaid gets shot dead in the St. Helena Island tale, the island's school at least provides us with a student-authored text of the spirit's demise. As coastal Georgia's Cornelia Bailey stated of the closing of Sapelo Island's school, "Once our kids went to the other side . . . what they were learning from the first grade on, was to look to the other side for everything."[83] Relating how local spirits were also murdered by the growing presence of University of Georgia marine biologists on the island ("When you explain it away, it goes away"), Cornelia Bailey adds that the elders' authority was diminished by diploma-oriented education: "Being in a culture where you didn't disbelieve your elders, it was hard to put aside what they believed . . . There were two worlds—the textbook world and their world of believing in the unseen and the unknown—and you were caught in between."[84] Cinderella's textbook fairy godmother and Prince Charming displaced the one-legged crone who initiated Kumba, just as certain textbook modes of worshipping the Trinity and evoking the Holy Spirit displaced the rites of bush arbor societies. But beneath the surface of a Cinderella-like Baptist orthodoxy, something else remains at work: restorations of behavior, in patterns we will trace in aggregate under the name "Kumba/Cumba" via her Baptist praise-house travels.

Kumba's travels were hardly over upon reaching Georgia. At the end of the American Revolution, a number of "Kumbas" gathered in British-held enclaves in Charleston, Savannah, and finally east Florida. From there, thousands of British subjects fled to the Bahamas in a mass migration of Loyalists, slaves, and liberty-seeking black refugees.[85] At least ten different "Cumbas" appear in Bahamian slave registries. One woman by the name of Cumba likely accompanied Loyalist slaveholder Charles Farquharson, who built a cotton plantation on the island of San Salvador where Cumba died enslaved in 1825, leaving an orphan daughter.[86] Kumba's initiation tale found staying power in the Bahamas and cultivated her daughters' broughtupsy on Andros and Cat Islands, where we may recognize the Senegambian motifs of Kumba's tale repeated act by act in local tellings.[87] Cumba carried her incorporation into Geechee praise societies with her to the Bahamas: in initiatory spirit travels, ring shouts, and baptismal immersion in Zion's waters. This transcultural experience of Zion "reborning" crisscrossed the anglo-Atlantic, carrying Afro-Baptist visions of freedom from the Revolutionary Gullah/Geechee lowcountry to the Bahamas, Jamaica, Nova Scotia, Sierra Leone, Trinidad, and Liberia, among other of America's close kin.

The War of 1812 spread Cumba's travels in a second wave that sowed the seed of black Atlantic Baptist faith anew. When the British arrived along the coastal Georgia plantations of Camden and Glynn Counties in January 1815, hundreds of enslaved Georgians accepted the British offer of liberation from Georgia masters. Men were enlisted as British Royal Marines and stood ready to bear arms against U.S. military forces to defend their newfound freedom. After the war's end, the black marines and their families resettled in the British colonies of Nova Scotia and Trinidad. Cumba's name appears repeatedly on the rolls of those who escaped Georgia for opportunities as independent farmers in Trinidad. Cumba Parker left a Crooked River rice plantation in Georgia with her husband and three children and resettled in Trinidad's Fifth Company Village in 1815, while Cumba Goodbread came with husband and children to the same Trinidadian village from the same Georgia county, and Cumba Hamilton—from a St. Simons Island, Georgia, plantation—settled in Trinidad's 6th Company village with her husband and two children.[88] These are the villages from which Trinidad's very first black Baptist congregation emerged. The Baptist praise houses founded by these coastal Georgians proved capable of a profoundly cosmopolitan reassembly of religion to suit Afro-Atlantic needs. Cumba's travels also attest to the porousness of the Americas' histories and borders.

British colonial slave registries place Cumba throughout the Caribbean. With approximately 160 different enslaved women listed under the name Cumba in Jamaica, 30 in Antigua, 46 in St. Vincent, 40 in Grenada and Carriacou (along with a slaveholder in Grenada named Cumba Moore), 9 in Trinidad, 30 in Tobago, 22 in Guyana, 30 in Barbados (augmented by 117 Coombas and 109 Coombahs where the names became surnames), Cumba turns up everywhere, her name being repeatedly bestowed upon babies in the last decades of British slavery.[89] Grenadian author Merle Collins recently underscored Cumba's steady witness in an Emancipation Day address. Collins referenced a Grenadian newspaper ad from 1823 in which a slaveholder listed Cumba, her two daughters, son, and two granddaughters for sale, all "merely for want of money."[90]

Wherever we find it, Kumba's initiation tale navigates challenges she and her daughters faced in their plantation societies. On St. Kitts, Alexander Hazel's tale "The Good Child and the Bad" restores Kumba's agency (under a well-marketed name) in narrating Cinderella's forced night journey to the Johnson River to wash a drop of mouse blood she had spilled on her mistress's punch bowl. At every mile along the ten-mile journey, Cinderella greets a terrifying "zion" (interpreted by collector Elsie Clews Parsons as "giants") until she meets a ten-headed zion, who refrains from devouring her only because she has respectfully hailed as "mahstah" each of the ten "zion[s]." Let us insist on the Zion-encounter here: the notion that Cinderella has allowed herself to be swallowed up by Zion experience. Cinderella shows herself to be a daughter of Kumba's broughtupsy when she makes it past the ten zions to her mentor, greets her respectfully as "Granny," scrubs her back (which cuts Cinderella's fingers "like a nutmeg grater"), cooks the single grain of rice and the bit of ham bone, is kind to the crone's cat, and chooses the proper eggs. Busted correctly, the eggs give Cinderella a lovely house and garden (but no Prince Charming here). When her stepmother finally passes by the new Zion/crone-bestowed abode, Cinderella confronts her: "You don' know me, Cinderella, what you done dat wicked evil to? When I kill de mouse and dob de mistress punch bowl, you sen' me unbeknown to me fader fah ahl dese wil' beas's eat me up." Cinderella survived the plantation's infanticidal tasks and set up a protected Zion-house "t'rough good behaviour an' manners" in contact with Kumba's bush crone. But when the stepmother gets her own daughter to kill a mouse, daub the mistress's punch bowl with blood, and go on the Zion-encounter, the girl gets devoured by the ten-headed zion since "She so sassy an' rude, tell dem word dat do hu't dem." The tale insists "all dat was God work," restores the behaviors of African broughtupsy, and reminds us that every planter's punch bowl bears this bloodstained inheritance: the traces of girls "you done dat wicked evil to."[91]

This Caribbean Cinderella tale sends its girls with their bloody punch bowls to the waterside to find their eggs. They have more on their minds than fitting into a pair of slippers. A look into the archives at the last wills of the plantation's Prince Charmings offers contrapuntal perspective. Pierce Butler's will conveyed "Quakoo and Cumba" (aged sixty-two and fifty-two) as a couple among 58 other pieces of Georgia slave "property" (along with carriages and punch bowls) to inheritors in 1800.[92] Quakoo's and Cumba's offspring were probably among the 138 Butler slaves from St. Simons (with 238 from neighboring Hamilton Plantation) who escaped to the British and freedom in 1814, settling in places as far-flung as Trinidad, Nova Scotia, and Sierra Leone.[93] Of the U.S. constitutional delegate who conveyed Cumba and Quakoo to his son, we are left with his will's deathbed prologue: "Seeing that it is appointed unto all men once to die."[94] What differences of perspective—on life, death, and passage-between—we may perceive between the Anglican slaveholder and the punch bowl washer of Zion-rebirthings! How much dread must be attached to a one-and-only appointment with death? How much power is wielded in a text that can convey people as property and direct the binding will of the dead?

For an example of what a disfigured and transfiguring (one-armed/legged/eyed) creole writing can offer, we can turn to an exemplary text from the anglo–New World mother-colony of Barbados: Kamau Brathwaite's *Mother Poem*. Brathwaite's *Mother Poem* (1977), substantially revised for his *Ancestors* trilogy (2001), would foster its children through a restoration of respect for the performance structures and community networks that have sustained the generations. In response to renewed mercantile devourings of Barbados and its "plantation ground" (16), Brathwaite's revision of *Mother Poem* allows the basilectal imagination to be swallowed up by the typographic possibilities of computer technology and by the hypertextuality of contemporary media in what he calls "video Sycorax" style, presenting new poems confronting the island's failed initiations ("Pixie") and failed initiatory housings ("Heartbreak Hotel").[95] In *Mother Poem* we meet a schoolgirl lost to the nihilism of sexed, drugged, and brand-name consumption. The poem that bears her name, "Pixie," presents its own "versioning" of the local media's spectacle-reportage of an island scapegoat and daughter of the streets, a virtual orphan who could just as easily be from any of Dixie's postplantation diasporas.

The Elvis Presley–imbued "Heartbreak Hotel" opens with a pixelated design (like *vèvè* ground drawings used to call Vodou spirits): a spread-tailed mermaid or contact zone siren (be she Kumba Bang, the orisha Yemaya, or the Starbucks trademark). Pixie's representation moves from newsprint to voice transcription from a radio call-in show. Pixie faces a calabash-washing challenge but has no access to fostering authority: "I want my Mum to tell me what to do and I'm bleeding for it" (69). Amid the streets' buzz of commerce and the development of island space to serve the tourist industry, "Heartbreak Hotel" calls for a genuine home-making ethic: "o city building houses houses houses w/out homes // o homeless daughters needing love," needing basilectal respect or base *groundation* in "iron ritual of bells // where very words need love" (72).

"Hex" depicts a mother island with "none left to comfort her" (73): "her inheritance is swallowed by strangers / her houses her beaches the views of her landscape," her time-space all "tuned over to tourists" (74). Disposession results: "she mothers us as if we was orphans" (74). And the education system reproduces this hex:

> . . . the chillren lock-way in their factories of schools
> know nothing of these matters
> they cannot change nothing that is theirs/not theirs
>
> they eat paper. they spit out half-
> chewed words. they burn king alfreds cakes
> but cannot help w/the housework (78)

What the untrained young cannot help with is the bringing of spirit(s) into the house, the assembling of a Vodou *houmfort*'s (or house's) comforts against nihilistic threat.

So *Mother Poem*'s final movement ("Koumfort") undertakes this housework, beginning with the praise-house assemblage of "Angel/Engine." An island mother whose "godma bring her up" (131) announces, "I tek up dese days wid de zion" (132):

> & uh holdin my hands up high in dis place
> & de palms turn to
>
> praaaze be to
> praaaze be to
> praaaze be to **gg**
>
> an the fingers flutter an flyin away
> an uh cryin out (132–33)

The poem's "praaaze" passages move "thru crick/crack" of the self's reassembly and through sharply exhaled "gg" sounds as the page scripts its hyperventilating escape of print and first-person consciousness in adoption of angel engine powers

                    who haunt me
                         huh

                 my head is a cross
                    is a cross-

                  road. (135)

A "horseman" comes down the "tracks" (136), releasing *huhs, hahs,
shhhaaaaas, shangs,* and *ggs* as overbreathing to the "praaaze"-callings builds
more toward "Shango" than "God," and a Zion conversion accrues steam to
counter homelessness.

    As container of uncontainable housings, *Mother Poem* finds "Koumfort"
in a steadily risked submersion in folk authority and in the island's fossil
(coral) spaces of the sublime. Brathwaite's long poem does not finally conclude as much as it signs off through pixelated invocation of an Atlantic genie
who "knows that her death has been born" (150) where erosions of Bajan
limestone meet the beaches' tidal pulse:

                 the ancient watercourses

            echo of pebble trickle worn stone
   the sunken voice of glitter inching its pattern to the sea

            towards the breaking of her flesh w/foam (153)

The last "word" of Brathwaite's re-visioned *Mother Poem* is, in fact, a pixelated design of the island's cliffs morphing back/into an Atlantic mother-fish
siren—a ritual vèvè of all our born(e) gulfs and engulfments.

Hot Boudin—Orphan Cumba and the Gonbo Pot

When most North Americans think "creole," they think "New Orleans." At
the Gulf mouth of America's heartland watershed, the city is historically
tied to Latin Caribbean and Atlantic ports as well as to globalizing revolu-
tions. Between the Senegambians sent to Louisiana by the French Company
of the Indies and an influx of Saint-Domingue refugees following the Haitian Revolution, New Orleans was set to become North America's enduring Afro-creole base. Its famed architectonic ingredients—gumbo, Voudou,
carnival, and jazz—summon (in nationalizing master narrative) a kind of
"make-believe art" of fabrication and affect by which the city also serves as a
receptacle for much of the nation's shame, projected on a marginal and tropi-
cal elsewhere.[96] New Orleans remains both an exceptional receptacle city or
govi (ancestral spirit-pot) and a rather ordinary Atlantic rim location crucial
to re-imagining America(s) in relation.

A slave inventory from Louisiana's Chaouaches Plantation for 1737–38 lists four Kumbas: Comba Fagiguy, Comba Guy, Comba Nea, and simply Comba.[97] These four women and two more "Combas" recorded by Gwendolyn Midlo Hall probably traveled from Senegambia to Louisiana on ships that stopped in French colonies such as Grenada, Martinique, or Saint-Domingue.[98] From Senegal to Grenada, St. Lucia, Dominica, Guadeloupe, Haiti, and Louisiana, franco-creole tellings of Kumba's experience served as thriving vessels of Afro-creole language, authority, and social reassembly.[99] This body of creole tales bears the trace-mechanisms whereby black subjects evaded reduction to consumable chattel within the symbolic order of plantation slavery and insisted on remaining consuming subjects in a world of their own making.

Still, we must never underestimate the violence of the plantation system, an abjection that would seem to negate or skew every religious and aesthetic response, certainly including the responses of its perpetrators. The American Leonora Sansay's epistolary travel novel of Haiti, *Secret History; or, The Horrors of St. Domingo* (1808), conveys a tale of "jealousy . . . terrible in its consequences" and bears Euro-creole witness to initiations into colonial capitalism's cannibal culture:

> One lady, who had a beautiful negro girl continually about her person, thought she saw some symptoms of *tendresse* in the eyes of her husband, and all the furies of jealousy seized her soul.
>
> She ordered one of her slaves to cut off the head of the unfortunate victim, which was instantly done. At dinner her husband said he felt no disposition to eat, to which his wife, with the air of a demon, replied, perhaps I can give you something that will excite your appetite; it has at least had that effect before. She rose and drew from a closet the head of Coomba. The husband, shocked beyond expression, left the house and sailed immediately for France, in order never again to behold such a monster.[100]

In a circum-Atlantic society of superabundance wherein consumer desires must remain stimulated in competition, the planter-patriarch has lost appetite and the Euro-creole wife is consumed by a demonic jealousy of the girl who had been her beauty accessory.[101] The plantation world of savage capitalism must view "tenderness" as a weakness since only the hardest of players keep the Cinderella mansion. In this tale, Coomba—as accessory or sex-thing—gets severed from community well before her beheading. She exists only in a narrative of the masters' transformations, a dish to be consumed in their gumbo. The whole backdrop, however, of *Secret History; or, The Horrors of St. Domingo* keeps us aware that the Coombas of the world have turned the tables, becoming global-cannibal consumers themselves. This is the initiatory global-historical moment that would have to be reported in secret against forces of censorship and blockade.

Coomba's fate (whether consumed by vultures, zion, or cannibals) is hardly new to her tale. Bad broughtupsy, jealousy, and narcissistic inflexibility in the face of other worlds lead to her demise in the conventional Afro-creole tales. But in Sansay's repetition of Euro-creole folklore, there is no one to foster Coomba. Since no sacred grove can harbor her within this tale's imaginary realm, Coomba can only aspire to become a sexually hyped, colored Cinderella in the masters' world of punch bowls. Coomba's own ritual families, of course, guard their own transformational tales, none of which follow Kumba's Senegambian prototype closer than does a Louisiana version featuring a girl's reception of three eggs from a one-armed, one-legged, one-eyed crone.[102] A Haitian variant, however, offers the most compelling counterperspective on Leonora Sansay's tale of Coomba—with the orphan receiving her inheritance from a Vodou *houmfort* (spirit-house or "congregation") that serves as guardian force of Afro-creole agency. This Vodou tale, bearing witness across two hundred years of Haiti's revolutionary initiation, may raise the hermeneutic stakes in its fetching of gumbo, ancestor pots, and a password song from across dread gulfs.

The Haitian storyteller (and Miami resident) Liliane Nérette Louis begins her tale in familiar fashion with a stepdaughter forced to do the household work of her stepmother and two stepsisters.[103] Here though, a secret inheritance has been set aside for all three girls since their dead father buried three jars of treasure to be revealed in dream. In this tale, Vodou accesses a world of buried inheritance and imaginative/dream literacy, instructing its *serviteurs* in the work of developing a ritually steeped *tendresse:* the permeable spirit and possessable body capable of service to the *lwa* (*mystères*, saints) and to spirits secreted in clay jars (*govis*) or found in nature. This orphan's initiatory task calls for a journey to a priestess's grove (Manbo Cia and her okra garden) to bring fifty cents' worth of okra back for dinner. Anyone who does not know Manbo Cia's praisesong lacks the passwords to her sacred grove. And any uninitiated person who intrudes without first paying proper ritual respects will be tossed into the gonbo pot, a fate that is the stepmother's clear expectation for the orphan girl. The girl, however, learns the occulted song from a spirit. The song's grooves open the path to a grove that is potential grave. After the orphan goes to the garden gate and performs the praisesong with such power that Manbo Cia dances a salute to the four directions—giving the girl a basket of okra as reward—the stepmother sends her own two daughters, who do not learn the song and get thrown into the pot, with the stepmother joining them in Manbo Cia's soup. Our orphan, freed of stepmother and stepsisters, and with a lovely basket of okra, sleeps such a blessed sleep that her dreams reveal the location of all three inheritance-jars buried beneath a village tree. The Manbo's song and gonbo lead the girl to the *govi*-pots of an occulted patrimony.

Émigrés from the Haitian Revolution insured the survival of an Afro-Latin Creole inheritance during the first decade of U.S. possession of Louisiana. Over ten thousand émigrés re-Africanized and re-creolized the whole material, psychological, and spiritual matrix of New Orleans, fostering Vodou and gumbo values, Catholic and carnivalesque aesthetics, at a time-place of the endangerment of New Orleans' African and Latin Creole urban cultural mix.[104] The jazz that New Orleanians swung thereafter in service to their own *lwa* and *govi* has proven to be an inheritance of worldwide reach.

For an example of jazz-driven vision supple enough and Vodou hermeneutics complex enough to reassemble so much transatlantic material, we can look to *the* great initiatory poem of black modernism: the Martinican Aimé Césaire's *Cahier d'un retour au pays natal* (1939), which coined "négritude," black modernity's valorization of a black aesthetic.[105] Like jazz great Sidney Bechet's grandfather in Congo Square, Césaire in *Notebook of a Return to the Native Land* must throw out devils and bring down powers, and the poem acknowledges the depths of its devils' internalization. His autoethnography of négritude faces creole assemblages that won't quite assemble. Césaire's poem begins under surveillance, beneath colonial monuments whitewashed "up there above the nigger scum," and the text's evocation of a tongue-swallowing, bulimic silence turns to emetic performance in a vomiting out of colonizing authority's classrooms and police (37).

Notebook may then whet an appetite for Christmas rites familiar to New Orleans celebrants: "You eat good, and you drink hearty and there are blood sausages [boudin], one kind only two fingers wide twined in coils, the other broad and stocky, the mild one tasting of wild thyme, the hot one spiced to an incandescence . . . and all sorts of good things which drive your taste buds wild or distill them to the point of ecstasy" (41). The congregational body without organs (like boudin encased in emptied-out viscera) sizzles in song: "And not only do the mouths sing, but the hands, the feet, the buttocks, the genitals, and your entire being liquefies into sounds, voices, and rhythm" (41). A heated-up swinging performance transforms the real—till the sacrificial fete ends and its *serviteurs* face "aborted dreams . . . hesitant to flow," the speaker's mother gone back to work on a silencing "Singer" sewing machine she "pedals for our hunger day and night" (41). *Notebook*'s colonial machineries return readers to a native land of savage capitalism by which Coomba's body and soul may still be commandeered to thicken the stews of the world's haute cuisine: "But *can* one kill Remorse, perfect as the stupefied face of an English lady discovering a Hottentot skull in her soup-tureen?" (43).

To the question of inheritance ("what is mine?"), *Notebook* responds with an altar set up with containers of seemingly disparate stuff: the native "cala-bash of an island"—Martinique—and an "archipelago," with its currents "separating one America from another," linked to "Haiti where negritude rose for the first time and stated that it believed in its humanity and the funny little tail of Florida where the strangulation of a nigger is being completed" (47). In this very first appearance of the word, négritude emerges from Hai-tian uprising and from the *govi*-pot of Toussaint Louverture's French prison grave: "What is mine also: a little cell in the Jura" (47). As "death gallops in the prison / like a white horse" (49), Césaire's return to native land reclaims maligned possessions at "a full gallop" (51)—"what neighing!" in the text's rising from "the vomit of slaveships" (61) to become mount of a Vodou *lwa*, négritude's *génie*. This notebook of return demands the death of the diplo-maed author's first-person singularity (a *go-and-be-swallowed* imperative) and calls coiling winds of Atlantic storm to mount and consume its host (figured like viscera-bound coils of spicy boudin served in Creole sacrificial economies):

> devour wind
> to you I surrender my abrupt words
> devour and encoil yourself
> and self-encoiling embrace me with a more ample shudder
> embrace me into furious us
> embrace, embrace us
> but after having drawn from us blood
> drawn by our own blood! (83)

This is not the affect of the lynch-rope. Rather, in the coiling of the orisha of Atlantic storm (Oya), the coiling of the Vodou serpent (Damballa), and coiled Christmas sausages, *Notebook*'s sacrificial rites assemble an energy-generating ritual body out of négritude's radically excluded subjects. This process of "swing" works via Haiti and Vodou, and draws its incandescent valorization from New Orleans jazz.

"Walking on the Other Side"—Florida's Muck-born Saints

When we recall that "the funny little tail of Florida" was a Spanish outpost administered through Cuba for over three hundred years, we gain perspective on its enduring frontier status. As we might guess, "Comba" can be found in Spanish Florida too, living on a St. Johns River plantation within the prox-imity of other Havana-purchased Senegalese women.[106] Spanish Florida was unusually open to black agency, welcoming anglo-creole maroons (reaffiliated as free Spanish subjects and border militia) through Catholic conversion and baptismal name change. Florida was also Indian country, stretching across a Gulf South inhabited by a stunning array of peoples. At least one Black Seminole girl was given the name Cumba.[107] In an Alabama court in 1831, a Creek Nation claimant contested the ownership of another slave named Cumba.[108] In 1836 on the eve of Chickasaw removal, Hac La Cum Ba sold a parcel of land to John C. Whitsel for twelve hundred dollars.[109] Surely some of Cumba's daughters walked the Trail of Tears, some got converted to cash before the journey, some fled by boat to Bahamian or Cuban havens, and some hunkered down, allied to Indians or held by them, in southern swamps.

Back in Cuba, Kumba's daughters orphaned by transatlantic slavery had recourse to African mutual aid societies (*cabildos de nación*) patterned after Spanish religious fraternities. These orphans could affiliate with the *cabildo* of the Mandinga *nación* or find adoption into one of the thriving Yoruba cabildos that served as lodges for the emergence of Regla de Ocha, popularly known as Santería, "the way of the saints."[110] The cult of the island's Yoruba-inflected patron saint, the Virgin of Cobre, dates to 1611 or 1612 according to the deposition of Juan Moreno, one of three hagiographic witnesses of the Virgin's rescue of their small "open boat" from a storm.[111] This Virgin traveled many water-borne paths to creole canonization, her dominant ones emerging from the Yoruba deity Oshun's intersections with Catholic forms that seemed to engulf African ways. As Antonio Benítez-Rojo reads her, the Virgin of Cobre reaches us via a triptych incorporation of the Arawak mother-of-waters, the Byzantine cult of Our Lady, and the orisha Oshun's fluvial pathways. Each triptych piece, however, has consumed others; for example, Oshun's coalescence in Cuba swallowed up African spirits such as the Senegal River's Kumba Bang.[112] For Benítez-Rojo, the Virgin of Cobre's cult may thus be reread in a provocative "confluence of marine flowings that connects the Niger with the Mississippi," working to "sublimate apocalypse and violence" in a calling-responsive hermeneutic of "performance and rhythm" that "takes away the space that separates the onlooker from the participant."[113] Oshun/the Virgin of Cobre gives birth to sacred space in each new housing of her image.

As Bishop Felipe Estévez remarked of the Florida shrine of La Ermita de la Caridad del Cobre, "[f]or Cubans in Miami . . . Our Lady's shrine is the most sacred space outside their longed-for patria."[114] Bishop Estévez regards Miami's shrine as both a comfort-space of holy land left behind and a sacralization of the land on which one now stands: "A child is always at home with its mother. For a people suffering from being uprooted, expelled, la Ermita nears them to their land. For a diaspora, dispersed throughout the whole world, la Ermita completes its identity."[115] She, the creole Virgin, the *mulatta* mother of God, removes the space of orphaning separation and sublimates the contact zone's violence. Interestingly, black virgins were among the divine mothers who traveled best with the Spanish as they left *patria* behind to conquer the far shores of a world new to them.[116] The black virgins of Regla and Candelaria, like the *mulatta* Virgin of Cobre and Mexico's *morena* Virgin of Guadalupe, emerged recharged from the hailings of natives, Africans, and creoles washing their calabashes in seas afloat with Catholic signs.

Authors from all sides of the Florida Channel (between the Gulf and the Atlantic) hail from cross-cultural sea-changes. Orisha religion reconfigured as Santería informed Lydia Cabrera's body of work in Cuba as well as during her decades of exile in Miami. A Euro-Cuban born to privilege (and thus to a certain ladylike silencing), Cabrera found reaffiliating voice in the orphan narrative that opened her first book, *Cuentos negros de Cuba* (1940).[117] The initiatory story "Bregantino Bregantín" is set in the mythic time-space of "Cocozumba" (suggestive of orisha divination's simplest form utilizing coconut pieces) with fifteen-year-old princess Dingadinga in "full blossom."[118] Dingadinga soon finds herself married to a bull who usurps all power in the kingdom, lays claim to every woman of Cocozumba, slays every male they bear, and proclaims Jehovah-like authority over his female herd each day: "Me, Me, Me, Me, Me / There's not a man in the country but me, me, me!" (8). After years of such rule and infanticidal sacrifice, "[t]he only novelty was that after a while, all masculine words not directly related to the bull were eliminated from the language" (16). The cognitive realm of Cocozumba shrinks. And as Edna M. Rodríguez-Mangual asserts, "If the bull's domination is the root of the annulment of the masculine, the result is a space that by the reversal of gender re-creates a linguistic universe ruled by a feminine ontology."[119]

Cabrera's story speaks of initiation into the other side of the plantation's symbolic order. Its heroine is not Dingadinga (who disappears utterly into the herd) but a young woman named Sanune, native to this agency-voided space. Her babies (her eggs) are destroyed by order of the Bull-God, the only one who is real. Pregnant yet again after the killing of her sixth son, Sanune finally goes "somewhere she could scream out her hate," where she can be "totally alone and rebellious" on "the other side of the river": "She crossed the old abandoned bridge as quickly as in a dream and continued walking on the other side. She came to the edge of the fearsome forest, guided by the spirit of her mother who, while she was alive, was a faithful servant of the saints of iron, her protectors (arrow, bow, nail, chain, and lock), Ogun and Ochosi, Saint Peter and Saint Norbert" (10). On the other side, via an abandoned bridge (allied with dream and imaginative literacy), lies the orisha realm of Sanune's mother, secreted in vessels of the saints. Here the text steps into *el monte* (the deep bush) and into well-known Afro-Cuban myths of the hunters Ogun and Ochosi—myths underscoring these hunters' affiliation with more experienced female orishas whose knowledge in many ways exceeds theirs.[120]

Cabrera's orphan tale crosses over into *el monte* to evade plantation patriarchy and to find a space of women's agency. Fleeing the bull, Sanune is led by her dead mother's spirit to the mother's orishas and to initiation under the godparentage of a diviner-priestess. At the foot of an Ochosi altar in the bush, Sanune enters a deeper version of the sublime swoon so familiar to the belles of plantation fiction. She dies and is born *there:*

> Sanune touched the earth and kissed it on her fingertips. Prostrate at the men's feet [the orishas Ogun and Ochosi], she lost consciousness. When she opened her eyes, she was surrounded by night, in a room thick with the smell of warm foliage and guavas, as if a crowd of blacks had just gathered there a few minutes before. She found herself before an altar made of two wildcat skins and two freshly cut poplar branches propped against the wall. On the ground she could see several soup tureens with their lids on, a horseshoe, two huge pots of rice, some red beans, and popcorn. Beside her, an old woman with her head wrapped in a veil held in her kerchief twenty-one little snails [cowrie shells]. (13)

At this priestess's Ochosi altar, Sanune is instructed to make an offering of cloth color-coded to seven orishas, and prepares to return to the bull's kingdom to birth her seventh son. Her newborn—killed under the bull's standing orders—gets revived by Ochosi back in *el monte.* Sanune can then die "with a smile on her lips" since she has Ogun's word that her child of initiatory labor will be known for the tree-toppling power of "one thrust of his horns" and in twenty years "the world will know his voice" (16).

The bull-child's voice sounds out the maturation of Sanune's initiate rebirth. But years pass while all feminized meaning in Cocozumba must cohere around the "Me, me, me!" boast of "the One and Only, the Peerless One with the final word, the Unique and the Absolute" (17). Since in Cocozumba, all nouns must be feminized and "the only man anyone could speak about was God, given that God and the bull were one and the same" (17), Cabrera sets up an allegory of patriarchal monotheism and plantation monoculture in contestation with the polytheisms, polycultures, and polyrhythmic capacities of the subaltern and enslaved. Natural forces intervene to point to the coercions of bull-headed law: "A surprise hurricane [*un ciclón*] blew through leaving everything topsy-turvy, and people couldn't get its horror out of their minds" as "[t]hey talked for a long time about the 'hurricaness' [*ciclona*] that had reaped so many lives" (16). Cabrera shows us that in bull-ruled Cocozumba, any challenge presented to "the Man" must come from the other side's conceptually feminized, strategically occulted space of becoming. Sanune's son, whose voice "broke a half-century of adoring silence" with the counterpoint of response—"me, me, me, me! / Now I'm the Thick Forest" (*Yo yo yo yo / Yo mismo soy Monte Firme*)—steps forward as avatar of composite assembly, born and compounded of Sanune, her dead mother, the initiating godmother, Oya (the buffalo-avatar storm orisha), and the deep bush of *el monte* (19). With *Monte Firme*'s killing of the bull, "nature reclaimed its rights [*sus derechos*] and men were born again in Cocozumba" (19). Once *la naturaleza* receives the *derechos* of the Santería economy (the *derecho* being a ritual fee of cash or goods), women are freed from giving their children, or "eggs," to feed the bull's monotheistic, monocultural rule. In Santería's sustainable economy, the one-legged, one-armed initiator of the bush familiar to us from Kumba's tale (Osain) is the orisha charged with receiving and distributing nature's share of the *derechos* for every herb used in every rite.[121]

Kumba's orphan tale shares a matrix of relations with Sanune's initiation narrative, starting with the name "Sanune," known best by frequenters of the bush. One set of tales from Kumba's Senegal and Gambia headwaters (where Sanene-Kontron is the paired divinity, like the orishas Ogun and Ochosi, of hunting fraternities) links Sanune to Sanene-and-Kontron. Their names are "condensations of a proverb: 'We have tasted of death and returned to life.' " The divine hunting pair's altar, made of horns mounted atop a mound by a crossroads, testifies to the hunters' knowledge of violence committed against a refugee mother and newborn.[122] Tales of Sanene-Kontron collapse the two hunters and female refugee into a single paired assemblage, "not actually mother and son, but . . . in the same relation."[123] In this sacral bush, as with Cabrera's story and the cult of the Virgin of Cobre, one myth swallows another one—though we can hardly tell the consumer from the consumed.

Afro-creole narratives and performance authority have reconstituted the psyches and cultures of the peoples who have marked Africans and black creoles as enslaveable others: Euro-Cubans like Cabrera, white Louisianans and Mississippians, Cherokee and Choctaw planters. As Cabrera's *Afro-Cuban Tales* remind us, in a world in which the bull lays claim to all *derechos*, resistance must seek apprenticeship within illegitimized spaces of alterity. Whether facing the bayous and Gulf waters of Kate Chopin's cornered women, the low path traversed by Eudora Welty's Phoenix Jackson, the pool from which Toni Morrison's Beloved rises, the swampy mangroves of Maryse Condé, or the bayous of LeAnne Howe's *Shell Shaker*, gulf narratives of initiation pass through the abject's fluidities, unmarked dump sites of throwaway bodies, sloughs of confluence and conjunction.[124]

The chapters that follow are grouped in travels across southern/circum-Caribbean space. Chapter 1 traces rites of community and authority emergent from Gullah/Geechee praise-house societies. It turns to migrations and synchronicities between coastal Georgia and the anglophone Caribbean to place novels by Paule Marshall, Toni Cade Bambara, Toni Morrison, Erna Brodber, and others in a unified tradition. Chapter 2 focuses on a major author of black Atlantic modernity, James Weldon Johnson, whose autoethnographic investment in Afro-creole sacred forms demands our reconsideration of his relevance to contemporary Sea Island and Bahamian reterritorializing claims.

Chapters 3 and 4 examine Franco-Caribbean legacies of New Orleans. Chapter 3 argues that the re-creolizing of the Louisiana territory by the arrival of refugees from Haiti set a framework for Vodou's ritual authority to shape the emergence of jazz. Chapter 4 looks to franco-creole Caribbean writing to reassess New Orleans's ritual economies in a post-disaster landscape. The city's writers offer crucial guidance to its gulf sublime, as I argue in discussing Brenda Marie Osbey's *All Saints* and Eileen Julien's *Travels with Mae*, among other texts.

The book's last set of chapters turns to frontier space in Florida and the Gulf South. Chapter 5 argues that Zora Neale Hurston's various initiations played an underappreciated role in sustaining her circum-Caribbean/Floridian travels into a submerged authority. Chapter 6 reads some of northeast Florida's early contact narratives in dialogue with Santería-inspired Miami-based work by Lydia Cabrera, Adrian Castro, and Ana Mendieta. Here too, Seminole and Creek bodies of memory carry a crucial witness tied to Afro-creole agency from Florida's "First Coast."

Finally, the conclusion explores some of the antiphonal limits of black Atlantic spirituality and enculturation, using a Choctaw novel and Yoruba-based Cuban and Creek turtle tales to reveal sacrificial, calabash-washing needs in Faulkner's *The Sound and the Fury* and Welty's "A Worn Path." Most pointedly, I argue that holistic authority in the Deep South emerges from apprenticeship to geniuses of the nonstandard time-space of our contact zones. The reassessment of gulf writing, rites, and needs-to-make-right calls forth a sacral rubric underscored in blood-red, its first criterion bearing the most demanding challenge: "*Go and let yourself be swallowed . . . be swallowed into the wilderness.*"

PART ONE

The Ancestral House

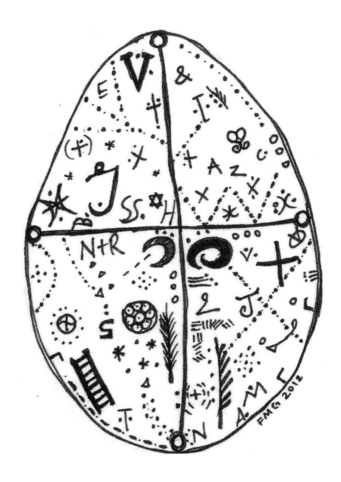

We're the first potential parents who can contain the ancestral house.
—Wilson Harris, *The Whole Armour*

CHAPTER ONE

Down to the Mire

Travels, Shouts, and Saraka in Atlantic Praise-Housings

African Guardian of Souls,
Drunk with rum,
Feasting on a strange cassava,
Yielding to new words and a weak palabra
Of a white-faced sardonic god—
Grins, cries
Amen,
Shouts hosanna.
—Jean Toomer, "Conversion," *Cane* (1923)

Jesus been down
    down to de mire
Sister Josie, you must come
    down to de mire
—"Down to de Mire," *Slave Songs of the
    Georgia Sea Islands* (1940)

From W. E. B. Du Bois to Jean Toomer, several key early authors of African American modernity turned southward to Gullah/Geechee terrain—the Altamaha, the Georgia rice fields, the shout-driven rhythms of the Charleston—to dip their art into living waters of a folk authority more complex and transfiguring than they could know. Their texts bear poignant, often opaque witness. As Toomer's *Cane*, for example, depicts a Georgia folk culture in urban migration and modernizing transition, it also registers a conservative remnant, the "African Guardian of Souls" who, though "converted," remains present as another kind of converting force working from within a counterculture of modernity. Toomer's "Conversion" reveals that whatever else Afro-Atlantic Protestant conversion has been, it has emerged from a creolizing double agency wherein the Soul Guardian says *Amen*, shouts liminal grooves that congregate workings of old African genius.[1]

Along *Cane*'s swamp trails, African goat paths, and Dixie Pikes, we enter a limbo gateway between Africa and the Americas. This "limbo imagination of

35

the folk"—with Toomer's Guardian of Souls—passed supply through "the gateway complex between cultures" conceptualized by Wilson Harris, and herein readers too are called ever-lower into saltmarsh and mire, to identify "with the submerged authority of dispossessed peoples."[2] Going down to the mire entails a journey into deaths and birth-crampings of global modernity. In the lowcountry of coastal Carolina, Georgia, northeast Florida—and its routings into/from a wider Atlantic world—Afro-creole praise societies used ring shouts like "Down to the Mire" to construct limbo gateways of conversion, testing flexibility, restoring suppleness, undoing and redoing the calling-responsive boundaries of individual members, to build structures of corporate and even judicial agency.

Language also emerges converted and converting from this gateway. Especially at the creole contact zone—the most charged site of the African linguistic substrate's submerged authority—the word bears stunningly limber witness. How can we know this "mire" down to which the seeker may be called? Is it the "area of wet, soggy, and muddy ground" of *Webster's New College Dictionary*?[3] If it is the "myuh" recorded by WPA interviewers from Georgia ring shouters descended from African Muslims, might it be the Pulaar *maayo* (or "river") recalled by the Muslim headman Salih Bilali to the Georgia "master" who held legally defining title to him? Or the " 'Mighty Myo,' which figures as a river of death" in a "sorrow song" noted by Du Bois?[4] Might this ring-shouted "myuh" also have ties to the emergence of Jamaican *myal*, which Edward Long first described in 1789 as a recent establishment, "a myal dance . . . a kind of society" that renders its initiates "invulnerable" to whites through its spirit-guarding ring dance performed—as a missionary wrote from Jamaica in the 1840s—mostly by women, backed by the ritual circle's humming and timekeeping: "by hands and feet and the swaying of their bodies"?[5] How comprehend the word given so much linguistic and performative supplement? This gateway of limbo performance calls for respectful apprenticeship (sacrificial expenditures of ego), as we see in Lydia Parrish's description from Georgia: "Of all the ring-shouts I know, 'Down to de Mire' is in more ways than one the most interesting. In the center of the ring, one member gets down on his knees and, with head touching the floor, rotates with the group as it moves around the circle. The different shouters, as they pass, push the head 'down to the mire.' "[6] Here, the "mire" or "myuh" signifies in performed, embodied relation to restored black Atlantic behaviors. But what are the convergent memories that find restoration in this myuh/maayo/myal/mire? Christian and Islamic prayer? The "I bow my head to the ground" of the *moforibale* and *moyuba* (Yoruba ritual greetings or prayer) in which "[o]ne head honors another by going to the floor"?[7] When we encounter a word, say "death" or "god," we must ask how it travels and has reached across the gulfs of various contact zones. We should reconsider, in this context, the Latin *religare* ("to bind back," "retie," "bond") basing our "religion," and its closest Yoruba equivalent: the *awo* ("secret" or "initiate knowledge") embedded in divinations of the *babalawo* (guardian-father of secrets).[8] We may recognize that Toomer's African Guardian of Souls, in saying "Amen" to religion while also channeling nations of guarded knowledge, asserts a reciprocal model of agency that challenges Americans' genealogical assumptions.[9]

More than any Anglo–North American contact zone, the Sea Islands of Carolina, Georgia, and northeast Florida have served as sacred groves of the African Guardian of Souls' submerged authority. From lowcountry landings, commercial lines of triangulation connected the Sea Islands to the British Isles, Africa, and the West Indies. We may first notice lines running from Barbados to Charleston along routes of "the odyssey" of Barbadian settlement of Carolina—founded as the colony of a Caribbean colony.[10] In the wake of the American Revolution we may chart routes from Charleston, Savannah, and St. Augustine ports, moving Loyalists and enslaved or allied Africans and creoles to the Bahamas, Jamaica, and throughout the Atlantic world.[11] The War of 1812 left more crosshatching on our nautical maps, moving free black refugees from coastal plantations to repatriation in Trinidad.[12] These flows of people, goods, ideas, and language shaped complex anglo-creole assemblages in interface with other Atlantic assemblages. Along with Deleuze and Guattari, we find "*[c]ollective assemblages of enunciation*" moving in rhizomatic patterns, "agglomerating very diverse acts, not only linguistic, but also perceptive, mimetic, gestural, and cognitive" in "a throng of dialects, patois, slangs, and specialized languages."[13] The lowcountry's creole language (Gullah or Geechee) offers vital perspective on complex machineries of globalization and countercultural feedback.

The salt marsh is rhizome. Amid tidal flows over oysterbeds and mudflats, groves of arborescence (live oak hammocks) rise over sediment-trapping baffles of sweetgrass and spartina that extend precarious terrain. Resurrection fern and Spanish moss cover gigantic limbs of the oaks prized for use in the curved ribs of sailing ships. The lowcountry is a gateway of terrestrial, riverine, and marine flows. Any effort to territorialize this space within a strictly national narrative can account for only part of the Sea Islands' cultural history. Indeed, the creole cultures around Charleston, Savannah, and Jacksonville test the waters separating the plantation South from the West Indies, and the Americas from Africa. Here we may find rites of psychic and social reassembly that work points of maximal Afro-creole authority to form a deep nexus of Afro-Atlantic Protestantism. It is an orphaned authority, however, long seen as "mumbo jumbo" or as a pinch of marketable local flavor thickening a vacation economy's okra soup. Its temporal-spatial perspectives of relation are rapidly being vacated as gated "plantation" communities reterritorialize

Geechee space and insert themselves over marsh grasses' old baffles and expensively "renourished" beaches. The hold of Gullah/Geechee communities upon ancestral land and ties to transgenerational embodied knowledge—what French historian Pierre Nora terms "environments of memory"—has grown so tenuous that Congress passed the Gullah/Geechee Cultural Heritage Act in 2006, allocating $15 million over ten years to establish the "Gullah/Geechee Heritage Corridor" for the "preservation and interpretation of the Gullah/Geechee cultural heritage."[14]

The notion that Afro-creole rites and environments of memory might offer epistemological value is new to most people of Western education and upwardly mobile aspiration, be they white or "of color." Could the enslaved really have fashioned, in their hodgepodge "mumbo jumbo," model reassemblies of cross-cultural desire and authority? The Presbyterian slaveholder, Rev. Charles Colcock Jones of Liberty County, Georgia, voiced his frustration over the slaves' unwillingness to stick to the script of their standard hymnals: "The public worship of God should be conducted *with reverence and stillness on the part of the congregation;* nor should the minister . . . encourage . . . responses or noises, or outcries of any kind during the progress of divine worship; nor boisterous singing immediately at its close," adding that "[o]ne great advantage in teaching them good psalms and hymns is that they are thereby induced to lay aside the extravagant and nonsensical chants, and catches and hallelujah songs of their own composing and when they sing . . . they will have something profitable to sing."[15] Similarly, one Methodist contributor to the *Southern Christian Advocate* in 1846 complained of the "deplorable exhibition of pseudo religion" in Gullah praise societies and of the "remarkable tenacity" of "ancient superstitions, handed down by tradition and propagated by so called *leaders.*" He asserts that "[i]nstead of giving up their visionary religionism, embracing the simple truth . . . our missionaries find them endeavoring to incorporate their superstitious rites with a purer system of instruction, producing thereby a hybrid, crude, and undefinable medley of truth and falsehood."[16] Such hybrid medleys seem to have traveled well.

The 1843 complaints of the English Baptist missionary James Phillippo in Jamaica point to a regional black Atlantic religious movement: "[A]t the conclusion of the war with America, some who had been imported from that continent, mysteriously blending together important truths and extravagant puerilities, assumed the office of teachers and preachers, disseminating far and wide their pernicious follies."[17] Likewise, the *Bahama Argus* printed an editorial in 1831 arguing against official sanction of black Baptist preachers who had established island congregations following the (mostly Gullah) Loyalist migration of 1783–84: "[A]lthough temporary fear of censure may induce a degree of demure decorum among them, yet there would be a proportionate want of real reverence for what they deem a 'John Canoe' exhibition . . . more in conformity with the noisy rites of Bacchus, than with the sober doctrines of the Christian faith."[18] While Rev. Phillippo, Rev. Jones, the *Bahama Argus*, and the *Southern Christian Advocate* sought to block the flows and production of black sacral desire and authority—and organize them along lines of plantation profitability—African guardians of soul performance were not easily stilled. A certain carnivalesque "noise" unsettled white missionaries. But their real fear was of countercultural black authority in congregation: an orphaned agency of gulfs that may still baffle the "purer system" of instruction to which we are all variously subject.

As Sea Island and West Indian cultures developed in interface, Afro-Christian praise societies channeled conversions of ancestral spirits and Holy Spirit in three key ways: (1) via initiatory patterns of seeking and narrating authoritative vision in spiritual "travels"; (2) via polyrhythmic ring shouts that sustained linkages of body, mind, and spirit; and (3) via sacrificial economies of remembering the dead and feeding the children. This chapter essays an archaeology of rites by which lowcountry praise societies spread Afro-Atlantic Baptist congregations to places as far-flung as the Bahamas, Trinidad, Jamaica, Nova Scotia, and Sierra Leone.[19] We will examine how these praise-housings have fed contemporary literary stepchildren. Calls issued in 1993 by Cornel West for a "politics of conversion" and Paul Gilroy for a "politics of transfiguration" had indeed already been sounded in a literature by (or of) women seeking to conserve and remodel (post)plantation praise-house assemblies.[20] These Geechee-infused novel travel-tracts (Toni Morrison's *Song of Solomon*, Toni Cade Bambara's *The Salt Eaters*, Paule Marshall's *Praisesong for the Widow*, Gloria Naylor's *Mama Day*, Erna Brodber's *Myal*, Earl Lovelace's *The Wine of Astonishment*, and Julie Dash's *Daughters of the Dust*, to name a remarkable artistic congregation assembled in a fifteen-year period between 1977 and 1992) have contested the white-supremacist, patriarchal filiations of the church. These works often take shape as conversion "tracks" under the spiritual parentage of a powerful female "pointer." They foster alternative spaces of sanctuary and bear witness to a cosmopolitan conservatism emergent from forced navigation in a globalizing world.

"You Compel to See That Baby"—A Heterodox Conservatism in the House

With independent African Baptist congregations formed in Savannah and Augusta by 1777, Georgia became a gateway from which black missionary agency spread throughout the U.S. South and the anglo-Caribbean.[21] Mechal Sobel has described the attractions of the Baptist faith for enslaved Africans, the compatibility of Baptist rites and worldview with African practices, Baptist grounding in ecstatic regeneration of the spirit, and the appeal of congregational independence.[22] While the highly visible ministries of George Liele,

David George, and Andrew Bryan were spreading black Baptist institutional agency in Georgia, the predominantly Africa-born plantation communities of coastal Georgia, which had experienced a surge of slave population—increasing from about 420 in 1751 to 16,000 in 1773 after massive importations—were bringing conversions to bear on Christianity.[23] Although documentary evidence for the emergence of antebellum bush arbor and praise-house societies is sparse, colonial Christian activity, coupled with the prestige of Savannah's independent Afro-Baptist ministries, appears to have been strong enough that Protestantism became the dominant element of black religion in Georgia between 1775 and 1815, and Georgia émigrés proved seminal in transporting their Baptist faith across an Afro-Atlantic world.[24] By making use of a variety of older sources—augmented by interviews with ex-slaves collected by the Georgia Writers' Project (1940), Lydia Parrish (1942), and Lorenzo Turner (1949)—and comparing this material with practices presumably carried to the Bahamas, Jamaica, and Trinidad by Georgians between 1783 and 1816, we may chart assemblage-structures by which Geechee praise societies helped to initiate a creolizing Baptist faith in the Caribbean.

Margaret Creel has described how Gullah praise societies served as the social, spiritual, and judicial force of the enslaved, building such community alignment that "reportedly there were no orphans on the Sea Islands."[25] Entry into Gullah societies found initiatory culmination in a period of spiritual travel known as seeking or mourning. This journey "in the wilderness" began with the seeker being apprenticed to a spiritual parent who monitored the seeker's travels (dreams, visions, prayer) for signs that the seeker was prepared for examination.[26] Head bound with white cloth or a single string, the seeker/mourner chose a secret retreat for repeated daily and nightly prayer over a period of months. Something of the mourner's prior construction of self would be sacrificed in the process. The mourner, usually but not always near the liminal age of twelve, would face a ritual rending of accustomed first-person perspective in the face of the sublime, a series of spirit-signs (accompanied by the spiritual parent's interpretive guidance into the society's symbolic order), followed by a resacralization of the extended self's new first-person plurality (as composite "I" bound of body-soul-spirit, serving as vessel of spirit-entities and as a responsible society member).[27] The "leader" was charged with preparing the seeker to deliver a testimonial of her travels to the congregation's examining committee. Recalling her own experience, Rosina Cohen spoke of how

> If you seek religion, you compel to see that baby. And what is that baby? Your soul, your soul is the baby, you understand. And you got to go to him and ask, "Lord, I ain't see my baby this month." And you beg him and beg him; and at last when he give [it to] you, you wash it off nice and clean. Oh Lord! I so glad

to have a baby. Oh, I run around, carry it to my leader; tell him. He say: "That's your soul; that's your soul. The baby is your soul. Don't let nobody fool you; the baby is your soul."[28]

These "travel" narratives, three of which Lorenzo Turner collected in his landmark *Africanisms in the Gullah Dialect* (1949), appear to be a key Sea Island genre for allowing society members to find voice and witness for their wilderness experiences via congregationally shepherded conventions of co-operative agency in the face of an otherwise devouring chattel slavery. This process of "seeking Jesus" was a Christian rite, informed by the first Great Awakening of evangelical Protestantism with its emphasis on visions, dreams, prayer retreat, catching the spirit, baptismal initiation, and public "taking of experience."[29] Yet something else found play here since Georgia's black population harbored a rich set of linguistic and travel experiences from various African nations, southeastern Indian nations, and much of the Caribbean— from St. Kitts to Curaçao.[30]

The lowcountry was populated by peoples familiar with rice culture—the Gola, Kissi, Vai, Mende, and various Senegambian peoples—for all of whom, according to Creel, the experience of bush initiation's incorporations into spiritual personhood "was a shared memory."[31] As Creel remarks of Sande and Poro initiations among the peoples of upper Guinea who proved crucial to the development of Gullah/Geechee culture, youths were sequestered in the bush for initiation where, guided by elders, they "underwent a travel, a series of terrifying dreams in which they were symbolically eaten by the Poro or Sande spirit . . . and then reborn by the same spiritual force."[32] Praise-house processes of initiation coalesced from the many sources that shaped the members' travel experiences. One missionary complained in 1847 that there was "no distant element of Christian experience involved in the whole affair," as he wrote disparagingly of the authority accorded to the spiritual mother "to whom the seeker relates all his 'travel.'"[33] His *Southern Christian Advocate* report insists, "This word *travel* . . . is one of the most significant in their language, and comprehends all those exercises, spiritual, visionary and imaginative, which make up an 'experience.'"[34] Geechee praise societies used their congregationally valued travel genres to help members claim the authority of their own experience. When Katie Brown (whose great-grandfather was a Bahama-purchased Fulbe Muslim and leader of a considerable Muslim presence on Sapelo Island, Georgia) sang of seeking, for example, her song ("Believer I Know") testified to her initiate travel-authority. And it offered spiritual parentage to new seekers as they gave up something of the self in a process incorporating free wild agency into extended families of a sequestered plantation society: "The way to get to Heaven / Believer I know / Go in the wilderness / Believer I know / Fall on your bendin / Believer I know."[35]

Following ritual death and rebirth beneath living baptismal waters ("wen duh tide is goin' out so duh watuh will wash duh sins away"), congregants often celebrated in a ring shout.[36] William Francis Allen's Port Royal diary entry from 1863 offers one of the clearest early representations of the ring shout's counterclockwise movement and polyrhythmic call-and-response improvisation. Considering that "[p]erhaps it is of African origin, with Christianity engrafted upon it," Allen described how

> Billy sang or rather chanted, and the others "based" him as they say, while . . . [six dancers] moved round the room in a circle in a sort of shuffle. This is the shout. Some moved the feet backward and forward alternately, but the best shouters—and Jimmy, I was told to-day, "is a great shouter," keep the feet on the floor and work themselves along the floor by moving them right and left. It seemed tremendous work for them . . . and I saw that the most skillful ones moved very easily and quietly. The shouters seldom sing or make any noise except with their feet, but work their bodies more or less; while the singers clap their hands and stamp the right foot in time.[37]

Reworking dances honoring various African spiritual nations, and incorporating Sufi repertoires, Protestant hymns, and perhaps even elements of Creek stomp dances, the ring shout—according to historian Michael Gomez (echoing Allen's arborescent 1863 observations)—was the primary vehicle by which Christianity was "grafted onto the tree of African tradition."[38] Ring shouts like "Down to the Mire" enabled both the becoming-African of creole Christianity and the becoming-Christian of creole Africanity. Parrish's *Slave Songs of the Georgia Sea Islands* contains other performative rememberings of Islamic and African prayer. We find "Knee-bone in the mornin' / Ha-ah Lord knee-bone bend," as well as shouts in Mende, and maybe even creolizations of Yoruba songs for the orisha Oshun passed down by the Georgia African Dublin Scribben: "My soul sine de *oshun*."[39] The iron orisha Ogun most likely found manifestation in the house via the overturned iron pots often placed on praise-house floors.[40]

Although disquieted whites such as Rev. Charles Colcock Jones attempted to silence and reseat Geechee worship, African embodiments of sacred authority refused to be stilled. As contemporary shouter Odessa Young explains, the shouters' steps must come into rhythmic agreement with the song's words and the beat of the "rapper's" broomstick: "If your feet can't say what the song say, you might as well not to do it. Because it ain't done right. Your feet got to say exactly what that song and stick say, and our feet got to say it exactly—if not, they're not set right."[41] A key rule was that the feet must not cross, which would result in the prohibited actions signified by the English word "dance." Shouting was clearly not "dancing," but something quite beyond English significations. Shouters integrated mind, body, and spirit in ritual swinging that has "set" much of Afro-Atlantic Protestantism's and global popular music's complex conversions.

The most conservative realm of Geechee life may lie in rites for the dead and the memorializing of ancestors—who, as in much of the diaspora, often find transitional linkage with the unborn and with children. Funeral ring shouts described by Georgia ex-slaves reveal that the shout restored behaviors from well beyond the realm of orthodox Christianity.[42] Exemplifying this conservatism is coastal Georgia resident Amelia Dawley's rendition of a funeral song identified as Mende and transcribed by Turner, recorded by Parrish, and collected from *Drums and Shadows* informant Tony Delegal in lines that fed the lyric core of Toni Morrison's *Song of Solomon:* "Come booba yalle, come booba tambee."[43] Work undertaken by Joseph Opala and Cynthia Schmidt facilitated the homecoming travel of Amelia Dawley's daughter Mary Moran from Georgia to Sierra Leone in 1997 to sing the family song in a Mende village with Baindu Jabati, who recalled the song from her mother's generation's now disavowed burial rites. Moran remarked, "I didn't know it was a funeral hymn . . . I used to dance to it."[44] Indeed, Liberty County's James Rogers, who sang a version of the song to Lydia Parrish in the 1930s, recalled learning it from Africans who "shouted" it in ritual ring-stepping.[45] This is how the lowcountry dead have been laid to rest, served, remembered.

The documentary film of Moran's travel to Sierra Leone (*The Language You Cry In*) portrays services of intergenerational "rescue."[46] Something of the circum-Atlantic complexity of this service appears when Moran's Georgia family and friends sing gospel in a Sierra Leone church. Moran may carry the Mende funeral song from Georgia back to Sierra Leone, but in Sierra Leone she meets not just her Mende sources but also Afro-Baptist congregations founded by David George in 1792 when he carried the gospel from Georgia to Sierra Leone.[47] According to Joseph Roach, performances such as these are important precisely because "the voices of the dead may speak freely now only through the bodies of the living," and he insists that cemeteries, historical markers, and pulpits take on a special charge "as behaviors," that is, "as occasions for memory and invention" within "an oceanic interculture."[48] Unsurprisingly then in Georgia, before entering Sapelo Island's Behavior Cemetery for the burial of her nephew, Cornelia Bailey writes, "We stopped at the old iron cemetery gate when we got there and asked the spirits for permission to enter. We have always done that over here."[49] Cemeteries such as Behavior have grounded transgenerational ties to specific spaces and times of behavior, as a South Carolina Committee on Behalf of the People insisted in 1865, demanding " 'promised Homesteads'—in terms of 'getting land enough to lay our Fathers bones upon.' "[50]

The Senegambian tradition of "saraka" cakes was passed down across generations on the Georgia coast. Made on key days of the Muslim calendar or as a thanksgiving to the ancestors for blessings received, sweetened "saraka" cakes (from Arabic *sadaqa*, to make sacrifice, give charity) have been distributed in rites of "feeding the children" throughout West Africa's diaspora.[51] On Sapelo Island, Katie Brown spoke of her grandmother, Bilali Muhammad's Bahamian-born daughter Margaret, who "make funny flat cake she call 'saraka.' She make um same day ebry yeah, an it big day. When dey finish, she call us in, all duh chillum, an put in hands lill flat cake an we eats it . . . 'Saraka' she call um."[52] Shad Hall recalled his own grandmother's saraka: "She make strange cake, fus ub ebry munt. She call it 'saraka.' She make it out uh meal an honey. She put meal in bilin watuh an take it right out. Den she mix it wid honey, and make it in flat cakes. Sometime she make it out uh rice. Duh cake made, she call us all in an deah she hab great big fan-nuh full an she gib us each cake. Den we all stands roun table, and she says, 'Ameen, Ameen, Ameen,' an we all eats cake."[53] The saraka tradition that I encountered during my Peace Corps experience in Senegal faded away slowly in Georgia; however, these rites traveled to the Caribbean with Georgia slaves who chose the British offer of freedom during the War of 1812. The Georgians resettled in Trinidad where Spiritual Baptist congregants may celebrate a "saraca" or "thanksgiving," commonly known as "feeding the children," which involves setting a ritual table for the ancestors with honey, cakes, candies, flowers, etc., and offering it in the end to children of the family and neighborhood.[54] Throughout the Afro-Atlantic world we find a saraka ethos of sacrificial expenditure whereby the dead are fed and cooperative bonds of community behavior find rearticulation through ritual table-settings shared with the children (the ancestors' freshest representatives). Here is the truly functional "trickle-down" economy. The "old parents' plate" set with "all different quality of meats, chicken, pork, mutton, rice, vegetables, citrons," for "people who dead," for "everybody parents," may feed quite a global reach of creole family since humanity is "one family come from one God," as the Carriacou saraca leader, May Fortune, insisted.[55]

We hear much about isolation as a key to the lowcountry's deep African cultural substrate, but the more carefully we consider Gullah/Geechee culture in its Atlantic context, the more we may see a certain cosmopolitanism and far-reaching intercultural agency. Mass migrations from the lowcountry in 1783–84 and 1815–16 included a diverse mixture of Africans and creoles and proved foundational to Anglo-creole cultures of the Bahamas and Trinidad. We should recall the charismatic black minister George Liele's flight from Savannah in 1783, his establishment of what became the Native Baptist Church in Jamaica, its influence on the development of Revival Zion and Jamaican popular religion.[56] These movements did not emerge from a people without knowledge of rapidly changing circum-Atlantic contact zones. In their culturally foundational years, the Sea Islands were hardly isolated from the world.

The Loyalist migration at the close of the American Revolution had its greatest impact on the Bahamas, more than doubling the population of the capital, Nassau, and providing initial settlement for most of the Out Islands.[57] Bahamian islands such as Exuma and Long Island were populated largely by Georgia slaves (with strong Muslim presence), and one missionary arriving on Exuma in 1802 wrote of meeting many who "called themselves followers of Mahomet."[58] The Bahamas' first Afro-Baptist praise houses were founded in the mid-1780s by Sea Island refugees such as Samuel Scriven and Prince Williams, the latter of whom appears to have been an African with country marks.[59] Gullah/Geechee migration to the Bahamas was, in fact, so formative that creolist John Holm has described contemporary Gullah and Bahamian as "sister dialects" of an eighteenth-century Sea Island plantation creole.[60] Despite its colonial Anglicanism, the Bahamas became almost a Baptist nation, shaped by the diverse repertoires of lowcountry praise societies and their navigation of truly heterogeneous cultural conditions.

The Loyalist exodus to the Bahamas was largely a forced exodus of enslaved peoples, but the decision of slaves from the Georgia Sea Islands to side with the invading British Royal Marines during the War of 1812 (and their readiness to take up arms against U.S. troops) was a calculated risk that led to their eventual relocation as free farmers in Trinidad in 1815–16. Seven hundred eighty-one black American refugees escaped from Georgia and Virginia to find resettlement in Trinidad in the six "Meriken" Company Villages.[61] A Georgia migrant from St. Simons Island, William Hamilton, founded the first black Baptist church in Trinidad in the Fifth Company Village made up of Georgia ex-slaves (with an especially strong St. Simons contingent consisting of eighteen households supplemented by another forty-one St. Simons households in the neighboring Sixth Company Village).[62] This Geechee church, according to Trinidadian Spiritual Baptist archbishop Ahram L. Stapleton, provided foundations for one of the most cross-culturally open faiths of the Anglo-Caribbean world: the Spiritual Baptists, also known as the Shouters.[63]

Like the migrant Georgians, Trinidad's Spiritual Baptists may refer to their churches as praise houses. Spiritual Baptist praise houses also valorize an initiatory period of spiritual "travels" undertaken under the watchful eye of a ritual "pointer" in a period of vision-seeking known as "mourning," followed by the public testimony and validation of the "tract" or "track" of the mourner's travels. These "tracks" narrate journeys beneath the wonders of the sea to otherwise unaccredited transnational spiritual "schools" in Africa, India, China, or Assyria.[64] The music of services can be so ecstatic that disquieted colonial authorities banned Spiritual Baptist worship in Trinidad in the Shouters Prohibition Ordinance of 1917, and banned Baptist "Shakerism" in St. Vincent in 1912.[65] Lorna McDaniel has observed striking similarities in song texts and style shared between Spiritual Baptists and Geechee shouters, kinships of sound she attributes to the Baptist " 'Mericans" of the Company Villages.[66] Spiritual Baptists' polyrhythmic training of mind, body, and spirit to come into agreement makes use of dreams, spirit possession, and readings of scripture; thus, Trinidadian Baptist rites "devote attention to the entire person" as the shouters "march" around the church's center pole and stamp feet to engage grounding vibrations.[67] While body, spirit, and mind need rites of synthesis to "pull together" in fully functioning ways, Spiritual Baptists organize their aesthetically rich rites and altars along a mosaic principle of spatial and temporal juxtaposition that conserves the integrity of each strand of creole ritual tradition.[68] Spiritual Baptists thus manage to be both heterodox and conservative as they juxtapose and accumulate ritual traditions from Orisha, Hindu, Muslim, Catholic, and Pentecostal traditions.[69] What Trinidad's Spiritual Baptist faith suggests is that conservative religion need not be exclusionary but may be open to a consensus of diverse practices—conserving and honoring the various spirit-roots of creole peoples. Indeed, the conservative ritual openness of Spiritual Baptists in Trinidad, St. Vincent, and Grenada and in early Gullah praise societies has been troubling to many "orthodox" Baptist congregations.

The Spiritual Baptists' diversely spirited worldview is evident in many members' use of saraka rites to honor the dead by feeding the children. As revealed in a narrative by the Oshun ("African power") devotee Norman Paul, "saraca" rites have been common structures of spiritual consensus in Grenada and Carriacou (often coupled with Big Drum nation dances and elements of Catholic or Baptist worship) as well as in Trinidad, where a Spiritual Baptist leader read one of Paul's dreams as a call from Oshun to "fix a table" and "feed the children" with an altar offering "sweets, cake, bread and ginger-beer" amidst nightlong song.[70] These traditions have many sources, but we should acknowledge likely migrations of saraka rites from Georgia to Trinidad. I seek here to offer a saraka in memory of Sea Island refugees willing to fight U.S. military forces for freedom and who gained a new start in the Caribbean: people like William Hamilton who founded the Baptist faith in Trinidad, and descendant Samuel Ebenezer Elliott (Papa Neezer) who received the Baptist faith of his 'Meriken ancestors and the Yoruba orisha work of his matrilineage for a life devoted to inspiriting both paths.[71] Papa Neezer's life, practices, and personae—as orthodox Baptist deacon, as Trinidad's best-known orisha house leader, and as "obeah" subject of carnival calypsos—are exemplary of the heterodox conservatism and suppleness of Afro-Atlantic performance. From such angles we may see Gullah/Geechee experience as more than an amassing of primitive survivals in splendid isolation. Here, in the soul-guardian's traveled authority, are "tracks" to a counterculture of modernity. This was a culture impoverished by chattel slavery but nevertheless far from being without means and vision to feed its children.

Steady callings to the mire and a compulsion to "see that baby" in ritual mourning brought generations through captivity and fostered extended kinships, limbo suppleness, a saraka ethos.

Amidst salt marshes and plantation landings, a spiritually mothered post–civil rights/postcolonial congregation of Afro-Atlantic writing has taken stock of its ritual repertory and reentered old mourning grounds. The travel-tracts of Georgia's Alice Walker—in essays such as "In Search of Our Mothers' Gardens" (1974) and "Looking for Zora" (1975)—pointed a generation of women writers southward—back to Hurston and to unmourned "mothers and grandmothers . . . moving to music not yet written."[72] From Toni Morrison's *Song of Solomon* (1977) to Julie Dash's *Daughters of the Dust* (1992), a transnational congregation answered the call to risk identification with the submerged epistemologies of seemingly dispossessed ancestors. The hybrid medleys, John Canoe exhibitions, and broken Englishes inscribed in these novel praise-housings point us toward reconsideration of Wilson Harris's "limbo imagination of the folk" and its "crucial inner recreative response to the violations of slavery . . . [which] needed its critical or historical correlative, its critical or historical advocacy."[73] For initial entry, we can follow one of the clearest and most comprehensive pointings into lowcountry/circum-Caribbean spiritual travel: Paule Marshall's *Praisesong for the Widow* (1983).

"Somewhere a Baby Needed Changing"—*Praisesong*'s Novel Travel Tract

Praisesong for the Widow demands to be read intertextually or congregationally, within the "single calling-responsive unit" that emerges from postplantation literature, according to Valérie Loichot, when the reader works "*to foster the text.*"[74] Since *Praisesong* revitalizes and enacts the "Gullah 'seeker's' initiation rite," as Elizabeth McNeil observes, the novel's travel of "[i]nitiation also involves the reader as a participant in . . . a rhetorical 'call and response'" that moves us between the Gullah Sea Islands, New York, Grenada, Carriacou, and various vessels at sea.[75] *Praisesong* opens aboard ship as we meet our avatar, the upper-middle-class, middle-aged widow, Avey (Avatara) Johnson, gathering her six suitcases after a sudden decision to abandon her cruise aboard the *Bianca Pride*. Widowed not just from her husband but also from so many others (daughters, ancestors, and lost components of self), Avey moves in both a zombie and a mourner state. She must face an unrecognized need for a different kind of travel: not a recreational getaway on the *White Pride* but the re-creative marooning of a "Runagate," as the title of the novel's first of four chapter sections underscores in pointing to Robert Hayden's poem.[76]

As Avey packs her overstuffed bags in her ship cabin, her bare feet help her recall small acts of eros and balance that once sustained her marriage:

The 78s on the turntable in the living room: Coleman Hawkins, Lester Young, The Count, The Duke. Music to usher Jay in the door. Freed of the highheels her body always felt restored to its proper axis. And the hardwood floor which Jay had rescued from layers of oxblood-colored paint when they first moved in and stained earth brown, the floor reverberating with "Cottontail" and "Lester Leaps In" would be like a rich nurturing ground from which she had sprung and to which she could always turn for sustenance.[77]

Starting its rescue work of realignment via barefooted stepping and a blood-red hardwood floor, *Praisesong*'s musical memory activates old habits of self-possession. Aware that she "hadn't thought of that floor for decades" (12), Avey recalls her first glance at the cruise ship's high-tech consoles and how she found "There had been no resisting it!" (15). What has been occupying her mind has been the stuff and upwardly mobile aspirations of consumer culture. Nevertheless, much as her feet activate memory, her body offers resistance—via an intense case of indigestion in the ship's opulent Versailles Dining Room. And within the three-day time frame of Christ's death and resurrection, Avey quits her cruise to mourn, shout, and open herself in saraka acts of reclaimed kinships.

As with the initiatory rites of praise-house seeking, Avey is guided by a spiritual parent and hailed by dream. In one of Avey's dreams aboard the *Bianca Pride*, her dead great-aunt Cuney comes calling her "out of her cotton-picking [mind]" to the walks they shared "during the Augusts she had spent as a girl on Tatem Island . . . on the South Carolina Tidewater" (32). Aunt Cuney steps forward as Avey's pointer to call her away from cotton-picking service to consumerism . . . via the ring shout's soul guardianship:

> Only their heels rose and then fell with each step, striking the worn pineboard with a beat that was precise and intricate as a drum's, and which as the night wore on and the Shout became more animated could be heard all over Tatem. They sang: "*Who's that riding the chariot? / Well well well . . .*"; used their hands as racing tambourines, slapped their knees and thighs and chest in dazzling syncopated rhythm. They worked their shoulders; even succeeded at times in giving a mean roll of their aged hips. They allowed their failing bodies every liberty, yet their feet never once left the floor or, worse, crossed each other in a dance step.
>
> Arms shot up, hands arched back like wings: "*Got your life in my hands / Well well well . . .*" Singing in quavering atonal voices as they glided and stamped one behind the other within the larger circle of their shadows cast by the lamplight on the walls. Even when the Spirit took hold and their souls and writhing bodies seemed about to soar off into the night, their feet remained planted firm. *I shall not be moved.* (34)

The shout works to reconcile African worship styles with Anglo-Protestant prohibition of dance and drums. As structure of both authority and freedom, the counterclockwise steps and polyrhythms of the shout enact the psychic grounding and flight signified in Avey's name, Avatara—"bird-earth"—and enable the steadiness the late Georgia shouter Lawrence McKiver observed in an accomplished holy dancer: "she could be just as level . . . Her meats'd be shakin', but she could be—so level in time."[78]

Although the shout supports *Praisesong*'s level movement and psychic flight, the object of Avey's childhood walks was Ibo Landing, where a group of chained Ibo, as the historians recount, committed suicide by leaping into the tidal river on which they were docked.[79] What Aunt Cuney imparted, however, is the marvelous witnessing of the event received from her grandmother, who spoke of the visionary gift of Africans who "could see in more ways than one" and how "when they seen what was to come" (37),

> They just turned, my gran' said . . . and walked on back down to the edge of the river here . . . They just kept walking right on out over the river. Now you wouldna thought they'd of got very far seeing as it was water they was walking on. Besides they had all that iron on 'em. Iron on they ankles and they wrists and fastened 'round they necks like a dog collar. 'Nuff iron to sink an army. And chains hooking up the iron. But chains didn't stop those Ibo none. Neither iron. The way my gran' tol' it . . . 'cording to her they just kept on walking like the water was solid ground. Left the white folks standin' back here with they mouth hung open and they taken off down the river on foot. Stepping. (38–39)

Providing precedent for Avey's escape from the cruise ship, this lowcountry narrative, passed from Cuney's "gran" Avatara, tests our good faith. When young Avey expressed doubts, asking, "how come they didn't drown, Aunt Cuney?" Cuney chastised her: "Did it say Jesus drowned when he went walking on the water in that Sunday School book your momma always sends with you?" (40). We see that the Christian miracles are accepted because they are scriptural, authorized by canonical texts, while Afro-creole encounter with the sublime faces dismissal as folkloric fantasy. The Ibo Landing tale, which Marshall reworked from the Georgia Writers' Project's interviews with exslaves (1940), asks us "to see in more ways than one," to nurture an ear for what John Chernoff calls a "profoundly pluralistic," polyrhythmic perspective that extends to matters of social and epistemological import.[80] As Chernoff insists, the music trains us to "expect dialogue . . . there is always an in-between, always a place to add another beat . . . beyond any one perspective a person can bring to it."[81]

If Ibo Landing is such "consecrated ground" (39) that Cuney "made the Landing her religion" (34), we may ask what consecrates it and allies it with the "rich nurturing ground" of Avey's early marriage? Consecration comes ultimately from continued *performance* of the Ibos' refusal to bow to an authority that would consume their agency. This restored behavior allows the landing's dead to shout-step in other (godchildren's) bodies in other times, places, and media of representation.

Aunt Cuney's spirit hails Avey on the *Bianca Pride*, "exhorting her, transformed into a preacher in a Holiness church imploring the sinners and backsliders to come forward to the mercy seat. 'Come / O will you come . . . ?'" (42). Issuing a call from the grave's pulpit, Cuney demands seekerly response. And *Praisesong* builds here from African notions of personhood since Avey bears some reincarnate component of Cuney's grandmother's soul. Old Avatara, Ibo Landing's witness, had come to Cuney in a dream divining Avey's birth, gender, and name, leaving Aunt Cuney to announce, "It's my gran' done sent her. She's her little girl" (42). Complicating individualist notions of personhood, authorship, filiation, or salvation, *Praisesong* presents Avey as an avatar of lives that have preceded her, an avatar ritually bound to generations past and future.[82] Aunt Cuney's whirlwind charge, "like one of those August storms" over the marshes (43), forces Avey down to the mourning ground of self-eviscerating travel familiar to Gullah/Geechee and Caribbean praise-house initiates.

Avey resists furiously. However, a parfait from the *Bianca Pride*'s Versailles dining room brings on the purging indigestion described by one contemporary Caribbean Spiritual Baptist mourner as healthy rejection of a bejeweled fruit more pleasing to the eye than to the soul or the stomach: "the snake had filled Adam and Eve with a desire for that which they could not digest."[83] Initiatory transmission of knowledge in Afro-Atlantic traditions insists on multiple stagings in preparing the seeker for the rechanneling of desire. Such moments of liminal inscription face real risk. When Avey walks up to the *Bianca Pride*'s top deck, she encounters a skeet shooter. Each clay pigeon blasted to shards in its "stiff-winged trajectory" gives her a sense of the danger her avian spirit faces. When an old man in red and white trunks and blue visor reaches out to her in a pirate-zombie's skeletal dissolve of flesh and organs (58–59), readers are hailed by Uncle Sam himself. As Elizabeth McNeil has noted, Uncle Sam doubles here as a Vodou Gédé figure of the grave's ravenous ability to digest and recycle, and he steps forward as the threshold figure through whom all ritual action and cosmic dynaflow must pass.[84] When Avey finally escapes the *Bianca Pride* and arrives dockside in Grenada, the text scripts more such hailings of consumptive dispossession when Avey's Grenadian cabdriver (in Gédé's mirrored shades) responds to her request for a hotel: "'Plenty hotels, oui!' . . . 'That's all we got 'bout here now'" (80). Escaping the reaches of the *Bianca Pride* proves no easy matter in the bejeweled markets of its capitalized landings.

Ever since the novel's first critical respondent, Barbara Christian, asserted that "a visceral understanding of their history and rituals can help black people transcend their displacement," *Praisesong*'s readers have been coming to a growing awareness of how the text works to reassemble its congregational performance.[85] Black secular and sacred music, Gullah praise traditions, Spiritual Baptist mourning, nation dance, Vodou, and Orisha houses all contribute to its transnational response to historic displacements. Viscerally acute displacements drive Avey off of the *Bianca Pride* in the novel's second section of chapters, titled "Sleeper's Wake." The "Sleeper's Wake" section begins in an unlikely sacred room of mourning (a hotel) on Grenada's Grand Anse Beach where Avey is confronted with visions of her once-tender marriage dispirited by relentless focus on material progress. Awakening to her dead husband's ghostly question, "What the devil's gotten into you, woman?" (87), Avey revisits old rites of soul-guardianship whereby her husband, Jay, would shed his workday-mask and ease back into self-possession: "as if it was something apart from him, the sore spent body of a friend perhaps, he would lower his tall frame into the armchair, lean his head back, close his eyes, and let Coleman Hawkins, The Count, Lester Young (Old Prez himself), the Duke . . . work their magic, their special mojo on him. Until gradually, under their ministrations . . . his body as he sat up in the chair and stretched would look as if it belonged to him again" (94). The enthroning grooves of this royal music create a protective grove for Jay: "In his hands the worn-out album with its many leaves became a sacred object, and each record inside an icon" (94). An erotic power undergirds the "special mojo" of this music. This is an erotic that has been well described by Audre Lorde as a "power which comes from sharing deeply any pursuit with another person," a "sharing of joy" that "can be the basis for understanding much of what is not shared . . . and lessens the threat of . . . difference."[86]

Polyrhythms of the creole saints do not celebrate asceticism and celibacy; they rise from spirited dialogue with the sacred source of life. Nowhere is this more clear than in Avey's mourning vision of how Jay would enter her body's "sacred room" in awestruck silence, sensing himself surrounded by living mysteries—Erzulie, Yemoja, Oya—"ancient deities who had made their temple the tunneled darkness of his wife's flesh" (127). Then the marvelous lit grid, the saintly blues rhythms of her miracle coming:

There would be the thick runaway beating of her heart ("Just the beat, just the beat of my poor heart in the dark": Lil Green on the record they loved), the heat and her dissolving limbs. And then, without warning, a nerve somewhere in her body which had never before made itself felt would give a slight twitch, and growing stronger take over the work of the pulse at her wrists and temples and throat, and begin beating. But in a more forceful way. And in a swift chain reaction—all of it taking less than a second—the upheaval would spread to a host of other nerves and muscles, causing them to erupt also. Until pulsing together they brought to life the other heart at the base of the body. And the miracle . . . took place. She slipped free of it all . . . [of] her ordinary everyday self. (128)

This gospel experience finds evangelical testimony too in blues singers' shouts and Baptist praise-house mourners' tracts. As Spiritual Baptist leader Mother Haynes asserts, "you . . . tell others about your 'tracks,' that is your story about traveling in the spirit."[87] One mourner says simply of the travel narrative she shared with praise-house members: "I shouted the good news that I had visioned . . . I was an authoritative energy."[88]

But remaining in possession of this authoritative energy requires maintenance of the infrastructural lines of erotic connection and calling-responsive communion: "The small rituals that had once shaped their lives . . . an ethos they held in common, had reached back beyond her life and beyond Jay's to join them to the vast unknown lineage that had made their being possible. And this link, these connections, heard in the music and in the praisesongs of a Sunday . . . had both protected them and put them in possession of a kind of power" (137). Individualist service to Mammon leaves the "lineage," "links," and "connections" in disrepair, leading Avey and Jay (and entire communities) to consumptive states of dispossession. If Marshall's novel speaks to a black bourgeoisie's distancing from collective soul-guardianship, it also leads us to see that soul-sustaining power lines might still be accessible. This is true in the text and in the saraka rites and Spiritual Baptist churches that inform it. As Mother Samuel, a St. Vincent pointer, insists, "When you are a spiritual elder . . . you will see the lines. They look like white telephone lines. They connect you to all the places where you can travel. Sometimes I see a line that is broken: it's not lit up. I then have to go repair it to keep the connection alive."[89] Tropes of power lines, phone calls, and shining lights pervade *Praisesong* in erotic gospel figurations.

In abandoning their rituals of music and dance, along with their annual summer pilgrimage to the Carolina coast, Avey and Jay cut the lines of their shared power. And as Avey's reopening to mourning takes her back to Jay's funeral, she discovers no trace of her erotic partner, only "that other face she sometimes thought she detected hovering pale and shadowy over his," matching "the unsparing, puritanical tone that had developed in his voice" (132). Jay fell victim to the professional face he had worn only as workplace mask—and became the driven, stiffer "Jerome Johnson." Looking back into his casket from the trance-space of her Grenada hotel room, Avey sees "in the face of her great loss" (133) what she had feared to acknowledge: "she and Jerome Johnson . . . could almost pass for twins" (141). Avey Johnson, unable to think of herself as "Avey" or "Avatara," and now hailed by her own zombied corpse, has lost access to something of her deep self, the reincarnation of her ancestral witness to Ibo Landing—what Yoruba people would call her *ori* or "head." She must mourn her losses and awaken to respond to Cuney's call "at the mourner's bench" (143). One thing, however, must be kept in mind: the altar call—"*Come / Won't you come . . . ?*"—of "Sleeper's Wake" (143) is not simply for Avey, who is, after all, only an avatar for the text's readerly experience.

Praisesong's third section—"Lavé Tête," opening with an epigraph of pointsong (Vodou praise song) to the path-clearing crossroads deity, Legba—moves toward "head-washing" whereby Avey is prepared to receive the *lwa* (mystery or guardian of soul) planted within her head. First she must smell her own stink, and history's too. The "Lavé Tête" head-washing section commences with Avey as both mother and infant: "In the final turn of her sleep she smelled it. An odor faint but familiar. Somewhere a baby needed changing" (149). Of course, as praise-house pointers would insist, "the baby is your soul." Awakened to "the staleness of her own flesh" (150), Avey leaves her hotel room for a beach stroll, "clumsy as a two-year-old" (151). She feels "the caul over her mind lifting" (154) before the sun sends her to shelter in a rum shop tended by an old man from the Out Island of Carriacou. Here, Lebert Joseph, an agile but limping "old man with one leg shorter than the other" (160), an avatar of Papa Legba (the Vodou path-opener), takes on the role of Avey's pointer "[a]s if she were a schoolgirl again and he a teacher she disliked" (161). He speaks of the weekend's Carriacou "excursion" and explains the need for remembrance of the "Old Parents," who may "get vex and cause you nothing but trouble" if not honored in the Big Drum's nation dances and assuaged with the Beg Pardon dance (165). In stating "I's a Chamba!" and asking, "What's your nation?" (166–67), he deterritorializes Avey's accustomed boundaries of identity. Mystified, she nevertheless relates her dream of Aunt Cuney, and Lebert realizes Avey is one of those vexed subjects "who can't call their nation" (175).

Although Avey recognizes only one of Lebert's dance demonstrations (not a nation dance but the creole Juba dance she knows from Carolina), she watches him perform another creole dance most poignantly: the Bongo. When he "of the mismatched legs" (178) performs the Bongo for her, "it didn't seem that the story was just something he had heard, but an event he had been witness to," the song's enslaved parents enchained and sold off to different islands, the song's children "left orphaned behind" (177). Such danced, embodied mourning fosters remediating responses to the traumas of diasporic orphaning. In the contemporary Caribbean, we see this remediation take form in Baptist rites of "adoption." Spiritual Baptist Mother Superior Sandy advises her initiates to "[m]ove when the spirit adopts you."[90] According to St. Vincent's Mother Samuel, "'Doption is when the spirit gets into your belly. When you feel it making your body tight, you must stand up and stomp the ground. Then let it come out of your mouth."[91] She explains how a tutelary spirit adopted her and showed her "how the stomping of the feet and the shaking of the earth sent a pumping spiritual energy into the belly."[92] In Grenada, Avey recalls her own childhood experiences of antiphonal adoption—a Tatem Island ring shout and a Harlem boat excursion up the Hudson—and how she felt "what seemed to be hundreds of slender threads streaming out from her navel and from the place where her heart was to enter those around her" (190), till suddenly it would seem that "the threads didn't come from her, but from them . . . issuing out of their navels and hearts to stream into her" (191). This memory of adoption's erotic threads or power grid marks Avey's final preparation for her unanticipated travel on the Carriacou excursion.

Avey goes back to the docks that very afternoon, boarding a Carriacou sloop with Lebert Joseph, who opens "a swift path for them" (192). Once aboard the packed boat, she sits amidst women so much like "the presiding mothers" who brought "sinners and backsliders . . . [through] their shamefaced calvary up to the pulpit" of her childhood church (194) that she gets transported to a childhood Easter sermon, "Affrighted and filled with wond-a-a-h!" (199). As Avey's waterborne vision fills with the Holy Ghost power of that old Easter sermon, which can "roll away the stones sealing up our spirits" (200), the minister's remembered voice becomes supplemented with the power-flow (or *ashé*) of "saints" like Shango, fiery orisha of electric storm, establishing electric lines by which "*Jesus called and God acted*" (201), as Avey travels back into that Easter Sunday's intoned launching of "This little light of m-i-n-e" (202). The preacher's summons—"*Just call Him*," "*Call Him in the midnight hour*"—evokes "*the thrilling response*" of a fully lit congregational assemblage: "*Call Him*" (202). The restored powerlines of that childhood Easter, twinned to the boat's turbulent sea-passage, have Avey vomiting in seasick voidings and in purgings of a deeply lodged indigestible "*chocolate Easter egg*" from childhood (203). Here is the over-rich unincorporable gift-egg given to the failed initiate girl in the narratives that charted our introduction. Tended by the "mothers" on "the bench" of the schooner (204), the infantilized Avey finally shits herself in a detoxifying release of "the stench" (205) common to Afro-creole initiatory rebirthings, which often use herbal emetics and laxatives in production of the freely flowing body without organs, realized for Deleuze and Guattari, we may recall, in the Dogon cosmic egg's distribution of intensities.[93]

This ritual evisceration moves Avey into the limbo of what Gay Wilentz termed a "Middle Passage back" across the Atlantic.[94] It also repeats a harrowing vision described by a Spiritual Baptist mourner who experienced "spiritual surgery" in the sacred room of his travel: "All my inner organs and tissue were scraped out and then washed with a small fire hose. I was completely emptied. They poured salt inside me and sewed me up."[95] To travel or mourn is to enter a gutting of individual agency that paradoxically works to open the initiate to energy flows (grace, *ashé*) of potentiality via travel through abject mires—shit, bile, undigested matter, the sacrificial blood of animal surrogates. If flow is blocked, Legba/Lebert can clear a path through stagnation, as he does for Avey down to the deckhouse where, though she is left alone, a "multitude it felt like lay packed around her in the filth and stench of themselves, just as she was" (208). Afro-creole initiations often revisit these limbo-mires of Middle Passage. Métraux describes how the Vodou *laver-tête* ceremony calls supplicants to have their heads washed and then bound with a shampoo of herbs, syrup, milk-soaked starches, and blood, challenging them with an itchy, decomposing stench throughout their lengthy retreat to aid their own passage's adoptive purpose: to instantiate the link between initiate and *lwa*.[96]

Praisesong's final section, "The Beg Pardon," opens with an exhausted Avey, bathed and massaged by Lebert's daughter, finding the saraka offering of lit candle and corn set on a side table for the ancestors "no more strange than the plate of food that used to be placed beside the coffin at funerals in Tatem" (225). She meets Lebert that evening by the crossroads to attend the Big Drum rite, and at the gate Lebert again manifests as the path-opening *lwa* Legba: "his body more misshapen and infirm than ever before" (233). Leading Avey to a rum-wet clearing where the "long-time folk" gather, Lebert soon falls to his knees, calling the "Old Parents" with a falsetto "*Pa'doné mwê* . . . !" (236).

After the "Beg Pardon," the nation dances call those who identify themselves by performance of African "nation" (Cromanti, Manding, Congo, etc.). When the creole dances begin with fresh drum-mistings of rum, an iron gong summons "Ogun Feraille" (246), iron deity of metallurgic creative/destructive cycles. With Ogun's "[i]ron lending its authoritative voice" (242), Avey watches the dancers' "ever-widening ring" till "the reverberation of their powerful tread in the ground" brings her to take "a single declarative step forward" (247). Moving "cautiously at first, each foot edging forward as if the ground under her was really water—muddy river water" (248), Avey rejoins the Ibo stepping across the waters back home: "She had finally after all these decades made it across" (248). Making it across means tapping into structures outside the self—as "she felt the threads" (249)—those power lines of connection with other people, places, times. Moving now toward flight, "working her shoulders in the way the Shouters long ago used to do, thrusting them forward and then back in a strong casting-off motion" (249), Avey steps a "shuffle designed to stay the course of history," till suddenly her "arms went up and her body seemed about to soar off into the night" (250).

It is at this point that Lebert drops the proud glow of spiritual parentage and bows low, followed by the other older dancers prostrating themselves, one by one, to some awesome manifestation from the Old Parents incarnate in Avey's dance. When a bearded woman, a "Tiresias of the dried dugs," bows and asks, "And who you is?" Avey replies, as Aunt Cuney had insisted, "Avey, short for Avatara" (251). Finally, she has made it across to becoming avatar of her own reclaimed head (ori): both that reincarnate transgenerational spirit which makes the prenatal choices of destiny we may work to maximize, and the orisha or "head-source (ori-sha)" that is a guardian-source of this consciousness.[97]

Avey's travel to restored behaviors of orisha consciousness finds fullest vetting in the final recognition scene between the dancing Avatara and the bearded woman, a scene that reincarnates masks from Yoruba Gelede and Efe spectacle. Practiced in Nigeria's Yoruba communities, Gelede pays homage to transformational powers of the Mothers. Gelede's nighttime component, Efe, begins with ijuba incantations—activating personal and relational potentiality—followed by praises to the path-opening deities Eshu-Elegba and Ogun, then songs of social commentary, and finally the appearance of ancestral mother-masks, embodying powers of shape-shifting and becoming.[98] These masks "dramatize the spiritual side of womanhood in two of its aspects—a bearded crone, often called the Great Mother (Iyanla), and Spirit Bird (Eye Oro)."[99] Women's birthing powers and their relatively open access to the "head" allow the mothers a share in the primary Yoruba emblem of the spirit: the ever-reincarnate spirit-head (ori) or white "bird of the head" that enters each physical head at birth.[100] When these bodies of knowledge migrated to the New World, they met virgin saints and the white dove of annunciation. In Carriacou, the "Big Drum" rite reaches Avey with such deep affect that—upon being recognized with a bow from the bearded mother—she introduces herself as Avatara (both avian and of terra firma), avatar of an ancestor who bears witness to the Ibo hierophany.

As Avey goes to the mire, makes it across, and becomes avatar of "the Longtime folk," the Big Drum moves her to mourn transgressions against her "spirit-head." She begs pardon for her submission to consumer materialism and for her subsequent shirking of an elder's responsibilities. Facing this disorganization of personal and community energy flow, Avey reaches, in Baptist terms, salvation. Augmenting Avey's ancestral restoration is the potential renovation and conversion of the Tatem Island church itself, which "looked as if it had never recovered from the blow dealt its authority one evening long ago when Avey's great-aunt had raged out of its door never to return" (33). Praisesong anticipates Cornel West's 1993 call for "some kind of politics of conversion," working locally, within "those institutions in civil society still vital enough" to counter the nihilism of an "ever-expanding market culture that puts everything and everyone up for sale."[101] West grounded his appeal for conversion in a "love ethic," a kind of lapsed saraka ethos that he found exemplified in fiction, especially in Marshall's and Toni Morrison's novel "tracks."[102]

"To dare transition," that is the achievement of *Praisesong for the Widow.* It undertakes a politics of conversion and transfiguration in its remodeling of Afro-Atlantic assemblages. A restored Avatara leaves Carriacou vowing to repair the family house in the Sea Islands to host her grandchildren each summer in the manner in which Aunt Cuney pointed her. Advancing an Afro-conservative politics of conversion, she will convert the house into a summer camp, inviting her daughter's schoolchildren too—those "sweetest lepers" of the poor—to travel Ibo Landing's "consecrated ground." In *Praisesong*, the novel functions as assembly house of old rites that begin to find a new social legitimization through the very print networks that had steadily dismissed black Atlantic religion as an "undefinable medley of truth and falsehood." Marshall's praise-novel performs a remarkable redefinition-and-conversion medley on reclaimed terrain.

Transfiguring Conversions—"Lower lower . . . down to de mire"

Recent novels set in creolized postplantation spaces return us to a saraka ethos and the travels of mourning on trauma-consecrated ground. In *Partial Faiths: Postsecular Fiction in the Age of Pynchon and Morrison*, John McClure points to a widespread seekerly impulse in American fiction. McClure utilizes Robert Wuthnow's description of two modes of contemporary religious orientation, "dwelling" and "seeking," and charts a postsecular turn in North American fiction in texts in which "religiously unhoused spiritual seekers" enact "practices of open dwelling that have not closed the door to otherness."[103] Nevertheless, as McClure admits, apprehensions of spiritual homelessness are hardly new to the Americas or to transatlantic plantation economies. Afro-creole praise societies faced incredible challenges of fostering community via occluded modes of resistance to white-supremacist fundamentalisms. McClure's *Partial Faiths* rightly insists, however, that even these hard-won Afro-creole housings find healthy contestation in the work of contemporary writers who "project a spiritually charged cosmos" while seeking to avoid "turning this cosmic house of the spirits into a prison house of religious dogma."[104] Speaking of how Toni Morrison's "power as a postsecular novelist arises in part from her culturally sponsored investment in a spacious, creolized spirituality," McClure adds that "it rises as well . . . from her culturally grounded knowledge of the dangers of religious enclosure."[105] What gets fashioned in texts like *Praisesong* is the housing of another kind of authority—out of subalternized, discredited, and just plain dissed sources—

and particularly out of women's ministration of what Karla Holloway has called "endangered wisdom," born of "whatever smacks of survival."[106]

The term "postsecular" is hardly apt for describing these novel texts from traditionally "spirited" cultures of the South and the Caribbean that have never fallen into lock-step with metropolitan secularization. Contemporary works of a lowcountry sublime (Marshall's *Praisesong*, Morrison's *Song of Solomon*, Bambara's *The Salt Eaters*, Naylor's *Mama Day*, Dash's *Daughters of the Dust*, Brodber's *Myal*) have contested the church's scripturally engendered enclosures of deity in Father, Son, and Holy Spirit. They especially contest what Caribbean theologian Dianne M. Stewart describes in *Three Eyes for the Journey* as Christianity's "Afrophobic ideas," its hermeneutic burials of "'local awareness' of constructed suffering."[107] In resisting Christianist Afrophobia, these works of bush-arbor reassemblage often remain constructed as conversion tracts under the godparentage of powerful female pointers, bringing initiates into alternative spaces of sanctuary. Although the virtual praise houses constructed in this seekerly womanist lineage have been charged (most influentially by Hazel Carby and more recently by Madhu Dubey) with privileging a southern/circum-Caribbean folk aesthetic of nostalgia and romanticism, I would insist—along with Wilson Harris and Dianne Stewart—that much of the submerged authority of the folk has been so censored and devalued that it has hardly received its critical and historical advocacy.[108] We absolutely must open our eyes to a wider body of orphan literary "tracts" in which a virtual *hippikat* congregation may move in counterclockwise ring fashion beyond mere nostalgia—into a true-true creole cosmopolitanism.

Morrison paid intertextual homage to Sea Island initiatory authority in *Song of Solomon* (1977).[109] Macon and Pilate Dead, "[t]he orphans [who] called to Circe from the vegetable garden," both have their mourning to do in this novel.[110] But the storyline follows the belated journey of Macon's son, Milkman—with Aunt Pilate serving as the pointer whom Milkman meets at the seekerly age of twelve when she offers him a boiled egg. From Pilate's perpetual offer of eggs, to a best friend's assertion that "somebody got to burst your shell" (129), to an inheritance appearing "like nest eggs" (187) and "like the green of Easter eggs" (203), the object of Milkman's travel is the misrecognized golden egg of initiatory desire. This gold also appears in power lines of erotic connection, in the "thread of light" in his mother's milk, "as though she were a cauldron issuing" a "secret power" in the "golden thread stream[ing]" into Milkman's mouth (20). The novel tracks Milkman's southward travels into various sacred spaces presided over by hunters, godmothers, and lovers. In a hunting scene, briar cuts "stinging . . . from the leaf juice" (298) medicinally hasten Milkman's mourning process by which "his self— the cocoon that was 'personality'—gave way" (300), enabling thereafter the remnants of ring shout in a children's song to connect him to a more composite vision of self. Morrison's building of this *song* of Solomon ("Come booba yalle, come booba tambee") around the funerary Mende ring shout performed by Amelia Dawley (and by Georgia ex-slaves in *Drums and Shadows*) gives uncanny testimony to its gateway power. Furthermore, the ringplay's encoded mention of "Saraka cake" (303) speaks to how *Song of Solomon* sets an ancestral "table" of intergenerational service and reciprocity. Its saraka sweets feed its children in a manner far different from the "Divinity" candy given to Guitar Baines (Milkman's one friend) as a child by a Florida sawmill owner as consolation following the sawmill-evisceration of his father. *Song of Solomon* is hardly concerned with orthodox Christian divinity. Adhering to its own politics of conversion and transfiguration, the novel refabricates its corporate models of mercy and grace from Geechee nation's southern limits: from ex-slave narratives in the WPA *Drums and Shadows*, and from the Jacksonville, Florida, entrepreneurship of A. L. Lewis—founder of the Afro-American Life Insurance Company and American Beach (the Jim Crow–era black-owned beach of Amelia Island, Florida).[111]

Perhaps the most crucial literary co-initiator of a saraka ethos was Toni Cade Bambara's *The Salt Eaters* (1980). *The Salt Eaters* opens with its seeker, a nigh zombified social activist (Velma), being treated by the acclaimed local healer Minnie Ransom. Inhabiting the fictional Geechee town of Claybourne, Georgia, Minnie Ransom leads an assembly of healers who cure by laying on hands and by psychic travel. Bambara's textual praise house is a most heterodox one, moving away from church enclosures to do its seeking down low amidst the marsh's "crusty short grass and salt-stiff calamus," near the sound's "merging of the waters."[112] Moving steadily "toward a clearing, toward a likely sanctuary of the saints, the loa, the dinns, the devas" (247), and seeking to "tap the brain for any knowledge of initiation rites lying dormant there," *The Salt Eaters* works thresholds of a "new spiritism" (248). Velma finally limbos through, backed by her mourning vision's drum-fed "Feedback and contagion" (250), "travel[ing] the streets in six-eight time cause Dizzy said righteous experience could not be rendered in three-quarter time" (264)—to emerge "like something heaved up from the marshes" (267). Righteous experience gets produced in this text's heterodox tract of it, in the knowledge that it is "only proper to do one's seeking on one's knees" (266), down in the marshes where a dance of mud women and a transfiguring storm remove Velma's blocked flows. Here we find the taste of salt that wakes the zombie, and the initiate language of power-gridded connection between Velma and "the healer, the people circling her" in "silvery tendrils . . . extending out like tiny webs of invisible thread" (267).

Gloria Naylor's *Mama Day* (1988) introduces yet another initiation tract into this lowcountry web. Set on a tempest-struck island on the Carolina–Georgia border, the novel locates authority in Miranda Day, a midwife and rootworking healer who takes on much of the parentage of her sister's orphaned granddaughter, Cocoa, and eventually tends to Cocoa's New York orphanage–raised husband. Eggs are put to use in ritual, in divination, and as initiatory travel-objects in *Mama Day*. Hands carry an electrifying erotic power. Miranda Day calls her niece's husband beyond self-reliance, telling him to place his hand in hers "so she can connect it up with all the believing that had gone before," to have him enter her chicken coop to reach beneath "an old red hen that's setting her last batch of eggs," and "bring . . . back *whatever* you find."[113] Unable to reconnect that power grid in full, he brings back his own sacrificially bloodied hands and subsequent heart attack. The novel, with its Candle Walk rite linked to Thomas Dorsey's gospel plea ("Take My Hand, Precious Lord"), aims to recharge Afro-creole networks of mutuality. Naylor's text remains mistrustful, however, of the church's fundamentalist Afrophobia. Mama Day responds to Rev. Hooper's condemnation of her diasporic rootwork in terms true to Toomer's Guardian of Souls: "[D]on't make me no nevermind. Been here before he came and I'll be here after he's gone" (187).

Let us be clear. These texts do not call us to get right with the Lord, or his Father or the King James version of His Word and Holy Ghost. But they do regard the spiritual and institutional spaces of reassembled black society with respect for their history of soul guardianship. While *Praisesong for the Widow*, *Song of Solomon*, *The Salt Eaters*, and *Mama Day* present initiating female pointers (Aunt Cuney, Pilate Dead, Minnie Ransom, Miranda Day) who have few compelling ties to church or organized religion, it is perhaps Marshall's novel, the one with the most reach outside of North American territoriality (and a novel written by the daughter of islanders), that treats praise-house assemblies with the most attentiveness to their transfiguring limbo work. It is in Caribbean fiction that we find some of the most wholehearted embraces of praise traditions emergent from spaces beyond mainstream Christianity's censorships.

From Jamaica, Erna Brodber's *Myal* (1988) assembles a heterodox cooperative (of Methodists, Baptists, Myalists, Rastafarians, Revival Zionists) to support the healing of Ella O'Grady, who suffers spirit thievery, being "tripped out in foreign," and whose body passes in hurricane force "the stinkiest, dirtiest ball to come out of a body since creation."[114] Ongoing colonialist work of "separating people from themselves, separating man from his labor" (37) requires Grove Town to recharge its local grids, going down to remnant forces of Myal societies that protected enslaved Jamaicans against ideological and psychic invasion. But the novel reminds us that spirit thieves operate within the community itself—as we see when Myalists root out a sexual predation perpetrated on a fifteen-year-old girl by an orthodox Baptist deacon. Drawing especially from *The Salt Eaters'* pointing, *Myal* adopts a challenging language of bush telegraph, telepathy, and rhythmic grooves serving an assembly of fabulous reincarnate souls and their animal doubles. Insisting that the printed word has hosted spirit thievery, *Myal* models a tract that would transform the script(ure). The healed Ella O'Grady, foster daughter of a naïve (but educable) Methodist minister, serves as a schoolteacher and manages to change (via interdenominational help), if not the curriculum, then her pedagogy. Assigned to teach the subalternizing primer of *Mr. Joe's Farm*, Ella learns to turn the tables of colonialist education by raising questions about how the primer's "sub-normals" pay the costs of Mr. Joe's farm life (97). Her teaching makes literacy and education function as a saraka table, a feeding of the children and a reclamation of the initiatory eggs of their own potentiality:

> The lesson described the strike on Mr. Joe's farm . . . Mrs. Cuddy resented having her milk taken away from her: she would have preferred to have given it to her calf. Mother Hen and White Hen felt the same resentment at their highhanded alienation from what was their own. Nobody asked them whether they wished to sit on their eggs and produce more chicks. Instead, their eggs were summarily taken away and eaten by Mr. Joe and Benjie and those others in his house who walked upright and on two feet. These ladies had been vexed for a long time. (99–100)

Brodber's allegory of independence and collective healing fights contemporary spirit thieveries, whereby postcolonial consumers are reduced to "empty shells" and "living deads capable only of receiving . . . from someone else" (107). For Brodber—as for Jamaica's Native Baptists of George Liele's era— both the printed word and countercultural institutional agency offer key means "to put us back together" (110).[115] In response to colonial practice "that splits the mind from the body and both from the soul and leaves each open to infiltration" (28), *Myal*'s balmyards prepare readers to host, interpret, and transfigure received script(ure) "for an antidote" to dispossessions (68).

Earl Lovelace's *The Wine of Astonishment* (1982) engages the similar struggles of a Trinidadian Spiritual Baptist congregation to keep from "growing more away, astray from ourself" during the period of British colonial prohibition of Baptist/Shouter practice.[116] Although a male-authored text, *Wine* narrates its struggle for sociopolitical legitimization through the voice of Eva, the Baptist pastor's wife, who witnesses the community's slipping hold on their own potentiality. *Wine* presents only one power-generating scene of illegal worship during which the Baptist assembly breaks colonial law to foster its sacral desires along grids of spirit adoption:

> Sister Lucas . . . she go to the Centre Post and she spin and she twist and she turn and she ring the bell and fall on her knees and she pray to the Lord and her

Spirit pick her up and she talk her language and she dance around like a bird going to fly, and I get up and go and meet her and my Spirit come on me, and all over the church people was getting up with their Spirit on them and we meet there in the centre of the church and we hold hands and salute one another, and we was there, the whole church, rocking and humming and talking our language, and the bell was ringing and water was sprinkling and the Spirit was in charge and I was shaking and shouting, Ooh God. (62)

The price paid for this going low and rising up to humming, rocking, ringing, sprinkling, hand-holding thresholds of spirited authority—police beatings, jail, and fines—turns out to be too much to bear. They submit to colonial silencing, knowing "we is still illegal and illegitimate" (112). The resultant loss of power leaves "Everybody living for theyself" (120). When the ban on Baptist worship is eventually revoked, the congregants no longer have the facility to generate their own gnosis, but Eva finds hope in the most secular and bacchanalian of sources: "the music that those boys playing in the steelband have in it that same Spirit that we miss in our church: the same Spirit; and listening to them, my heart swell and it is like resurrection morning" (146). The church must then recover by conducting its "travels" near or within the seemingly profane carnival tent.

From these long submerged (and outlawed) housings of translocal authority, novel black Atlantic bush arbors work to keep hope of initiatory reaffiliation alive. There is something ever new and simultaneously old about this reconstructive intergenerational process, as we can see from Julie Dash's acclaimed film *Daughters of the Dust* (1992). Responding explicitly and deferentially to Marshall's *Praisesong*, and even purchasing sampling rights to some of the language of the novel's Ibo Landing tale, Dash's *Daughters of the Dust* draws a cinematic convergence of Protestant, Catholic, Muslim, Sande/Poro, Orisha, and Vodou rites around Ibo Landing's canonized ground. The film's ministration flows through its primary pointer, Nana Peazant, possessed of the spirit of the orisha Obatala who created humanity from African dust. Through Nana, Dash calls viewers to a process of conversion whereby the mourner must submit to Nana's spiritual parentage as well as to the converting eye of the camera, to step into the film's hermeneutic circle: the cinematic praise house it constructs in this first nationally distributed film by an African American woman.

Narrated by an unborn daughter potentially conceived in a rape, *Daughters* honors the violated womb that is sacred grove of New World space. Sara Clarke Kaplan calls attention to the film's cinematic task of mourning this womb-space's historical mires: "In *Daughters'* slow fades, moments of dreamy slow motion, asynchronous flashbacks, and scenes of spiritual possession, Dash gestures to the continuing ghostly presence of that history, as sedimented in and animated by displaced spirits and ancestors."[117] Following gorgeous scenes of travel across marsh waterways and a series of baptismal rebirthings in Ibo Landing's waters, we witness the island community gathered to enjoy a last supper or saraka table of lowcountry culinary glamour. After this key feast, Dash scripts her directions: "We find them resting. We focus on their eyes and facial expressions, it is a time of conversion, of rebirthing to journey North."[118] In the traditions of spirit-integration practiced by elders like Pilate Dead, Minnie Ransom, Aunt Cuney, Miranda Day, and *Myal*'s Miss Gaitha before her, Nana Peazant then fashions a convergent "hand" from cuttings of her slave mother's hair; adds her own hair, a "dressed" root, a Catholic/orisha St. Christopher charm; lays the fashioned "hand" on top of a Bible, and places a firm grip on fellow elder Bilal Muhammad's shoulder to include Muslim Baraka (the Islamic "grace" inherited from descendants of Muhammad and associates—which gave name to Barack Obama), as she blesses her migrating congregation: "We've taken old Gods and given them new names . . . Come children, kiss this hand full of me."[119] Here is the binding moment that would turn the space of the film house into a sanctuary of open dwelling wherein we may face, as Sara Clarke Kaplan insists, what "remains, sedimented in the bodies of the living and the dead, in communities and in nations, producing a spatial memory of a past that is not over and must be confronted."[120]

For the eye/I trained by Hollywood's "Nation-Birthing" ways of seeing, Dash's film can indeed be baffling, even foreign in its Gullah dialogue and its demand that the viewer travel with it. The film's submersion of narrative beneath "altared" imagery, its akimbo diva-ism (attentive to aesthetics of black women's self-fashioning), its patchwork catalog of Africanisms, all demand a ritual submission from the viewer in order for its conversions to take effect. From its signifying, reclamatory reverence for the Georgia earth of a Hollywood classic like *Gone with the Wind*'s "Tara," *Daughters of the Dust* layers its fashion sense and glamour with the ritual respect that shapes every detail of an altar to an orisha such as Oya, goddess of the winds and of the shape-shifting dead. Dash remakes the screen as altar to cleanse it of ways it has received Afrophobic projections violating black women, family, and spirituality. *Daughters of the Dust*'s marsh-side "baffles" gather the sediments of graves to build terrain in an act of wetlands and praise-house restoration. This is another kind of conservatism and conservationist ethos.

The heterodox conservatism of *Daughters of the Dust*—along with that of Marshall's pointerly novel—finds creole kinship in Merle Collins's documentary *Saracca and Nation: African Memory and Re-creation in Grenada and Carriacou* (2008). *Saracca and Nation* looks to how African ancestors and nation networks get remembered and re-invoked in the Caribbean. Whole communities have begun dancing their own nation (as in River Sallée Nation in

Grenada, or as we may see in the coastal region of the contemporary Gullah/
Geechee Nation). In Grenadian and Geechee rites of restored behavior, we
may appreciate how nations have found remembrance by bending foreheads
and bodies low, limboing down to a mire/myuh/*maayo*/myal in the counterclockwise motion of Atlantic storms and West African "social medicine":

> Sister Emma, Oh, you mus' come
>> down to de mire,
>> down to de mire,
> Jesus been down
>> down to de mire
>> down to de mire
>> down to de mire
> You must bow low
>> down to de mire
> Honor Jesus
>> down to de mire
>> down to de mire
> Lower lower
>> down to de mire
>> down to de mire
>> down to de mire
> Jesus been down
>> down to de mire
> Sister Josie, you must come
>> down to de mire
>> down to de mire.[121]

The Guardian of Souls who shouts, the praise-house seeker who narrates
her travel tract, the saraka maker who honors ancestors by feeding their child-
avatars, all have resisted conversion by modernity's colonizations. But they
have also kissed modernity's hand and converted all of us from countercultures within. It is the Guardian of Souls's difficult double processes of conversion that we would do well to study and acknowledge with a bow of respect.
We can catch sense of lowcountry reconsecrations in rites and writings that
go down to the mire to wake nations of relations otherwise hardly charted.

CHAPTER TWO

Lift Every Voice and Swing

James Weldon Johnson's
God-Met Places and Native Lands

We have come over the way
That with tears hath been watered.
We have come treading our paths
Through the blood of the slaughtered.
—Rev. Martin Luther King Jr., closing his final address to the
    Southern Christian Leadership Conference (1967) with a
    rendering from James Weldon Johnson's "Lift Every
    Voice and Sing" (1900)

God of our weary years,
God of our silent tears,
Thou who hast brought us thus far on the way;
Thou who hast by Thy might
Led us into the light
Keep us forever in the path, we pray.
Lest our feet stray from the places, our God, where we met Thee,
Lest, our hearts drunk with the wine of the world, we forget Thee;
Shadowed beneath Thy hand,
May we forever stand.
True to our God,
True to our native land.
—Rev. Joseph Lowery, quoting from "Lift Every Voice and Sing"
    to open the benediction at the inauguration of President
    Barack Hussein Obama, January 20, 2009

There is a remarkable set of tensions between God and native land in the
Negro national anthem. Marking a path grown from "the places, our God,
where we met Thee," the song lays implicit claim to a countercultural knowledge of the sacred's blood-consecrated terrain.[1] Written by the agnostic
James Weldon Johnson (and set to music by his brother, Rosamond) for a
chorus of Jacksonville schoolchildren in honor of Lincoln's birthday, "Lift
Every Voice and Sing" traveled beyond its natal place and time—opening a
new century at the nadir of postbellum race relations in the state with the

65

highest lynching rate in America—to become a nation-anthem canonized amidst the spirituals it evokes.[2] Its patriotism and piety can seem utterly conventional. There is, however, in "Lift Every Voice" a yearning for integration of sacral inheritances that does not reduce to paths of assimilation into Anglo-American national norms. For the God and native land of this countercultural anthem of modernity differ from the God and native land of the republic's imaginary: a difference that made many Americans uneasy when Rev. Joseph Lowery intoned the song's closing stanza to launch President Obama's inaugural benediction. "Lift Every Voice and Sing" asserts a subtle, stake-raising claim to authority that we find repeated throughout James Weldon Johnson's later work. It seeks to produce a utopian space of nativity in the congregational labor of lifting voice and moving beyond fixed boundaries—an agency and affect that Brent Edwards has observed in Johnson's work as "swing."[3] The pathways to the god(s) and native lands of the black national anthem are to be found across deep time and as much across the Atlantic, the Gulf, and the Caribbean as within the territory or chronology of any single nation-state. This aspect of the anthem's rather un-American testimony affirms that seemingly impassable gulfs may prove treadable for fluid bodies of lifted voice.[4]

What Johnson's *The Autobiography of an Ex-Colored Man* (1912) ventriloquized one hundred years ago as that " 'great and impassable gulf' between the races 'fixed by the Creator at the foundation of the world' " gets exposed in the author's body of work as a make-believe gulf born of white supremacy's repression of the real, a repression nonetheless so ideologically tangible to our real conditions of existence as to exact a price for traversal of its boundaries.[5] In "Lift Every Voice and Sing" as in *The Autobiography of an Ex-Colored Man* and Johnson's other works, keeping "forever in the path" turns out to be a prayer-promise to remain close to a gulf-traversing practice of swing.

My own response to James Weldon Johnson's call emerges from rather commonplace orientations and from uncanny circumstances of creolizing fate: a civil rights–era white southern childhood (and many of the usual southern self-fashionings around soul foods and musics), Peace Corps experience in Senegal, a federal job at JFK Airport that introduced me to the cosmopolitan diasporas reassembled in New York City, and a first teaching position at black Baptist Selma University in Alabama. A deeper path into Johnson's God-met spaces began to open up when I finished my doctoral coursework and moved with my wife to St. Simons Island, Georgia, to begin teaching Developmental English at Coastal Georgia Community College. Our moving day happened to coincide with the Georgia Sea Island Festival held on St. Simons the same day. My unloading of the U-Haul truck got done between breaks for smoked mullet, deviled crab, and dirty rice, and found longer sabbatical in performances from both the McIntosh County Shouters and a trombone shout band from Savannah's Ogeechee Road United House of Prayer. They laid down grooves to pull bodies and souls into a different kind of subject-verb agreement than what I would be instilling in Geechee speakers seeking a handle on writing in standard English. I would come to recognize that some of the most self-possessed of my students carried a certain base or basilectal understanding of aligning subjects and verbal action, a gnosis fostered within them by their elders' and ancestors' long work at keeping zombifications at bay.

Steady travels to Sapelo Island (Georgia) over the past eighteen years have augmented my respect for Geechee environments of memory. One particularly charged travel experience came when one of my students invited me to attend New Years' Watch Night Services at her church on the mainland just across from Sapelo Island. Her mother and grandfather were core members of the McIntosh County Shouters, who were set to ring in the new year with a shout in the church annex from past midnight until the wee hours toward dawn. From the moment I stepped inside the packed annex, the "rapper's" stick (almost a pestle) thumping a drumlike beat against pine floorboards, coupled with the polyrhythmic clapping and stamping and chanting of ring-circling shouters and choral "basers," gave the event a complex durational pulse that my body carried long after the actual rhythms finished. The ring shout undertakes travel into a deeply antiphonal time-space, a travel I experienced from the outermost edges of the rite's hermeneutic circle, to be sure, but one open nonetheless to any hosted body through which the spirit(s) can be shared—in a kind of saraka—along with the congregational potluck of hopping John and greens, sweet potato and pecan pie.

Four years later, when I left my job at Coastal Georgia Community College for a position at College of the Bahamas in Nassau, I found that the journey from coastal Georgia to Nassau entailed an increasingly uncanny crossing through submerged kinships and history. The kinships of Sea Island and Bahamian creole languages made for one strong route of passage. Once again it was musical rites that swung a basilectal creole authority to spectacular apprehensions: the New Year's Eve masked junkanoo "rush out" restoring behaviors of the African dead in goatskin drum and cowbell rhythms that displace the individual psyche and ally it in reassembly with others—a feeling in the pit of the stomach when the goombay drums pass like a roller coaster's swoosh and drop . . . rocking a body long after the event. During the year I taught in the Bahamas, my wife and son and I heard brass bands move funeral mourners down the road past our apartment to the cemetery, with shades of a junkanoo beat emerging along the route. We shared vicariously in a night-long wake below our apartment as our neighbors faced death's transitions with the singing of anthems (spirituals) in slow meter, building in amassed waves into the night. My students discussed assigned texts even as the drum-beats and "rush outs" of a spirit-filled "Jumper Church" filled the air of our Wednesday-night "Introduction to Literature." Unfathomable kinships and recognitions emerged for me, my father, and our Bahamian hosts at a rum-soaked "rake and scape" quadrille hoedown near the Out Island community of Cartwright's. These kinships kept growing. Each month when rent was due on my Nassau apartment, I would walk the cash payment across town to the landlady, who ran a bed and breakfast (Dillet's Guest House) out of her home. It took a while for me to register that she was from the prominent Bahamian family of James Weldon Johnson's mother, Helen Louise Dillet. It took a while too in my relocations from the Georgia coast to Nassau and eventually back to my present home in Jacksonville for me to open my eyes to the Gulf Stream currents that shaped Johnson's vision. To put it plainly and by way of preface, my own circum-Caribbean orientation to Deep Southern time, creole spaces, and gulf authority owes a tremendous debt to lives and God-met places that initiated Johnson. Johnson and his elder-guides intro-duce us to a realm of authority that swings accustomed bonds and historici-ties, taking us deeper south—into a truer cosmopolitanism.

In the preface to his classic "passing" novel, *The Autobiography of an Ex-Colored Man*, Johnson established a rubric of initiatory challenge to readers: "In these pages it is as though a veil has been drawn aside: the reader is given a view of the inner life of the Negro in America, is initiated into the 'freema-sonry,' as it were, of the race."[6] As Brent Edwards has insightfully observed, this novel "signals a small but crucial shift of authority" in its revision of Du Bois's veil of race as something more than a shadow-haunted incarceral state.[7] Here, Edwards notes, "it is the white readership that is shut out, and which must by implication undergo a transformation, an initiation 'into the freemasonry' of the Negro race, in order to cross what now seems to be a much more unsettling frontier" as "the book offers not the thrill of access to a 'veiled' world, but the threat of incomprehension, of indistinguishable lim-its."[8] The *Autobiography* is indeed "a *tricky* African Atlantic text," Heather Russell adds, one that "simultaneously veils and conceals while unveiling and revealing," leaving its readers "tasked with standing at the gateway": the testy, transfiguring space of "Wilson Harris's limbo gateway."[9] Johnson forces his reader into creole frontiers whose guides are those native to shape-shifting terrain. A secular-minded and agnostic product of Jacksonville's (and also a Bahamian) black bourgeoisie, Johnson returned almost prodigally to low-country sacred forms and to the effort, famously expressed in his preface to *The Book of American Negro Poetry*, to do "something like what Synge did for the Irish . . . to find a form that will express the racial spirit by symbols from within rather than by symbols from without, such as the mere mutila-tion of English spelling and pronunciation."[10] While his body of work has been fruitfully approached from northern Atlantic and black Manhattan perspectives, readers are only beginning to comprehend how Johnson drew his "symbols from within," his vision of deepest basilectal time and space, from Geechee and circum-Caribbean (Cuban, Haitian, and especially Bahamian) routes of passage.

More than any other literary figure, James Weldon Johnson's authorship, activism, and curatorial/performative cultural agency authorized the jazz era's fetching of "symbols from within" Afro-Atlantic experience. However, because of Johnson's remarkable cosmopolitanism and partly because his Jacksonville, Florida, hometown lies at the southern limits of a Sea Island region more commonly linked to the environs of Charleston and Savannah, Johnson has hardly been considered a native son of the Sea Island lowcountry. Jacksonville, nevertheless, lies well within Geechee cultural space. It is the largest city within Congress's recently established Gullah/Geechee Cultural Heritage Corridor (2006) and marked the southern limit of lands reapportioned in 1865 to coastal freedmen by William T. Sherman's Special Field Order No. 15.[11] But *really now* . . . a Geechee James Weldon Johnson? Such a prospect may sound laughable as a description of the man fellow Floridian Zora Neale Hurston once described, tongue-half-in-cheek, as a King James "just full of that old monarch material," who "took up being colored as a profession" and has "been passing for colored for years."[12] Still, Johnson remains, hands down, the most accomplished author to emerge from Geechee native land.

James Weldon Johnson, quite frankly, was as accomplished as any American has ever been. No early American modernist found as much success in as many venues as he did. First winning recognition as a dominant pitcher for Jacksonville's top black baseball club, Johnson had such a good curveball that he would probably have made his path in a later era as a professional baseball player. But in the four years after graduating from Atlanta University in 1894 and returning home to Jacksonville, he founded and edited a black daily newspaper in the city, became principal of Stanton School (making it the first public high school for blacks in the region), and was the first black man to be admitted to the Florida bar and to open a law office. In 1900 he wrote the lyrics to "Lift Every Voice and Sing." The following year, after narrowly escaping lynching in his fire-ravaged hometown, he moved to New York and, along with his brother, Rosamond, and Bob Cole, became an international pop star, writing hits for Broadway ("Congo Love Song," "Under the Bamboo Tree," "My Castle on the Nile") and touring Europe. In 1906 Johnson made yet another career change to serve as U.S. consul in Venezuela and then later in wartime Nicaragua while making a name as a poet (with poems like "Brothers," "O Black and Unknown Bards," and "Fifty Years"). Meanwhile, he completed the signal novel of African American modernism,

The Autobiography of an Ex-Colored Man (1912). Following his resignation from the consular service in 1913 and the movie production of one of his screenplays, Johnson took charge of the editorial page of the oldest black newspaper in New York City. He joined the NAACP, organized New York's famous "silent march" of 1917 protesting lynching, and participated in the founding of the ACLU. Johnson soon thereafter became the first black leader of the NAACP (1920), and traveled to Haiti to investigate U.S. Marine occupation there. In 1921 Johnson turned his full energies to lobbying for the Dyer anti-lynching bill (blocked in the Senate). In a five-year period of busy political and civil rights activity, Johnson managed to publish the first major anthology of African American poetry (1922), the first black-edited and arranged volumes of spirituals (co-edited with Rosamund, 1925, 1926), and a key book of poetry based in sermonic motifs, *God's Trombones* (1927). After a career as public school principal, newspaper editor, lawyer, pop star, theater figure, diplomat, NAACP leader, antilynching activist, poet, novelist, and black cultural anthologist, Johnson published a history, *Black Manhattan* (1930), and the autobiography *Along This Way* (1933), taught at Fisk, and became the first person to teach a course on African American literature at a primarily white institution, New York University.[13]

One would expect such a legacy to be secure—especially in Johnson's native Jacksonville. Surely in the achievements of Johnson, local readers must encounter the authorial figure so canonized that Roland Barthes felt compelled to announce "The Death of the Author." But in my teaching at the University of North Florida, I have come to expect graduates of James Weldon Johnson Middle School or Stanton High (where Johnson served as principal and where "Lift Every Voice and Sing" was first performed) to be unable to say anything at all about the man. These are students from the best college-preparatory magnet schools in Florida. Stanton presents nothing of Johnson's significance in its website's history of the high school, mentioning only that a man by that name once served as principal. And the website of James Weldon Johnson College Preparatory Middle School offers no information other than listing him as co-author of the school song.[14] It is enough to make one wonder about the alienation fostered in public schools and about the costs of such partial education on our communities . . . since most of my students have something to say about the namesakes of Jacksonville's Robert E. Lee High School and Nathan Bedford Forrest High. Clearly, some public memories are authorized and passed on, and some, perhaps those most unsettlingly close to home, go ignored. Johnson remains largely unremembered in his natal city, a city that has had the highest (and quite racially skewed) rates of murder, infant mortality, sexually transmitted diseases, school dropouts, incarceration, and poverty in an unusually distressed and dysfunctional state. As Russ Rymer writes, "No one has ever accused

Jacksonville, Florida, of putting on airs . . . Its sparse outcropping of corporate skyscrapers, surrounded by unrestrained generic-American urban sprawl, gives the impression of salted earth, a desiccated soil in which nothing sophisticated or genteel can thrive . . . The city also, of course, has a history, a prominent one. The history stays invisible because the prominence resides almost exclusively on the black side of town."[15]

Johnson's work is not a politically easy read. But his texts also point to a cosmopolitan cultural history that could be mobilized to combat the nihilism and low corporate self-esteem of a city (and region) orphaned from its inheritance and left with little other than the NFL Jaguars and numerous mega-churches for cultural capital. Something vital in Jacksonville's and the region's memory has been silenced in the kind of electroshock treatment given to the main character of Ralph Ellison's *Invisible Man* (1952), a character drawn in response to the tricksterish call of Johnson's unnamed Ex-Colored Man. Johnson's narrator was a man driven by "shame, unbearable shame" and violent trauma out of the region and away from the potentiality of an initiatory "birthright," a man driven instead to "make a white man's success; and that, if it can be summed up in any one word, means 'money.' "[16] No wonder policemen tote Tasers to keep order in our public schools. No wonder an underground drug economy has so much appeal in a postplantation region founded upon enslavement of people to mass-produce tobacco, sugar, rum, chocolate, coffee, and, in a word, money. Writing of his hometown, Johnson makes painfully clear how a city that "was known far and wide as a good town for Negroes" became "a one hundred per cent Cracker town," a bastion of the "Solid South."[17] A Jacksonville that Johnson lauded in 1895 in the pages of the city's own *Daily American* as being "regarded by colored people all over the country as the most liberal town in the South" would be disparaged after a series of disenfranchisements and lynchings led him by 1919 to exasperated confession in the *New York Age:* "one is taken up entirely with the shame of this city."[18]

"That Hell-Border City of Babylon"—Johnson's Nassau and Jacksonville

Although *The Autobiography of an Ex-Colored Man* charted a remarkable fictional range for the travels of its protagonist, Johnson's own autobiography, *Along This Way* (1933), stretches the seaways of our literary cartography even more. Haiti's revolutionary agency launches *Along This Way*'s initial story of Johnson's matrilineal great-grandparents as the opening sentence sweeps us into currents that still shape his native Florida: "In 1802 Étienne Dillet, a French army officer in Haiti, placed Hester Argo, a native Haitian woman, together with her three children, aboard a schooner bound for Cuba."[19] We read of how the schooner, intercepted by a British privateer, was commandeered to the Bahamas and how one of Hester's sons by Étienne Dillet, Stephen Dillet, eventually became chief of police and postmaster after having been—in 1835—one of the initial free men of color elected to the Bahamian House of Assembly. We learn of his marriage to Mary Symonett, daughter of a white Bahamian ship captain and an African girl (who was seized by the British from a Brazil-bound slaveship), and of the birth of Johnson's mother, Helen Louise Dillet.

Against the far-reaching matrilineal stories, Johnson's patrilineage is less richly narrated, working back only to the forceful presence of his father. We are told how James Johnson, a freeman from Richmond, migrated to Nassau during the Civil War to wed Helen Dillet, whom he had met in New York after being struck by her vocal performance on the concert stage. After a lull in Nassau's tourist and maritime economy, James Johnson, who worked as headwaiter of Nassau's Royal Victoria Hotel, moved to Jacksonville, Florida, in 1869, and sent for his wife, child, Bahamian in-laws, and their "faithful retainer" Mary Bethel—who served the family in Jacksonville for over thirty years.[20] He soon became headwaiter of Jacksonville's St. James Hotel, "for many years the most fashionable of all the Florida resort hotels" at a time when Jacksonville was Florida's primary winter haven for the wealthy.[21] When baby James was born in Jacksonville in 1871 to a mother too ill to nurse him, the infant was breastfed by a white neighbor and cared for by the two Bahamian women who, along with his mother, would be fixtures in his early life: his maternal grandmother and Mary Bethel. Thus, from the opening pages of Johnson's autobiography, complex blood, sweat, and milk bonds of Haiti, England, Africa, France, Virginia, and New York cross in Nassau and Jacksonville along routes linking Atlantic plantation economies and an emerging tourist trade. Any project, therefore, to seek "Aframerican" expression of "spirit by symbols from within rather than by symbols from without," as Johnson urged in his preface to *The Book of American Negro Poetry* (1922), must call for extraordinarily comprehensive efforts.[22]

I recount Johnson's opening narrative of genealogy, geography, and economy to point to the Afro-creole backstory of globalizing hegemonies and their accompanying forces of displacement that have shaped trade and travel in the Atlantic world. Metropolitan "spaces of flows" turn out to have been cut and interrupted by all sorts of other ebbs and flows: the performance rites of counterpoint and polyrhythm that Benítez-Rojo locates in "peoples of the sea."[23] Attentiveness to any New World port underscores the polyvocality and heterogeneity of its creole cultures. Even as we open our eyes to historical kinships between the Gullah lowcountry and the Bahamas, the more we look at the tourist plantations and gated communities visible in both locations, the more we may see forces of displacement. Prodigally, we start to recognize environments of memory evoked in the sermonic call of Johnson's *God's Trombones:* "Young man, come away from Babylon, / That hell-border city of Babylon."[24] Babylon, as my Sewanee Agrarian mentor Andrew Lytle, the reggae great Bob Marley, a number of Bahamian poets, and the Geechee preacher of *God's Trombones* have all typologized it, rules as invasively as ever.[25] No cultures know the globalized Babylon better than those enslaved and reassembled within it: the diasporic creoles of the Afro-Atlantic world.

The ties between the Bahamas and the Gullah/Geechee coast run so deep that the Bahamas is easily the South's—and black America's—closest national cousin. As Saunders and Craton have shown, the Loyalist migration following the American Revolution made the Gullah/Geechee coast the strongest single source of Bahamian population and culture, with Loyalist immigration (largely out of British St. Augustine from 1783 to 1785) more than doubling the black population of Nassau and providing the source of initial settlement of most of the Out Islands—where a black-white ratio of 20:1 was soon established.[26] So it comes as no surprise that the Bahamian writer Cleveland Eneas could say of his wife's coastal Georgia, "Their accent of the spoken English was almost identical with that of the people among whom I grew up," or that linguist John Holm has described Bahamian creole syntax as so "similar to that of contemporary Gullah" that they are "sister dialects" of a North American plantation creole.[27] Flows between the Bahamas and ports in Key West, Miami, Jacksonville, Savannah, and Charleston have continued to circulate new creolizations via the routes of tourism and commodity culture that brought "long staple" Sea Island cotton, James Weldon Johnson, Sidney Poitier, and the Baha Men to the United States and that bring Nassau most of its cruise ship passengers, as well as the bulk of its foodstuffs—imported for years via Jacksonville's Winn-Dixie and now trafficked through chains like McDonald's, KFC, and Pizza Hut.

Since creolization processes have long been likened to the gumbo approach to cookery over rice or grits, we might turn, as Johnson did, to the cultural grounding provided by New World culinary arts. In *Along This Way,* Johnson writes nostalgically of crosstown (Jacksonville) family visits to the Gibbses, who would generally serve gumbo:

Mrs. Gibbs was a native of Charleston, South Carolina, and knew how to cook Charlestonian gumbo. Into the big pot went not only okra and water and salt and pepper, but at the proper intervals bits of chicken; ham first fried then cut up into small squares; whole shrimps; crab meat, some of it left in pieces of the shell; onions and tomatoes; thyme and other savory herbs; the whole allowed to simmer until it reached an almost viscous consistency; then served in a deep plate over rice cooked as white and dry as it is cooked by the Chinese.

This gumbo, a dish for—reference to the epicure and the *vrai gourmet* are not in place—this more than a savory dish—the dish irresistible—the most soul-satisfying of all the dishes that Negro cookery has given the South.[28]

Here as much as anywhere we get a clear sense of *haute*-creole cosmopolitan authority, King James version. The Gullah foodways that were brought to the Bahamas with the Loyalist migration were recreolized and then brought back to the lowcountry in the Bahamian cooking of Johnson's Jacksonville home:

My grandmother was especially skillful in the preparation of West Indian dishes: piquant fish dishes, chicken pilau, crab stew, crab and okra gumbo, pop-pin' John, and Johnny cake. She also knew how to make the Southern delicacies. We talk a great deal about impressions made upon us in childhood that influence us through life, but we seldom recognize the importance of the tastes formed for the things we loved to eat. Whether I am eating in a humble home or an expensive restaurant, it is difficult for me to understand why there is not hominy for breakfast and rice for dinner—not the mushy, gruel-like messes some people make of these staple foods, but hominy cooked stiff and rice cooked dry.[29]

Publishing his autobiography while he was teaching at Fisk, Johnson seems sympathetic to the arguments of Vanderbilt's Agrarians that the material and aesthetic base of culture is rooted in our incorporating relationship to foods, the culinary arts, and agriculture: what Allen Tate called "spiritual soil."[30] While Tate's essay reveals how the white supremacy of a Solid South blocked Euro-southern tillage of aesthetic and spiritual soil, Johnson introduces us to rich Afro-Atlantic ecologies from across the Florida straits.

James Weldon Johnson's gumbo tastes rose from a rice plantation economy, from mortar and pestle poundings of grits, from the benne candies of childhood in Jacksonville and Nassau, and from songs accompanying the cultivation, preparation, and vending of soul foods. He nurtured respect for how the folk-authored products of Afro-creole spiritual soil link the Americas' humblest homes and our global metropoles' most elite clubs. These products need no pedigree. The produce of creole urban plots finds confident marketing and theorization in Johnson, who attested in his preface to *The Book of American Negro Poetry* that "The earliest Ragtime songs, like Topsy, 'jes' grew.'"[31]

Johnson swings us to embrace our composite (gumbo) origins. And we can come to appreciate why Allen Tate adamantly refused an invitation to a Nashville dinner party to which Johnson had also been invited. Tate insisted, "there should be no social intercourse between the races unless we are willing for that to lead to marriage."[32] And Tate was right insofar as that our universities' programs of humanistic studies have yet to enter into a real marriage with other bodies of knowledge. Tate was not ready to marry a pedigreed child of his own to any body of knowledge that jes' grew, nor to any gumbo epistemology. The English departments of southern universities may now admit black students, faculty members, and texts, but few universities, if any, show a readiness for marriage that might alter the fundamental base of the curriculum—nothing that would reroute lineages of Anglo-Saxon patrimony, nothing bringing Caribbean and Latin American creole cousins into full in-law relationships.

Like Du Bois before him, Johnson would have us respect a pioneering Afro-creole presence that has given the US "the only things artistic that have yet sprung from American soil and been universally acknowledged as distinctive American products."[33] Repeatedly he offered the spirituals, the "uncle Remus" fables, ragtime (then jazz and blues), and the cakewalk (black dance) as an indispensable base of America's artistic originality.[34] For Johnson this distinctive gulf-traversing gift, internationally appropriated but never accorded proper respect, was "the touchstone, it is the magic thing, it is that by which the Negro can bridge all chasms."[35] He further presents "[t]his power . . . to suck up the national spirit from the soil and create something artistic and original" as a "transfusive quality" of "Aframerican" artistry, proliferating across gulfs while "still hold[ing] the racial flavor," much like a lowcountry gumbo.[36]

Johnson's perspective on the way the spirituals worked to bridge chasms came from inseparably intertwined Geechee and Bahamian sources: a historically shared body of songs and performance styles that had traveled back and forth across the Florida straits. This relation was first explored in detail by the amateur musicologist Lydia Parrish in her work in the Sea Islands and the Bahamas. The pioneering Bahamian scholar E. Clement Bethel later addressed it, noting that the Loyalists' slaves brought with them a liminal spirituality "that finds expression in the church music, rushing songs, wake songs, settin' up songs, and the music associated with funerals."[37] One of many shared contexts that Parrish cited for the performance of Geechee and Bahamian spirituals was the tradition of night-long singing at a "settin'-up" or wake.[38] Ex-slaves interviewed by the Georgia Writers' Project offer insights into the numinous area of transition underlying these wakes and funerals:

Dey alluz use tuh beat duh drum wen somebody die tuh let duh udduh Folks know bout duh det.

Dey kill a wite chicken wen dey hab set-ups tuh keep duh spirits way.

We all sit wid duh body an sing an pray an keep duh spirit company.

Wen a person die we have a settin-up and then we leave sumpn wut we got to eat in a dish by him to eat.

They stretch a sheep-hide ovuh a roun bucket . . . they beats the drum in the fewnul cession wen they mahches tuh the buryin groun.

At duh fewnul wen we beat duh drum we mahch roun duh grabe in a ring.

Den at duh time fuh buryin, duh drum would beat an all would lay flat on duh groun on dey faces befo duh body wuz placed in duh grave. Den all would rise and dance roun duh grave. Wen duh body wuz buried, duh drum would give signal wen all wuz tuh rise an fall an tuh dance an sing.[39]

Bahamian wakes continue to use spirituals or "anthems" to help swing the transition between worlds. Ian Strachan points to the fact that Bahamian funerals "still include processions in which the dead are marched, danced, drummed and sung to their resting places, particularly using brass bands."[40] Given that one of Johnson's earliest ambitions was to be a drummer in "a crack brass band" like Jacksonville's Union Cornet Band, whose drummer was noted for the way he "beat a continuous and unbroken roll on his muffled drum all the way from the church to the cemetery," we can bet that crosscurrents of Geechee/Bahamian hermeneutics shaped the man who wrote the Negro national anthem (as well as the lyrics to "O Didn't He Ramble," which became central to the repertory of New Orleans jazz funerals).[41]

Despite his commitment to "seeking symbols from within," the *haute-creole* Johnson put up considerable resistance to the sublime power of the ring shouts (known as "rushin'" in the Bahamas). Referring to shouts in his preface to *The Book of American Negro Spirituals* as "not true spirituals nor even truly religious; in fact, they are not actually songs," he conceded that they "might be termed quasi-religious or semi-barbaric music."[42] Recalling from his Jacksonville memory how the shout was seen "as a very questionable form of worship," allowed only "after the regular services" and banned by "the more educated ministers and members, as fast as they were able to brave the primitive element in the churches," Johnson met his limits of flexibility in facing soul-guardians of the ring shout.[43] But to his credit Johnson describes this disquieting rite with care in both his preface to *The Book of American Negro Spirituals* and in his autobiography. In *Along This Way*, his description of shouting in Jacksonville is tied to a woman whose shouterly skills of vacating the self could have caused her in other places to be "classed among those 'possessed with devils'":

When there was a "ring shout" the weird music and the sound of thudding feet set the silences of the night vibrating and throbbing with vague terror. Many a time I woke suddenly and lay a long while strangely troubled by these sounds . . . The shouters, formed in a ring, men and women alternating, their bodies close together, moved round and round on shuffling feet that never left the floor. With the heel of the right foot they pounded out the fundamental beat of the dance and with their hands clapped out the varying rhythmical accents of the chant; for the music was, in fact, an African chant and the shout an African dance, the whole pagan rite transplanted and adapted to Christian worship. Round and round the ring would go: one, two, three, four, five hours, the very monotony of sound and motion inducing an ecstatic frenzy.[44]

In spite of the evocations of "monotony," "frenzy," and "vague terror" by which he maintained authorial distance from the shout's power, Johnson carefully noted the rite's circum-Caribbean omnipresence. When on a fact-finding mission to Haiti during the first U.S. Marine occupation, he traveled to a village where he observed a feast day's drummed ring dance: "There was the same ring going round and round on shuffling feet, one heel stamping out the rhythm of a monotonous chant, in the same manner that I had seen as a child in the African village in Nassau, and observed later in the 'ring shouts' in Negro churches in the South."[45] Sounding to Johnson like the far edge of babble while also moving folk out of Babylon, the much-censored shout offers polyrhythmic encounter with gateways of transition that defy Kantian or Calvinist mastery. Surviving in the United States only "in some backward churches of a backward community" like the La Villa neighborhood of Johnson's Jacksonville childhood, the shout marks a tenacious assertion of "African cultural and religious ideas" that found practice in rites he had observed throughout the plantation zones of Venezuela, Haiti, the Bahamas, and Jacksonville.[46]

As with the shout, many basilectal forms such as junkanoo—described in evocative detail in Harriet Jacobs's narrative from coastal North Carolina—disappeared from black American mainland culture as powerful voices of racial uplift looked askance at the lower classes making a spectacle of themselves.[47] The Christmas "carnival" of junkanoo has been a widespread feature of the anglophone black Atlantic, linking Jamaica, Belize, St. Vincent, Bermuda, and the Bahamas with the U.S. southeast coast in performances similar to the Edenton, North Carolina, description given by Harriet Jacobs:

> Every child rises early on Christmas morning to see the Johnkannaus. Without them, Christmas would be shorn of its greatest attraction. They consist of companies of slaves from the plantations, generally of the lower class. Two athletic men, in calico wrappers, have a net thrown over them, covered with all manner of bright-colored stripes. Cows' tails are fastened to their backs, and their heads are decorated with horns. A box, covered with sheepskin, is called the gumbo box. A dozen beat on this, while others strike triangles and jawbones, to which bands of dancers keep time. For a month previous they are composing songs, which are sung on this occasion.[48]

In junkanoo, ruling taxonomies give way to the gumbo box, and other kinds of intercourse between human subjects and animal, vegetal, and ecosystemic becomings emerge in performance.[49] Following jazz age revalorization, Bahamian junkanoo became valued, perhaps "saved" in appropriation, by Nassau's tourist economy. The Bahamian government, according to Ian Strachan, keeps working "to impose greater 'order' and 'organization' to an activity that existed for centuries as a resistant cultural form."[50] In spite of its commodification and domestication, junkanoo clings to a resistant role that makes it "among other things, a New World reincarnation of the spoken, danced, masked physical re-embodiment of the living dead" in rites "meant to bring the dead and the living closer and . . . to energize and empower the living thereby."[51] With junkanoo's disappearance from U.S. tidewater regions by the 1880s and censorship of the ring shout, spiritually disembodying forces threatened to hold communal sway until black popular music and race records emerged with counterbalancing agency. It is at this crossroads that we can best understand Johnson's authorial interventions, his articulations of a swing agency from the gumbo-limbo rites of his Geechee native lands.

Swinging That Subtle Undertone—Grooves Not Susceptible to Fixation

Johnson's catalytic efforts as anthologist and theorist of the spirituals attest to his respect for a body of song that enabled, as he put it in his preface to *The Book of American Negro Spirituals* (1925), "physical and spiritual survival of two and a half centuries of slavery."[52] Brent Edwards has identified Johnson as one of the most astute evaluators of the spirituals. Locating their power in a dynamic feel for swing, which "in its verb form," Edwards insists, is a "paradigmatic black cultural *action* or *process*" resistant to commodification, Johnson opened a path toward swing theory.[53] In describing swing, Johnson drew on antiphony and polyrhythm, a sway and balance between congregational and individual embodiment, articulated through a marine language of surge and wave:

> The "swing" of the spirituals is an altogether subtle and elusive thing. It is subtle and elusive because it is in perfect union with the religious ecstasy that manifests itself in the swaying bodies of a whole congregation, swaying as if responding to the baton of some extremely sensitive conductor . . . It is the more subtle and elusive because there is a still further intricacy in the rhythms. This swaying of the body marks the regular beat or, better, surge, for it is something stronger than a beat, and is more or less, not precisely, strict in time; but the Negro loves nothing better in his music than to play with the fundamental time beat. He will, as it were, take the fundamental beat and pound it out with his left hand, almost monotonously; while with his right hand he juggles it. It should be noted that even in the swaying of head and body the head marks the surge off in shorter waves than does the body. In listening to Negroes sing their

own music, it is often tantalizing and even exciting to watch a minute fraction of a beat balancing for a slight instant on the bar between two measures, and, when it seems almost too late, drop back into its own proper compartment.[54]

Edwards sees Johnson's articulations of swing as a "stammering" or "telling inarticulacy" that points toward what refuses to be transcribed, what sways between notions of individual and congregational agency, and moves through a body in almost infinitely fractal expression beyond easily located notions of call-and-response.[55] Here, we enter Deleuze and Guattari's "field of immanence of desire," the assemblage of their body without organs (BwO) that "swings between two poles, the surfaces of stratification . . . and the plane of consistency."[56] Deleuze and Guattari insist "the BwO is always swinging between the surfaces that stratify it and the plane that sets it free."[57]

Not only in his 1925 preface to *The Book of American Negro Spirituals* but in his entire oeuvre, Johnson presents the spirituals' swing as a quality so fluid and effervescent that it may slip past the dominant organs of hearing, leaving us to ask of the performance—along with Johnson's "O Black and Unknown Bards" in 1908—"How did it catch that subtle undertone, / That note in music heard not with the ears?"[58] We meet the same charged wonder four years later in *The Autobiography of an Ex-Colored Man* in a passage introducing the Georgia "Big meeting's" song leader, Singing Johnson. The novel uses "Swing Low Sweet Chariot" both to demonstrate the workings of congregational call-and-response to the reader and to rev up a whole machinery of desire whereby "The solitary and plaintive voice of the leader is answered by a sound like the roll of the sea, producing a most curious effect."[59] As the novel's ethnographic ex-colored narrator observes of these songs' curious affect, "there is sounded in them that elusive undertone, the note in music which is not heard with the ears."[60] If the ears do not hear the elusive undertone (or undertow) of swing's sea-roll and surge, how then do we hear, feel, and assemble such vibrational intensities of desire?

Musicologist Katherine Hagedorn takes up swing's elusiveness in asking, given the infinite possibilities of improvisation, "what exactly is taught to potential performers?"[61] How teach apprentices, as Singing Johnson does, to "improvise at the moment lines to fit the occasion," to know "just what hymn to sing and when to sing it" and "pitch it in the right key" to set the assembly in motion?[62] According to Hagedorn, a process of teaching via "imitation ultimately leading to (improvisatory) difference" keeps swing performance tied to socially performative intent. Intent to swing, coupled with a studied preparedness, produces the grooves' subtle crests and undertows: "this swing, this extra microvariation in interpretation, that propels the sound forward, and that excites a physical reaction from listeners. Playing the bata rhythms 'straight' will still sound good; it just won't move the room.

And if you don't move the room, you won't bring down the santo [saint]."[63] In her apprenticeship to Afro-Cuban sacred drumming, Hagedorn learned to "get" the rhythms but struggled to "make them swing" since "[s]ome apparently intangible feeling or ability to interact rhythmically was missing."[64] Johnson's observations about European performers' difficulties in swinging a song are worth noting here: "They play the notes too correctly; and do not play what is not written down."[65] For Hagedorn, it may indeed be a matter of learning to read what is not written and of learning to hear or see outside of the dominant organs: "One could argue that I was almost getting the rhythms, but that certain microrhythmic differences (all but indiscernible to the human ear) were making swing unattainable."[66] She came to feel that swing rises from intent, skill, and a contextual *social* knowledge that is always unwritten and trailing off into gulfs of individual/collective experience. Hagedorn knows that swing may sound like an assault on the organized self, for "in order to swing, one has to be relaxed . . . enough to propel and be propelled by the collective impulse of the moment," and "all of these sounds assault the body, in the same way that one's 'intentful' hand assaults the head of the drum to provoke possession, propelling the moment, pushing the creyente over the edge of consciousness and control, into a vehicle driven by the orichas."[67] This is the chariot swung low to limbo possessions.

The "big meeting" songleader of *The Autobiography of an Ex-Colored Man* is the text's alter-ego of folk authority. Attending the revival as a secular-minded ragtime apprentice to sacral swing, "a non-religious man of the world" who had come as seeker with his notebook "trying to catch the spirit," the narrator witnesses a sublime trembling at "the mourner's bench" that almost opens, revives, or converts his own voice: "I, too, felt like joining in the shouts of 'Amen! Hallelujah!' "[68] His previous organizations of knowledge and self are set aflow "with the tears rolling down my cheeks and my heart melted within me" (110). Here, heart-melt opens each ego-stripped self to songs of such unsettling performative authority that "[t]he educated classes are rather ashamed of them, and prefer to sing hymns from books" (110). They sing only what is safely fixed.

But this big meeting's swinging past shame serves to move the novel itself from the sublime assembly of a black revival to a white lynch mob's displacement of shame. This is the text's counter-initiatory, antiswing passage, the moment when "I strayed into another deviation from my path of life . . . an entirely different road" (110). It begins with the narrator's lodging in a house with parlor and organ (the kind of place that harbors shame for the spirituals), owned by a decidedly unswinging fellow "tremendously in earnest," (111) and leads to a white-supremacist meeting taking sudden assembly down the road, with "everything . . . done in quite an orderly manner," and "no extra noise or excitement, no loud talking, only swift, sharp words of command"

(112). The lynch mob finds catalytic hailing in "that terror-instilling sound known as the 'rebel yell,'" and our narrator becomes a nonperformative, utterly stiffened witness: "I was fixed to the spot where I stood, powerless to take my eyes from what I did not want to see" (113). The burning alive of the black victim takes oceanic affect—"A great wave of humiliation and shame swept over me" (113)—as this meeting concludes in sacrificial reassembly of that "'great and impassable gulf' between the races 'fixed by the Creator at the foundation of the world'" (114). Ironically, it is this white-supremacist "fixing" rite of terror (maintaining the great gulf as impasse) that propels the narrator's crossing over, like "a man who had lost blood," moved by "shame, unbearable shame" (115) into the white world.

It may be outrageous to suggest that the unswinging musician (or English Department) fixed to the charted score and unable to "play what is not written down" may share a time-space organization of stratifying violence with the lynching spectator, "fixed to the spot . . . powerless to take my eyes from what I did not want to see." But we must nurture a capacity to read what is not presented to our gaze, what has been submerged in service to the "great and impassable gulf . . . fixed by the Creator" if we are to swing both the text and our frontier capacities. Fortunately, we have homegrown models and teachers. In Johnson's estimation, the spirituals provide an exemplary model through their "curious turns and twists and quavers" and "certain notes just a shade off the key," through the power of swing that "has baffled many of the recorders of this music" and rendered the songs' deepest power "not susceptible to fixation."[69]

Jacksonville and the Georgia coast gave Johnson his gateways into an initiatory basilect beyond easy shaming. Doing his seeking of "symbols from within" via reimmersion in remembered Geechee terrain, Johnson observed that "the dialect spoken in the sea islands off the coast of Georgia and South Carolina remains . . . farther from English than the speech of American Negroes anywhere else."[70] His native Jacksonville, where he encountered the ring shout, a vibrant circum-Caribbean culture, and two avatars of performance of the spirituals—Singing Johnson and "Ma" White—served his seeking well. Of "Ma" White, he recalled how "each church meeting found her in her place ready to lead the singing, whenever the formal choir and organ did not usurp her ancient rites."[71] With her "shrill, plaintive voice quavering above the others," she would lead the church body (without organs) in rites of intent organized prior to the assembly's bourgeois aspirations. Johnson recollected how "even as a child my joy in hearing her sing these songs was deep and full."[72] The spirituals, under such leadership, bear a profound capacity for time travel. Johnson observes that when "the foot is not marking straight time, but what Negroes call 'stop time,' or what the books have no better definition for than 'syncopation,'" the "down beat is never lost, but is playfully bandied from hand to foot and from foot to hand" in an embodied time-machinery that rags time, stops time, and serves in counterpoint to swing's propulsions of time.[73]

Johnson's discussion of "stop time" mechanics occurs in a section of his preface to *The Book of American Negro Spirituals* wherein he addresses black secular music and popularization of a dance named for *the* exemplary lowcountry space: "the Charleston." He remarks how "white people everywhere . . . count it an accomplishment to be able to 'do the Charleston.'"[74] The Charleston's New York stage introduction, he insists, did not draw its success so much from its "extraordinary jazz band" but from the stage chorus that added juba-patting, hand-clapping, and foot-stamping to an "effect [that] was electrified and contagious" and "the best demonstration of beating out complex rhythms I have ever witnessed."[75] In moving from place to action, "Charleston" swings from noun to verb. And it is with this chronotopic Charlestoning authority in mind that the Johnson brothers sought to arrange the spirituals without the kinds of high-art "innovations" that could result in the tradition being " 'opera-ated' upon," seeking "above all else to retain their primitive 'swing.' "[76] In his anthologies and prefaces, his novel and poems, James Weldon Johnson moved steadily to provide the critical and historical advocacy of folk forms that had been long censored by ideologies of racial uplift. His swinging of the Geechee body without hymnals or church organs helped open an era to modes of swinging low without shame . . . across gulf-impasses.

In terms of his own experience of the sacred, Johnson recounts a complex oscillation. Prodded by his Bahamian grandmother to conversion at a revival meeting in Jacksonville and "led to the mourners' bench" when he was nine years old, young James fabricated a conversion experience "based on a remembered illustration in *Home Life in the Bible* that purported to be the artist's conception of a scene in heaven."[77] He notes, "I was called upon to repeat the vision many times thereafter—to my inward shame."[78] Shame remains a steady source and byproduct of Johnson's swing narratives. Upon being received into the church, however, and "welcomed . . . into the bond of Christian fellowship," there came a feeling of being "lifted up, transported," and "[t]he vision I had recounted came back a reality."[79] Fairly soon thereafter, Johnson lost any investment in Christian theology: "At fourteen I was skeptical. By the time I reached my Freshman year at Atlanta University I had avowed myself an agnostic."[80] Old rites of swing, however, worked as spiritual ballast. In *Along This Way*, he essayed "what has come to me from this early religious experience, this swing from almost the one extreme to almost the other," and judged that "[i]n that swing through the arc, rapidly forth and gradually back, I came to that conception of religion and philosophy of life that are now my guideposts, and I feel that if my experience had been otherwise I might not have come to an adjustment as nearly in emotional and intellectual balance as that which I have reached."[81]

Although he described antebellum Christianity as a "narcotic doctrine" and black America as "the most priest-governed group in the country," Johnson clearly respected the black church for its historic ability to reclaim a space of social autonomy.[82] In his preface to the sermonic poems of God's Trombones (1927), Johnson traced the formal history of the black church to George Liele's ministry in Georgia in 1773 and to Andrew Bryan's ministry in Savannah after Liele left with the British for Jamaica. Johnson insists that establishment of "independent places of worship" fostered the growth of independent black authority in this "first sphere in which race leadership might develop and function."[83] These Afro-Baptist spaces of flows provided the place where voices attuned to swing and stop time, and "saturated with the sublime phraseology of the Hebrew prophets and steeped in the idioms of King James English," could forge "another language": a sermonic "intoning" punctuated "by a quick intaking and an audible expulsion of breath" (the "trumpeting" of spirit adoption in the Caribbean, referred to as "honking" in southern churches and jazz circuits), a "syncopation of speech" with silent beats left open to be "filled by a hand clap."[84] Johnson attested that from "memories of sermons I heard preached in my childhood" in Jacksonville, he found the grounding and language for the poems of God's Trombones: poems like "The Creation" (first published in 1920) that helped spark the vernacular poetics of the Harlem Renaissance.[85]

God's Trombones calls its prodigal congregants out of exile in "That hell-border city of Babylon."[86] Speaking to "the man in the mire of Babylon," the book references a different mire/maayo/myal of exilic memory and restored behaviors.[87] The poem "Go Down Death" locates its seekerly ground in the Geechee heartland near Savannah (Yamacraw) . . . where Death takes one of the church's sisters "up like a baby" to where "the angels sang a little song / And Jesus rocked her in his arms."[88] Sampling steadily from lines, stanzas, and themes from the spirituals, God's Trombones points readers to a rocking body of wisdom literature and to vehicles of performance that swing low.

Johnson's repeated valorizations of the body of folktales popularized by Joel Chandler Harris's Uncle Remus stories show that he regarded these fables as another font of Afro-creole authority.[89] Elsie Clews Parsons's Folk Tales of Andros Island, Bahamas (1918) and her Folklore of the Sea Islands (1923) reveal a profound narrative kinship between Gullah and Bahamian orature. Parsons recorded several versions of the orphan Kumba tale on Andros Island, along with many animal fables familiar to Gullah narrators.[90] One widespread tale recorded by Parsons in both South Carolina and the Bahamas features a woman who vows not to marry a man with a single blemish on his body and subsequently weds a perfectly "airbrushed" devil who aims to devour her. Of particular contextual interest here is a Georgia version recorded by Charles Spaulding Wylly as recalled from his black nurse. Wylly, from St. Simons Island, was the paternal grandson of a Loyalist who emigrated to Nassau and eventually returned to Georgia with all his human property. Wylly's maternal grandfather, Thomas Spalding of Sapelo Island, Georgia, had also fled to the Bahamas and returned to Georgia, where he helped initiate the cultivation of Sea Island cotton from Bahamian seed and with Bahamian slave expertise. So while it is indisputable that Sea Island Creole speakers had a major influence on the development of Bahamian creole culture, we must also recognize that the Bahamas played a role in lowcountry culture, especially through the impact of slaves (re)imported by returning Loyalists.[91] The Bahamas and the lowcountry intermarried, blemishes and all, as Lawrence McKiver, elder leader of the McIntosh County Shouters, insisted in speaking of the "Nassau-ified" currents in his "Geechee talk": "The old folks talk bad, jus' like I do. My mama wasn't a slave. My mama's mama was. My mama told me they was more like Nassau-ified people. She always would say that. From some kinda island. My daddy's side, they come from Carolina, me being mixed Nassau and Geechee . . . Geechee, that's true! So therefore I'm in the midst of danger!"[92] The lowcountry's Nassau-ified pathways of exchange swing the historical record and reveal a whitewashing of U.S. cultural history that does much to "airbrush" out real and perceived blemishes or dangers of the United States' natal bonds to the Caribbean. We end up, however, in the midst of greater danger: matrimony with our perfectly constituted devil.

Johnson was writing in an era when the United States was reconsolidating its patrimony as a white nation (as in the film *Birth of a Nation*) and expanding beyond its continental frontiers.[93] With the Spanish-Philippine-American War, the annexation of Puerto Rico, the virtual annexation of Cuba (and subsequent bloodbath wrought upon Cuba's Independent Party of Color [1912]), Marine occupation of Haiti (1915–34), and the purchase of the Virgin Islands from Denmark (1917), the United States asserted itself over Caribbean peoples and territories ripe for the extension of its southern plantations. Addressing the "place" of black cultural authority in imperialist Anglo-America, Johnson sums up the turf wars of his era: "White America has for a long time been annexing and appropriating Negro territory, and is prone to think of every part of the domain it now controls as originally—and aboriginally—its own."[94] Johnson did not so much begrudge the inevitable appropriations of creolization at the contact zone as he did the radical asymmetries of power that naturalize and aboriginalize white territorialization of the bodies, repertoires, property, and gravesites of others. His autoethnographic reterritorializations reasserted "native" Afrocreole claims. James Weldon Johnson is *the* major author of Geechee and

Bahamian broughtupsy, *the* great underappreciated public figure of a city (Jacksonville) and a region deep "in the midst of danger."

"Outta the Swamp Grass and Hammocks"—"Mangrove and Marsh"

The coast between Savannah and Jacksonville has been swamped with researchers and their projects over the past eighty years. This is especially true of Sapelo Island, Georgia. It is still possible, nevertheless, to read the extensive ethnographic literature on Sapelo without getting a sense of the import of the island's long culture of witness or of the need to listen carefully to the witnesses themselves. Recently, Cornelia Bailey's autoethnographic work— a cookbook, a set of interviews with community elders, and especially her memoir *God, Dr. Buzzard and the Bolito Man* (2000)—has staked clear claim to her own Sapelo-born-and-raised authority.[95] Bailey's memoir works from knowledge of "the body, the soul, *and* the spirit, just like the people in Africa had believed" (31). She details Sapelo women's ministration of endangered modes of wisdom: midwives who have divined future births by reading "the knots in the afterbirth" (76) and who saw to the burial of the afterbirth to mark "the first part of you that went back to earth . . . that connected you to the earth . . . and to Sapelo . . . your true home" (77). Bailey's wry trinity of belief "in God, Dr. Buzzard, and the Bolito Man" (Bolito being a Cuban-affiliated underground lottery) (187) introduces readers to a flexible spiritual orientation that serves the Lord, serves the spirits of the earth, and cultivates opportunity to make-do.[96]

Nobody needs to inform Bailey of her island's ties to the Bahamas and to a wider Atlantic world. She roots her narrative in lineages going back to the Bahama-purchased Bilali Muhammad, "the first of my ancestors I can name" (1). Bailey speaks of the "special seed" of long-staple "Sea Island cotton" that the Loyalist planter Thomas Spalding brought back to Sapelo from the Bahamas with Bilali and his family (286), and notes islanders' ties to Creek and especially Seminole peoples (311). From her travel to Sierra Leone she asserts, "because of the freedmen who returned to Sierra Leone, we had ties both going across the Atlantic and coming back" (311). Bailey knows we are not the isolate individuals, races, or nations we so often imagine. As she describes it, Sapelo's creole language, like its culture and people, emerged from a low, marshy contact zone: "a lot like throwing everything into a huge pot, blending it together and simmering it into a delicious soup served over rice" (4). Hers is a cosmopolitan "Saltwater Geechee" text drawing networks of knowledge from Muslim ancestors and from the Atlantic trickster An' Nancy (87), and drawing inspiration from a song of conversion composed by a British slaveship captain ("Amazing Grace").

Bailey may be from the first and last Gullah/Geechee generation to write from an authority vetted in initiatory travels in the praise-house tradition. She writes of how she picked her teacher (a deacon in the church) and her "secret place," "a pine tree off in the woods" where "[m]orning, noon, and night" each day for several months she would go "into the wilderness and go seeking" (164). Young Cornelia narrated her travel vision of meeting an angel in a yellow robe before a proving-board of deacons and passed the test, leading to her baptism in the living waters of a tidal inlet and acceptance as "a bona-fide member" of Sapelo's African Baptist Church (168). This, of course, is the familiar lowcountry initiation. But here we see this rite needing complement and fulfillment later in life, with another seekerly travel: Bailey's journey to Sierra Leone as part of a guest Gullah/Geechee delegation. This travel, as she reports it, extended her sense of kinship in meaningful ways across the Atlantic. Upon being presented in Sierra Leone with "a skirt of gold fabric" and "matching tunic" and anointed as "an honorary woman paramount chief" (309), Bailey recounts her African travel as an authorizing conversion: "The experience was absolutely out of this world . . . It changed me, it made me feel stronger, and I knew then I could do anything, go anywhere, and say what needed to be said from then on. I had this new power within me and I would never again be the same" (310).

Her memoir, however, also reveals how her Sapelo experiences prepared her for this travel's transatlantic flight. In Sierra Leone, the old flying angel in yellow robe receives her golden dress and tunic, her enlarged sense of purpose and authority, along with rice-based communion meals that "stirred up all kinds of memories in me" (303).

God, Dr. Buzzard, and the Bolito Man invokes the swing-rites of the ring shout. The text's key ring-shout scene does not take place in church but during a Friday-night corn liquor session around "The Buzzard Lope." In this secular shout, the men's becoming-buzzard still does sacred work of cleansing the stench of their long workweek under the buckra's (white man's) authority and gaze. As Bailey's father and friends moved to a broomstick's pounding beat, "[t]heir arms were stretched out wide, gliding like a buzzard" (180) circling over a folded handkerchief placed in the center of the ring. Swooping lower with each pass, "bending a little bit lower each time," Papa "was going lower and low" (181) until he—in his fifties and drinking—could pick the handkerchief from the floor with his teeth without falling. The men's limbo of becoming buzzard links them to the rootworking powers of the famed Dr. Buzzard and nurtures a shared assemblage of desires: "The men had a camaraderie out of this world when they were together, a sharing from the soul" (183). Such sharing from the soul could take place on a Friday night or on a Sunday morning when "the whole church was rocking" and "[e]ven the building seemed like it was swinging gently with you" (161). It is this swing that Bailey channels in closing her memoir with a Sapelo New Year's Watch Night service—the night when the shouts were brought into the church in her youth: "You can feel the beat of the stick in the rhythm of the music and the way the women clap their hands and the men stomp their feet, and all of a sudden, the church comes alive" (321).

Sapelo residents have long been placed in the position of Barthes's ethnographic societies, nostalgically envied by metropolitans for masterful performance of an oral tradition. But as Bailey asserts of such local folk authority, "there were huge holes in it, so many it was harmful to our view of who we were. You respect yourself more when you know you're someone with a history and we needed that over here" (279). Her Sierra Leone travel gave her the "oomph!" to fill these holes, "the inner power to back them up" (319). Like Avatara Williams of *Praisesong for the Widow*, Bailey concludes with projects of saraka-work: "I want to build a praise house on our property . . . so that my grandchildren will see what a praise house is like and visitors will learn about them" (331). Her Sapelo praise house will be adorned by a small stained-glass window featuring a bird, that "symbol of freedom" (331). Cultivating a relation in deep time with the island's sacred groves and graves, Bailey asserts that "there's no markers for about half the people buried there" (237). She points to a general dispossession of Geechee communities "turned into fancy shops and high-priced homes" (251) on St. Simons Island where the Ibos "chose the water as their grave, rather than live out their life as slaves" (281). For Bailey as for James Weldon Johnson, such unmarked paths and God-met places ground the restorability of behaviors. Reciting the Mende funeral song from Sierra Leone passed down in nearby Harris Neck ("Come quickly, let us all work hard / The grave is not yet finished" [313]), Bailey asserts ancestral tenure to land that "in every way but legally . . . is ours," presenting her memoir as an act of profound reterritorialization since Sapelo residents "feel threatened every day" (327), "like a special list of endangered peoples had been drawn up and that our names were on it" (266).

Marquetta Goodwine's anthology *The Legacy of Ibo Landing: Gullah Roots of African American Culture* (1998) takes an even more politically assertive stance worthy of her inheritance of a visionary preservationist mission pioneered in part by James Weldon Johnson. A St. Helena Island, South Carolina, native, the Fordham- and Columbia-educated Goodwine founded the Gullah/Geechee Sea Island Coalition in 1998 and traveled to speak at the United Nations Commission on Human Rights in Geneva in 1999 to seek international response to economic and political assaults on Gullah lands. Goodwine's travel to the UN and her history of organizational activism helped her forge Gullah/Geechee Nation and become enstooled as Queen Quet. Among her many international engagements was the holding of the 1997 Gullah/Geechee International Music and Movement Festival in the Bahamas to draw attention to Gullah/Bahamian kinship ties. Her travels to the Bahamas, Nova Scotia, and Mexico (to confer with the Afro-Seminole Muscogas) point to a Gullah/Geechee Nation conscious of its transnational affiliations even as her focus remains on a certain homeland security along the historic coastal base from North Carolina to northeast Florida.[97]

Queen Quet's text opens with a call to memorialize Ibo Landing and gives an address for readers wishing to contribute to the effort.[98] Named for a site that "remains unmarked" (6), *The Legacy of Ibo Landing* converges directly with Cornel West's call for a nihilism-combating politics of conversion. Queen Quet intervenes on behalf of "rebuild[ing] our families, our organizations and our institutions" in order "to recapture the interest and respect of our youth and pay attention to and care for our elders" (8). Her signature essay contribution, "Destructionment: Treddin' een We Ancestas' Teahs," insists that "[t]he words 'development' and 'developer' ring hollow within the Sea Islands" since their result has been "family removal and the breakdown and dissolution of cultural ties," more aptly termed "destructionment" (164). Once the destructioners hold title to tracts of Gullah/Geechee land, community members may "no longer even be allowed on the property again because a gate was going up which would only be opened for those with passes . . . on this resort 'plantation' " (170). Queen Quet marshals a righteous indignation against the "ethnocide" enacted when Sea Island communities get turned into "recreation areas" or gated plantation communities (184). Her final two essays offer pointers and guidelines. "Holdin' Pun We Culcha: Sites, Individuals and Organizations Preserving the Gullah and Geechee Heritage" provides contact information for connecting with community groups and their custodianship of key sites, while "Excavating Gullah Seeds: Guidelines for Conducting Research on the Gullah" underscores the need for ethical work that might serve community interests rather than merely authorizing ethnographers and their vitas (202).

The Legacy of Ibo Landing contains not just its editor's essays and prescriptions but anthologizes the stories, art, scholarship, recipes, and recollective visions of many contributors. Y. N. Kly's "The Gullah War" presents the U.S.-Seminole wars as a long struggle between the United States and Seminole-affiliated Gullah maroons. Drawing from General Jesup's 1834 assertion that "[t]his, you may be assured, is a negro and not an Indian war" (29) as well as from Ian Hancock's insistence that Florida's maroons spoke "Afro-Seminole, a creole related to Gullah" (25), Kly cites a remarkably long-memoried account (from a 1972 interview) of an 1818 battle from the First Seminole War given by an Afro-Seminole descendant on the Bahamian Out Island of Andros: "The Old Ones used to talk 'bout the look on them white soldiers' faces when they see Black fighters looking like they grow outta the swamp grass and the hammocks . . . that kind of thing does give the white man nightmare and day-fever all at the same time . . . wherever my blood-seed scatter, they will spread the word 'bout how Black and Seminole ancestors fights side by side at Swanee" (34). We come to see that much of the Seminole diaspora ("blood-seed" scatterings to the Bahamas, Texas, and Mexico, as well as to Oklahoma) is also a Gullah diaspora. In the ongoing struggle over native land and its ecologies of human relation, today's "nightmare and day-fever stricken" developers are trying to see to it, as MaVynne Betsch observed, that "All this is going to condos" (84).

Also tending the ecosystemic roots of *The Legacy of Ibo Landing*, Josephine Beoku-Betts's contribution focuses on the symbolic value of a "make-do" culinary culture tied to the environment, and draws on Emory Campbell's assertion that Gullah see themselves as an "endangered species" (146). Linguist Salikoko Mufwene argues that Sea Island Creole (Gullah) "is not endangered by debasilectalization [the loss of features that make it distinct from more prestigious varieties of the language] but by factors that are largely ecological" (175), that is, by the "potential demographic erosion of its speakers" (181) tied to lost community lands. Mufwene points out that "[i]n the case of Gullah, one must distinguish the question of debasilectalization from that of endangerment" (181). In other words, the base of language and culture may well thrive if the communities can continue to "grow outta the swamp grass and the hammocks."

On many islands now, one must gain permission from golf club security guards to enter old plantation cemetery grounds. As land prices and property taxes soared (at least until the real estate crash that further eviscerated investment in public infrastructure and in each other), new gated communities and tourist developments morphed devastatingly from the old plantation economy. The naming of resorts (Amelia Island Plantation) and subdivisions (Dunbar Creek Plantation) speaks of Old South nostalgia coupled with indifference to the losses inflicted on the communities they displace. Highway markers substantiate stories of local (white) color while the saraka-memory of the one-time black majority goes unmarked. "Freshwater Geechee" communities like Harris Neck, home to the Mende funeral song that fed Toni Morrison's *Song of Solomon*, are also being displaced by the hell-border condos of Babylon.

The activism of Gullah/Geechee organizations and of individuals such as Emory Campbell, Cornelia Bailey, and Queen Quet has enabled umbrella groups like the Sea Island Coalition to partner with the congressionally funded Gullah/Geechee Corridor Commission to preserve the agency and staying power of Geechee cultural networks and to foster respect for them as a national treasure.[99] An orientation to the islands' deep time-space, however, teaches us that when we speak of "nation" we speak of something more porous and less sovereign than we are often led to think. Multiple nations awaken into assembly through Geechee shouts, anthems, and sarakas. As this chapter has steadily argued, the Bahamas offers the closest cultural-historical and linguistic kinship to the Gullah/Geechee Nation. Bahamians can learn much from study of the Gullah/Geechee cultures that played a foundational role in Bahamian life as well as from Gullah/Geechee peoples' ongoing struggle for survival and self-determination. But we in the southeastern United States (and especially those of us who inhabit the Gullah/Geechee coast) may look to the efforts of Bahamians—our closest national cousins—to feed the children of a culture that is simultaneously local, national, and open (vulnerably) to global economies. Bahamians certainly face their own modes of endangerment documented in an emergent national literature of potential import to the Gullah/Geechee Nation.

If there is one Bahamian whose life and multifaceted artistry best parallels that of the Jacksonville/Bahamian James Weldon Johnson, it is the Miami-born, Cat Island and Nassau–raised Sir Sidney Poitier, whose autobiography, *This Life* (1980), may well be read alongside Johnson's *Along This Way* as a testimony of cosmopolitanism from below.[100] Poitier's and Johnson's autobiographies bear witness to the most accomplished twentieth-century self-authored "lives" of a transnational Geechee Nation. Cleveland Eneas's *Bain Town* also deserves mention as a remarkable autobiography pointing to cultural and linguistic ties between his own Nassau and his wife's native coastal Georgia. The autobiographies of Poitier the actor, Eneas the dentist, and Johnson the son of a headwaiter also bear uncanny witness to how the islands have served as a stage or "set" where the "natives" have had to tend consciously to self-possession, smiles, and the maintenance of dignity. All of these tensions converge in the multigeneric literary output of Nassau's Ian Strachan. Strachan—who has produced and published a number of plays, a collection of poetry, a novel, two films, an activist blog archive, a weekly newspaper column, and the scholarly monograph *Paradise and Plantation* (2002) while devoting his considerable energies to teaching at the College of the Bahamas—has been one of the most visible Bahamian heirs to the legacy of Johnson.

In *Paradise and Plantation,* Strachan underscores the dangers of investment in a tourist economy that produces a "paradise" serviced by smiling "natives" who keep a "well-oiled plantation economy" rolling.[101] The result is that Bahamians become consumers of a brochure art and paradise iconography fabricated in the service of others and tied to longstanding racial ideologies. We all certainly perform our identities in the face of others, but there is a perniciousness of scale to the Bahamian performance. Strachan shows us that the "contradictions between an imaginary paradise and the lived experience of most Bahamians," coupled with educational directives limiting "Bahamians' knowledge of the lives their ancestors led," leave many Bahamians mired in an infantilizing dependency and passive consumerism (125). He insists that many factors combine to "make an industry founded on white leisure and black labor more than an ordinary consumer-producer relationship" (116).

Strachan's focus in *Paradise and Plantation* on Bahamians' "increasing land alienation and disinheritance" (142) speaks to concerns of his Geechee cousins. Perhaps even more pernicious than the construction of South African–owned mega-resorts such as Atlantis, which limit beach access and control much of the economy, is the growth of gated communities. The Bahamas' prototypical gated community, Lyford Cay, was built in the early 1960s as a residential retreat for North Americans and other millionaire expatriates and has been duplicated throughout the island nation. According to Strachan, "the wall and gate constructed to separate Lyford Cay's white residents from the rest of the Bahamas has become a metaphor for the disparity between rich and poor and between white and black. The phrase 'living behind the gates' passed into popular language as the standard means of discussing the Lyford Cay lifestyle of North American millionaires" as well as the lives chosen by the increasing number of "wealthy African Americans and black Bahamians [who] have jumped the gates, so to speak" (139).

If James Weldon Johnson's novel was drawing a veil aside to show his reader how the guarded gates of racial privilege were "forcing an unascertainable number of fair-complexioned colored people [to jump the gate] over into the white race," we may sense in our own time a voodoo-economized expansion of scale of apartheid.[102] In the gated-community destructionment of the circum-Caribbean, a concentrated privatization of power and wealth gets stashed "behind the gates," intensifying the alienation and disinheritance of Afro-creole historical majorities. That these gated communities are often called plantations—and quite often restrict public access to waterfronts, cemeteries, and sacred memorial spaces—rubs salt into old wounds and widens historic gulfs.

Coastal southerners would do well to examine Bahamian responses to the islands' Afro-Atlantic history, efforts to support local production and maintain environments of memory. In "Everything Babylon," Jerome Cartwright (likely my distant cousin descended from a Virginia Loyalist who settled near Dead Man's Cay on Long Island in the Bahamas) urges Bahamian prodigals away from satellite TV dishes wherein "everything Babylon is good":

I am thirsty
But I shall not lap
These poisoned drops
That splash my saucer

From some distant, alien cup.
The food I crave falls not from heaven
But must spring from deep within me
To name me
Who I am.[103]

Cartwright's "Everything Babylon" advocates self-assertive production, like the "rake and scrape" quadrilles swung (on accordion, goatskin drum, and carpenter's saw) by Thomas Cartwright and the Boys out of Clarencetown, Long Island; or the erotic conjure conveyed by Cindy Cartwright Armbrister's narrative of Long Island's local gumbo—an okra-based "cuckoo soup" infused with obeah.[104] The cuckoo soup, of course, needs to be consumed by enough outsiders to feed the gene pool. Still, however, creole cultures of cuckoo soup tend to be adept at finding ways to add and mix new ingredients, avoiding valorization of the pure breed. Consider the Bahamian term "potcake," which refers to the rice that crusts-up on the bottom of the pot when cooking peas 'n' rice, and is most often used to signify the kind of mutt (or common island "yellow dog") that draws its sustenance from what is left on the crusty bottom of the pot. Thus, we get Patricia Glinton-Meicholas's playful Bahamian dictionary entry: "potcake, *n*. A hybrid dog whose pedigree includes more streams than the Mississippi," "the dog that will eat raw corn."[105]

Marion Bethel's *Guanahani, My Love* (1994) moves readers in similar directions, reclaiming a sacred native Guanahani (the Lucayan name for the island of Columbus's first landfall) and acknowledging an enduring potcake identity even while recognizing Bahamian self-possession as "a species endangered."[106] "On a Coral Cay" depicts a postplantation place "where tourism is king / divine and banking, a silver prince" as Bethel signifies upon local complicity: "we do not pain for what / we do not know we have lost" (26). Currents that brought James Weldon Johnson's father from his job as headwaiter of Nassau's Royal Victoria Hotel to Jacksonville's St. James Hotel (along with the family's "retainer," Mary Bethel) still link Bahamian and Sea Island economies:

On a coral cay where we live
on a tourist plantation, a banking
estate where the air is conditioned
and so are hands that do not know
the fishing line or pineapple soil
We produce nothing, or hardly and
we service the world, or nearly
In our air conditioned service
We are blessed waiters of grace divine. (26)

Marion Bethel's prizewinning book announced the arrival of a Bahamian national literature 502 years after Columbus's landfall on Guanahani. Yet, as is signified in the book's Cuban publication, its Haitian cover painting, and its placement of the Lucayan Guanahani as New World touchstone, *Guanahani, My Love* embraces a regional cosmopolitanism that exceeds any isolate nationalism. Bethel also evokes the old Geechee connections in "Miss Jane's Hands," which takes readers back to the midwifing hands of "a slavechild from Georgia / A freed woman in Abaco," an ancestor whose birthgnosis may serve as antidote to Babylon's epidural conditioning. With hands "stretched into hiccoughing / wombs untying their death knots / reaching deep within herself / she knifed her own child's bellystring" (30). Bethel's response to the islands' shared dilemmas packs an especially timely message conveyed in the six-line poem "Creativity": "I decided not to consume / anymore / I learned starvation / is not the opposite pole / of consumption / Now I am producing."[107]

Urban centers along the historic Gulf Stream region—from Charleston, Savannah, and Jacksonville to Nassau and Freeport—swell with people displaced from rural and Out Island homes. In Jacksonville, a model of the sprawling hell-border Babylon, one may find urban gardens and orchards planted to suit Geechee needs and tastes, "root" shops such as Mystic Keys Botanica (founded by a Bahamian in the 1930s), and churches guarding a spiritedness of Afro-creole worship that James Weldon Johnson feared was passing. Against a Babylonian urbanity's violence, we find pockets of creole urban space that have restored and transformed behaviors of Afro-creole broughtupsy. Here are hard-won spaces nurtured like the one in the Cat Island tale of the good-hearted orphan Camille whose tossing of her third "egg" gave her "a well-appointed house set in a grove of orange, grapefruit, and lime trees": a modest enough inheritance that leaves her "dumbfounded at her good fortune."[108] To remain habitable, cities like Jacksonville or Nassau must carry a sustaining image of themselves—in the *hippikat* vision of authors such as Johnson or in orphan tales such as Kumba's or Cat Island Camille's. Anyone who has inhabited a Jacksonville or Nassau knows City's zombifying cycles of violence and despair, the edgy music of profanity—its commodifications (in "explicit" and "clean" versions)—and worse yet, the silencing of its response. One also notes the changes in the air of depopulated and repopulated Out Islands—as golf, jet skis, and the "Margaritavilles" of Jimmy Buffet cover bands cover over a loss of long-lived relation.

When the G8 summit took place on St. Simons Island back in June 2004 (near the unmarked site of Ibo Landing), I found myself wishing that participants could see something of the process of "replacement" whereby in the place of once dynamic Geechee communities a landscape became transformed with chain stores, supersized homes, and golf courses peopled by supporters of a War on Terror that had caused the summit to be held on such a "secure" island. This kind of security displaces people behind its occupying gates. It also redirects a systemic violence that finds venting and scapegoated targets among the peoples who keep being ghettoized and displaced. Along with the G8's discussions of political and economic response to a certain kind of terrorism, the G8 participants would have done well to attend to the local dynamics of their hypersecured island meeting space and to read (and risk being swung by) the authors of that space's long witness: James Weldon Johnson, Cornelia Bailey, Queen Quet, or Nassau cousins such as Marion Bethel and Ian Strachan.

All of us pay a price when we are unable to lift voice and respond to the challenges of a James Weldon Johnson. We are encouraged to be brand-name consumers but not cultivators of our own produce: Disney Cinderellas (with requisite Walmart accessories from Haitian sweatshops) rather than Kumbas with washed calabash and fresh eggs.[109] Strolling golf courses built on plantation cemeteries holding the bones of those whose descendants no longer hold the soil bequeathed to them by ex-slaves, Babylon's movers and shakers have to be moved by the vital struggle for symbols from within being fought in hell-border cities and souths everywhere.

PART TWO

Les Invisibles

Il me pousse
invisibles et instants par tout le corps,
secrètement exigés, des sens,

et nous voici pris dans le sacré . . .
—Aimé Césaire, "Les pur-sang"

CHAPTER THREE

Fe Chauffe, Balanse, Swing

Saint-Domingue Refugees in the Govi of New Orleans

When objects are taken off an altar to be introduced into ritual action, or when they are moved from one ritual arena to another, they are first swung from side to side, or the people carrying the objects turn around and around themselves, often with the sacred pots or bottles perched on their heads. When the yams were cut and ready to be cooked, Madame Jacques's daughters were told to pick them up and balance, balance by turning round and round, as they headed up the stairs to the kitchen. To "balanse" in Haitian Creole does not mean to achieve equilibrium. It means to activate or enliven, to dance in a back-and-forth way. To raise energy by playing with conflict and contradiction is to "balanse." Balancing is a way of exposing the true nature of something by bringing it within the forcefield of clashing energies and contradictory impulses.
—Karen McCarthy Brown, "The Ritual Economy of Haitian Vodou"

A prayer
holds me in place,
balancing this sequined
constellation
—Yusef Komunyakaa, "No Good Blues"

To *balanse* is to bring a catalytic ritual heat to bear on an otherwise stag-nant situation. Balancing acts help swing us beyond the fixed score or script through otherwise uncharted, invisible, inaudible, or unthinkable zones of experience. Whether it be the time-space of a Haitian yam harvest celebrated in Brooklyn or the stage of a club in New Orleans's Faubourg Marigny, the black Atlantic's "balancing" systems of service to *les Invisibles* (the *lwa* and ancestral dead) have enabled adepts to make a way out of no way and to move through seemingly impassable gulfs. From such a ritual swing-perspective, it is easy to see that the most profound balancing act of New World (and new World) history is to be found in Haitians' revolutionary self-emancipation from chattel slavery and the French Republic. From other, mainstream per-spectives, however, Haitian legacies can appear utterly marginal—even invis-ible—save for news of the latest catastrophe.

Coming out of the world's most profitable colony, Saint-Domingue (where roughly half a million enslaved Africans and black creoles were held in bondage beneath thirty-one thousand French citizens as some twenty-eight thousand free people of color navigated a variety of niches in between), the Haitian Revolution of 1791–1803 "entered history with the peculiar characteristic of being unthinkable even as it happened," according to Michel-Rolph Trouillot.[1] The spectacularly violent consecration of Haiti's initiation as the first Black Republic rendered fundamental change immanently imaginable all across the Atlantic world, but it also amplified white responses of censorship, repression, and denial of the real and the known. Just over fifty years after ten thousand refugees from the revolution had arrived in New Orleans, the *Daily Picayune* remained so utterly bound to the ideologies and economy of "the Peculiar Institution" that it could confidently editorialize in January 1861: "Real estate owners are not at all disposed to sacrifice their property, and slaveholders have no fears—negroes are selling at advanced prices. Fashionable ladies dress as splendidly as ever; fast gentlemen go to the races . . . and imbibe champagne as readily as of old" since—as the paper announced a few days later—"Not only the colored population of New Orleans, but the slaves of Louisiana will stand by us in the moment of danger."[2] What the hegemony of the market works to keep unthought has the uncanny ability to *make* a history that ruling authority fears to acknowledge.

The slaves' violent response to the revolutionary spirit of the age and to the French Republic's "ethnocentric appropriation of the universal," Michael Dash insists, "made for a radical application of universal human rights," a profoundly creolizing cultural action.[3] What erupted from the most profitable colony in the eighteenth-century world was a cosmopolitanism from below that proved "world-historical in its implications."[4] But we (even those of us who may identify ourselves as black, African American, Caribbean, or Latin) inhabit a world ideologically conditioned to pretend not to hear Haiti's call. Recent work of Atlantic intellectual history has been tracking a black Atlantic cosmopolitanism of inescapable interface with what creolists term the acrolect: the prestige language and metropolitan print-oriented forms of books, ledgers, and legal code. I take up something of this project too. I seek response, however, to hailings from the other side of things: coming from what in relation to Africa, Haiti, and New World plantation zones may get dismissed as occult "Voodoo." Louisiana Voudou quickly became linked—like the Haitian Vodou of Bois Caïman—to the swamps and bayous surrounding the plantations, spaces where humans inescapably meet with ecosystemic entanglement.[5] Haitian Vodou and its New Orleans cousin (Voudou) have not shied away from what is truly basic to human and ecosystemic relation, what New Orleans–born "ritual designer" and spiritual consultant Luisah Tesh calls a "primal life culture."[6] Primal, not necessarily primitive or primitivist, but base, basilectal, open to alternative, combinatory readings of our extended sets of relation.

"Voodoo" has been maligned as true religion's other, its devil. "Voodoo" has been sensationalized and often even overemphasized in accounts of Haiti's revolutionary agency and essential(ist) difference. Nonetheless, reengagement with Haitian Vodou's and Louisiana Voudou's complex bodies of knowledge may be necessary to opening ourselves to otherwise unregistered or hardly accessible strata of experience—even to aspects of something integral to American and global sensibilities, which "for lack of more specific phrase, we call swing," as jazz critic Gary Giddins explained in his evaluation of the early recordings of Louis Armstrong and his Hot Fives laying out the grooves that "created modern time."[7]

Any true history of "modern time" must turn at some point to a Haitian New Orleans matrix and to the *govi* pots of Vodou: the fired clay *canari*-pots from which funeralized spirits of the dead may speak. After Haitian chattel "servants" resisted the zombifications of colonial rule by acting, in part, on the inspiriting authority accessible to them as *serviteurs* of the Vodou spirits (*lwa*), the entire plantation complex felt the reverberations of a balancing swing. It is almost impossible to overstate the dread impact of Haiti's specter upon the slave states of the early Anglo-American republic. Something of the unthinkability of the Haitian Revolution, its refusal to be contained within Western categories of analysis, remains with us, affecting what we read and how we read, whom we collectively see and whom we don't.[8]

According to Alfred Hunt, it was in reaction to the Haitian Revolution and through increasing censorship and restrictions on black agency "that the South began to erect its intellectual blockade against potentially dangerous doctrines."[9] New Orleans, however, has been a notoriously leaky borderspace. In the wake of Haitian independence (and the Napoleonic Wars that caused Cuba to deport over ten thousand Franco-creole aliens in 1809), Louisiana faced uncontainable modes of demographic and political swing. Although the whole eastern seaboard of North America received as many as twenty-five thousand refugees from Saint-Domingue (including the Florida exile of one of the insurrection's key generals and initiators, Jorge Biassou), it was in Louisiana that the Haitian revolution's reverberations continued to move with the dynamism that had forced an embattled Napoleon to offer France's Louisiana Territory for U.S. purchase, finding a new home space in what Ishmael Reed has called "the Govi of New Orleans."[10]

If New Orleans is to be conceptualized as a *govi*, we must consider the stakes of presenting Creole City as sacral pot of *les Invisibles*. New Orleans has been described by one jazz historian as "perhaps the most seething ethnic melting pot that the nineteenth-century world could produce."[11] But New Orleans was hardly exceptional in the Atlantic world, was no more "seething" with multiethnic transculturation than was Havana or Rio de Janeiro. The melting-pot metaphor also projects a metallurgist's homogeneity that exists neither in Vodou nor in the head of any individual who serves spirits such as the iron-working Ogun. In keeping with a West African "multiple soul complex," Vodou ontologies move us away from the unified subject of European identities and help us see that we are all composite, nigh-polyrhythmic relational assemblages composed of at least four components beyond the *corps-cadavre* (the physical body): (1) the *nam* or "animating force of the body"; (2) the *gwo bonanj* or big guardian angel that travels in dream and departs in possession states and may be described as "the consciousness and essential personality of the individual"; (3) the *ti bonanj* or little guardian angel, an intuitive "spiritual reserve tank" of ancestral fossil fuels; and (4) the *zetwal* or star, a celestial double or prenatally divined fate.[12] Beyond this there is the divine *lwa* enshrined at initiation as *met tet* or "master of the head." Each individual thus constitutes something of a simmering gumbo pot in need of careful tending in life and also in death. Those who serve the spirits acknowledge that we are all composite and multiple. This is why we need rites of balance or swing if we are to pursue any path with sustainable momentum. Every first-person consciousness, every "I," is an assemblage, a plural *we*. Since much of one's living self remains as opaque to the composite nonautonomous self as it does to others, we can hardly be surprised that the funerary spirit pot or *govi* can hold only one component part of the dead individual—his or her *gwo bonanj*. The rest of the "passed" person escapes us, as uncontainable in death as in embodied experience.

Facing the gulf-abyss, funeral rites in New Orleans and the creole Caribbean maintain the possibility of restoration of the behaviors and gnosis of the dead. After death, the *gwo bonanj* must be detached carefully from the body, to dwell in the waters of the abyss for a year and a day. This abyssal year and a day coincides with the period of time during which a single occupant must occupy the sealed, leased tombs (collective family vaults) in New Orleans's cities of the dead, the time officially required for the body to decompose before another is interred inside. At some point after the year-and-a-day, the Vodouist's family must reclaim the departed's spirit from the abyssal waters and install it in an earthenware *govi* from which the spirit may be summoned for consultation or blessing in times of family need. A major ceremony, usually involving a collective of families pooling resources on behalf of a number of dead, the "reclamation rite" or *rele mo nan dlo*, requires the ritual *konesans* (knowledge/power) of an initiated priest who (accompanied by drums and chorus) functions "as midwife, assists the third birth, the rebirth of the soul from the abysmal waters."[13] Without this reclamation of the initiate soul from gulf waters, there is no peace between the dead and the living, no way of keeping the dead and their *konesans* in the family, no access to the experience toward which we gesture with the word *history*. Ancestors must be reclaimed from the abyssal waters in elaborate rites aimed at performance wherein the dead speak spectacularly "through a kind of ventriloquism possession" to the living, consoling or advising them, prescribing medications, offering pointed critique.[14] Once lodged in a *govi*, the dead may be reactivated in rites swinging or heating the pot. Since, as Joseph Roach puts it in *Cities of the Dead*, "the voices of the dead may speak freely now only through the bodies of the living," we may understand the importance of New Orleans's ritual calendar to the activation of the city's sense of deep time—tending to *les Invisibles* of its long *durée*.[15]

The two chapters in this section of *Sacral Grooves* seek to aid in the widespread work of reclaiming something of the soul(s) of New Orleans (and really of all of us in relation to it) from Gulf waters, from economic and political neglect, environmental and social devastation. In paying respects to the *longue durée* of New Orleans, these two chapters also aim to bolster our acknowledgment of kinships with a Haiti owed long overdue economic, social, and ritual respects. If we cannot serve these key *govi* of creole modernity, we risk losing contact with crucial guides to modern Gulf time and space. We risk entrapment in the cultivated naïveté and thoughtlessness of the French colonials of 1791 or of *New Orleans Picayune* readers of 1861. Few of us would elect to remain so vulnerable or stupid as we consider recent Gulf disasters like Hurricane Katrina and the BP Deepwater Horizon oil spill. Our corrective effort to go to the mouth of the *govi* of New Orleans, however, calls for difficult acts of listening to subalternized voices that are often poorly represented, if recorded at all, in available texts. These voices that would balance our vision and open our eyes to clashing energies and contradictory impulses have been censored, silenced, and ignored. Nevertheless, we have available more (and richer) textual resources in New Orleans's literary corpus than we tend to realize. Haiti-swung readings of Louisiana's francophone literature, early Anglo accounts of New Orleans Voudou rites, foundational jazz autobiographies, and recent African American literature invoking Creole City's Legba-ruled hermeneutics can help us, in the words of Louis Armstrong, to "swing . . . away from the score."[16]

"Makebelieve Art"—Swinging the Most Disparate Stuff

The linguistic and cultural agency of francophone New Orleans was sustained and re-energized in the nineteenth century by a single event: the Saint-Domingue (Haitian) migration to Louisiana, about which George W. Cable writes, "it might be easier to underestimate than to exaggerate the silent results of an event that gave the French-speaking classes twice the numerical power with which they had begun to wage their long battle against American absorption."[17] While Louisiana's Afro-Creole culture owes much to its foundational Senegambian slave presence, the mass migration from Saint-Domingue (with 9,059 refugees coming in the final wave of exodus from Cuba during the last nine months of 1809) re-creolized the newly acquired U.S. territory.[18] Following the 1809 arrival of 2,731 whites, 3,102 free people of color, and 3,226 slaves, the population of New Orleans increased to 6,331 whites, 4,950 free people of color, and 5,961 slaves.[19] Coming just six years after the Louisiana Purchase and more than doubling New Orleans's francophone creole population and black majority, the Saint-Domingue migration allowed French (or franco-creole) speakers to remain a majority presence until around 1830 and likely enabled New Orleans to hold onto its French and Caribbean heritages of language, culinary arts, religion, music, and its three-caste racial society.[20] Beyond this demographic re-creolization of New Orleans from revolutionary Haiti, the refugees brought considerable technical expertise and cultural verve to frontier Louisiana. Nathalie Dessens outlines their roles in developing Louisiana's lucrative sugar industry; their founding of newspapers, schools, theaters, and opera; as well as their contributions to military defense, medicine, law, freemasonry, religion, architecture, the arts, fashion, and other areas of life for which Louisiana is celebrated.[21]

Among the refugees, it was probably the free people of color whose presence made the most distinctive mark. As Paul Lachance's study of antebellum Louisiana marriage contracts has shown, "Saint-Domingue refugees were not only an important addition to the number of free persons of color living in New Orleans, but also to the wealth of the group" as "female refugees of color arrived with more property than local free women of color had been able to accumulate."[22] This was no small matter since of the 3,102 émigrés who were free people of color, only 428 were men, with 1,377 women and 1,297 children among them.[23] New Orleans's free black populace, most of whom could claim Saint-Domingue descent, soon possessed land and wealth beyond the reach of any other black population in the United States. Key contributors to *Les Cenelles* (1845), the earliest anthology of poetry published in North America by authors of African descent (including Camille Thierry, Michel Séligny, Victor Séjour, and Armand Lanusse), were descendants of the Haitian Revolution's free refugees of color, as were newspaper editors and activists Louis Charles, Jean-Baptiste Roudanez, Paul Trévigne, and Rodolphe Lucien Desdunes.[24]

Saint-Domingue émigrés carried not just the acrolectal orientations of a sophisticated and wealthy revolutionary colony but profound basilectal orientations too. They re-Africanized and re-creolized the whole material, psychological, and spiritual matrix of New Orleans. Donald Cosentino's discussion of contemporary Haitian altars does a remarkable job of conveying the power of the improvisational assemblage-aesthetics that migrated from Saint-Domingue in the heads of the *lwa*'s servants:

> This totalizing vision belongs to Vodou, which doesn't blink before any of Haiti's brutal, and often obscene, history. The vision doesn't lie, but it does force meaning out of every event, including those which more secular societies repress, or even deny. To look at a Vodou altar cluttered with customized whisky bottles, satin pomanders, clay pots dressed in lace, plaster statues of St. Anthony and the laughing Buddha, holy cards, political kitsch, Dresden clocks, bottles of Moët-et-Chandon, rosaries, crucifixes, Masonic insignia, eye-shadowed kewpie dolls, atomizers of Anaïs-Anaïs, wooden phalli, goat skulls, Christmas tree ornaments, Arawak celts . . . is to gauge the achievement of slaves and freemen who imagined a myth broad enough and fabricated a ritual complex enough to encompass all this disparate stuff.[25]

Cosentino repeatedly utilizes jazz analogies to give readers a sense of the sophistication of a demonized religion's sacred arts. He notes David Byrne's description of Vodou altars as "visual jazz, constantly reworked and reactivated," and practitioners' reinterpretations of Catholic lithographs and iconic hagiography: "The process is centripetal, pushing out into new forms like a jazz riff."[26] If jazz serves as valorizing analogy for maligned Vodou, we may also see that Vodou has worked as primitivist analogue for the syncopating powers of jazz. Whether from a *Ladies' Home Journal* (1921) attack on swing's origination as "the accompaniment of the voodoo dancer, stimulating the half-crazed barbarian to the vilest deeds," or whether we find it in Sidney Bechet's homage to a Congo Square drumming grandfather who turned to the songs of Vodou "to throw out the devils and bring down powers," jazz's swinging power has been tied to fantastic figurations of Voodoo.[27] It would take New Orleans writers a long while to embrace the totalizing vision of a maligned basilect. Nevertheless, an intriguing body of nineteenth-century New Orleans writing points to how a totalizing Voudou-jazz aesthetic emerged from cross-currents of Catholicism, Senegambian *nyama*, Masonic rites, spiritualism, revolutionary Romanticism, opera, carnival, Congo Square dance, and prior ritual activity in Saint-Domingue and Santiago de Cuba.[28] Louisiana's Franco-Creole literature encompasses all this disparate stuff.

Pre-revolutionary Saint-Domingue provides the setting of "Le Mulâtre" (1837), by Victor Séjour, the New Orleans–born son of a free man of color from Saint-Domingue. The story of a slave's vengeance against his planter-father, "Le Mulâtre" offers a sympathetic representation of rites that stand as precursors to New Orleans jazz funerals. In one scene, proto-Vodou practitioners bury the main character's Senegal-born mother. We see that "[e]ach of them, having blessed the remains of the deceased, kneels and prays," and "[w]hen this first ceremony is finished, another one, no less singular, commences" with "songs, and then funeral dances!"[29] The funeral asserts a danced rapport with death in this story set in Saint-Domingue by a first-generation New Orleans descendant.

An important element in the creolization of relations with the dead in the circum-Caribbean was the rise of nineteenth-century spiritualism. Spiritualist séances and mesmerism emerged as popular forces, engaging black mediums such as New Orleans blacksmith J. B. Valmour and white mediums such as Charles Testut in shared, often politically radical dialogue with the dead.[30] Testut's "new age" novel *Le Vieux Saloman* (1872) evokes a freemasonry-informed spiritualist organization that stretches from Louisiana across North America, Europe, and the Caribbean (Guadeloupe) in its abolitionist activity, working to free "those who possess men as well as . . . those possessed."[31]

While Testut's work depicts spiritualist and Masonic activities linking black and white creole elites, Alfred Mercier's *L'habitation Saint-Ybars* (1881) represents Afro-Creole life with a more intimate grounding in the basilect, providing dialogue in Creole (or "gumbo French") and acknowledging a fuller range of creolized music and authority in Louisiana. The white Creole protagonist grows up listening to the banjo music of his nurse's Bambara father while the Afro-Creole nurse learns classical repertoires on the piano. Much of the gothic storyline follows the body and blood of a phenotypically white slave woman whose mixed-race grandmother "was raised by a good master . . . who came here after the disasters of Saint-Domingue."[32] Mercier's novel depicts a stunning material, psychological, spiritual, and linguistic matrix of Europeans, Africans, Choctaws, and Creoles in southern Louisiana's transcultural contact zones.

New Orleans's most famous nineteenth-century composer, Louis Moreau Gottschalk, was the son of Saint-Domingan refugees and brought a basilectal Creole respect—like Mercier's—for goatskin drums and banjo into his "high art" composition. His 1848 Parisian debut of "Bamboula" and compositions such as "Danse des Nègres" worked to integrate Louisiana's and the Caribbean's Afro-creole music into the "world" music scene.[33] While Mercier and Gottschalk drew upon the spiritual and musical basilect, Marie Augustin, a Louisiana-born descendant of Saint-Domingue exiles, beat a different drum for strict white-supremacist mastery in her novel *Le Macandal: Episode de l'insurrection des noirs à St Domingue* (1892). Published in the peak year of lynchings in the United States, Augustin's narrative takes up the question of whether "the blood of Macandal [the famous one-armed insurrectionist of Haitian memory] could engender anything other than a monster."[34] This amounts to a question of whether Haiti itself (or independent black authority) can give rise to anything other than monstrosity. She dramatizes an inevitable racial atavism of orgy and terroristic savagery as Macandal's Paris-educated son returns to Saint-Domingue to direct the "monstrous ceremony" of Bois Caïman, "impregnated with an electricity charged from the agglomeration of these human bodies." The rest of the novel is anticlimax, leading to the killing of the white would-be "rehabilitators," to a flotilla of surviving exiles with their loyal servants, and to a last wistful look upon Saint-Domingue as winds push them "toward the hospitable shores of Louisiana" and to new plantations and narratives of monstrosity.[35]

George W. Cable's *The Grandissimes* (1880) treats New Orleans Voudou in sharper detail than the Franco-creole fictions do, noting, for example—and perhaps with the voyeurism of an anglophone outsider—"an oblation of beer sweetened with black molasses to Papa Lebat [Legba], who keeps the invisible keys of all the doors."[36] An exotic alterity moving between fear and longing pervades Cable's representation of Voudou rites. In one ritual he perceives "a frightful triumph of body over mind," but later observes the nigh-unrepresentable physical education that draws a servant of the spirits to "turn, posture, bow, respond to the song, start, swing, straighten, stamp, wheel, lift her hand, stoop, twist, walk, whirl, tip-toe with crossed ankles, smite her palms, march, circle, leap—an endless improvisation of rhythmic motion to this modulated responsive chant."[37]

In similar but far more appreciative vein, Karen McCarthy Brown has described how Haitian Vodou works past "the mind/body splitting that has characterized Western thought," and demands practitioners' commitment to developing "mindful bodies" in order "to understand what it means to be human in the world."[38] Voudou's supple resistance to white-supremacist inflexibility comes across in powerful counterpoint when Cable's white center of narrative perspective, Frowenfeld, reacts with dread as "the cathedral clock struck twelve and was answered again from the convent tower; and as the notes died away he suddenly became aware that the weird, drowsy throb of the African song and dance had been swinging drowsily in his brain for an unknown lapse of time."[39] "Swinging" in spite of itself through unknown lapses of clock time—into other knowledges and temporalities—the novel's gothic core lies in the story of Bras Coupé's rebellion nurtured by the Voudou priestess Palmyre Philosophe, who "had heard of San Domingo" and knew "the lesson she would have taught . . . was Insurrection."[40] What the book also conveys (almost in spite of its author and narrative center) is an intuitive, late-nineteenth-century textual feel for the deep time of New Orleans.

We find something more of the initiatory vision of this performance culture in Alcée Fortier's *Louisiana Folk-Tales* (1895), which reconfigures (as "Rose and Blanche") the Senegalese orphan initiation story of two girls' journeys to receive their magic eggs from a bush crone.[41] Louisiana's ritual bush has remained a destination for receiving not only Kumba's eggs or Manbo

Cia's initiate gombo but—as Muddy Waters well knew—it's where "mojo hands" get made and traded. Fortier's *Louisiana Folk-Tales* presents Compé Lapin (Brer Rabbit) as a mojo-icon of authoritative Creole moxie. Rabbit, whose "mouth was so honeyed that no one could refuse him anything," is the master drummer and fiddler who swings the Creole balls and makes the strongest gris-gris amulets, and he is a Legba-like "player" of spaces Joseph Roach describes as "liminal zone[s] in which dances, masquerades, and processions could act out that which was otherwise unspeakable."[42] *The* liminal zone, of course, for acting out what is otherwise unspeakable in New Orleans has long been Mardi Gras.

Cable, in *The Creoles of Louisiana* (1884), didn't know what to make of this totalizing performance—the deep play in deep time of Mardi Gras.[43] He noted carnival's "gorgeous, not to say, gaudy, tableaux drawn through the streets under the glare of blazing petroleum and frequent lime-lights, on tinseled cars, by draped teams, to the blare of brass music and the roar of popular acclamation, in representation of one or another of the world's great myths, epics, or episodes," all of which he could then dismiss as "makebelieve art, frivolous taste, and short-sighted outlay."[44] This, like the Voudou drumming of *The Grandissimes*, is an art swinging in the lapses of monumental and progressive clock-time. New Orleans's "makebelieve art" drew from creolization's assemblage aesthetic, remixing myth, history, material culture, and local or world events in limelight to brassy syncopations. *Serviteurs* of the Vodou spirits have certainly been among the most adept make-believe ritual artists. According to Mintz and Trouillot, Vodouists "successfully 'patched' what *had* been believed to what *would* be believed."[45] That they had the patchwork wherewithal to make autonomous belief possible on sugar plantations almost beyond belief marks a wondrous achievement: the maintenance and behavioral restoration of one of the world's most powerful limbo gateways.

New Orleans's nineteenth-century literature provides a vision of Saint-Domingan/Haitian cultural vitality as well as a sense of the material, psychological, and spiritual resources available to this Creole City's make-believe arts. Only a basilectally grounded aesthetic would be able to use the whole palette. We must turn now to accounts of nineteenth- and early-twentieth-century Voudou practice in New Orleans if we are to enter the liminal zones of *konesans* shared by Vodou and early jazz *serviteurs* and opened up across global gulfs.

Papa Limba and "Them *Fe Chauffe* Dancers"

Prior to the influx of refugees from Saint-Domingue, Louisiana's Afro-creole spirit world had taken shape in practices maintained by Senegambian slaves in contact with Catholicism, other Africans, and Gulf Coast Indians. But with the arrival of the refugees and the ascension of Sanité Dédé (a free woman of color from Saint-Domingue) as New Orleans's first-recorded Voudou Queen, Haitian Vodou appears to have taken root.[46] A white teen, brought to Dumaine Street's abandoned brickyard on St. John's Eve (June 23) in 1822 by a woman enslaved by his father, recalled Dédé, "the high priestess or Voudou queen" (accompanied by an herbalist-musician named Zozo), presiding over possessions induced by the *calinda* rhythms of a sheepskin drum, a drummed barrel, a gourd rattle, a banjo, and Zozo's swinging of a ritually balanced snake. The music moved one *serviteur*, a "lithe, tall black woman, with a body waving and undulating like Zozo's snake . . . to sway on one and the other side" as "the undulating motion was imparted to her body from the ankles to the hips." The white Creole witness recalled over fifty years after this possession scene how "she tore the white handkerchief from her forehead" and the lead drummer called: "Houm! Dance Calinda! / Voudou! Magnian! / Aie! Aie! / Dance Calinda!" This long-memoried testimonial of a New Orleans Voudou ceremony places "half a dozen white men and two white women" among those submitting to the *konesans* of a Haitian *mambo* and the spirits she served.[47]

We are left to wonder about the needs or desire that drove this white teen to be guided there by his father's and the spirits' servant. The teen-become-adult narrates a classic moment of the Western sublime in a scene of his own momentarily swung abjection and his resistance to it (in a well-rehearsed language of Voudou's "discords," "noise," and "orgies"): "an indescribable horror took possession of me. With one bound I was out of the shed, and with all speed traversed the yard. I found the gate open, and I was in the street and near home sooner than I can tell. If I ever have realized a sense of the real, visible presence of his majesty, the devil, it was that night among his Voudou worshippers."[48] Here, in an old man's narrative of 1875 recalling a teenager's gateway moment in 1822, one gate's opening (back to the white home) marks another gate's closing (to fostered affiliations). Our written record of the event comes through the closed gulf-gateway—from a narrative authorized in turning away from the sublime encounter ("the horror, the horror")—rather than in apprenticeship to its sacral border-crossings.

In the early written record it is often the law and police that bring us to the scene, and the newspapers report it. The *Louisiana Gazette* (August 16, 1820) provides our earliest criminal record of a New Orleans spirit house wherein several slaves, free people of color, and a single white man were arrested for illegal night-gatherings in a Faubourg Tremé home "used as a temple for certain occult practices and the idolatrous worship of an African deity called *Vaudoo*." The *Gazette* reports the seizure of ritual objects, including "the image of a woman, whose lower extremities resemble a snake."[49] Able to see the seized image now only through the eyes of an antebellum police blotter, we are left with a perhaps suspect (but repeatedly witnessed) icon of the limbo discipline required to have the *lwa* Danballa dance in the head of an initiate. No easy passage. It points the servant's way to a legitimate master (the *mait-tet* or "master of the head"), the *lwa* that is the sacral other of the law (French *loi*, Creole *lwa* or *lalwa*).[50]

While Sanité Dédé may have helped to install the revolutionary *lwa* from Saint-Domingue in New Orleans houses, the key figure in the popularization of New Orleans Voudou, Marie Laveau, was born in New Orleans on September 10, 1801.[51] Married in 1819 to the Saint-Domingue émigré Jacques Paris, she was known as "the Widow Paris" after Paris's disappearance. Sometime around 1826 she entered into an enduring relationship with a white Louisiana Creole, Christophe Glapion (often remembered as a free man of color from Saint-Domingue) and emerged soon thereafter as New Orleans's preeminent *mambo*, leading rites in her home (152 St. Ann Street), presiding at various locations in Faubourgs Tremé and Marigny, and perhaps even—as legend has it—on Sunday afternoons at Congo Square.[52]

Under Laveau ("the Widow Paris"), Voudou appears to have permeated all strata of Creole society. One Louisiana Writers' Project interviewee, a playmate of Marie Laveau's grandchildren, recalled the front room of the Laveau-Glapion residence as being full of burning candles, with "all kinds of saints' pictures and flowers on the altar."[53] Marie Laveau's altar probably looked something like the one described by the *Daily Crescent*, on July 30, 1850, after Betsy Toledano and followers (both free and slave) were arrested at Toledano's French Quarter home for "unlawful assembly." We read of "the rude chapel walls hung round with colored prints of the saints," bowls on an altar holding a variety of stones, and "goblets and vases filled with unknown liquids," all congruent with contemporary Vodou altars.[54] These reports of private spirit houses and their rites "[c]arried on in secret," according to an 1850 *Picayune* article, frightened whites for their capacity to "bring the slaves into contact with disorderly free negroes and mischievous whites."[55] It is this "occult" contact under the ritual time-space of free black authority that most worried the *Picayune*'s white readership. Perhaps because of her connections and sagacity, Marie Laveau herself eluded the 1850s crackdown on Voudou. She petitioned the court to retrieve a religious icon seized in the raid on Betsy Toledano's house ("a quaintly carved figure resembling something between a centaur and an Egyptian mummy") and enters the record again as subject to a neighbor's disturbing-the-peace complaint issued in 1859 against Marie "Clarisse" Laveau, "Queen of the Voudous," for "infernal singing" at a home she owned in Faubourg Marigny.[56]

While guarding private rites for initiates and sincere or paying seekers who contributed to the society's ritual economy, the Widow Paris may have helped a younger successor or spiritual daughter, also known as Marie Laveau (Marie II), to develop the annual festival of St. John's Eve as a carnivalesque midsummer attraction held near old Milneberg on the shores of Lake Pontchartrain. We do not know the official civic identity of this second, younger Marie Laveau, who reigned over Reconstruction-era St. John's Eve fests. But journalists' reports, coupled with recollections by Louisiana Writers' Project interviewees, testify to the ritual leadership of a second, younger, lighter-skinned Marie Laveau. The effect was to augment what was becoming legend—a Marie Laveau who ruled New Orleans Voudou for over a hundred years, hardly losing a dynamic step, a Marie Laveau who in apotheosis became one of *les Invisibles* herself, and also (in the market parlance of our time) "branded" New Orleans Voudou with her legendary name.[57]

The flamboyant Marie II appears to have used journalists to hype the spectacle of St. John's Eve and bring "great crowds" to the lake, according to one reporter in 1872, for festive rites that continued until dawn.[58] Robert Tallant, the sensationalist historian of *Voodoo in New Orleans* (1946), insisted, "To go see Marie Laveau became one of the things a tourist in New Orleans must do, just as he was supposed to eat once in each of the famous restaurants and attend a performance at the French Opera House."[59] A visiting traveler could traverse opera house, Creole restaurant, and Voudou in a single night. But what do we make of the basilectal cosmopolitanism capable of incorporating this matrix of experience? In contemporary Haiti, according to Cosentino, "[t]here is no grander realization of 'le mélange' [creolization's whole mix] than the patronal celebrations for St. John the Baptist" bringing Catholics, Freemasons, and Vodouists to parties, ceremonies, and St. John's Eve bonfires from which—as with the Pontchartrain fetes of Marie II—the ashes are saved for luck and healing.[60]

From the responses of Louisiana Writers' Project interviewees, the second Marie Laveau appears to have been admired as much for being a lithe dancer and "hot" spirit-woman as for her religious devotion to the saints, qualities neither unusual nor oppositional for a *mambo* of power. As Karen McCarthy Brown explains, "connection between sexuality and life energy [is] pervasive in Vodou spirituality. All Vodou rituals aim to *echofe* (heat things up). To raise heat, to raise luck, to raise life energy, to intensify sexuality in the broadest sense—these are all more or less the same process."[61] The second Marie's best-known praise song, sung by congregants on Pontchartrain's shores, was "Mam'zelle Marie, fé chauffez. Mam'zelle Marie, chauffez ça" (Ms. Marie, make it hot, turn up the heat, feel the power).[62] All this, of course, got remembered quite variously. In the LWP interviews, Raoul Desfresne recalled how "them *Fe Chauffe* dancers balanced lighted candles on their heads the whole time they danced and the candle flames never went out. They was a sight!"[63] The mark left on Desfresne's memory by participation in those dances (and by his singing at rites in town) comes across clearly: "There was a gang of white ladies what had money and they'd pay Marie Laveau ten dollars each to come to them *Fe Chauffe* dances. You'd see 'em come, all dressed up and wearin' thick veils, but when they sent their carriages away, they'd take off their shoes and stockings and all their clothes 'cept their chemises. Then they'd dance on the barges with lighted candles on their heads. Marie Laveau would stand in the middle and shake and sing, and they'd dance around her in a circle. You can't see nothing like that nowadays, no."[64] For some, this heat was a bit much. But considering journalists' reports of thousands lining the shore for St. John's fetes, with dancers and spectators in various states of summertime undress, we may feel Martha Ward is right to speak of the Pontchartrain rites as a forerunner of events like the New Orleans Jazz and Heritage Festival.[65]

Voudou's considerable kinetic power appears in the lawyer Moreau de Saint-Mery's 1797 report from colonial Saint-Domingue. Moreau wrote of practitioners dancing "to the edge of consciousness" and added that "never has any man of the constabulary, who has sworn war upon Voodoo, not felt the power which compels him to dance and which without doubt has saved the dancers from any need for flight."[66] Having watched Vodouists "spin around endlessly," Moreau was savvy enough to see that these reenergizing balancing acts—given their independent authority to convert legally possessed chattel into *serviteurs* possessed by master *lwa*—"can be made into a terrible weapon."[67] This understanding is reinforced by one man's recollections of the powerful charge he felt after attending one of the Friday-night rites held at the Laveau residence on St. Ann Street: "[W]hen you left you surely had the belief."[68] A make-believe art under the control of the supposedly subaltern could strike fear of the gods into anyone, dissolve and redo the ego, and launch the master class into currents shaped by Afro-creole agency. Thus a *Times* reporter wrote in apocalyptic wonderment of a white celebrant dancing with the St. John's Eve Voudouists in 1872: "[H]er pallid wanton face actually beamed with exuberant levity," as there on Pontchartrain's shores, "set adrift on the rapids of depravity, she had reached the center of the vortex."[69]

In New Orleans, for about fifty years the embodied spirits of the two Marie Laveaus ruled the center of this vortex. The original (the Widow Paris) is remembered for reinvesting Voudou practice with the spiritual glamour of Catholic iconography. According to legend and variously corroborated by LWP interviews and the newspapers, she was a skilled yellow fever nurse, a healer and spiritual adviser, a social worker, a dedicated counselor of condemned prisoners, a dependable Catholic parishioner, and an inventive "player" of Louisiana's white-supremacist political system. In all this, her service to the saints worked to feed the *lwa*, as Josephine Green's recollection of the Widow Paris's Legba rites attests:

My ma seen her . . . back before the war what they had here wit' the North-erners . . . She went outside and here come Marie Laveau wit' a big crowd of people followin' her . . . All the people wit' her was hollerin' and screamin', "We is goin' to see Papa Limba! We is goin' to see Papa Limba!" My grandpa go runnin' after my ma then, yellin' her, "You come on in here Eunice! Don't you know Papa Limba is the devil?" But after that my ma find out Papa Limba meant St. Peter, and her pa was jest foolin' her.[70]

We hear of Legba's *serviteurs* entering the lake, circling, holding hands, and singing as food is tossed to "Papa La Bas."[71] Another informant, Mary Ellis, recalled a song her aunt learned from Marie: "St. Peter, St. Peter, open the door, / I'm callin' you, come to me! / St. Peter, St. Peter, open the door" and added that "Marie Laveau used to call St. Peter somethin' like 'Laba'" and "called St. Michael 'Daniel Blanc,' and St. Anthony 'Yun Sue.'"[72] Legba (Laba) rules creolization's crossroads. He opens the doors to a space *là-bas* ("out there") connecting us to *les Invisibles*. Like St. Peter, he carries the keys and swings the gate.

Between the time of Marie Laveau's disappearance from active ritual leadership around 1873 or 1874 and her death in 1881, New Orleans Voudou may have lost something of its religious organization around spiritual family and the rites of initiatory reproduction and economy. But plenty of people continued to offer services. Jean Montanée ("Doctor John") practiced divination and gave medicinal prescriptions (or gris-gris) till his death in 1885. Lafcadio Hearn's memorial published in *Harper's Weekly* as "The Last of the Voudoos" presents Doctor John as a native of Senegal sold as a slave in Cuba, one who, after securing his freedom in Cuba, worked as a cook aboard Spanish ships till he settled in New Orleans as a fortune-teller.[73] When we look to Doctor John's chief method of divination, we find a system more common to Yoruba-centered Cuban Santería than to practices of Haitian Vodou. In 1866 a *Daily Crescent* reporter described his divination session with "Devil John," who took "a handful of shells" that he "held at some distance above the table and let fall. It was by marking the arrangement which these took . . . that a glimpse into the future was obtained."[74] While Dr. John may have been using forms of cowrie divination known in his native Senegal, it is even more likely that his divination system was informed (or initiated by) the sixteen-cowrie system of divination in regular use in Cuban Santería.

Voudou queens such as Eliza Nicaud and Malvina Latour are also remembered from this post-Laveau period that roughly parallels the rise of a proto-jazz music called swing. One early-twentieth-century New Orleanian, Marie Brown, recalled her great-grandmother, "Queen Eliza of the Dance," who "danced at all the Marie Laveau meetin's on St. John's Eve" and was the daughter of a migrant "from Santo Domingo . . . all hoodoo people." Brown informs us that Queen Eliza of the Dance was "named" by Queen Marie Saloppé (a Voudou contemporary of the Widow Paris), and this Eliza may well be the Eliza Nicaud (or Nicaux) often mentioned as a late-nineteenth-century Voudou leader.[75]

This was the era of the triumph of Jim Crow, culminating in the apartheid-supporting Supreme Court ruling against the Faubourg Tremé's own Homer Plessy during the nadir of both national and local race relations. New Orleans's three-tiered racialized society was forced to start shaking itself out in more black-and-white terms. Spirituality, music, and carnival all found reshaping in an ever-changing counterculture of modernity that has never quite squared with the rest of North America. We must recall too that New Orleans's position as the nation's Gulf port maintained a steady maritime flow of commerce and travel between the Creole City and ports in Cuba, Haiti, and Mexico. The more we look at change in early Jim Crow New Orleans, the more we may also look at old patterns of creolization.

During the wars of Cuban independence and the years preceding the U.S. occupation of Haiti, it is easier to imagine ongoing dialogue between New Orleans *serviteurs* and practitioners of Haitian Vodou or Cuban Santería than it is to imagine a New Orleans spiritual and musical scene in Gulf-isolation. It was, after all, Gaetano Mariatini's "Congo Circus" from Havana that—in its seasonal winter shows in the Place Publique until Mariatini's death in New Orleans in 1817—gave the place its enduring name: Circus Square or Congo Square.[76] Descriptions of St. John's Eve rites led by Malvina Latour in 1884 reveal practices shared with contemporary Haitian Vodou and Cuban Santería: an altar featuring a cloth placed on the floor with candles at the corners, and "on the cloth, there was a shallow Indian basket filled with weeds, or, as they call them, *herbes*. Around the basket were diminutive piles of white beans and corn . . . outside of all several saucers with small cakes in them."[77] Charles Raphael, who sang at weekly Friday services in a home in Faubourg Tremé in the early 1880s, described a circum-Caribbean ritual scene: "A feast was spread for the spirits on a white tablecloth laid on the floor. Certain foods were always present . . . congri [rice and peas], apples, oranges, and red peppers. Candles were lighted and placed in the four corners of the room."[78] Charles Dudley Warner, writing in 1887 of a New Orleans ceremony he had attended, described the process of rapping invocations on the floor, offering candles and brandy on the altar, and dashing libations. He depicts a ritual music intent on dissolving the space between participant and observer: a "rhythmical shuffle, [moving] with more movement of the hips than of the feet, backward and forward, round and round, but accelerating . . . as the time of the song quickened and the excitement rose in the room . . . [which] made it almost impossible for the spectator not to join in the swing of its influence."[79] Joining this collective "swing," newly made or reheated believers were misted in brandy sprayed from the mouth of an initiate elder who, as in Haitian practice, washed their heads, "shampooing them" and took each one, "spun him round a half a dozen times, and then sent him whirling."[80] Such acts of balancing left folk both heated up and ritually cooled, ready to face whatever Jim Crow New Orleans might throw at them.

In this proto-jazz era of widespread spectacle lynching in America, a believer in other structures of authority would have to be ready to see her experience depicted as the *Times-Democrat* described the St. John's Eve rites of 1896: "impassioned black savages danced as naked as islanders to the beating of ox skulls and tom-toms, the weird crooning of the hags, and the sharp ejaculations of bucks and wenches."[81] Media circulation of the rhetoric of black savages dancing naked as islanders obviously had more to do with the radical racism of an apartheid nation-state on the verge of island-occupying empire and banana republicanism—Hawaii (1893, 1898), Cuba, Puerto Rico, Guam, and the Philippines (1898), Samoa (1900), Honduras and Panama (1903), Nicaragua (1912), Haiti (1915), Dominican Republic (1916), the Virgin Islands (1917)—than it does with "real" Afro-creole spiritual practice in a New Orleans that was principal port to the U.S. banana trade.[82] But black New Orleanians would come to complex self-identification with other so-called savages, not just with islander forebears and cousins but also with their Choctaw and Zulu kin. Charles Raphael (born around 1868) described the St. John's Eve *Fe Chauffe* rites of his youth as resembling the "bands of Negroes who dress in Indian Chief costumes on Mardi Gras and dance on the Claiborne Avenue neutral ground."[83] The Mardi Gras Indians, active in ritual carnival families since Becate Batiste masked in 1885 with his Seventh Ward Creole Wild West Gang, famously assert an independent native and circum-Caribbean authority that refuses to bow down, refuses to let anyone take its elaborately wrought crowns.[84] They do so within a deeply Voudou-inflected spirit—"that natural rhythm that goes back to that Marie Laveau thing, that Vodou thing"—which draws not only upon old black-Indian contacts and a Saint-Domingue carnival ethos but also upon the sequin art, feathered assemblages, conga lines, calypsos, and raras of twentieth-century carnival in Haiti, Trinidad, and Cuba through travel fostered in part by the United Fruit Company's shipping routes.[85] In the Jim Crow–era onslaught on Voudou's family values, Mardi Gras Indian and jazz families emerged to serve both New Orleans's and Creole modernity's complexly countercultural spirits.[86]

Multiethnic relations of reciprocity in the Gulf region had long been fostered among Indians, Africans, and subalternized or chattel Creoles. The Choctaw and Natchez were known for harboring black maroons. And a number of LWP interviewees recalled Choctaw market women camping regularly in the backyard of the Laveau-Glapion residence on St. Ann Street.[87] The

Choctaw almost certainly contributed to Marie Laveau's store of ritual and medicinal knowledge, as she and her spirits did for them. The result over time was a creole mélange thickened with African gombo and Choctaw filé asserting other grammars, shell-shaking stomps, and spirited authority. Voudou's swinging of multiethnic authority and make-believe affect—nigh impossible to resist—must be considered in any invocation of the *racine-lwa* (rhizomatic root-spirits) of jazz.

"A Certain Cure"—Making It Hot

Although the Voudou leaders' ritual authority suggests a unique Afro-Creole agency that prefigures much of what jazz would swing into accomplishment, Congo Square is more often invoked by jazz historians and musicians themselves "as the originating locus of American jazz."[88] Saxophone pioneer Sidney Bechet opened his autobiography with the story of an enslaved grandfather who used to "beat out rhythms on the drums at the square—Congo Square they called it . . . No one had to explain notes or feeling or rhythm to him."[89] Le Page du Pratz, in his *Histoire de la Louisiane* (1758), observed that the Sunday market at what was then called the "Place des Nègres" was a site where "[u]nder pretext of the calinda, they sometimes get together to the number of three or four hundred, and make a kind of Sabbath," dangerous both for its potential for rebellion and for its underground economy.[90] Moving to restrict the slaves to a predictably policed place and time, the New Orleans city council finally decided in 1817 to sanction Congo Square as the singular site for the Sunday dances (held previously in multiple locations). The earliest detailed description, from an 1819 entry in Benjamin Latrobe's diary, suggests what Congo Square's music likely shared with the Voudou rites led by Sanité Dédé. Latrobe notes ring dances utilizing antiphonal patterns of song along with instrumentation consisting of a banjo prototype, percussive gourd instruments, and a variety of drums.[91] Accompanying Latrobe's careful drawings of the instruments and his wonder over an "extraordinary . . . incredible noise" comes requisite Kantian remastery of the sublime in his dismissal of the scene as "brutally savage . . . dull & stupid."[92] We recognize the repeating pattern: white-supremacist "reason" remastering its encounters with the slave sublime but also tending to be swung by it.

The Congo Square we know from travelers' accounts was a well-policed tourist attraction and a medicinal or narcotic chronotope. Herbert Asbury insists that "sometimes there were almost as many white spectators surrounding the square to watch the slaves 'dance Congo' as there were black dancers."[93] James R. Creecy, in his 1834 travel observations, found there "a certain cure for ennui, blue-devils, mopes, horrors, and dyspepsia."[94] Congo Square's proto-jazz/blues of "banjos, tom-toms, violins, jawbones, triangles, and various other instruments," and the dancers "fancifully dressed, with fringes, ribbons, little bells, and shells and balls, jingling and flirting about the performer's legs and arms, who sing a second or counter to the music most sweetly," offered a shell-shaking, calinda-strutting pharmacy that swung observers like Creecy through bouts of blue-devils. He advertised, "[e]very stranger should visit Congo Square . . . once at least, and, my word for it, no one will ever regret or forget it."[95]

Any jazz history that turns to Congo Square for narratives of origin also alerts us to ways in which jazz freedoms have been circumscribed by paternalistic tourist stagings, racial commodification, and police surveillance.[96] All this remains a key part of the story, and Congo Square is indeed a sacred chronotope of New Orleans and its black musical tradition. However, we should also look to underground Voudou houses for the *govi*-vessels of jazz's ancestral spirits. Musicians and dancers appear to have moved fluidly between the public Congo Square gatherings (diminished after 1835 and held sporadically into the 1850s) and the more private (or at least autonomously staged) Voudou rites—with Saint-Domingue émigrés playing key roles in both arenas.[97] While Sanité Dédé and Marie Laveau may have attended the Sunday Square gatherings in addition to their presiding over Friday-night Voudou services, key differences of authority and agency exist between the Congo Square dances and Voudou rites. After 1817 at least, the Congo Square gatherings were regulated slave meetings held under the watchful eyes of police and white spectators. Antebellum Voudou meetings were almost always in violation of laws of assembly, gathering free and slave, red and white and black, in nighttime balancing acts of service to the spirits, often under the leadership of free women of color backed by musicians. Whites tended to be *participants* in such spirit houses even more often than they were spectators, thereby submitting to Afro-Creole authority in an unparalleled manner. Furthermore, the Voudou houses remained active well after Congo Square had been fenced off and renamed Beauregard Square.

Before *swing* became a jazz-age noun, it was a verb of ritual, syncopating movement. As we have seen, Vodou insists on the paradigmatic act of "balancing" or swinging ritual objects and bodies to raise their energy. According to Karen McCarthy Brown, Haitian Vodou services address "a pervasive contrast between being immobile and blocked and having a life of energy and flow," with rites most often aimed "to *echofe* (heat things up) so that people and situations shift and move, and healing transformations can occur."[98] The necessity of swinging individual and congregational bodies in order to raise their energy (in the face of enormous blockages) appears in late-nineteenth-century New Orleans descriptions of *Fe Chauffe* dance. Swing makes ritual *konesans* possible. One learns to serve the spirits by learning to embody them and become their "horse" in musically induced possession. All this, of course, is a widespread Afro-Atlantic phenomenon, but one that found powerful secular transformation in New Orleans.

Vodou works to evade the chattel ideal of zombifying stiffness, an inflexibility that too often accompanies the mind/body splittings of religions or disciplines of the book.[99] Early New Orleans swing worked similarly to free its players from strict reproduction and idolatry of a written score. As Louis Armstrong observed in his autobiography, *Swing That Music* (1936), "it takes a swing player, and a real good one, to be able to leave that score and to know, or 'feel,' just when to leave it and when to get back on it." The key would be to activate "something new swinging into the music to make it 'hot,'" a term used "when a swing player gets warmed up and 'feels' the music taking hold of him so strong that he can break through the set rhythms and the melody and toss them around as he wants without losing his way." So for "[w]e 'cats' (all jazz musicians from New Orleans called each other 'cats' and still do)"— as the *hippikat* Armstrong asserted—there is a "liberty that every individual player must have in a real swing orchestra that makes it most worth listening to." Heating things up and swinging them, breaking up metronome rhythm, defamiliarizing and refamiliarizing space, New Orleans jazz—like Vodou— prepares the *gwo bonanj* to vacate the head so the *serviteur* may become "horse" of the *lwa*. As Armstrong writes, "when you've got a real bunch of swing players together in an orchestra, you can turn them loose for the most part. 'Give 'em their head,' as they say of a race horse. They all play together, picking up and following each other's 'swinging.'"[100] Armstrong knew that this manner of ritually unloosing bound bodies and repertoires could embrace any material. The New Orleans drum great Baby Dodds (who played in Armstrong's Hot Sevens) speaks, for instance, of hearing the Buddy Bolden and John Robichaux bands "play classics in swing," and says of those transitional days, "they didn't call it jazz, but they called it swing."[101]

Swing appears to have been a rhythm-unloosing or "ragging" of the calindas of Voudou houses and Congo Square that got routed rhizomatically through Mardi Gras Indians, brass bands, ragtime, and black Protestant and Spiritualist church music. Bunk Johnson said, "We'd take all of those old spiritual hymns and turned them into ragtime." Ragging the hymnals' scored time was something the black churches had been doing especially well in New Orleans, most notably in Sanctified and Spiritualist churches. Mahalia Jackson spoke of how Sanctified services in New Orleans used "the drum, the cymbal, the tambourine, and the steel triangle" and "had a beat, a powerful beat, a rhythm we held onto from slavery days . . . it used to bring tears to my eyes." After Congo Square was silenced, and after the shape-shifting Damballah spirit of Voudou was driven underground (and crossriver into Algiers), we may accept Louis Armstrong's assertion that jazz and second-line culture "all came from the old Sanctified churches."[102] These were the independent institutions wherein the rhythm held onto from slavery days got fostered with most public regularity among English-speaking Protestants in Armstrong's childhood. For a vision more attuned to Franco-Creole routings, however, we would do well to listen to another key early jazz genius—Jelly Roll Morton.

Jelly Roll Morton, born Ferdinand Joseph Lamothe in New Orleans's Creole Seventh Ward in 1890, claimed to have "started using the word [*jazz*] in 1902 to show people the difference between [the new] jazz and ragtime."[103] One of early jazz's most important composers, players, and practitioner/theorists, Morton was steeped in the music's "Spanish tinge" and its Haitian lineages, and steeped too in the lingering power of Voudou.[104] Pierre Monette, Morton's maternal great-grandfather, was a free man of color from Saint-Domingue who had purchased a slave from the Laveau-Glapion household on St. Ann Street and was close enough to Marie Laveau (the Widow Paris) that Laveau was summoned to court to testify on behalf of Monette's son Julian in a claim to the deceased father's estate.[105] Morton's Nan-nan (godmother) Eulalie Hecaud, who became his main maternal figure after his mother's early death, was a Voudou practitioner/consultant who ministered to the working women of Storyville.[106] Morton recalled how "[t]here were glasses of water around her house and voices would come out of those glasses. Very prominent people would consult my godmother."[107] He speaks of having been "worried with spirits when I was a kid," and of having received a set of three rites and baths from a New Orleans healer, Papa Sona, the last of which Morton claims concluded three days before his first piano gig in Miss Hilma Burt's house (perhaps the most upscale sexual pleasure house in the Storyville district) where "Jelly Roll" made his name. He was given poppy seed to chew, which was "supposed to make you highly successful—you could swing people your way."[108] Morton's "King Porter Stomp" (1906) would become "the anthem" of swing dance bands in the 1920s and '30s, and his "Georgia Swing" (1907) channeled the behavioral vortices of a New Orleans broughtupsy steeped in Franco-Creole language, in shows at the French Opera House, in the power of Voudou and in the ludic space of Storyville's "homosocial pleasure dome."[109]

The Morton composition that speaks most uncannily to this mix is "Milenberg Joys," which Morton recorded with the New Orleans Rhythm Kings (a white Chicago band) in a 1923 session in Indiana.[110] As Martha Ward points out, Milneburg, the site on the Pontchartrain lakefront where St. John's Eve fetes were centered, was an antebellum getaway from New Orleans' summer fever season. After the Civil War, Milneburg was perhaps "the most integrated and lively place in Reconstruction New Orleans," featuring a battle of the bands most nights. Sidney Bechet gave greater credit to Milneburg's fostering of pioneer jazzmen than he did to Storyville's houses of pleasure.[111] Milneburg may also have been where Eliza Nicaud made her name as a dancer in Marie

Laveau's *Fe Chauffe* rites. A great-granddaughter reported that Eliza "used to wrap her legs wit' ribbons and she'd have a big red bow on each knee. Madras handkerchiefs used to cost five dollars each then, but that wasn't nothin' to Queen Eliza of the Dance. She wore ten of 'em for a skirt."[112] Eliza may well be the dancer praised for how "The way she syncopates don't leave nothing out" in "Milenberg Joys" and its homage to lakefront sessions that "Separate me from the weary blues. Hey! Hey! Hey!"[113] The dance's medicinal power of separation from blue-deviled stasis "pushes at people," as in Vodou rites, "forcing them to find in themselves a way of staying steady in the midst of conflict."[114] A child of Haitian descent and godchild of a turn-of-the-century hoodoo-spiritist practitioner, Jelly Roll Morton carried an appreciation for creole balancing acts and their ritual heat. Like Louis Armstrong's Hot Fives and Hot Sevens, Jelly Roll and his Red Hot Peppers kept the *Fe Chauffe* of Voudou's "danced religion" stirring in New Orleans even as they rerouted its "social medicine" in evermore secular housings of what Richard Brent Turner has called "jazz religion" and "second line culture."[115]

Home of Mystery—Papa LaBas and Voudou Contagion

Any honest discussion of a creole religion like Haitian Vodou (itself hardly orthodox, highly heterogeneous) or a form like jazz cannot look in any single direction for origins, must keep in mind Glissant's notion of creolization as "confluence," and will find much of its subaltern agency unrecorded, misrepresented, and "undisciplined."[116] This is the ultimate case of the history of Voudou in New Orleans and the early development of jazz. Still, we can note certain shared places and aesthetics of assemblage, an embodying emphasis on swing, and a polyrhythmic antiphonal perspective described by John Miller Chernoff as "profoundly pluralistic," allowing for symbiosis between "the aesthetic conception of multiple rhythms in music and the religious conception of multiple forces in the world," an orientation that has provided much of the agency of creolization, for "there is always an in-between, always a place to add another beat."[117]

The *lwa* Legba holds a crossroads "authority over mix and transition" that, as Nathaniel Mackey writes, has "made him especially relevant to the experience of transplantation brought about by the slave trade."[118] Given the benchmarks provided by formal schooling and ideologies of racial uplift, black writers took their time in turning consciously to Legba for mediatory reorientation. Led by the modernist trailblazing (and primitivist reception) of jazz and blues performers, black American writers reappraised what had been emanating from New Orleans. As we shall explore in more detail in chapter 5, something of this Voudou hermeneutics fed the innovations of Zora Neale Hurston, whether in her Haitian fieldwork on Vodou, in her writing of *Their*

Eyes Were Watching God in Haiti, or while initiating with New Orleans Voudou doctors. With the Harlem Renaissance, the international popularity of
jazz, and a reorienting vision exemplified by Hurston, Legba's crossroads
agency found increasingly dynamic, gulf-traversing circulation.

Ralph Ellison's writing points to New Orleans as an initiatory *hippikat*
locus of modernity. The second-sighted ability of Ellison's *Invisible Man* to
see around corners owes much to a chronotopic New Orleans, "home of mystery," the bounce of its reefer-imbued swing, that "slightly different sense
of time . . . its nodes, those points where time stands still or from which it
leaps ahead."[119] Louis Armstrong emerges in Ellison's novel as master figure of invisibility and modern time. In *Shadow and Act*, Ellison slipped into
chronotopes transported from Storyville's "Basin Street Blues" into Minton's
Playhouse in Harlem, which became "a shrine" where "an audience initiated
and aware" might sway with the musicians' rites of "apprenticeship, ordeals,
initiation ceremonies, of rebirth."[120] Ellison brings a Voudou trial-by-fire passage and praxis (reassembling all the disparate stuff of his Western, global,
and black vernacular formation) to an art that—like jazz—would exclude
nothing. He praises the New Orleans–born gospel singer Mahalia Jackson as
"the high priestess [who] sings within the heart of the congregation as its own
voice of faith." Hers is "an art which swings."[121] Then turning to Voudou-
jazz hagiography to make a *lwa* of "the legendary Bird," Charlie Parker, and
noting how " 'legend' originally meant 'the story of a saint' . . . often identified with symbolic animals," Ellison reveals how much his own mythopoesis
or gulf-*konesans* stems from jazz re-creolizations of the *lwa*. *Invisible Man*
opens our eyes to a most complex crossroads modernism allied with *les Invisibles*.[122]

Legba finds tricksterish invocation from New Orleanian/Haitian routes
in Ishmael Reed's *Mumbo Jumbo* (1972), as PaPa LaBas and Mumbo Jumbo
Kathedral serve the *lwa* "Jes Grew" in its movement from "the Govi of New
Orleans" to Chicago, New York, and beyond.[123] Jes Grew, like early jazz, gets
cast by those who resist it as a "psychic epidemic" spreading from an assumed
"local infestation area" of Congo Square via far-flung networks of jazzcats
and hipsters, morphing through folk like Charlie Parker "for whom there
was no master adept enough to award him the Asson," the gourd-rattle of
ritual authority (16). Jes Grew's bypassing of entrenched chains of authority
unsettles those who would stop the contagion, for "it's nothing we can bring
into focus or categorize; once we call it 1 thing it forms into something else"
(4). It is this difficulty in pinning down creolization's material, psychological, and spiritual agency that Reed underscores in *Mumbo Jumbo*'s embedded epigraphs, beginning with Louis Armstrong's description of second-line
dancing, "*The spirit hits them and they follow*" (7); moving to Hurston's description of the birth of new *lwa* in Haiti, "Some *unknown natural phenom-*

enon occurs which cannot be explained, and a new local demigod is named"; to James Weldon Johnson's awareness that "the earliest Ragtime songs, like Topsy, 'jes' grew'" (11). *Mumbo Jumbo* insists that texts are a play of signs and power, scores to be settled or swung, bopped, spaced out. And in spite of Jes Grew's multiplicity (or lack) of origins, Reed locates its matrix of subaltern powers most firmly in New Orleans via Haiti. The new spirit's key *serviteur*, PaPa LaBas (or Legba), maintains "22 trays which were built as a tribute to the Haitian loas" (28). LaBas worries, however, "I don't know the extent to which the Haitian aspects of The Work can be translated here" (52).

Mumbo Jumbo's primary assumption, however, is that this translation has already occurred, via "the Govi of New Orleans," housing a "*gros-ben-age* of the times, that aura that remains after the flesh of the age has dropped away" (20), most discernible in the jazz-blues coalescence of "a loa that Jes Grew" (128). Reed's novel presents the U.S. occupation of Haiti from 1915 to 1934 as a desperate front in the long Western crusade against alterity, an "attempt to kill Jes Grew's effluvia by fumigating its miasmatic source" (214). In response to the Marines' "Holy War in Haiti" (147), *Mumbo Jumbo* follows a group of powerful Haitian Vodou priests, Harlem Freemasons, jazz-age artists, multi-ethnic art-napping *Mu'tafikah*, and the hoodoo work of PaPa LaBas, all collaborating in a counter-Crusader insurgency to feed Jes Grew's reemergent agency in North America. Noting how "our loas adapt to change" (137), the Haitians work to encourage Jes Grew's jazz *lwa*—in its extension of ritual kinships allowing folk (of any ethnicity) "to go out of their minds so that spirits could enter their heads" (213). What we may see in textual assemblages of the *lwa*'s key North American literary *serviteurs*—from James Weldon Johnson to Hurston, Ellison, and Reed—is a Legba/limbo-supported embrace of a submerged Afro-creole authority and its resistance to binary rule.

In practice, Vodou, of course, is no more "saintly" than is any world religion. Vodou—with its decentered organization, charismatic leadership, traditions of aggressive or judicial sorcery, and its demands of ritual secrecy and of trust in ritual elders—has been as ripe for sexual abuse as our churches and universities have been, and has provided bases for collaboration with political terror (as the CIA-backed Duvalier regime's cooptation of Vodou revealed). But Vodou's "danced religion" consistently finds performance as "social medicine" producing an integral embodied knowledge unmatched in scripturally oriented religions of the Book.[124] Any medicine may become drug or poison, but the peculiar maligning of Vodou's pharmacy comes without justification. Those who serve the spirits learn to navigate a world uncharted by binary structures of thought. *Serviteurs* learn to open themselves to a dance that, "[f]or the possessed," as Joan Dayan puts it, "is not a loss of identity but rather the surest way back to the self, to an identity lost, submerged, and denigrated."[125] This self, however, is not selfsame, is finally composite and other. Vodou balancing rites ultimately work, in the words of Laënnec Hurbon, to "evoke our own strangeness to ourselves, as human beings: they bring us to *das Unheimlich*, to the 'disquieting strangeness' of which Freud speaks, and not to *Heimat* (to the comfortable, the rooted, the familiar), and it is for this reason that they open the path to the encounter, to intercultural communication."[126]

Balancing Komunyakaa's Piety Street and *Pleasure Dome*

In *Symbioses d'une mémoire: Manifestations religieuses et littératures de la Caraïbe* (2006), Anny Dominique Curtius attends to the ways in which Caribbean literary artists, by returning repeatedly to representations of long-submerged Caribbean religious practices, manage to contest both the pretexts of the Western colonial mission (Christianization and civilization) and the ways in which texts have worked to legitimize this mission in its various ongoing economic and political forms.[127] For her study as for my own, writing grounded in Santería, Obeah, Vodou, Rastafari, or Quimbois most often amounts to a deconstructive act, questioning—and generally sabotaging—the authority of Western disciplinarity and universalism. I will conclude this chapter on a Gulf South/Haitian Voudou hermeneutics by looking closely at jazz manifestations of *les Invisibles* in the work of a single South Louisiana–born poet: Yusef Komunyakaa. Komunyakaa has repeatedly affirmed the primacy of jazz to his poetics: "Jazz discovers the emotional mystery behind things; it provides a spiritual connection to the land, reconnecting us to places where its forms originated."[128] For Komunyakaa, jazz restores memory and behaviors of lapsed time-spaces. It reconnects us to the *longue durée* of spaces that may not feature prominently in the canons of national, regional, or Western narrative, or that call for differently authorized perspectives. He reasserts the notion of jazz origin in Congo Square only to find therein a powerful indebtedness to the balancing acts of Voudou: "It's easy to recognize contemporary American culture in the graceful shadows swaying with the night in Congo Square. They committed an act of sabotage merely by dancing to keep forbidden gods alive."[129] By implication, jazz carries memory and behaviors of this danced sabotage within it. Jazz changes the way we inhabit time and space, how we approach what Alejo Carpentier termed a "marvelous real" that is "not the unique privilege of Haiti [or Louisiana] but the heritage of all of America, where we have not yet begun to establish an inventory of our cosmogonies."[130]

Danced sabotage. Reconnecting forms of knowledge (*konesans*) to places and terrain more marvelous and dread than we've been trained to know. Komunyakaa takes this up in his poetry, exemplified in *Pleasure Dome: New and Collected Poems* (2001). This is what grounds him in jazz, "the one thing that gives symmetry—shape and tonal equilibrium—to my poetry."[131] He concludes his essay on "Shape and Tonal Equilibrium" with an example from the first and last stanzas of his "No Good Blues":

> I used to think a super-8 gearbox
> did the job, that a five hundred dollar suit
> would keep me out of Robert Johnson's
> shoes. I rhyme Baudelaire
> with Apollinaire, hurting
> to get beyond crossroads & goofer
> dust, outrunning a twelve-bar
> pulse beat. But I pick up
> a hitchhiker outside Jackson.
> Tasseled boots & skin-tight
> jeans. You know the rest.[132]

The rest that we know of the age-old blue-devil encounter gets figured as that provocative virgin of "sublime luxury," "desire beyond adequacy," the "Madonna" and "material girl" emergent from reimaginings of plantation pleasure domes.[133] She takes shape as Erzulie-Freda, a most demanding *lwa* who troubles every effort of containment:

> I'm cornered at Birdland
> like a two-headed man hexing
> himself. But the no-good blues
> come looking for me. A prayer
> holds me in place,
> balancing this sequined
> constellation. I've hopped boxcars
> & thirteen state lines to where
> she stands like Ma Rainey.
> Gold tooth & satin. Rotgut
> & God Almighty.[134]

In both exemplary stanzas, Komunyakaa's "No Good Blues" is accompanied by the two-headed language and ethos of hoodoo: crossroads and goofer dust. The poem's balancing (with a sequined constellation that brings Vodou flags, Rara, and Mardi Gras Indians to mind) packs a heat that has little to do with Western notions of equilibrium. Legba's no-good crossroads modernity excludes nothing and transports the whole *durée* of black Atlantic experience into "A prayer / [that] holds me in place."[135]

Working as jazz palimpsest to deconstruct and swing certain classics or standards, *Pleasure Dome* takes Coleridge's "Kubla Khan" ("In Xanadu did

Kubla Khan / A stately pleasure-dome decree"), its opiate-induced invocation of a chasm of desire "haunted / By woman wailing for her demon lover," and covers it from vantage points taking in New Orleans's Superdome and its postplantation pleasure domes.[136] In "Providence," the collection's opening poem, Komunyakaa works from "the shadow of the dome of pleasure" (4), bringing renewed Abyssinian music of holy dread to the damsel with a dulcimer and the "honeydew" that fed Coleridge's romantic imagination. The muse of "Kubla Khan" carries "a pear-shaped lute" and becomes "a honey-eating / animal reflecting in shop windows" (4). She haunts the shadows of Xanadu's and Basin Street's pleasure domes: "Opened by a kiss, / by fingertips on the Abyssinian / stem & nape" (4). Xanadu's caves of ice and the dope-anodynes that sustain it find remix in the "Ice. Ecstasy. Crack" (9) fueling contemporary underground economies tied to the plantation era's drug trade (sugar, tobacco, coffee, chocolate, rum).

A palimpsestic approach to the text brings with it a certain sacrificial "balancing" ethos that is sacral to Vodou, integral to creolization, and essential to jazz. The long multisection poem "Palimpsest" offers a key to *Pleasure Dome*'s reactivation of a jazz-fed Gulf sublime in revisitation of buried (but undead) time-space. The poem's first section, "Modern Medea," begins by returning to the infanticidal action of the historical Margaret Garner (or the fictional Sethe of *Beloved*): "Apex, triangle . . . a dead child / on the floor between his mother / & four slavecatchers," as "she stands listening to a river / sing, begging salt for her wounds."[137] Another section of "Palimpsest" resteps the Vodou yanvalou dance from a poem to the *lwa* by the Haitian René Depestre in an act of long-memoried sabotage: "The dead rise / when the gods bend me into this / Yanvalou, & nightbirds / sing in the redbuds" (355).[138] When the poem's speaker (like Depestre's) becomes Legba's "horse," he enters an Alabama judge's household on judiciary mission:

I am Papa-Legba
From the backwoods

& the cock's blood
metamorphoses my hands
into five-pointed stars
holding down the night. (355)

Returning later in the poem, Legba takes choral voice in "Gutbucket," his blues cutting a path through a terrain superabundant with numbing violence:

I'm back, armed
with Muddy's mojo hand.
Take your daughters & hide them.

Redbuds cover the ground
like Lady Day's poppies
kissed beyond salvation & damnation. (358)

Here, Legba's postplantation mountings carry the white noise of "ghettos fenced-in by freeways" (361) and an incessantly reloaded sacrificial logic. Intense yearning for beauty fills this infanticidal space, "but all you can see / is the bitch eating her puppies / under the house" (362). We face what René Girard termed "the sacrificial crisis" as ruling judicial law has lost both efficacy and legitimacy, and efforts to decrease violence only increase it: "You load the gun / when you think you're unloading it" (362).[139]

"Palimpsest" keeps returning to the sacrificial grounding of the sublime and to a jazz spirituality that raises psychic energy by swinging objects, poems, and historical actions in a contradictory back-and-forth *balanse*. It kills (or overwrites) something—a beloved child, a cock, the innocence of an Alabama judge's daughter or of an earlier reading of a text—so that something else may be born. "I kill a part / so the other lives," the ritual artist of "Palimpsest's" closing section, "Balance," announces (363). This living "other" survives and evolves only via sacrifice. Stunned by

how the sky's balanced
by the ground underfoot.
I think of Count Basie,
what he knew

to leave out. Leverage
determines the arc,
& everything else is
naked grace. (364)

"Leverage" or swing's "arc" moves through the killing of certain desirable possibilities, through necessarily violent selection or revision, or as René Girard would put it, via "[r]itual . . . the regular exercise of 'good' violence."[140]

Homeopathic good violence gives initiatory agency and *balanse* to another of *Pleasure Dome*'s poems, "Mismatched Shoes." Here we get a backstory of how the poet came to sacrifice his received patronym (and not without a certain violence to the beloved father who bequeathed it) so that something else might find leverage and arc. Here, too, Legba resurfaces—in familiar hermaphroditic and limping forms—via the mismatched boy's and girl's shoes that Komunyakaa's Trinidadian grandfather wore:

My grandfather came from Trinidad
Smuggled in like a sack of papaya
On a banana boat, to a preacher's

Bowl of gumbo & jambalaya, to jazz;
The name Brown fitted him like trouble,
A plantation owner's breath
Clouding each filigreed letter.
He wore a boy's shoe
& a girl's shoe, with the taste
Of mango on his lips.
Gone was his true name
& deep song of Shango,
But for years it was whispered
Same as a poor man might touch
A lover's satin glove
From another life. (292)

From calypso music and "Shango" orisha rites, the Trinidadian grandfather
arrives in a banana boat to jazz and a Baptist gumbo. The poem balances
what is supposedly "gone" in the crossing to U.S. nation-space—the whispered name "Komunyakaa" and "deep song of Shango"—to bolster a marooning from plantation "owner's breath":

. . . my grandmother
Never stopped whispering his name.
I picked up those mismatched shoes
& slipped into his skin. Komunyakaa.
His blues, African fruit on my tongue. (292)

Ultimately, such balancing acts suggest there may be no escape from "owner's
breath." This is a lesson revealed everywhere in New Orleans. Even the dead
call on descendants to inherit or "own" them in ritually balanced *govi*, and in
our responses we are often pushed into owning much we would deny.

We can pick a specific time and physical address initiating Komunyakaa's
authorial ownership of his own gulfs of memory: spring and summer of 1984
when he was renovating a historic home at 818 Piety Street in the Bywater
district of New Orleans's Ninth Ward. Komunyakaa explains, "here I was
in New Orleans, with the weight of the Old South pulsating underneath a
thin façade" and wanting "to get the hard high work finished first, where
the stifling heat collected," when suddenly Vietnam's humidity and violent
machinery interrupted his home remodeling work.[141] From Piety Street, Komunyakaa's first essaying of his Vietnam experience emerged in the opening
lines of "Somewhere Near Phu Bai": "The moon cuts through / night trees
like a circular saw / white hot. In the guard shack / I lean on the sandbags, /
taking aim at whatever" (193). Something more than an uncanny home renovation moment brings Phu Bai and New Orleans together in *Pleasure Dome*'s

reconnection of Franco-imperial space. Beyond their subtropical climate and Creole architecture, New Orleans and Saigon are marked by the *longue durée* of their colonial matrix: linked by the Senegalese (sent as slaves to Louisiana by the French and pressed into colonial military service in French Indochina) as well as by revolutionary ties to Haiti.[142]

Komunyakaa states that Louisiana prepared him homeopathically for Vietnam: "that kind of vibrancy didn't frighten me." Having incorporated extreme verdure, violence, and vertiginous wonder into his imagination from childhood in Bogalusa, he insists that in Vietnam "I did not fear the land. I realized a kind of beauty in the overall landscape, beauty and violence side by side."[143] It may have taken the Piety Street renovation project, however, for him to delve into his Vietnam experience. That process seems to have catalyzed the writing of the much-reprinted "Facing It," which engages the Vietnam Veterans Memorial in a way that prefigures the nation's televised gaze on Katrina-flooded New Orleans. The speaker's "black face fades, / hiding inside the black granite" (234), and what is seen becomes a matter of predisposition overdetermined by a screen of blackness simultaneously opaque and transparent. Komunyakaa describes meditating on the Memorial "as if the century's blues songs had been solidified into something monumental and concrete" in a "dance between the dead and the living."[144] Interestingly, his Vietnam poetry conveys a dance-between-life-and-death more attuned to the deep time of New Orleans than is much of the work often used to provide literary windows into the city. Renovating his Ninth Ward house while "reading some of the Negritude poets . . . Aimé Césaire, Nicolás Guillén, René Depestre," Komunyakaa tapped into currents connecting Piety Street and Saigon's Franco-creole gulfs.[145] He is hardly the first writer to explore Vietnamese/Afro-creole kinships. Back in 1954, Paul Robeson published a piece entitled "Ho Chi Minh Is Toussaint L'Ouverture of Indo-China," and Ho Chi Minh's biographer reports the revolutionary leader's frequenting of Marcus Garvey–led meetings during Ho's years in New York (1917–18). Invisibilized kinships swing open all around. If Ho Chi Minh had his finger on the pulse of the jazz age, might we rethink a New Orleans known then for opium dens on St. Ann Street and songs such as the Armstrong-led Hot Fives' "Cornet Chop Suey"?[146]

In this vein, Komunyakaa has also insisted that Vietnam "connected me to the place and people I had come from," as his wartime ability to "identify with the peasants and their rituals" restored empathetic memories of the Gulf South.[147] The Piety Street remodeling work also helped him face his Louisiana childhood (explored in *Magic City* and later books): "yes, the writing of the Vietnam poems helped me to get to *Magic City*" since "I had very systematically written around this, in the same way I had systematically written around the Vietnam experience."[148] How much have we systematically written and read *around* in our literatures and schooling? The Piety Street writing that led to *Dien Cai Dau* (1988) and *Magic City* (1992) has swung open a vision for essaying what the Gulf Coast's sizeable Vietnamese communities may share—especially in their networks of mutual aid, urban organic gardening, and Catholicism—with the creole worlds of Louisiana's early Senegalese and Haitian arrivals. The Gulf's recent traumas render such kinships more necessary and more thinkable. As Kim Dung Nguyen observed, Hurricane Katrina gave South Louisiana's Vietnamese new visibility and "made us stand up and become more united as a community."[149] In the aftermath of the Deepwater Horizon oil spill, Vietnamese-Louisianan shrimpers again became visible in America's disaster-prone Gulf. Tapping into unthought Gulf-matrices beneath our pleasure domes, Komunyakaa's work houses a *konesans* of abyssal waters. Embracing the body as govi, identifying with tropic and swamped landscapes, *Pleasure Dome*'s jazz-Voudou aesthetic ushers us lower into places "where life accumulates its energy, its essence—out of darkness" (82).

Attending to how this Bywater cosmopolitanism builds rapport with spirits *en ba dlo* (beneath abyssal waters), the chapter that follows engages contemporary New Orleanian and Antillean ritual economies of energy generation. In the wake of Hurricane Katrina and the BP Gulf oil spill, the project of reimagining New Orleans takes on greater urgency. Books like *Pleasure Dome* grow more valuable for their guidance into a Gulf *konesans* . . . going down to the mires amidst "salt marshes that move along like one big / trembling wing" and "insects / shiny as gold in a blues singer's teeth" (161). *Pleasure Dome* totes calabashes to reclaim a "Landscape for the Disappeared": "this lovely face so black / with marsh salt. Her smile, / a place where minnows swim" (173). It has readers follow a bass line in "Copacetic Mingus" through a "New Orleans / years below sea level" (112). These below sea level, swamped, and underground paths provide the bass line to swinging a cosmopolitanism we "don't supposed to know" (258), the *Fe Chauffe* of a poetics of deep time wherein "Legba mends / hope" (102).

Making Faces at the Sublime

Momentum from within Creole City

There is no way to imagine America without New Orleans.
—President George W. Bush, from Jackson Square in
    New Orleans, September 15, 2005

I am New Orleans
A perpetual Mardi Gras
Of wild Indians, clowns, lords and ladies,
Bourbon Street Jezebels, Baby Dolls, and Fat Cats;
Peanut-vendors, flower-sellers, organ-grinders, chimney-sweepers,
    and fortune-tellers;
And then, at the end, bone-rattling skeletons and flying ghosts.
I am New Orleans—
A city that is part of, and yet apart from all America;
A collection of contradictory environments;
A conglomeration of bloods and races and classes and colors;
Side-by-side, the New tickling the ribs of the Old;
Cheek-by-jowl, the Ludicrous making faces at the Sublime.
—Marcus Bruce Christian, "I Am New Orleans" (1968)

New Orleans has been America's Creole City of the Sublime: a city both part
and apart, a collection, a conglomeration that assembles ritually, seasonally,
and as need or desire calls, to shake its parts together into an "I" (or Creole
mo)—the componental soul of its *ti-bon anj* ("little good angel"), *gwo-bon
anj* ("big-good-angel"), *nam* (animate force), *zetwal* (astral fate), and all the
hipbones-reconnecting-to-thighbones of the dead stepping in revivification.
The genius "*mo*" of New Orleans rises from an undead time-space of imagination that has crossed through erasures of history and waves of trauma.
"Mo oulé mourrir dans lac-là!" (I want to die in that lake!), Marie Laveau is
recalled shouting after stirring up a Voudou storm on Pontchartrain's shores.[1]
"M'o get me a mojo hand," blues and zydeco frontmen wail amidst waves
of slide guitar or accordion from clubs in the French Quarter and Faubourg
Marigny.[2] To step into that assembly's living memory or to walk the streets
of that genie's *mo* is to feel, at very least, the potential for parts of one's "I"

to be swung and displaced. In New Orleans's urban space, mosaic modes of being and relation find restored momentum in what Joseph Roach describes as "the behavioral vortices" of the city, "a kind of spatially induced carnival."[3]

New Orleans occupied my imagination well before I ever set foot in the city, especially during my Peace Corps service in a Senegalese village upriver from the old colonial capital of French West Africa, St. Louis. Situated near the mouth of the Senegal River, St. Louis has its own historically and behaviorally charged French Quarter, its own culinary and musical genius, all of which have inevitably shaped my responses to New Orleans.[4] My first visit to the Crescent City came four years after I left Africa: on honeymoon with my wife, Amanda, on the threshold of a marriage that has undone and kept swinging our separate and collective boundaries. We were finishing a cup of coffee near our hotel in the French Quarter when we heard nearby drums, tuba, and trombones tuning up in a strangely restive sound check. We followed to St. Ann Street and Royal, where two motorcycle cops and a tuxedoed grand marshal were holding folk back. The Olympia Brass Band started up a beat. Blue lights and the band pushed forward, and "A Closer Walk with Thee" sent waves of formal paraders in steady march up the street. Then the drums suddenly shifted to a strut-inducing backbeat that swept folk free. And we—after the photos Amanda snapped of the band, the Zulu Club president, the crème de la crème of black New Orleans, and T-shirted second-liners— fell into place behind, to wherever this conga line wanted to go. It was only when the whole bouncing parade crossed Rampart and Basin Streets, pausing at the iron gates of St. Louis Cemetery, that the two of us really came to recognize what we'd been swept into and the stunning amassment of people gathered behind us. Limousines pulled in and opened up. And suddenly— with huge swell and press all around him—Jesse Jackson was working the crowd with chants of *Keep Hope Alive!* Something had indeed come alive, stomping and shouting by the cemetery gates. As the funeral party finally moved into that city of the dead to the vault of the deceased, a line filed through to lay hands in farewell upon the casket. The next day the *Times-Picayune* reported the event as the second largest jazz funeral the city had ever seen (exceeded only by the funeral for the patron saint of contemporary New Orleans music, Professor Longhair). The city's first black mayor, Dutch Morial, Creole descendant of Haitian refugees, had been laid to rest just around the corner from the vault holding the bones of Marie Laveau.

Amanda and I lingered that late December afternoon in the cemetery, soaking in its sunny labyrinths, sitting on the "stoops" of the houses of the dead, amidst white marble geometries and slave-bricked vaults, virgins and angels, corporate skyscrapers rising strangely—almost organically—on the city horizon behind. That evening we would sip wine on a bench in Jackson Square. I would have blackened redfish and turtle soup sprinkled with sherry at a popular restaurant on Chartres Street. We toasted a life begun together—away from our frozen water pipes in Arkansas—amidst heated up spirits in a city that guarded and stretched certain boundaries and invocations of the sacred even as it remained dogged by an enduring bad air made more festering by Reaganomics and crack cocaine. We poured libations to the living and dead of Creole City.

In an evocative post-Katrina essay, New Orleans native Ruth Salvaggio has put ancient Greek and New Orleans Creole lyric traditions into intense relation, calling us to reread Sappho from a flooded and gutted-out Desire Street, and from the horrifically poor refuge of the New Orleans Convention Center where streets named after all nine muses converge. Salvaggio takes us to Desire and Abundance Streets to rethink surviving fragments of Sappho's eros-imbued texts: "If we want to think hard about what it means to come into desire, to long for what is missing, for the limits of eros in the social bond, for the place where that bond unraveled in a great modern flood, maybe we should listen for Sappho precisely here."[5] We recognize that social bonds between groups in postplantation spaces have long been braided by lash and rope, bills of sale and lading, law and ledger, marriage licenses or their impossibility. Nevertheless, as Salvaggio insists from her study and experience of New Orleans, a creole erotics of desire (a longing for what is missing) has worked integrally within and between groups—especially in the *Fe Chauffe* balancing rites of Marie Laveau, the swing of Armstrong's Hot Fives or Jelly Roll's Red Hot Peppers, and the bounce of New Orleans's Hot Boys and Hombres Calientes. Drawing from readings of Sappho's legendarily fire-censored fragments, Salvaggio observes that the "effort to take stock of the city in the wake of Katrina" sends us "in search of something missing in history, as if we are recovering a past never fully acknowledged or even understood, a past often couched in shame." She locates that "something missing" in a "wellspring" of "voices," "songs," and "sound waves" forming creole grammars and calling-responsive structures of desire that have provided the lyric base of *"relation"* from which to engage "our most intimate and social bonds."[6]

So we take stock of the city and its Gulf relations, seeking something missing. In late August 2005, after Hurricane Katrina stormed in from a wetlands-denuded Gulf to overwhelm New Orleans's vulnerable levees, what we began to see more clearly were a number of gulfs—political, ecological, economic, and psychic—that had widened while being occluded in denial over the years. We faced real gulfs of vision and imagination. Two post-Katrina *PMLA* essays emphasize the vexed role New Orleans has played in the national imagination: Judith Jackson Fossett's "Sold Down River" and Tara McPherson's "No Natural Disaster." Jackson Fossett, speaking of the "willed ignorance" of U.S. media and politics, argues that "New Orleans is betrayed by its unique position in the national imaginary as a metropolis at once raucous and mythic, paradisiacal and seedy, elegant and corrupt."[7] McPherson agrees, asserting that New Orleans "looms large in the national—and the literary—imagination," and has performed "powerful ideological work for the nation, functioning throughout the twentieth century as a convenient repository and origin story for much that ails the country."[8] As with Salvaggio's focus on relation, McPherson sets out to tell "a story about New Orleans and its relation to the world, a story that refuses to freeze the city in its southern past," one that would "think the city in relation, in context."[9] Given such a charge, orienting us implicitly to Édouard Glissant's vision in *The Poetics of Relation*, I launch my own story about New Orleans via certain regionally transnational (circum-Caribbean) and local (neighborhood) chartings. New Orleans is a space imbued with multiple temporalities fueled by the fossil structures of its colonial past. All of us, of course, bear the evolutionary and linguistic traces of our antecedents and could be considered living fossils. But we have not all cultivated the practice of moving through multiple time signatures in ritually charged spaces. For Wilson Harris, cityscapes like creole New Orleans may invoke "a rhythmic capacity to resense contrasting spaces and to suggest that a curious rapport exists between ruin and origin as latent to the arts of genesis."[10] New Orleans remains especially hospitable to this kind of "rhythmic capacity" and its "curious rapport . . . between ruin and origin."

I would have us look closely at what McPherson calls the city's clichéd "hallmarks of tourism," New Orleans's "gumbo, jazz, voodoo, and architecture." We may agree with McPherson that "[t]he familiar tourist images of old New Orleans—tied up in the blackness of another era—allowed a disavowal of the racism that elsewhere was writ large across our television screens" during the Katrina debacle.[11] But New Orleans's hallmark fossil signs may still point out crucial (and inadequately explored) routes into the durational city's imaginative agency, its "rhythmic capacity" and restored behaviors. What, we may ask, might the still active fossil fuels of gumbo, jazz, Voudou, and carnival offer as exemplary challenge, and why might the remembering of New Orleans and its culture-bearing rites be a (trans)national priority? What is imperiled in New Orleans and the Gulf, and what remains tenaciously guarded there?

We can follow Salvaggio's and McPherson's calls for relational response and keep Judith Jackson Fossett's metaphor in mind of New Orleans as the "most important domestic market in the United States for slaves, the antebellum world's 'fossil fuel.'"[12] We must account for the violence and exhaust-energies released by a modernity built on the consumption of fossil fuels. In such living "environments of memory" as New Orleans, prone to becoming mere "places" of memory (archival, monumental, tourist-oriented), we encounter a performance culture that sustains its own networkings of community.[13] Even nigh-clichéd staples of tourism may be enduringly charged with a relational ethos and a performative Gulf-authority. As Eileen Julien told Shona Jackson in a gumbo-fueled interview, "when I cook things like this, I feel like I am in a relationship with my mom, with my aunts, with my grandmother, that somehow I'm giving testimony to them and affirming my own capacity to perpetuate these acts of culture."[14] Born of specific relational environments, gumbo assemblages (like those of jazz or carnival) speak to that "vision thing" so absent from our public life and so fully present in Julien's discussion of love, loss, and the culinary restoration of social joy: "a question of a certain confidence, of confidence that you can put these things together, and this is going to work. That you've got either enough skill or you've got a guardian grandmother," and as she laughingly added, "Yeah . . . it's all related to this food thing."[15]

To tell a story of New Orleans in relation, writers tend to speak in terms of energy industry—as Andrei Codrescu has in naming New Orleans "a generator of human and cultural energy for centuries."[16] Charles Rowell, the founding editor of the remarkable journal *Callaloo*, pulls no punches in referring to New Orleans as a "magical and mythical city," the one refuge "which always fed my imagination." His editing of *Callaloo*'s special issue on Katrina, most of which consists of interview testimony from New Orleanians, is a "praise-song," a "call to action," and a reminder that any effort to tap into the city's energy work must first listen carefully to the witnessing of New Orleanians.[17] Rowell's editorial act of listening is of utmost importance. Careful listening opens our ears and eyes to a poorly reciprocated New Orleanian hospitality. We come to acknowledge that much of what we call "southern hospitality" has been built most inhospitably and asymmetrically on the backs of those who have provided its most basic goods and services.

Like other creole cities, New Orleans is steeped more deeply in performance poetics than in any literary tradition we have been schooled to receive. Much of the literature for which New Orleans is widely known was written by outsiders, and the city's exemplary historic works are scarcely read (colonial and nineteenth-century) texts written in French, with smatterings of Creole expression. This chapter seeks reassembly of a literature coming from within the interior of the city's ritual economies and from rapport with the *longue durée* of creolization. For a Franco-creole gateway to such a reading, two paradigmatic texts from Martinique—Édouard Glissant's *Poetics of Relation* and Patrick Chamoiseau's novel *Texaco*—offer crucial precedent. For guides into a New Orleanian neighborhood perspective, I turn to Brenda Marie Osbey's *All Saints: New and Selected Poems* (1997) with its long view from Faubourg Tremé, and to Eileen Julien's memoir *Travels with Mae* (2009) from the old Creole Seventh Ward, to essay challenges and resources discernible in a locally grounded literature. Bearing a cultivated opacity, and working from the interstices of accredited systems, Creole City keeps reassembling itself from its basilectal core, its *mo*, in frequentation of the Gulf's limbo gateways.

An Air, Heavy with Gas—Voodoo Economies and Funky-Butt Relations

Franco-creole environments of memory still have a hold on spaces colonized by the French but claimed finally by Anglo-political control: from Catholic communities like Roseau on Dominica or Castries in St. Lucia to Gouyave in Grenada or New Orleans, Louisiana. A Jean Rhys novel or Derek Walcott poem may speak to readers interested in the Gulf Coast's durational histories with as much (trans)local insight on Creole City as do the Faulkner and Tennessee Williams texts usually associated with New Orleans. Walcott's "The Gulf" (1969) bears peculiarly prophetic witness, directing our gaze out the window of a "trans-Texas jet" over an oil rig–dotted Gulf of Mexico. Propelled by "fumes of the exhausted soul," by the fossil-fueled Molotov cocktails illuminating late 1960s racial gulfs, Walcott offers a flyover vision revealing

> the divine union
> of these detached, divided states, whose slaughter
> darkens each summer now, as one by one,
> the smoke of bursting ghettos clouds the glass
>
> down every coast where filling station signs
> proclaim the Gulf, an air, heavy with gas,
> sickens the state, from Newark to New Orleans.[18]

Walcott's long view upon a Vietnam-era globalizing Gulf points to a nauseatingly inhospitable state: "Yet the South felt like home. Wrought balconies, / the sluggish river with its tidal drawl, / the tropic air charged with extremities / of patience, a heat heavy with oil, / canebrakes, that legendary jazz" (107). Images of exhaust and flame, oil companies more sovereign than any elected republic, spread an oil-thick stench.

Responding to fossil-fueled economies by which "The Gulf, your gulf, is daily widening," Walcott's Jeremiad confronts apocalyptically driven forces that leave refuge for no one, "no rock cleft to go hidin' in" (107). He challenges those who traffic in Gulf politics of fear, in "filling station signs" that "proclaim the Gulf" and keep its air "heavy with gas" (107). Walcott's window-of-vision into archetypal bad air launches prophetic readings of a post-Katrina Gulf and an overheated, oil-slicked climate of consumption:

> The Gulf shines, dull as lead. The coast of Texas
> glints like a metal rim. I have no home
> as long as summer bubbling to its head

boils for that day when in the Lord God's name
the coals of fire are heaped upon the head
of all whose gospel is the whip and flame,

age after age, the uninstructing dead. (108)

Speaking in the 1960s from a St. Lucia–informed vision into deep time, Walcott laments our learning disabilities, our widening gulfs of economy and security.

Although Ronald Reagan's proposals to increase revenue by cutting taxes were derided in 1980 by his Republican primary challenger George H. W. Bush as "voodoo economics," a voodoo "trickle-down" economics became mainstreamed as both Bushes continued the Reagan-Thatcher free-market approach to flows of global capital increasingly unregulated and untaxed by the nation-state. Neo-liberal faith in "the invisible hand" of a free market seems, in retrospect, as oddly irrational and sacrificial as anything we may find in Hollywood voodoo films. Mario Degiglio-Bellemare, in his advocacy of Haitian Vodou as a model for a liberationist "crossroads theology," alerts us to the cynical workings of a "savage capitalism" that mocks and denigrates all it would disinherit (with terms like "witch doctors of Wall Street" and "zombie businesses").[19] Trickle-down policy may maintain consumer republics, but it erodes the spirit of democracy as money poured into the top of the machine reproduces moneyed interests—producing gated communities, a lockdown criminal justice system, environmental crises, infrastructural decay, and multifront wars on everything from Terror to Drugs. In all honesty, given how readily the white South has served the "trickle-down" economic and political machinery as a reliable base, we should speak more accurately of a Southern Baptist Convention economics rather than continue to denigrate Haitians and Vodou.

"Voodoo" scapegoatings certainly ran rampant in the wake of Hurricane Katrina. One of the most egregious affronts came from Rev. Dwight McKissic (of Cornerstone Baptist Church in Arlington, Texas) who charged his Gulf neighbors with being deserving of divine chastisement by way of Katrina since "[t]hey openly practice voodoo and devil worship in New Orleans."[20] Given American churches' wholesale embrace of a prosperity gospel, one thing is clear: it remains difficult to find "hidin' place" or refuge from a global voodoo economy and its trickle-down media. Being poor, victimized, or vulnerable counts as evidence of one's sin. We can expect Rev. Pat Robertson to find the divine cause of Katrina's wrath in *Roe v. Wade* or to blame the Haitian earthquake on Haiti's voodoo "pact with the Devil." It is a stake-raising thing, however, to see media outlets like the *New York Times* and *Newsweek* consistently publish articles that place blame on the victims of catastrophe (when those victims are largely black and poor). David Brooks wrote in the *New York Times* on January 15, 2010 (not three full days after a quake that killed over 200,000 people), that Haiti "suffers from a complex web of progress-resistant cultural influences," especially "the influence of the voodoo religion, which spreads the message that life is capricious and planning futile." Brooks, who clearly has no meaningful knowledge of Vodou, adds, "We're supposed to politely respect each other's cultures. But some cultures are more progress resistant than others, and a horrible tragedy was just exacerbated by one of them." With voodoo identified as the opaque heart of the problem—the reason for Port-au-Prince's mass poverty, substandard building construction, and 200,000 earthquake deaths—Brooks's *New York Times* op-ed piece proposes a rededication to colonial principles: "It's time to promote locally led paternalism . . . to replace parts of the local culture," to infuse Haiti "with middle-class assumptions" and progressive Judeo-Christian orientation.[21] This stunning piece of disrespect circulated by the *Times* at a catastrophic moment in a neighboring country could *only* find publication in relation to Vodou and African diaspora peoples (and perhaps especially in relation to a people who have resisted French, British, and U.S. Marine occupations of cultural replacement and material theft). Some of these responses were also evident in the aftermath of Hurricane Katrina.

Writing in *Newsweek*, columnist George Will chose a Hobbesian response to the hurricane's reminder of "how thin and perishable is the crust of civilization, and hence how always near society's surface are the molten passions that must be checked by force when they cannot be tamed by socialization." For Will, Katrina's reduction of New Orleans residents to "the essence of primitivism, howling nature" underscored a need for a growing commitment to law and order. In Will's comparison of looting in New Orleans to the Newark and Detroit riots of 1967, hardly concealed beneath the surface is the "howling" subtext of race. Reacting to "bodies floating in the sewage," Will's *Newsweek*-published choice of first response to Katrina focused on allegations of "raping, looting, and gunfire" in the hurricane's aftermath.[22] It would be up to the New Orleans *Time-Picayune* to show that early post-Katrina reports of predatory mayhem were dominated by urban folklore fed by hysteric racial fear. Five years later, the disastrous earthquake in Haiti summoned many of the dehumanizing preoccupations seen earlier in Katrina headlines such as *USA Today*'s story, " 'The Looters, They're like Cockroaches.' "[23]

Events surrounding the BP Deepwater Horizon oil spill made it re-apparent that the whole Gulf Coast is at stake in the market's (ultimately *our*) risk/cost analyses, that the preachers have had little to say about God's role in this, and that U.S. media had even less to say about how such a spill could affect Gulf neighbors in Cuba, the Bahamas, and Mexico. When we take a long view toward a Caribbean/Gulf Coast matrix of disaster and reparation, we may see that whatever it is that fuels resistance to the progress of global consumerism demands our attention. Vodou's crossroads theology, the communions of its own proper economy and energy industry, cannot be dismissed easily by anyone hospitable to rites or economies (we might say *ecologies*) of sacral exchange.

In "The Ritual Economy of Haitian Vodou," Karen McCarthy Brown introduces readers to the meaning of Vodou (rather than Reagan's "voodoo") economics and the "*travay*" which makes the Haitian ritual economy work. Extended Vodou families, "those who serve the spirits together," use ceremonies to establish a "context for continuous maintenance of family networks": people who "eat from each other's cooking pots" and "can be counted on in times of trouble."[24] The ritual economy Brown describes has arisen from long concern with fostering adoptive and adaptive networks under the most challenging conditions. Each member is called to work in support of a collective that is "the occasion for and the product of virtually all Vodou ritualizing," and this requires "skillful work with 'the mindful body'" (205). This energy industry's "dynamic exchange system" keeps the spirit-house functioning (205), as we see at a yam fest in which "an elaborate meal is presented to one of the spirits who then gives it back to the people" (209). The people's taxes thus support the infrastructure that gives meaning and social security to their lives. Anyone who has attended such a rite knows that serious healing work gets done, social medicine gets prescribed and dispensed in performance, and a good (ritually heated) time is passed by most all. Linkage of religion and good time can bewilder scripturalists as well as academics. But this is a hermeneutics familiar to the Gulf South—where the Haitian staple of Vodou *travay* (*riz national* or red kidney beans and rice) was recreolized in New Orleans house rites fed by red beans and rice. Any understanding of these culinary ritual economies must also, of course, reengage the historic workings of the plantation.

In *Poetics of Relation*, Édouard Glissant points to how many of our contemporary economic and social practices were put into early assembly on the plantation: "the territory of *créolité*" bearing "the modern vectors of civilization."[25] The literary consequences call for meaningful reassessment. Glissant insists that the oral literature of the plantation shares such a "web of filiations" that the vernaculars, musics, and novels of postplantation spaces have "made it no longer possible to consider these literatures as exotic appendages of a French, Spanish, or English literary corpus; rather, they entered suddenly with the force of a tradition that they built themselves, into the relation of cultures" (71). He can thus mention Alejo Carpentier, Kamau Brathwaite, Gabriel García Márquez, and Faulkner as writers of a literature born from the exploded "ruins of the Plantation" (72). This literary briarpatch draws from composite origins, multiple temporalities, and a "poetics of duration" (33) capable of navigating "entanglements of world-wide relation" (31). Any adequate rereading of (post)plantation texts and cultural history thus calls us to meet challenges of cross-cultural, postplantation hospitality and new ecologies of relation.

With Glissant's help, I want to consider how creole models of cultural production may move postplantation economies out of consumer dependency and into a "revised aesthetic connection with the earth" (150). Glissant, sounding sometimes like a neo-Agrarian in his fears that "all the prestige (and denaturation) felt in internationally standardized consumption will triumph permanently over the pleasure of consuming one's own product," steadily advocates nonstandard, localized patterns of production and consumption resistant to monocultural plantation-crop patterns (151). Without such localized action—whether in Martinique's departmental relation to France or in the Gulf Coast's relation to capitalizing "trickle-down" power— "[t]he entire country would become a Plantation, believing it operates with freedom of decision, but, in fact, being outer directed" (152). What trickle-down economies produce, at bottom, is a nihilistic consumer-dependency.

When nothing else seems to offer possibility, acts of violence may puncture otherwise closed space. As Carol Bebelle, director of New Orleans's Ashé Cultural Arts Center puts it, in a tourism-driven economy in which "reciprocity is absent," there is this "insidiously bad" thing: "It's young people living lawless and short lives because they can't count on the adults to create a world that has more to offer them."[26] Glissant insists that such disquieting violence "comes from having to consume the world without participating in it," from being positioned as "receivers" rather than "generators" of media spectacle, "cultures apart, who . . . have no thought that counts."[27] Given such positioning, violence becomes a way of counting, a participatory response to a globalizing economy, generating representation in flash media recountings.

Gangster rap emerged as a tricksterish integration of what Glissant calls "flash media" and the need of "cultures apart" to participate as players in global consumption and production. Working from the roux of their own tastes and gnosis, New Orleans rappers re-introduced the hip-hop world to Creole City's funky-butt carnivalesque bounce. "Out of the trunk" start-up labels (like New Orleans's No Limit and Cash Money) grew their own flash media and megamillions.[28] The social stakes were raised, however, in Katrina's aftermath, as we see in ex–Cash Money artist Juvenile's dismissal of the news media's disaster coverage (especially the spectacle voyeurism of Fox News) supplanted by his own reportage upon renewed gulfs of relation: "We livin' like Haiti without no government."[29] Hip-hop's most adept flash agents understand what Glissant notes about televised catastrophe and how "humanitarian movements that have sprung up in wealthy nations strive to bandage the open sores in poor countries, inflicted more often than not by the merciless economies of those same rich countries."[30]

Hip-hop clearly shares vernacular ethos and frontier exploration with the *hippikat* trickster tales of the plantations. Louisiana's trickster tales, featuring Rabbit's and Bouki's murderous struggles over victuals, sex, and markers of status, find amplification in New Orleans rappers' responses to savage capitalism. A first sign of imagination's atrophy, however, is when myth and allegory are given fundamentalist readings. Homeopathic doses of narrative violence (Lapin's/Brer Rabbit's ethical *play*) may cease to feed the imagination. Medicine becomes dope or poison, and Rabbit's violence or "bad" air reduces to a reductionist thug-life authenticity. As Riché Richardson observes, Dirty South rap often works to fetishize "the violence, money, and misogyny" that is primarily a mirror reflection and distillation "of the obsession with capitalist gain in the dominant national culture," and may present youths with the danger of "internalizing racialist myths themselves" in its commodified entertainment.[31]

Like their immediate elders—the Mardi Gras Indian tribes whose bounce and warrior-like refusal to bow infuses them—rappers representing New Orleans carry on a tradition of ludicrous face-making at the Sublime, at City Hall, and at the White House. Grammy-winning Lil Wayne sampled from Ray Charles in "Georgia . . . Bush" to drop his Gulf-critique of Bush's compassionate conservatism (or Southern Baptist Convention economics): "he aint gonna drop no dollas, but he do drop bombs."[32] This cut from a post-Katrina mixtape goes on to excoriate Confederate flag-flying supporters of the Bush regime's flushing of resources into Persian Gulf occupations. As Tara McPherson asserts, "The cost of the war for *one day* would almost have completed the levee repairs in Louisiana."[33] New Orleans bounce music lets some of the Gulf's bad air out. Its rap artists air out our wider disengagements from social responsibility, our abandonment of public infrastructure, and a potential death of collective imagination. Above all, and in counterpoint, bounce music rechannels old funky-butt *Fe Chauffe* in alliance with the dynamism of the Vodou *lwa* Gédé.[34] Still, given the misogyny and violence trafficked by the Cash Money and No Limit labels out of New Orleans, I want to engage the less hyped work of New Orleans' second-line imagination by returning focus to writers of Creole City who have hosted something of the ritual *travay* (work) modeled by Marie Laveau and cultivated in neighborhoods of relation across the Gulf.[35]

Swamp(ed) Hospitality—*Texaco's* Mangroves and *All Saints'* "Shallow Water"

We have already noted that the famous southern hospitality has been built upon an utter lack of hospitality, chattel slavery. Jacques Derrida has demonstrated that the conditions that make hospitality possible—requiring one to be owner or master of a house or space, requiring one to have the territorial control to host the guest—also constitute the conditions that render the ideal of hospitality impossible since the ideal requires a spirit of nonmastery (my house is your house) extended to anyone without precondition or judgment.[36] The reterritorializations of Afro-creole writing constitute the very conditions of a transcultural hospitality in postplantation contact zones, especially since writing has been one of the key tools of mastery. Those once possessed must assert their own possessions and territorializations (often via creole opacity, detour, and distancing) in order to be in position to host others as guests. Nothing speaks to the trying paradoxes of hospitality better than does the Afro-creole spirit house's fostering of initiates to become host or "mount" of spirits. It is the initiate's learned limbo permeability and *konesans* of mastery/nonmastery that makes possession and its adoptive spirit-hospitality possible. Gro(o)ves of the bush or wilderness constitute the "site" of this swamping of the subject in a process (whether ritual or literary) of becoming-host to matrices of relation with the other.

In Patrick Chamoiseau's *Texaco* (1992), the stakes are high as the novel thrusts readers into an unexpected sacred grove: the squatter community of Texaco hunkered on a hill on the outskirts of Fort-de-France, Martinique. An urban planner (a readerly avatar) whom the neighborhood will transform into its initiate Christ (or co-savior) arrives along a paved road appropriately named Pénétrante West, ready "to renovate Texaco," but "that really meant: to raze it."[37] The text's task then is to block and reroute this urban planner and his readerly mission. Texaco's community members must detour the urban planner (and reader) just enough to open eyes and ears to the *longue durée* of the island's composite culture and thereby initiate new modes of reading, writing, self-apprehension. Otherwise, Texaco's inhabitants face razing by forces of colonizing universality incapable of acknowledging the island's basilectal history or the people's enduring ties to the land. With the razing of local memory and community constructions, all of Martinique might then be reduced to inhabiting various "projects" in a Fort-de-France that, in its subsidized dependencies, is something of a project(ile) of France. This urban planner/Christ (along with the acrolectally oriented reader) gets the treatment of Glissantian distancing—being knocked unconscious by a thug's stone to the forehead upon entering Texaco. Only by being dazed and bloodied by a rock upside the head (or by dizzying creole-styled prose) can he/we be initiated as a *hippikat* apprentice to Marie-Sophie Laborieux, the community's founding mother who, with her baptismal rum and language of performative memory, wages "the decisive battle for Texaco's survival" (27).

As novel, *Texaco* comes at us like a second-line parade but also (for the progressive, linear-minded) like a rock upside the head. It is not an easy read: a mosaic of voices, notebooks, tall tales, a "creole circus" (7), defamiliarizing and refamiliarizing relations to the printed word. Once readers begin to follow the forehead-wounded/third-eye opened urban planner's apprenticeship into the basilectal currents of "THE SERMON OF MARIE-SOPHIE LABORIEUX (not on the mount, but over some dark rum)," *Texaco* builds momentum (29). From Marie-Sophie's recipes of creole building and gardening to her proverbs and tales, this *"femme-matador"* conveys the tenacity of Texaco's ever-reassembled will to insert itself into the Creole City, not to be merely a project or false copy (faubourg) of City. The key opening, however, is the blow to the head of the urban planner of *Pénétrante West*, the seclusion of the wounded initiate in "a magical clump of trees that the Texaco béké (white owner) had left untouched, probably because of stories about the she-devils around there" (265). *Texaco*'s initiation of its Christ then moves into the bleeding of becoming woman . . . with a folk narrative of an orphan's having "her wash to do" under the tutelage of a guiding crone/mermaid-genie: "This is not a wound which bleeds, the mermaid would sing, but the divine window that women still have on life, it bleeds not with pain but with regret for life. Man, the mermaid would sing, has lost touch with the divine power. Those invalids desired to close this portal to women. And their blind wood released not life but a kind of cement for a grave without All Saints' Day" (145). The creole text's divine window on Marie-Sophie's hosting of life secretes *Texaco*'s sanguine knowledge of a *longue durée*.

Through his own wound and momentary incapacity, the rum-and-word medicated urban planner becomes able to acknowledge creole urbanity's violent history: "Urbanity is violence. The town spreads with one violence after another. Its equilibrium is violence. In the Creole city, the violence hits harder than elsewhere. First because around her, murder (slavery, colonialism, racism) prevails, but especially because this city, without the factories, without the industries with which to absorb the new influx, is empty. It attracts without proposing anything besides its resistance . . . The Quarter of Texaco is born of violence. So why be astonished at its scars, its warpaint?" (148). Here "the city is danger, our danger" (346) as it "rises monstrously, multinational, transnational, supranational, cosmopolitan—a real Creole nutcase in a way, and becomes the sole dehumanized structure of the human species" (356). The urban planner comes to recognize the necessity of supporting *"a counter city in the city"* (361), "an urban mangrove swamp" (263). For him, the Creole City's household gardens represent restorative ecosystemic behaviors and a ritual economy of creolization itself, creating "a kind of magical *we*" (122), working a "space of brand new solidarities" (320), tending "what békés call secondary crops and we call food crops," grown "all tangled up with each other [which] never tires the soil" (128). The food crops and medicine plants of Creole permaculture keep the larger urban space habitable: "Texaco was what City kept of the countryside's humanity. And humanity is the most precious thing for a city, the most fragile thing" (281). In *Texaco*, this postplantation urban humanity guards a fragile hospitality extended to plants and the soil, and across generations.

In this spirit, *Texaco* generates a sustainable energy from the ruins of the plantation and from beneath the abandoned gas reservoirs of the Texaco Oil Company. There, Marie-Sophie finds a remnant grove of origin offering its own fossil fuels: "a world out of this world, a place of sap and of dead life" (24). This grove of remnant impenetrability, inhabited by an old "Mentoh" (mentor) of Afro-Creole gnosis, provides an alternative energy source beneath the reservoirs of globalizing corporate energy. Around this volatile old Texaco fuel depot, Marie-Sophie and her neighbors founded "our very own Texaco, a company in the business of survival" (24), generating for her "my life's gasoline" (312). Marie-Sophie draws her initiate authority from mosaic sources and from following the directive of Texaco's remnant Mentoh: "Find yourself a secret name and fight with it. A name that no one knows and that in the silence of your heart you can howl for courage" (294). Her chosen name braces her with a "Faith [that] is wonderful because it brings a momentum from inside when everything else is petrified" (370). This "momentum from the inside" sustains her individuated agency in the face of City's consumer markets. It puts Marie-Sophie in position to be our own readerly Mentoh—"the Old Woman who gave me new eyes" (165), who "taught me to see the city as an ecosystem" (257). "*Texaco*"—as secret name and fuel of Marie-Sophie's initiate agency, as the name of a creole community in its self-authorizing fight with City for recognition, as multinational oil company (City writ large) as well as pre-Columbian city-state conquered by Cortés (Texcoco), and as title of Chamoiseau's text of relation—vibrates with a stunningly high-octane creole energy.

The primary struggle of *Texaco* is a matter of reciprocal enculturation and agency: to assert itself so fully that City "admitted our existence" (381) and in fact "gobbled us," but also to plumb language, memory, and nature "to conquer ourselves in the Creole unsaid which we had to name—in ourselves and for ourselves—until we came into our own" (390). In New Orleans and the Gulf South, these struggles remain matters of intense engagement. If we were to search for a book in which a Marie-Sophie Laborieux's vision (and momentum fueled from inside) finds New Orleanian articulation from the fuels of the city's enduring *génie*, the search could be surprisingly difficult. New Orleans hardly possesses—as the island of Martinique does—a modern literature in which its genius finds expression in notebooks of its native land scripted and read by its own.

Modern New Orleans has found most of its literary marketing in writing by outsiders—Faulkner, Tennessee Williams, Walker Percy, Ishmael Reed. New Orleans–born-and-raised poet Brenda Marie Osbey has also observed this lack of literary native grounding, insisting in an interview with John Lowe that "I can't think of anyone, really" other than "those French-language writers, the Les Cenelles writers, Victor Séjour."[38] Osbey's own *All Saints: New and Selected Poems* (1997) fills this lack as well as any single text, bearing a tenacious vision akin to the creole-fueled imagination of *Texaco*'s Marie-Sophie. Osbey accepts that there is something sacred about New Orleans and makes the city almost her sole topic. As she told John Lowe: "New Orleans is the spiritual core of everything I write," adding that "everything that comes through New Orleans is black in spirit."[39] An unparalleled neighborhood poet addressing her own Faubourg Tremé in a city famed for neighborhood culture, Brenda Marie Osbey maintains an unfading sense of the sacred in New Orleans's deep time.

The central and longest poem of Osbey's *All Saints*, titled "Faubourg Study No. 3: The Seven Sisters of New Orleans" (remembering the Seven Sisters of hoodoo and blues fame), introduces readers, like *Texaco* does, to what is literally a "false town," "a city within the larger city," and hosts what *Texaco*'s Marie-Sophie Laborieux named faith's "momentum from inside."[40] As Faubourg "Study," the poem addresses mosaic, affective aspects of Creole collective memory, presenting varied readings of the famed Seven Sisters who entered the city (according to the study's opening informant) "talking in that high-note, / that back-parish way."[41] Rather than melting under the "reading" given them by the poem's opening guardian of Faubourg memory and morays—"pack of run-down whores is what I took the lot of them for," "likely come down into the city / to pass," *"just trash passing for trash / on account of a little yellow hair and tail"*—the sisters do their own reading and rereading in this battle of Creole eyes: "the one called 'baby sister' / had read senorita. / and of course senorita couldn't take it."[42] A second informant asserts that the sisters arrived under their own authority: "they didn't come to pass or whore around. / they come to make a living / out of visions and such" (42). And by the time a third informant ties her memory of the coming of autumn rains to the arrival of the sisters' first client, "asking after a reading / with the seven sisters of new orleans" (42), the poem has assembled a Voudou economy (and ritual calendar) that calls readers to take a certain initiative of response.

Textualized like *Texaco* as an insider/outsider's ethnography, "Faubourg Study" presents many-voiced readings of the sisters' legacy. One skeptical or dissimulating informant states dismissively, "old-time hoodoo is what it sounded like to me / and I never did go in for all that" (43). This informant remembers the Seven Sisters as being "'island people' most likely, 'not even *from* here'" (43), and asks the poem's autoethnographic compiler a pertinent question:

and how come it's always got to be some *negro* woman
got to heal everybody?
what kind of colored woman *did you* ever meet
had time or inclination
to sit on a chair all day
dreaming and healing?
me, I had to work too hard.
and when I'm done over to the factory of an evening
them days I had children to raise.
had a man to feed.
had me a plot of ground I used to work out there in back.
yes ma'am.
misbelieve, collards, banana,
date palm,
melon here and there,
tomato,
sweet bell pepper.
even had a few camellia bushes out front the steps. (43–44)

In a narrative of detour and opacity, by urban gardens preserving back-parish humanity, this speaker insists, "I never had no time for no hoodoo" (44). But inhabitants of Creole cities have always had to *make* time for economies of sustenance and healing, have had to *make* belief around the gumbos of their own culinary authority and plots of patchworked ground. Creole gardening has been a key means of cultivating imaginative agency in the midst of plantation monocultures. As Osbey told John Lowe, "[M]y grandmother . . . talked about how her mother forbade all her daughters to live anyplace where they couldn't have a garden. . . if we couldn't tend a piece of ground, then there was something spiritually wrong with us somehow."[43] This grounding commitment to a certain kind of communion or hospitality links the Creole gardens and cuisine of Osbey's *All Saints* with those of Cornelia Bailey's Sapelo Island memoir, Gloria Naylor's *Mama Day*, Julie Dash's *Daughters of the Dust*, Kamau Brathwaite's *Mother Poem*, Chamoiseau's *Texaco*, and Glissant's poetics of the earth.

Ultimately, "Faubourg Study," like *Texaco*, conjoins its quest for Creole authority with a spiritual/literary hospitality. The Seven Sisters of "Faubourg Study" attend to the Holy Mother's combinatory namings and service in Vodou, Catholic, and Spiritist altars that re-make belief in the power of the feminine:

hail mary full of grace
    érzulie, mother of women

blessèd art thou
   there is truth to be made here
blessèd art thou
   dreams, mother, to be dreamt[44]

This is the *lwa* Ezili described by Maya Deren: "the divinity of the dream," who sustains our "capacity to conceive beyond reality, to desire beyond adequacy."[45] But Ezili also "subverts the roles she affects," as Joan Dayan points out, and calls her *serviteurs* to enact a "mimicry of [the] excess" modeled by plantation mistresses and masters.[46] And since "sooner or later / everyone comes to the city," her gumbo economy of desire, truth-making, dream-fetching, and restored hailings of behavior keep an open pot even as the tradition of her service guards certain opacities and modes of distancing.[47] "Faubourg Study" notes of Creole City's culture-bearers that "their hospitality is a way of teaching strangers / to know their place" (47). Since in this gulf "you cannot go without learning much / when you are not the stranger / you have so counted on being," guests may discover that "the next thing, of course is you begin to dream" (47) the dangerous dream of initiatory travel by which folk learn to know their place in gulf-relation.

The poem's final informant—orphaned "Mother Josefina"—bears witness to the sisters' adoption of her and to her own continuation of their ministry: "I could tell you how they changed my life, / the things I saw / or hoped or thought or dreamt I saw" (48). Mother Josefina reveals how the youngest of the sisters, Eulalie, "used to read my dreams" (50). The emergent dream-song Josefina shared with Eulalie (singing of the orphan's abyssal encounter with the mother in liminal floodwaters) is a repeating myth reenchanted by second-line culture and by *konesans* of the Gulf's seasonal storms:

oh mother I am on the pathway
oh mother I am on that road
   shallow water
   shallow water loa-mama
   shallow water loa-mama
érzulie
érzulie
  mother
where I find my mother
  along the shallow shallow water (51–52)

Osbey remarks in the book's glossary that "shallow water loa-mama" is "a traditional chant invoking the blessings of Spirit of the Waters" (126). The Mardi Gras Indian chant is likely doctored improvisationally under Osbey's poetic license.[48] Tapping into memories re-encoded in black Indian song,

"Faubourg Study" revivifies the connection between Mardi Gras Indians and Haiti's spirit-serving *rara* bands: a danced union of sequin artistry, second-line culture, and flag-flying initiate nationhood.[49]

As a carrier of Seven Sister authority, Mother Josefina shares New Orleans's periodic proneness to the floodings and possessions that link the abject to the sublime. Looking to impart something of "loa-mama" *konesans* just ahead of storm season—"the rains are coming in to the city / in no more than a week. / it never did take much rain to flood these narrow / streets"—Mother Josefina seeks a spiritual daughter:

can you look at me, daughter
and say you have not dreamt that journey?
'course you can't.
come over closer, baby.
come where mother can touch you.[50]

This dream and mother's touch, however, bear something grotesque, almost contagiously abject. To have "dreamt that journey" is to be called into a sacrificial path without clear remuneration or legitimacy. What follows in the conclusion of "Faubourg Study" is a gateway blues resonant with the many tales of Marie Laveau's passing in a storm on Pontchartrain, and resonant too with Bessie Smith's "Highwater Blues":

Oh it come up a mighty rain
And it blowed my house away
I said it come up a mighty rain
Just blowed all my house away (51)

Although the poem's initiate "compiler" states a refusal to pass Josefina's touch to spiritual daughters—"I keep my own counsel / and I touch nothing / no one"—this speaker-poet-compiler has inherited Josefina's position as custodian of the Faubourg house and the psychically swamping work of the Seven Sisters: "I will not seal or rent or close off any of this house. / and I do not lock doors. / I live among the sacred objects of their lives" (52). The unlocked doors of "Faubourg Study" carry us into a below-sea-level proneness. Many of the Gulf's water-borne characters and legendary women seem to move in choral step here with the poem's closing lyrics: "*I want to walk a little farther / along the shallow water / I want to live a little longer / with my dangerous dream*" (53).

The poem that closes *All Saints*, "Suicide City," emphasizes the inescapability of Creole City's dangerous dreamings, embracing the "obligations that remove us / from ourselves" (115). *Obligation*, etymologically bound to *religion* (Latin *ligare*, to bind), does indeed work to remove us from narcissistic illusions of autonomy. Creole City—with its ritual calendar, its obligations of rapport with death and sacral time—threatens to mount the unobligated "I" who would inhabit or traverse its spaces. In "Suicide City," New Orleans comes alive as a consuming assemblage that takes possession of its subjects: "we dream the city back to sleep / we shield our fears" till "the city dreams us back alive" (117), as abyssal memory of a "whole city of slaves" (118) rises "over waters of the dead" (120). The city itself remains a revolving or revolutionary govi-receptacle that demands service since "in this city nothing has been forgotten. / that one great sin we cannot claim" (120). Osbey posits the Creole city not only as an economy of obligation but also as a living totemic creature that—when fed—rides and feeds its *serviteurs*, generating a charged fossil energy:

> it knows we know it is the dreamer
> turning huge back
> away from us to hump
> toward us to dream
> to dream us back alive each night
> so that we wake
> thrumming
> eternal
> ever
> at the tracks. (121)

All Saints shares much of this thrumming fossil-fueled sublime with Chamoiseau's *Texaco* and its Mentoh-directed search for "life's gasoline" in quarters that have resisted Pénétrante West. In both the swamped faubourgs of *All Saints* and the shantytowns of *Texaco* we encounter something undead in Creole City: an awareness that "City smells like an animal," and an obligation to *"feel it so you can see that it is really alive."*[51]

New Orleans's urban planners (and university provosts) would do well to read the poems of *All Saints*, to become apprentice hosts of the city's and region's totemic *mo*, its corporate momentum from within.[52] Whoever would do cultural-educational work in this space must be able to see its "invincible duration" with Creole-mentored eyes: "I understood suddenly that Texaco was not what Westerners call a shantytown, but a mangrove swamp, *an urban mangrove swamp*. The swamp seems initially hostile to life. It's difficult to admit that this anxiety of roots, of mossy shades, of veiled waters, could be such a cradle of life for crabs, fish, crayfish, the marine ecosystem. It seems to belong to neither land nor sea, somewhat like Texaco is neither City nor country."[53] Only through his initial swamping does our bureaucrat from City Hall come to host this vision of grace. Like the Seven Sisters of *All Saints*, *Texaco* immerses its shallow-water/swamp traveler in the *travay* of reading and rereading tidal systems of entanglement with obligation: "Out of the urban planner, the Lady made a poet. Or rather: she called forth the poet in the urban planner. Forever" (341).

Woman from the South—The Carnival Spirit of Chacuni's *Travels*

If we have no literature capable of calling forth the submerged poets among our boards of trustees and urban planners, then we may need to restructure our departments of literature and our boards of trustees and planning. We need to relearn to read—both locally and translocally in a more carnivalesque manner—and risk making faces at the accredited Sublime. For a sense of Gulf repertory and stakes, we can turn to another quintessential Creole neighborhood: New Orleans's Seventh Ward, adjacent to Osbey's Tremé. The black business district on Claiborne Street that linked the Seventh Ward and Faubourg Tremé was a space of local autonomy sacrificed to the urban planning and overpasses of Interstate 10. What got bulldozed was the heart of a neighborhood that had produced many of the city's jazz musicians and Indian groups. The Creole Seventh Ward, however, still houses an overpassed but rich contemporary literature that calls for careful reconsideration. Two Seventh Ward poets stand out: Sybil Kein, who published the first collection of poetry written in Louisiana Creole, *Gombo People* (1981); and Mona Lisa Saloy, whose *Red Beans and Ricely Yours* (2005) appropriates Louis Armstrong's epistolary signature in a collection steeped in culinary richness. Kein's *Gombo* and Saloy's *Red Beans* contribute to a Seventh Ward/circum-Atlantic buffet (set with Haitian *riz national*, Cuban *ajiacos*, West Indian callaloos, and Senegalese *ceeb-u-jen*) hosted most recently and generously in Eileen Julien's *Travels with Mae: Scenes from a New Orleans Girlhood* (2009).

The vignettes of *Travels with Mae* testify to the cosmopolitan brought-upsy imparted both by the author's mother, Mae, and by New Orleanian extensions of family, society, and pleasure. Julien begins in Proustian style with chronotopic culinary memory: "Sit me down anywhere with . . . [she lists an almost Homeric catalog of Crescent City dishes] and I find myself miles and years away. All of New Orleans . . . springs right up out of my plate."[54] As with the orphan initiation tales of Senegalese Kumba and Creole Cinderella, the give-and-take *konesans* imparted by the mother travels well, finding carriage in the spiritually nourished child's deep confidence, respect, and savoir-faire, her remarkable capacity for being both guest and host.

In Julien's "Man from the South" (titled after a painting by her Senegalese husband), we meet the author's artist-husband, Kalidou Sy, on his first visit to New Orleans, "preparing a peanut stew, a mafe" in the Julien family home (90). The guest shows himself ready to host his in-laws in a household and city known for its potentially intimidating culinary élan. Later in the memoir, the author recalls her mother's preparation of gumbo in Bordeaux and Dakar. In Senegal, Mae's gumbo, because of its delicious similarities to the local dish *suppakanja*, is received as a masterful presentation of Wolof comfort food: "One friend. Fatou Sow, kept going back to the pot to serve herself, exclaiming, 'This is our food! This is our food'" (105). That the New Orleanian guest, Mae Julien, is able to cook a gumbo recognized as "our food" in the host country of Senegal testifies to a remarkably diasporic cosmopolitanism. In the artistry transported with this food, we find a swamping of territoriality enabling Kalidou Sy to be "Man from the South" in New Orleans and the Julien women to prepare "our food" in Dakar. Given that Kalidou Sy eventually "cooked for whoever was living on Havana Street" (the Juliens' Seventh Ward home), the narrative of *Travels with Mae* puts Senegal and Havana into familiar relation with a Seventh Ward counter-city in the city. Here, "[a]longside the fig trees in our backyard, Daddy grew tomatoes, cabbage, okra, and greens" in an urban garden that has hosted something of the countryside, as Mae signifies with her teasing aphorism: "You can take the man out of the country, but not the country out of the man" (104). *Travels* takes the woman and man out of the South, but hardly the South out of the cosmopolitan traveler.

The vignette composition of *Travels with Mae* uses the implied statement and signifying gesture to tease meaning out of the gaps between pieces. In its musical approach and its comfort with potentially opaque modes of creole performativity, *Travels with Mae* shares a journey with *All Saints*, *Texaco*, and *Poetics of Relation*. Truth-telling, which "could definitely be a liability" (39), is most often rhythmically embodied in *Travels*, subject to Daddy's prohibition and to the nuns' guarding the mysteries of "*minestration!*" (38). Truth gets told and articulated in the "kinetic energies of the body," with "the groove of the black South of my high school and college years" (75) pulsing in neighborhood dance parties, a "volatile space, where we worked out and communicated our real or hoped-for relationships. Where you could say things you couldn't say" (76). In vignettes like "Groovin'" and "The Carnival Spirit," New Orleans hosts second-line truth-telling where "real or hoped-for relationships" and the otherwise unsayable find expression. For Julien, parade rites and musically backed maskings create the conditions of possibility for assembly of the festive, conglomerate momentum of Creole New Orleans: "There is something sublime about throwing or catching a throw during a parade . . . in being part of the emotion, the event, the communion, sharing an hour or two in a crowd with people you don't know and will probably never see again" (119). Trips back home for her family's participation in the Krewe of NOMTOC parade return the memoirist to face-making, sequin-flashing make-believe arts: "Children who grow up in this tradition . . . believe in color, community, disguise, metamorphosis, fun, seasons, ritual, sensuality, luxury, plenty, the body!" (119). This *konesans* must be made and remade anew in the flash of what Julien titles "The Carnival Spirit."

"Carnival Spirit" may revel in oblique and satiric truth-telling, but its funky-butt *konesans* also fosters an incredible frankness about life and death. Sharing in the kinds of service and obligations to the dead modeled throughout Osbey's *All Saints*, *Travels with Mae* asserts, "New Orleans culture always seemed more marked by death. Even Mardi Gras . . . was followed by Ash Wednesday and was a reminder of loss to come" (46). Julien writes of her childhood frequentation of wakes and funerals and of there being "no attempt to shelter us kids from cold, lifeless bodies and mask-like faces or the pitch of emotion they triggered" from mourners who "would wail uncontrollably, as though possessed" (46). Afro-creole cultivation of life and community in "The Shadow of Death" (as the vignette is titled) hosts the psychic honesty and acumen to live a life in the groove with carnival skeleton krewes, to honor—as *Travels with Mae* does—the spirits of one's ancestors, loves, and nurturers, knowing all the while, "you next."[55]

One thing New Orleans's second-line culture exemplifies is a host-and-be-hosted respect for true luxury and plenty, for festivity, travels, exquisite food, artful adornment. The daughter of a schoolteacher and a postal worker, Julien recounts a childhood immersed in her family's activities as charter members of the Jugs Social Club in the early 1950s, "*the* black club of note in Algiers" where much of the extended family lived just across the river from the French Quarter.[56] The Jugs hosted annual balls and selected queens, growing "into the Krewe of NOMTOC (New Orleans Most Talked of Club) in the 1970s" (23). She writes of a middle-class community, family, and mother who value living well. And it may take more than a village—a whole city even—to live and reproduce this life's ritual style: "When the second line was done and that Cinderella feeling began to wane, we typically went out to eat, although there were years when someone more or less in the family would host a breakfast with grits and eggs, sausages or bacon. But most often, it was Dooky Chase, *the* black restaurant in New Orleans at that point. And this was true for proms and balls all year long" (24). Julien herself became too politically conscious to acquiesce to being queen of the Jugs' Ball when her turn came, and she acknowledges that "these traditions that I love to this day seemed to me too gender-, class-, and race-determined" (24). Nevertheless, given the precariousness of such assembled heritages (a spirit of solidarity and mutual aid shared loosely but with ritual seriousness among those "more or less in the family") in a contemporary consumer economy that reduces the imagined world of black realness to narrow ghetto-centric spaces, Eileen Julien's *Scenes from a New Orleans Girlhood* offers a necessarily Catholic and spirit-imbued perspective hospitable to initiatory possibility.

As we have seen in black Atlantic initiation stories, the orphan acquires her dream home from crone-guided bush travel rather than from what some Prince Charming may provide. Such travel narratives have been key to hosting two seemingly contradictory aspects of the sublime encounter: (1) the initiate's increased hold on self-apprehension, and (2) the initiate's ability to allow dislodging of the self in becoming hospitable to mountings or possessions by otherness itself—by *lwa*, orisha, djinn, even perhaps a Prince Charming. All ends of the Creole continuum may be tapped, of course, for sublime travel—from orientations in Shakespeare and European fairytales to the complex orientations of carnival. The bedroom at the third-story top of the house on Havana Street was built to Mae's specification as "a place of make-believe and dreams . . . the place where Mae stored all her ball gowns, her chic dresses, jackets, and hats from the 1940s. It was an oasis for reading" (15). Corpus Christi school is another initiatory locus directed by the nuns. An end-of-year school play casts young Eileen as "'Daisy'/Cinderella," the Virgin Mary's fairytale double: "Queen of the Angels, Queen of the May" (43). Mae, as queen of her own realm, shows her daughter through exemplary action that a woman's place is in large part a matter of a woman's own exploration, travels, and choice.

After thieves break in, bust the safe, and steal valuables from the house on Havana Street, Mae responds to her daughter's concern matter-of-factly: you "get over this or die" (85). In the vignettes following "Getting Over It," *Travels with Mae* moves its focus more fully upon metaphysical gulf-travels of transition. *Travels* draws closer to the dead, cultivating rapport with a hard-to-imagine continuum, "wonder[ing] more and more what it's like on the other side" (111). The memoir depicts a night during the Virgin Mary's month of May (and just beyond the year-and-a-day reclamation of the departed's soul from the abyssal waters) when Mother Mae revisits her daughter in dream: "Her hands on my forehead—joy, ecstasy to know that even though she was dead, she was somehow alive!" (113). Upon awakening, Eileen sees a firefly stuck, flashing between the windowpane and screen: "Was it she in spirit who visited me as touch, as light—leaving, behind her, joy?" (113). Some seven years later, when Katrina floods the family home on Havana Street, the author's Indiana journal and home altar become a portal of travel through more things to get over: "The jar of figs before me on my unfinished altar, between trumpet and candle, appropriately framed by Kalidou's *Man from the South*—recalling that other jar of figs [preserved from the trees prized by her dead father] now submerged in water on the floor of the pantry" (122).

Katrina's flooding of Havana Street evokes the kind of tenacious attachment evinced by the stakeholders of the communities of Texaco and Tremé: "It is not a rational decision. It comes from the gut. I cannot forsake or sell this house" (125). The house built to her mother's specifications by her father and his family remains as something of an altar for a life not finished with its New Orleans relations. Like *Texaco* and *All Saints*, *Travels with Mae* helps us appreciate Creole City's neighborhoods and homes as structures of a rich poetics of relation. The book's cover establishes its own powerful altar image. On the cover, juxtaposed above four smaller family photographs, a larger reproduction of one of Kalidou Sy's paintings, *Signares*, gives a spectral sense of motherlands and their *longue durée* of time-space morphings. In Sy's expressionistically smudged ancestral image, five *Signare* figures (from Portuguese *Senhora*, designating the powerful Senegalese trading women who dealt with the French Company of the Indies) stand poised as cosmopolitan women from the South in spirit-parade across the Great Gulf's suddenly shallow waters.[57]

A concluding vignette of revisitation, "The Keys," opens gateways to reading the long reach of *Travels with Mae*. On the morning of her flight from her daughter's home in Massachusetts back to New Orleans, Mae addresses Eileen with the Creole pet name "my lil' 'chacuni'" (127). This name summons a response charged with mother/daughter poetics of place and displacement: "I'd never heard that expression from anyone but her and it roused in me a deep sense of belonging and warm memories of home" (127). Mae's "chacuni" (having become an accomplished scholar and memoirist) offers the following note: "I learned in a Haitian Creole class in 2001 that *choucoune* means 'yellow bird' and, by implication, lovely young girl. It is the name of a poem by Haitian poet Oswald Durand (1840–1906), for which Michel Mauleart Monton, born in New Orleans of a Haitian father and an American mother, composed a melody in 1883. 'Choucoune' is Haiti's . . . most popular Creole song" (127). Durand's "Choucoune" gave enduring image to the prototype of the beautiful, straight-haired woman often linked in Haitian literature, as Myriam Chancy observes, to "the vodou mulatta goddess Erzulie," a figure (much like Zora Neale Hurston's Haiti-scripted Janie Crawford Woods) "to be pursued, desired, emulated and, ultimately retrieved by women."[58] Mae herself appears in her daughter's memoir-retrieval as a profoundly individuated, self-assured woman who must have been her own mother's "chacuni."

In this daughter's attentiveness to her New Orleans broughtupsy, *Travels with Mae* honors a mother's (and transgenerational/ancestral networks of a community's) guidance. As pianist and organizer of the Jugs Social Club ball (tending to the tableaux, curtsies, waltzes, and regalia of the queen and king), Mae appears as a guardian of all that is classic and regal in taste. But her classicism remains aligned with tastes for a jazz, gumbo, and second-line vernacular classicism. *Travels with Mae* moves with a New Orleanian élan similar to that which George Lipsitz observes in the developers and performers of "'world beat' music," crowned with the "peculiar prestige from below" that accompanies the music, "because it seems as complicated as the rest of contemporary cultural life and to reflect the insights of artists who appear 'a day older in history than everybody else.'"[59] The gumbo second-line and waltz broughtupsy of *Travels with Mae*, a day older and extra-prepared for global time-space, points its readerly initiates into a world citizenship that we have only gestured at in our use of the word *cosmopolitanism*.

Turtle Knows How to Talk—*Ti Cowan*'s Taste of Heaven

More than do the citizens of any other major U.S. city, New Orleanians speak of their city as sacred ground, a locus of ritual imagination bearing its own "peculiar prestige from below" and "day-older in history" gnosis. Cultural historian Jason Berry states, "This city is holy. This is where jazz began . . . there's a quaking spirituality about this place. You find it in the churches . . . in the Mardi Gras Indians."[60] Jazz musician and black Indian culture-bearer Donald Harrison Jr. points to warriorly surrogations by which the Indians kept "the sound of Congo Square alive" not only in New Orleans spaces but in their nurturance of that sound's travels throughout the world.[61] The Marsalis family speaks eloquently of the immanence and reach of Congo Square's and the Voudou spirit houses' sound. As Ellis Marsalis puts it, "In other places, culture comes down from on high. In New Orleans, it bubbles up from the street."[62] His more famous son, Wynton, points to the city's second-line performance of sacral time, how with each danced improvisation, "It's something that has never happened and something that has *always* happened."[63] But this street-level energy remains incredibly challenged. Too often divorced from its service to the city's composite, basilectally assembled *mo* (or momentum from within), Crescent City's bounce gets marketed plantation-style as a product for guests' personal consumption and self-fashioning. Carol Bebelle, director of the Ashé Arts Center, excoriates the tourist economy's parasitic drain on the city's sacred energy (or *ashé*) for the way it feeds on "the ambiance and allure of New Orleans' authentic neighborhood culture" while offering little in return other than the minimum required to keep its initiates in service roles.[64]

Attentiveness to cultural bubblings from the street points to an underutilized guide to Creole identity and desire: turtle (*cowan* or *cawain*). Turtle, who carries home on his back, whose flesh makes a lovely sherry-splashed soup, whose tales fill volumes of folklore, and whose shells Choctaw women shook at stomp grounds and perhaps in Marie Laveau's backyard, is an apt totemic figure of Crescent City's momentum from within. In a recent essay of uncanny brilliance, Ruth Salvaggio channels Sappho and has us listen to the strummed shell of Turtle/Tortoise for Sappho's/Turtle's peculiarly discernible lyric eros at post-Katrina crossroads of Desire and Abundance Streets:

I took my lyre and said;

Come now, my heavenly
tortoise shell: become
a speaking instrument.[65]

Salvaggio's essay pairs Sappho's lyric shell-strummings with an old New Orleans lullaby and calls us to the task of reimagining the eros of communal
bonds, "the delicate bond of person and creature and thing that make up the
city." Her choice of old Creole lyrics from New Orleans's flood-prone streets
could not be more exquisitely loaded:

Gae, gae soulangae
bailé chemin-là.
M'a dit li, oui,
m'a dit li,
cowan li connais parlé
ti cowan li connais parlé.

Gae, gae Soulangae,
Sweep the road.
I tell her, yes,
I tell her,
The turtle knows how to talk,
The little turtle knows how to talk.[66]

Like most lullabies, this song is a day or two older than the children it seemingly targets. It codes adult street knowledge born of Mama's travels over pud-
dled water. Mama knows Turtle is no innocent. And I think she knows this
from tales circulated about Turtle from West Africa to Cuba, New Orleans,
and the Indian nations surrounding the city.[67] Turtle's Gulf tale, which we will
explore more fully in this book's sixth chapter and in the Envoi (and which
gives affirmative, riffing response to Salvaggio's reading), may be summed up
in this brief narrative shell: Turtle likes to lie in low places to get a vision of
heaven as women pass over in their skirts. Always seeking access to life powers that women keep veiled, Turtle is a carnal/spiritual seeker with an eye for
occulted private parts. And Turtle likes to talk. We can leave the well-traveled
story ("Turtle Tries to Look up Women's Dresses") at that for now. Turtle's
capacity for erotic trash-talk and broadcasting of his/her *konesans*, however, is
what the Creole lullaby's mother has in mind by calling Soulangae (the likely
servant) to sweep the road of its minefield of turtles.

   Turtle lies in street puddles and knows how to talk. But Turtle also fuels
the erotics of desire. Seventh Ward poet Mona Lisa Saloy performs a contemporary Turtle road-sweep in "Word Works" wherein we meet a man styling

himself as "the women's pet / the sissy's regret / and the whore's lollipop."[68] Like Sappho, Choctaw shell shakers, and the mother of the Creole lullaby, Saloy's Seventh Ward women know how to put Turtle in his place and make his shell voice their own longings. Shook, strummed turtle shells give rise to the larger assemblages that bring *serviteurs* into stomps and struttings of the carnival spirit or *mo*. Turtle knows how to talk, but women have also long known how to make Turtle their speaking instrument.

If Creole City's sacral energy bubbles up from its periodically swamped streets, Turtle is its emblematic but little-recognized medicine man. The black Atlantic's sacred lore teaches us that Turtle is the main companion of the ventriloquial one-eyed, one-armed, one-legged herbal initiator of the forest.[69] No initiation, no real hospitality, can take place without one-legged Osain and Turtle. Accessing New Orleans's Creole pharmacy, Mona Lisa Saloy knows too that Turtle (*Cawain*) is the source of erotically powered Easter eggs and a potentially botchable aphrodisiacal stew:

> Springtime brought *cawain*,
> and Daddy's expert taking of its head,
> then gently removing the neck gland—
> a purple thing of poison if burst.
> He hung the headless turtle, it still
> kicking for three days on the wooden fence,
> even its head snapped for hours in the grass.
> Never lost a *cawain*, its 21 meat flavors tasting
> of beef, pork, fish, and then some.
> The turtle eggs, Mother's favorite, promised
> youth, health, and sexy eyes, Daddy said.
> When he shooed aunts, uncles, and Mother
> out of the kitchen, he blended herbs for
> sauté and his special roux before stewing.[70]

Springtime brings Daddy's becoming-Turtle, his roux *konesans* and egg-promise to Mother: youth, health, sexy eyes. Turtle simmers as communion chronotope of Mother's desire and Daddy's secret seasonings offered

> to food fed spirits
> when *cawain* is a spring event
> of 21 meat tastes stewed or
> red beans and rice raise the Monday
> blues to rhapsody
> for every feuding face that
> genuflects before grottoes,

of the Blessed Virgin,
the mini altars between
many shotgun steps,
the Blessed Mother,
the sweetest protector
of Catholic schoolgirl dreams
and prayers of the faithful. (68)

Uniting sexual healing and tricksterism, Saloy's *Cawain* and the Blessed Mother keep up a carnal dialectic at the heart of this Seventh Ward dreambook for the faithful—its momentum from the inside, from eros and private parts.

To conclude, we may turn to a culinary master, to hear from Leah Chase (of Dooky Chase restaurant) how Creole time was marked by Turtle since "Easter dinner was never complete without cowan," with "Females . . . preferred and . . . always prodded around the rear legs for eggs . . . cooked right along with the turtle in the spicy gravy."[71] Creole Easter makes its feast of complete assemblage around Turtle's flesh and eggs. This work of Easter hospitality—like masking Indian, apprenticing to jazz, or initiating into a life of serving the spirits—is a time-intensive labor that keeps contact with swamp(ed) time-space alive. Chase writes of being the cook for Mayor Dutch Morial: "I would always have to cook anything Dutch got dumped on him. Every time his friends would give him something, he would say we had to have a party and I would cook. One year someone had given him about ten or twelve cowan" (36). But the party that Leah Chase describes comes at considerable cost. She adds her thoughts on belief and payback: "Like my mother and all others who enjoy eating this tasty, spicy dish, I always get the turtle alive. Remove the head and meticulously clean the meat from the shell. If there are any eggs, remove and set aside. I know of no chef willing to take on such a task, but you can believe that this dish is well worth the work. It was always served over rice with a good potato salad on the side and a glass of claret—and that's heaven!" (36). This is, indeed, a heaven to believe in. But let us never forget—as Leah Chase makes clear—the demanding economy behind the ritual production and imagination of heaven. This is a heaven *made* through economies of environmental memory and their dedicated *serviteurs*. Neither the state's nor the nation's miserly trickle-down economy will pay the costs, but most of us still demand access to productions (real and symbolic) of New Orleans's and the Gulf's hospitality. The production of a gumbo or a turtle soup (or the maintenance of an ancestor altar or Virgin grotto) is work that hardly pays in cash. Heaven is its reward. Still, this below-sea-level heaven generates and sustains a momentum from the inside that is necessary to living a life in good faith. As trickster, ritual music instrument, and Easter dish, Turtle remains one of the primary avatars of the Gulf's basilectal energy industry and its Creole sublime.

Figures of Mardi Gras Indians, Yellow Birds, Skeleton Krewes, and Turtle point to an enduring authority that moves its *serviteurs* toward the steady project of "building the structure / the years have torn down," as Brenda Marie Osbey puts it in "House of Bones." New Orleanian to the core, Osbey's "House of Bones" knows how to talk and how to walk turtle's seekerly walk—in tenacious affirmation of a shell-shaking, ever-reassembling momentum from the inside:

> this is the house
> i have carried inside me
> this is the house
> made of artifact and gut
> this is the house
> all my bones have come from
> *this is the house*
> *nothing*
> *nothing*
> *nothing can tear down.*[72]

PART THREE

Sangre y Monte

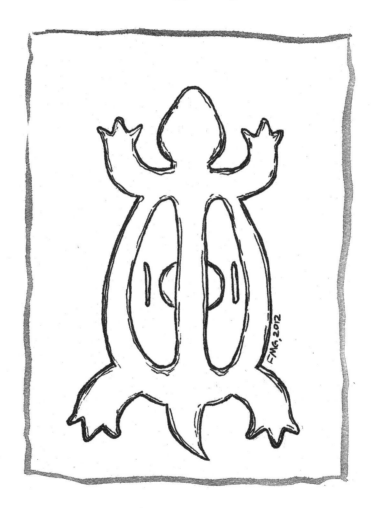

¿Ya conocéis mi sangre navegable,
mi geografía llena de oscuros montes,
de hondos y amargas valles
que no están en los mapas?
—Nicolás Guillén, "El apellido"

CHAPTER FIVE

"Come and Gaze on a Mystery"

Zora Neale Hurston's Rain-Bringing Authority

I was to walk with the storm and hold my power, and get my answers to life
and things in storms. The symbol of lightning was painted on my back.
This was to be mine forever.
—Zora Neale Hurston on her initiation as "Rain-Bringer,"
   Dust Tracks on a Road

Oya who causes the leaves to flutter
Oya, strong wind who gave birth to fire while traversing the mountain
Oya, please don't fell the tree in my backyard
Oya, we have seen fire covering your body like cloth.
—Praises of Oya collected by Fela Sowande and Fagbemi Ajanaku

"What is the truth?" Zora Neale Hurston was asked while doing what her
Baptist minister father might have called "two-headed work" as a novelist-
anthropologist serving the *Mystères* of Haitian Vodou. She received unforgettable ritual answer from a mambo who, "by throwing back her veil and
revealing her sex organs," gave bodily testimony that "this . . . is the ultimate truth"—"There is no mystery beyond the mysterious source of life."[1]
The mambo's flash of revealed truth would find publication in 1938 in *Tell
My Horse*, but it also shaped the "creaming" and "frothing" of the erotic
beneath the blooming pear tree of Hurston's best-known novel, *Their Eyes
Were Watching God* (1937), written while she was doing her fieldwork and
initiatory seeking in Haiti in 1936. There, "ever since the first tiny bloom had
opened," this ultimate truth inscribed in *Their Eyes* "had called her to come
and gaze on a mystery."[2] Hurston's Haitian encounters with the Vodou *lwa*
had been prepared by earlier travels of ritual seeking in the Gulf South and
the Bahamas and were fed too by her Florida broughtupsy and orphaning.
She carried all this—her initiate crowning in New Orleans as storm-walking
"Rain-Bringer," her experience in 1929 of a powerful hurricane in Nassau,
and her anthropological work in Jamaica and Haiti—into the storm-swept
hierophany of *Their Eyes Were Watching God*.[3]

The work that Zora Neale Hurston did in Haiti marks some of the deeper
channels of her reroutings of literary and folk authority. "You got tuh *go* there

tuh *know* there," Janie Woods famously insists to her friend Pheoby Watson (and to the readers of *Their Eyes Were Watching God*).[4] Such a journey may swamp an author (as well as her characters), make and break a career, and Hurston paid a steep sacrificial cost for her eventual literary canonization. In *The Nation's Region*, Leigh Anne Duck—assessing modernist skepticism toward folk culture (even in works shaped by attraction to it)—points out that the folk "allure" was often held to be "a dangerous nostalgia for an experience inaccessible to modern subjects": "too deep an immersion . . . must prove destructive to a modern, urban subjectivity."[5] Many a reader may feel that the overall-clad, vernacular-speaking Janie Woods of the opening and closing pages of *Their Eyes Were Watching God* has hauled herself back from too deep an immersion in the Everglades muck as she returns to her two-story central Florida home telling a tale of storm mayhem and of her trial and acquittal for the shooting of her much younger, rabies-possessed husband. Hurston's novel indeed becomes a vehicle of spiritual travel and of the annihilation of its primary avatar's bourgeois subjectivity. What we are left with is a novel of experiential female authority not bound by progressive models of temporality or by national models of space but given over to periodicity and antiphony, polyrhythm and heteroglossia. By the late 1930s Hurston had already answered Wilson Harris's 1972 call for a body of Caribbean/Gulf writing ready and able to risk the disparagement directed at artist-intellectuals who would step—with the limbo imagination of the censored (black) majority—into the Atlantic's submerged perspectives of time and space.

Hurston's entire body of work paid the accompanying price of critical disavowal or neglect, but her "Rain-Bringer" body of writing has also gifted us with openings to a Gulf sublime hardly accredited even now—despite the veritable Hurston industry sprung up to capitalize on the author. Hurston's most famous fictional avatar (Janie Crawford Woods) goes into the muck in her overalls to escape the limitations of certain bourgeois notions of femininity. She leaves the muck with an initiate orphan knowledge akin to that dropped on the anthropologist Ira P. Lowenthal in his study of market-women or "garden-women" in Haiti. The anthropologist was told by one of his entrepreneurial subjects that "Every woman is born with a carreau of land between her legs" (a plot of over three acres) for the cultivation of her garden.[6] Of course, we hear something of this postplantation *konesans* in the blues songs of Bessie Smith and Ma Rainey, perhaps in the ministry of Mother Catherine Seals, but hardly in the progressive literature of uplift expected by Hurston's critics.

In all of Hurston's writing, the abject and the sublime lurk together, in the muck, the jook, the storm, in looking up the skirts of the real—Janie's unforgettable seekerly time-space beneath a pear tree where "from the leaf-buds to snowy virginity of bloom," there comes "[t]his singing she heard that had nothing to do with her ears."[7] In what amounts to an altar (or alter) call, *Their Eyes Were Watching God* issues its doxology. It bids us to "come and gaze on a mystery," pushing its reader, like the Louisiana Creole (as well as Cuban and southeastern Indian) trickster Turtle, "face to face with the truth," whether this truth be the muck-raising period of some god or "monstropolous beast" immersing us all in her flows, or the mambo's ritually unveiled vagina, or any number of instances in which Death finds folk "watching, trying to see beyond seeing."[8]

Something of the *konesans* of both the Haitian *femme-jardin* (garden woman) and the Vodou mambo informs the initiatory narrative of *Their Eyes*. The text points to Seminole and Caribbean knowledge of God's reproductive cycles. And it follows a sacrificial, periodic logic. Like the St. Kittitian Cinderella sent to the river to wash a daub of blood from her mistress's punch bowl, Janie goes to the muck and returns to claim her own house, land, narrative, and womanly body. She becomes the text's readerly avatar for an initiatory gathering of *konesans* out of what had been "radically excluded," "what disturbs identity" and "does not respect borders."[9] In all this the text carries a powerful initiatory mythopoesis. This does not mean, however, that Hurston's vision excludes the historical and the real. Rather, it uncovers possibilities, identities, horizons, histories that our disciplinary categories and periodizations have excluded from consciousness.

Much question remains, however, about what Hurston may have excluded in her writing's charged hold on life. Among her most challenging critics, Hazel Carby insists that Hurston's work displaces an increasingly urban, northward-bound culture of the black masses by nostalgically keeping black folk culture in its place: the plantation South. Carby points to a reactionary displacement whereby "the geographical boundaries of Hurston's black folk are rural, but their Southernness is not defined through a difference to Northernness as much as it is related to cultural practices and beliefs of the Caribbean."[10] Hurston, in effect, is accused of not being national enough, urban-contemporary enough, *real* enough. As I underscore throughout this chapter, Hurston's spatial and spiritual positions *do* differ from the popular and academic norms of national (even U.S.-bound black national) culture, which is a big reason why her call went so long unanswered. Her earliest scholarly publication, a 1927 *Journal of Negro History* piece on "Fort Moosa" (Ft. Mose), an eighteenth-century outpost of black maroons commissioned by the Spanish to defend St. Augustine, points to Florida's foundational colonial difference and its strong ties to Cuba and the rest of the Caribbean.[11] Even before the founding of the fortified Gracia Real de Santa Teresa de Mose in 1738 (two miles north of St. Augustine) as North America's first free black settlement and as site of refuge for Carolina maroons, Florida had been a southern terminus of an underground railroad leading to a decidedly Caribbean space.[12] This station fed other southerly routes: Bahamian, Cuban, and Seminole. Given Hurston's knowledge of Florida's historical Hispano-Creole difference, her representation of the Okeechobee muck as fertile site of ongoing circum-Caribbean labor migrations—and the degree to which Florida remains shaped by Caribbean and Afro-Atlantic agency—her embrace of Florida's diasporic crosscurrents may be seen as pioneering and prophetic.

Their Eyes Were Watching God took on an even more unsettling poignancy in the aftermath of Hurricane Katrina. The novel's attentiveness to hubristic dismissals of storm warnings, its focus on economically driven decisions to stay in place rather than to seek a ride out, its depictions of high ground commandeered by whites, and its racially charged aftermath of segregationist burial crews testified anew to enduring gulfs of race, security, and belonging in America. Martyn Bone has done a good job of re-historicizing how the path of the storm in *Their Eyes* followed the trail of devastation left by the second deadliest hurricane in American history: the 1928 Florida storm that killed over 1,800 (and perhaps as many as 6,000) people when the levees holding Lake Okeechobee gave way, releasing an eight-foot tidal wave on the mostly Bahamian and black southern agricultural workers encamped on "the muck."[13] Hurricanes lay bare the plantation zone's systemically violent economy—one that has rendered Florida's poorest subjects and seasonally migrant "aliens" particularly vulnerable. Amidst the death and destruction such storms bring, they can also unveil much that is otherwise kept under ideological wrap. We think again of George W. Bush crony and FEMA director Michael Brown admitting cluelessly in the wake of Katrina, "We're seeing people that we didn't know exist."[14] Anyone who has read Hurston closely cannot doubt that she identified powerfully with storms, their time-space of climatic violence, their archetypally feminized (and inescapably colored) outings of invisibilized truth. Come Atlantic storm season, tropic nature asserts a sovereignty that black majority cultures of the Americas have recognized with long-memoried tropes of respect and dread rapport. In all the writing that followed her 1928 New Orleans initiation as "Rain-Bringer," Hurston showed herself to be the true autoethnographer of subjects periodically swamped (and rendered visible) by the powers of Atlantic storm.

Whoever would bow to kiss the mysterious source of life in *Their Eyes Were Watching God* would do well to consider what Hurston brought to the Haiti-scripted text from earlier initiations in New Orleans as well as how her investment in tropes of storm-walking found manifestation in her subsequent body of writing. My own re-readings of Hurston while teaching a University of North Florida seminar on her work just after Florida's perspective-changing 2004 hurricane season (when Hurricanes Charley, Frances, Ivan, and Jeanne struck the state) have convinced me that the coastal South's most celebrated author found signature authority in her 1928 "Rain-Bringer" initiation into repertoires of the orisha Oya—divinity of storms, death rites, and shape-shifting bush transformations. Oya provides indispensable keys to reading Rain-Bringer's texts.

Of all the New Orleans initiations represented in Hurston's earliest book project, *Mules and Men* (1935), the one in which she seems most deeply invested was her receiving "the crown of power" from Luke Turner (188), who traced his crowning to a famous aunt, Marie Laveau, in a storm-dominated narrative genealogy. After accepting entry into this ritual family and undergoing three days of intensifying visions in ritual isolation, Hurston emerged to receive Turner's spirit-divined re-naming: "I see her conquering and accomplishing with the lightning and making her road with thunder. She shall be called the Rain-Bringer" (191). She describes how Turner painted her face in red and yellow, then "painted the lightning symbol down my back from my right shoulder to my left hip." This was her sign: "The Great One was to speak to me in storms" (191).

Hurston would reinvoke this initiation years later in her autobiography, *Dust Tracks on a Road* (1942), insisting "it was not only elaborate, it was impressive. I lay naked for three days and nights on a couch, with my navel to a rattlesnake skin which had been dressed and dedicated to the ceremony," all of which led to sky-walking "dreams that seemed real for weeks," full of "lightning flashing from under my feet, and grumbling thunder following in my wake."[15] *Mules and Men*, then, presents a young "Zora" much like the Janie of *Their Eyes Were Watching God* who must go there to *know* there—in an initiating encounter with the sublime, in order to bring the text across gulfs of ritual and narrative authority. Hurston's storm-walking initiation as Rain-Bringer appears to have left its mark on all the writing that followed, inscribing itself most forcefully in the storm of *Their Eyes Were Watching God* but signifying as well in every book she authored.

Despite the fact that Hurston's first published story, "John Redding Goes to Sea" (1921), featured a deadly Florida hurricane, it was only after her crowning as Rain-Bringer in 1928 that her signature zigzag lightning sign and storm motif found steady inscription in her work. Her first novel, *Jonah's Gourd Vine* (1934), opens with God "grumbling his thunder and playing the zigzag lightning thru his fingers."[16] The horrific hurricane of 1928 gave dread inspiration and title to her second and most-celebrated novel, whose storm-struck characters "seemed to be staring at the dark, but their eyes were watching God."[17] Undergoing initiations in Haiti for *Tell My Horse* (1938), Hurston concluded that book with a tale deferring to her lightning sign: God summons "Shango, the god of thunder and lightning," to fashion "a shaft of lightning," allowing storm-music of the cosmos to land in "Guinea" to work its dance rhythms throughout the world (261). *Moses, Man of the Mountain* (1939) signs off as Moses lifted his hoodoo rod, "and the zig-zag lightning above him joined the muttering thunder."[18] *Dust Tracks on a Road* places Rain-Bringer's ritual signature in its final paragraph, signifying to and upon her readers: "You who play the zig-zag lightning of power over the world, with the grumbling thunder in your wake, think kindly of those who walk in the dust" (769). And Hurston's final novel, *Seraph on the Suwanee* (1948), has at its narrative center Jim Meserve's courting tale of "a terrible thunderstorm come up all of a sudden" with lightning "zigzagging around something awful," a tale in which Jim's violently taming husbandry of his wife, Arvay, and his anti-Puritan irreverence find flashpoint: "It's a habit of mine, Miss Arvay, when I catch a streak of lightning aiming at me, to stand in my tracks and slap it right back where it come from."[19] An initiate spiritual authority appears to root the work of one of our most celebrated writers, whose ritual death as Zora and rebirth as Rain-Bringer transformed what got authored through her reassemblies of dismembered mythic corpora. When Rain-Bringer is read in dialogue with Judith Gleason's articulation of the orisha Oya's manifestations as "I" of the storm's winds, spirit of death and ancestral representation, and spirit of shape-shiftings in wilderness, the counterclockwise spin of Oya's grooves and gateways may be recognized for giving Hurston's writing its hermeneutic integrity, its animation.

Ellease Southerland suggested in 1979 that "perhaps the culmination of Zora's folklore is the form it gave her religious thought," adding that "if one were to trace her religious thinking in her fiction, there would be discovered a new dimension of religious thought."[20] Since Southerland's provocative call, relatively few contributors to the booming Hurston critical industry have followed up on Hurston's immersions in circum-Caribbean ritual communities and her ministration of those rites in fiction. Most notably, Daphne Lamothe (1999) has examined the Haitian Vodou divinity Ezili as model for the characterization of Janie in *Their Eyes Were Watching God*. Edward Pavlić (2002) has recognized that Hurston was "clearly initiated into a New Orleans version of the cult of Oyá," but his crossroads modernist readings of Esu-Elegba's presence in *Their Eyes* lead away from tending more fully to the agency of Hurston's patron Oya.[21] More recently, Teresa Washington (2005) argued compellingly for recognition of Hurston as "African America's Iyá-Iwé, or Mother of Letters" and offered a fuller picture of Oya-typologies in the narrative formation of Janie in *Their Eyes Were Watching God*.[22] My own focus on Oya as hermeneutic key to Hurston's mythopoesis calls attention to real powers of storm read through folk narrative, fiction, and divination repertoires, but I also seek to point out how Hurston's Afro-conservative, preservationist aesthetic operates from another kind of conservatism—sustained through creolization's complex transformations. Her grounding in Florida's history, culture, and landscapes fed her efforts to muddy the water of national, disciplinary, and psychic boundaries, reopening the coastal South to currents of flow and exchange that have imparted to the region much of its cultural vitality as well as its foundational navigations of trauma. Rain-Bringer's textual reassemblies of "*Ajé*"—of woman-born(e) power or truth—may well bring us new dimensions of religious thought, new archives and affiliations of spirited knowledge.[23]

"De Wind Is a Woman"—Revolver Who Twists to Create

New dimensions of religious thought may be drawn from Rain-Bringer's storm-walking presence, and from how "[r]adical transformations in the weather," according to Judith Gleason, may "signal the need for radical transformations in human thinking and feeling," in economic and ecosystemic relation.[24] Although we may identify Rain-Bringer as a "road" of Oya, her energies share much with the fiery domain of the orisha Shango, with whom Hurston also likely identified. The south Florida *Regla de Ocha* (Santería) ritual leader Miguel "Willie" Ramos describes Shango as owner of "lightning and thunder" but notes that Oya wields and enables much of his repertoire, especially lightning, since Oya is the divinity "of the winds and tempests . . . represented by the lightning rod which she gave as a present to her husband."[25] Like her husband, Shango, Oya is fiery and charismatic. Her whirlwinds and storms ventilate and *work through* repressed or climatically imbalanced conditions. Oya's praise poetry speaks of her cosmic "housecleaning," including calls to "Let her rip" in "clean sweep."[26] In Oya, Gleason sees the means "to wrest women's fire back from Promethean culture-bearers of the Western tradition," a fire that includes the libidinal heat of Oya-Ajere, "carrier-of-the-container-of-fire," known in Brazil as "Oya de esteira" or "Oya of the mat"—an erotically charged manifestation of Oya performed in the "'plate-breaking' dance: hands on hips, buttocks prominently extended in saucy rotation."[27] The truth-and-rain-bringing Oya hyped in song—"Storm wind is arriving, strong wind / Oya likes a good hard lover, strong wind / Oya dances a wicked bamba, strong wind!"—performs a cleansing dance that may conclude "with a series of down-stroking flicks [of Oya's *ìrùkè* or horsetail whisk] . . . to get rid of negative energies clinging to whomever is whisked."[28] Oya, as musicologist Katherine Hagedorn affirms, is the ventilating whirlwind, "Revolver who twists to create."[29] Aptly situated for such steamy work, Hurston's home in Eatonville lies in a region of Florida that gets more lightning storms per year (over one hundred) than any other North American location.[30] Moving off West Africa's coast in trade winds that carried Africans to the Americas, Oya's tropic systems convey some of the most dramatic and traumatic linkages between Africa, the Caribbean, and the coastal South.

Hurston's initiations into Oya-energies led her to many mentors. Big Sweet, for example, models Oya's warrior role in Florida's Polk County jooks.

In *Mules and Men,* she warns Zora, "If anything start, Little-Bit, you run out de door like a streak uh lightning and get in yo' car" (147). The sermons of Rev. C. C. Lovelace of Eau Gallie (recharging memories of her father's Baptist preaching) were sampled for *Jonah's Gourd Vine* and offer another source for Hurston's ritual signature:

> You are de same God, Ah
> Dat heard de sinner man cry.
> Same God dat sent de zigzag lightning tuh
> Join de mutterin' thunder. (76)

Hurston witnessed a devastating 1929 hurricane in Nassau just months after her Rain-Bringer crowning and recounted the experience in *Dust Tracks on a Road* (702). In her Caribbean travels, Hurston received many pointers into the sublime. Instructed by teachers ranging from Mambo Etienne to Bessie Smith, Hurston nevertheless put a special significance on her New Orleans initiation under Luke Turner, so much so that even when studying Vodou in Haiti, as she writes in *Tell My Horse,* "Mambo Etienne tied my red and yellow handkerchief on my head in the proper loose knot at the back of my head" (418). These were the colors of Turner's earlier crowning of her.

There remains, however, reason to doubt Hurston's account of her Rain-Bringer initiation. She was such an accomplished fabricator that it can be tough to judge when she is telling the truth, when she is telling mythopoetic truths, and when she is telling bold-faced or evasive lies. Harry Hyatt, a widely successful white collector of hoodoo lore, was stunned enough by Hurston's account of her initiations that he traveled twice to New Orleans to confirm the vitality of religious Voudou there, only to be told such rites no longer existed in the practice of the 1930s. Other factors suggest fabrication of the Turner initiation. First, there is Hurston's plagiarism of material on Cudjo Lewis published in 1927, the year before her New Orleans studies. More vexing is language from the May 1928 publication of "How It Feels to Be Colored Me" that reveals either a jazz-fed oracular vision of her upcoming New Orleans initiation or a fictionalizing pattern of initiatory desire: "My face is painted red and yellow, and my body is painted blue."[31] The colors that would be painted on her face half a year later in New Orleans, red and yellow, also happen to be—along with blue and white—fundamental colors used to paint the crowned head in Afro-Cuban orisha initiations.[32] But if we couple this earlier body-painted "Colored Me" possession scene with Rev. Lovelace's sermonic zigzag lightning (1929) and consider possible "liftings" of material from ethnographic texts, the cynic may read a self-crowning story of Voudou initiation fabricated for literary consumption.

The bottom line is that Luke Turner could well have been teaching vital ritual traditions received from Marie Laveau via Saint-Domingue refugees who came to New Orleans after a six-year exile in Cuba. Afro-creole religious knowledge likely found continual lines of transmission in the Gulf South. The presence on the Gulf coast of people like the Cuban Tata Gaitán, a key Lucumi *babalawo* (diviner) and Ochosi priest in Havana who, according to David Brown, "was a *tabaquero* by trade and is believed to have worked in Tampa, Florida during the 1890s," could have contributed to sustaining initiations such as those Hurston describes.[33] Given the shipping activity and migrations surrounding the banana and cigar industries as well as the U.S. military occupations in the Caribbean from the 1890s to the 1930s, surely Tata Gaitán was not the only Caribbean priest who may have been crowning godchildren in the Gulf South during this time.

In the end, Hurston's investment in the "Rain-Bringer" initiation bears its own witness to the Oya authority inscribed in her life work. We can see that the primary object of spiritual seeking in *Mules and Men* is an initiatory quest, making the text, as Cheryl Wall argues, "a paradigmatic immersion narrative" in which the narrator, "Zora," finds transformation under the jook tutelage of Big Sweet and spiritual repertoires of a storm-ruling Marie Laveau.[34] Thereafter, all of Hurston's texts would be immersion narratives, journeys into storm-ruled mucks and low places of abject and sublime encounter. Even the Marie Laveau hagiography narrated (from Luke Turner to Hurston) in *Mules and Men* moves through immersion in Oya's windswept waters. Turner, who claims to have served the spirits under Laveau on the shores of Lake Pontchartrain and in her New Orleans residence on St. Ann Street, puts himself on the scene of what had become a widespread memory of Laveau's final hurricane transfiguration. He tells how Laveau set water on her altar and called on Lake Pontchartrain to answer: "lightning raced . . . and the lake heaved," and a "terrible strong wind at last tore the house away and set it in the lake." Although "the loving ones [ritual family members] find a boat and [go] out to where her house floats on one side and break a window to bring her out," the storm passes with Laveau's own willed passing. She famously insists, "I want to die here in the lake," but gets pulled ashore by her "loving ones," and she "sing a song and is dead, yes" (185). Here, Luke Turner (along with Hurston herself) narrates the lineage by which Rain-Bringer enters a ritual family of mutual aid and empowerment. In the end, Hurston would not remain within this "house" of loving ones to serve the spirit in the traditional sense. She writes, "He wanted me to stay with him to the end. It has been a great sorrow to me that I could not say yes" (195). We might insist, however, that Rain-Bringer's signature authority remained so much at the core of Hurston's subsequent work that she extended the housing of the spirit and its community of loving ones. Rain-Bringer's submerged authority seems to have called for transformations in emergent textual rites of passage, gathering and crowning new generations of "loving ones" in ways that foster new solidarities and commitments. *Mules and Men* marks an initial crowning of authority.

Like the fiction that followed it, *Mules and Men* intuits a unified reading of black Atlantic folk narrative and religious practice. Traces of the ritual domains of Afro-creole divinities emerge from folktales Hurston collected from the Gulf South, several of which feature diviners and the agency of Oya herself. These tales are a bridge between the authority of old divination corpora (such as Ifa) and the integral mythic vision of Hurston's fiction. When we look to a Yoruba Ifa tale associated with the figure Ofun Osa (one of the divination system's 256 *odu* or narrative "windows" on life), we hear how Oya in whirlwind form destroys many houses until she is finally welcomed and pacified with a sacrifice. Given ritual hospitality by the sacrificing diviner, Oya then vomits her storm-swept riches upon his floor. Judith Gleason writes that the oracle "stages the bringing in or 'owning' of one's own violence, thereby transforming its capricious, destructive aspects into creative, libidinal energy." Divination presents Oya as cosmic house-cleaner: "Swept-clean means Oya." And we are instructed that "Who knows how to calm me down / Knows how to prosper." In offering a sacrifice to Oya and applying part of it to our own eyes, we learn to encounter the storm "first by calming the eye of the beholder" and then by wooing the storm and hosting it while remaining open to the restorative balancing it may bring.[35]

In Hurston's final novel, *Seraph on the Suwanee*, Jim Meserve takes the place of the diviner who pacifies the eye/I of the female storm. Having developed the habit of having fits and fainting spells as a means of avoiding repressed desires, Arvay responds to Jim's courting like "a hurricane [that] struck the over-crowded parlor. Arvay gave a yell from the very bottom of her lungs." Jim pacifies Hurricane Arvay with a drop of turpentine in her eye, to which she responds: "That varmint! Ooooooooh! He poured teppentime right in my eye!" Her father adds, "Quickest cure for the spasm-fits I ever did see."[36] Arvay's yell, like Oya's guttural cry of arrival, *"heyi!"* or a Polk County blues cry, announces a turbulence that would refuse supplication but may find it in the act of vocalization.[37] The primary female warrior in the orisha pantheon, Oya brings sublimated rage and release to her storming fields of action.[38] She can reduce any of us to refugee status, as Janie and Tea Cake see clearly in Palm Beach following the storm of *Their Eyes Were Watching God*. Straggling in to their hoped-for "city of refuge," they come face to face with "Havoc . . . with her mouth wide open" (310). Oya may destroy those in her way, including the vulnerable and the hubristic who do not read or respect her signs, but she may also "whisk" and transform open-eyed devotees such as Janie at the novel's end: "The wind through the open windows had broomed out all the fetid feeling of absence and nothingness" (333).

One tale from *Mules and Men*, "Why the Waves Have Whitecaps," insists "[d]e wind is a woman, and de water is a woman too" (127). Here the women brag on their children, with Mrs. Water ending up drowning Wind's young seabirds. As their white feathers float, Mrs. Wind lets loose her storm of retribution on the waters. Oya's ritual dance often communicates this whirlwind energy and finds conclusion in akimbo warrior posture.[39] Such kinetic remembering figures prominently in *Jonah's Gourd Vine*, which carries strong currents of Oya's erotic charge, particularly in the appearance of Lucy, who "put herself akimbo" and, after flirtatious signifying, "was gone up the hill in a blue whirlwind" (34). Without such rain-bringing, embodied expression, we face drought conditions of the desiccated terrain forecast by the Oya-associated Ifa sign Irete Ogunda:

> Rain never falls again
> Penis has withered into whips all over town
> Vaginas have dried up like leather bags
> All the little rivers are dying of thirst
> And all the streamlets have put on garments of dried leaves.[40]

Hurston remedied such drought conditions (the drying up of life's mystery itself) in her blues immersions. In *Mules and Men*, when Ella Wall, for example, was toasted by Florida-flip players who sang "Oh, go to Ella Wall / If you want good boody," Wall eluded their objectification by shouting "Tell 'em 'bout me!" as she moved in subject performance, "snapped her fingers and revolved her hips with her hands" (146). Challenging her sworn rival, Big Sweet, Ella "stood up akimbo," unnerving Zora with the prospect of "dying in a violent manner in a sordid saw-mill camp" (147) until things were quieted by the patrolling "Quarters Boss" whose gaze and pistol would becalm without bringing release, keeping a turpentine and sawmill jook economy steaming, its bloodletting inwardly directed.[41] But as in *Their Eyes Were Watching God*, the boss cannot control the gathering storm, no matter how much he would segregate (or deny the costs of ignoring or blocking) basic, increasingly heated flows.

If folk blindly follow the boss in disregarding storm signs and trust to the boss's arrangements of security, the folk (especially folk of the global South) will stay caught in the trap Hurston describes in *Their Eyes* in the face of hurricane warnings: "The folks let the people do the thinking. If the castles thought themselves secure, the cabins needn't worry. Their decision was already made as always" (303). Clearly "folks" let "the people do the thinking" at folks' tremendous peril. We must all attend to this element of Rain-Bringer's recuperative project. Through the novel's storm, she brings us to a specific moment on the muck (but also to a larger global moment of authority) when "[t]he time was past asking the white folks what to look for" (304). Through ritually engaged thinking of the folk, Hurston gave *Their Eyes* sublime mythopoetic performance and eye-opening vision. Oya rites dispersed and creolized throughout the circum-Caribbean convey the importance of owning one's own violence, the need in facing a storm to becalm the eye of the beholder—even to host the storm (as climatic event or raging subaltern) with sacrificial offerings so as to seek reparation of the torn fabric of natural, social, or household domains. Oya's praise songs remind us: "Who knows how to calm me down / Knows how to prosper."[42]

"We All Bloody Bones Now in de Drift Together"—Egungun Oya

While our world may thirst because of an absent Rain-Bringer or be buried in a deluge of her rage, even the dead may thirst and trouble the living whose neglect ruptures lineage continuity and decenters every subject. This too is a realm of Oya and a signature concern of Hurston's; here, too, folk narrative and religion find recuperative, transfiguring convergence in Hurston's steady attentiveness to the dead. Oya is the only orisha who will attend to funerals and their transitional time-space between life and death. As Gleason observes, her "[s]torms, intrinsic to radical shifts of being, also mark the passage of life into death."[43] She is the mother of ancestor masquerades, the *egungun*, whose patchwork, multistripped cloth's "zigzag borders . . . speak lightning."[44] And Oya's repertory of restored behaviors calls us, perhaps uncannily, but also through initiate lineage and purpose, to keep in mind that Hurston not only signed all her initiate texts with storm or zigzag lightning but also with an unusual rapport with death and the ancestral dead. It is Rain-Bringer's re-creative capacity for mourning that can perhaps best help us understand her deep investment in the folk culture's saraka ethos—its sacrificial feeding of the children through ritual payment of ancestral respects.[45]

An Ifa oracle under the sign Irosun Osa tells how Oya founded the *egungun* masquerade of ancestral spirits. In order to give birth, Oya is called to carry nine whips in her right hand and nine in her left, to offer nine cocks in the market, and to cover her head in red cloth. Blessed afterward with nine children who later fall ill, she goes to two diviners, named "It-is-a-great-occurrence-when-rat-is-found-in-a-hole-of-water" and "It-is-a-great-occurrence-when-fish-is-found-in-grassland," both of whom direct Oya's children to continue the masquerade that enabled their births.[46] The *egungun*, in this Yoruba divination tale of their origin, are bound to Mother Oya, to storm floods, and to the blood-red periodicities of fecundity and women's power. The orisha mediating at funerals and the "owner" of cemeteries in much of the Caribbean, Oya works, as Judith Gleason writes, to "mend 'the broken connection' between ourselves and those who have gone before."[47] The *egungun* are figures of a lineage authority and localized judiciary that—under colonial, white-supremacist, and national conditions of modernity—account for something more than mere folk nostalgia. They assert a submerged yet enduring hold on authority from gulfs of unsurrendered resistance.

As mother of the nine *egungun*, Oya made her presence felt in Hurston's crowning in *Mules and Men:* from the nine days of ritual preparation (189) to the final blood sacrifice of a sheep in whose bleeding throat were inserted nine sheets of paper with Rain-Bringer's name written nine times on each (192–93). Befitting Oya, a broom was "dipped in the blood . . . and the ground swept vigorously" for "as long as the blood gushed" (193). Oya's ritual number nine is the most used number in Hurston's collected "formulae of hoodoo doctors" (258–59). In *Their Eyes Were Watching God*, Tea Cake cuts nine of Janie's hairs for good luck before going gambling in Jacksonville (277). And in the Caribbeanist text *Tell My Horse* (the anthropologically grounded twin of *Their Eyes*), Hurston observes that "[t]he most universal ceremony in Jamaica is an African survival called 'The Nine Night'" (309), an extended wake releasing the spirit on the ninth night after death, directed under the authority of women. In all of Rain-Bringer's texts, nine is the number associated with initiation and mourning, luck and fate.

We may read *Their Eyes* as both initiatory orphan text and as a Nine Night text of mourning, a wake. Claudia Tate has identified Hurston's early orphaning and specifically the mourning of her mother's death as a key component of the writer's steadfastness in pursuing a career as literary and anthropological professional, and as part of the orphan daughter's drive to conserve "the folklore of her mother's speech community."[48] Indeed, Hurston's first novel, *Jonah's Gourd Vine*, served as fictional wake for Hurston's parents (Lucy and John) as well as an attempt to mend broken connections and promises. These broken promises included the mother's admonition to her daughter to insist on departure from the community's traditional death rites. On her deathbed, Lucy instructs nine-year-old Isie (Zora) to intervene against the practice of pulling the pillow from the head (intended to ease transition into death) and the traditional covering of the clock and mirror. The child proves unsuccessful, and the adulterous John soon dreads Lucy's freed spirit in Oya's winds: "That night a wind rose about the house and blew from the kitchen wall to a clump of oleanders that screened the chicken house, from the oleanders to the fence palings and back again to the house wall, and the pack of dogs followed it, rearing against the wall, leaping and pawing the fence, howling, barking and whining until the break of day" (113–14).

John's preacherly, performative life is the focus of this novel dedicated to honoring (and transforming) something of the imparted broughtupsy of the mother. John's life gets funeralized at novel's end (and eulogized throughout) with an insistence on *African* American congregational rites. The text invokes

"O-go-doe, the ancient drum" and "voice of Death," swinging his Baptist funeral service: "With the drumming of the feet, and the mournful dance of the heads, in rhythm, it was ended" (168).

As contrarian modern text, *Their Eyes Were Watching God* calls for acts of mourning going lower than Zora's mother, Lucy Hurston, ever likely embraced—even as it may be driven by the mother's independent-minded savoir-faire. The novel moves (in)famously away from models of racial uplift, northward urbanization, and bourgeois ideological ascent (symbolized by the raised front porch and the organ in the parlor). Janie leaves behind her grandmother's desire for a sermon "about colored women sittin' on high" (187) and taking "a stand on high ground" (188) as she moves ever lower in social and geographic positioning, traveling southward into the Okeechobee muck, into the mires of a regional (circum-Caribbean) folk culture, to face death and its flows of abjection head-on: the "manure pile after a rain," the blood required of "[r]eal gods" (293), the "black earth clinging to bodies and biting the skin like ants" (282), the rabid slobber of her initiating lover as he is possessed by some strange snarling thing. Abjection and sublimity share low terrain in a Rain-Bringing text that summons "[t]he monstropolous beast" of the Okeechobee out of its diked bed (305).

Their Eyes commences with invocations of the Oya-deluged dead: "The beginning of this was a woman and she had come back from burying the dead . . . the sodden and the bloated; the sudden dead" (175). The novel's windswept breath of life moves through death-traps of bourgeois aspiration and patriarchal protection set everywhere. Janie's first husband, Logan Killicks, whom she married for his land, is already an ancestor: "He look like some ole skull-head in de grave yard" (185). To her second husband, Janie announces, "you ain't de Jody ah run off down de road wid. You'se whut's left after he died" (244). Following the deathly end of her first two zombifying marriages, Janie meets life in the muck with Vergible "Tea Cake" Woods. The Oya-driven sweep of the text, however, forces her to kill and bury that life as well. Finally at novel's end, "[c]ombing the road-dust out of her hair" and "[t]hinking" (333), Janie/Rain-Bringer honors the "roads" of an initiate life and recuperates the dust of ancestors as empowering sources.

So it is only after Janie's travels, after speaking of the brass band's funeral grooves for Tea Cake back in the muck, that Janie concludes the sharing of her tale with Pheoby by projecting another grove—the garden she intends to plant "for remembrance" (332), presumably at "the right time of the moon" from seeds Tea Cake bought just before his death (331). Janie's/Rain-Bringer's "liminoid" memory garden—allied to the Creole gardens of New Orleans and Fort-de-France—honors a *konesans* communicable within the gro(o)ves the novel constructs.[49] Like the hip-shaking Ella Wall of *Mules and Men*, Janie is ready to share her dawn and doom story: "[T]ell 'em [bout me]," she says to Pheoby, even as she has Pheoby realize that "they" cannot receive what has been shared in this narrative grove "cause dey's parched up from not knowin' things" (332). Indeed, ground may be so parched as to not be able to receive the rain brought to it, and this is a parching born of a cultivated lack of konesans.

All of Rain-Bringer's initiate work aims to remodel and cultivate the sacred in a manner similar to Nigerian and Afro-creole Ifa divination repertory. To get more accurately at Hurston's peculiar Gulf South conservatism, we may turn to an Ifa divination tale that found a place in the memory garden of Mules and Men. In an Ifa tale for the figure Otura Obara, Earth seeks divination to bear a child. Told "the child would wear a crown" but that Earth must sacrifice so that her child would be crowned while Earth "was still alive to see it," Earth neglects the sacrifice and dies while her son is just a boy. After the son becomes king, a farmer cultivating yams on Mother Earth's forgotten grave hears Earth cry to him: "Ha! Did you chop my head with your hoe?" When the farmer runs to tell the king of this strange talking skull—vowing on his own head to the veracity of the tale—he precipitates a cycle of violence. The king sends various officials to verify the tale, and the skull's subsequent silence leaves the oath-bound farmer decapitated, whereupon the hitherto silent skull asks the farmer's executioners accusingly, "Ha! Did you kill someone?" The scene is repeated with the official witnesses to the skull's speech being executed by other government officials, until the king intervenes directly and divination-prescribed sacrifices for the skull (Earth) bring reparation as well as a restoration of credibility linking speech and act. True to its prescriptive function, the tale ends with a plan of action for its client, announcing that a neglected ancestor demands proper burial or graveside attention: "Ifa says that there is a dead person who has not been buried. Ifa says we should hurry and bury this dead person in fine style, so that it will not draw many people to their death after it." Amidst cycles of violent contagion, a forgotten ancestor, Mother Earth herself, insists on ritual respect and sacrificial reparations to be carried out by the son for "sins" of the parent.[50]

The Ifa divination tale of Earth's speaking skull is reassembled and given voice in "High Walker and the Bloody Bones," a tale from Mules and Men. Here, High Walker, who "had power" to get cemetery bones to rise and shake and do an egungun dance, encounters a skull that speaks back to him, telling him "My mouf brought me here and if you don't mind, your'n will bring you here" (170). After rushing to report this incredible oracular experience to the white man, Walker attests to his credibility with an oath: "If it don't speak, you kin chop mah head off right where it at" (170). It should come as no surprise that when the skull refuses to speak, the white man lops off Walker's head, after which the "skull head" remarks to his new neighbor, "Ah told you dat mouf brought me here and if you didn't mind out it'd bring you here" (170). The bones then rise and shake, terrifying the white murderer and speaking collectively, in congregation: "De bloody bones say, 'We got High Walker and we all bloody bones now in de drift together'" (170). The "High Walker" story carries occult warning and sacrificially fed instruction from the African dead. It speaks from enduring Afro-creole junctures of the religious and the juridical and especially from a *konesans* of the difficulties of reliable two-way communication across gulfs of our contact zones. The white man is left haunted by a nondisclosable secret knowledge. Hurston herself seems well aware that this body of gulf knowledge—from the bloody bones in the drift together to Mother Earth's talking skull—places dread claims on humanity itself. Thus, Hurston took up obligations to the skull-head of Earth herself, a conservatism that would seem anachronistic but which she found necessary to the establishment of any credible practice of holistic relation. If we ask then, May folk remembrance speak to moderns? (or "does the subaltern speak?"), the answer is clearly *yes . . . but don't stake your head on having other folk hear it.*

Hurston's respect for ancestors and their landscapes of residence is one key unifier of her entire body of work. A recuperative vision drives *Mules and Men* and *Their Eyes Were Watching God* to conjoin subalternized knowledges to new openings in diasporic modernism for women's agency.[51] Yet Hurston herself was to lie forgotten—her gravesite unmarked, her body of work out of circulation—until Alice Walker took it upon herself to honor this most indispensable of American culture-bearers.[52] When Hurston wrote to W. E. B. Du Bois in 1945 with a plan to establish a national "cemetery for the illustrious Negro dead," she asserted, "[l]et no Negro celebrity, no matter what financial condition they might be in at death, lie in inconspicuous forgetfulness." She further insisted, "We must assume the responsibility of their graves being known and honored." Hurston knew the spiritual and political costs of such neglect since "the lack of such a tangible thing allows our people to forget, and their spirits evaporate."[53] She proposed a hundred acres in Florida's subtropical lake country, starting, she suggested, with reburial of the dust of the bones of Nat Turner. To plan to open such a memory garden with ceremonial reburial of Nat Turner is to assert another kind of authority. As her first two books insisted with "High Walker and the Bloody Bones" and the novelized wake for her parents in *Jonah's Gourd Vine*, and as *Their Eyes Were Watching God* brings to rich detail in its funeralizings (for a mule, Jody Starks, and Tea Cake), Hurston attended to death rites in order to conserve a full range of potential resources for the living so that our spirits might not evaporate in patterns of drought, dread, and violence.

It makes sense that death rites have marked some of the ultimately policed color lines in the South, with the resting places of the dead being among the last legally desegregated spaces. Hurston writes of the Palm Beach hurricane aftermath in *Their Eyes:* "miserable, sullen men, black and white under guard had to keep searching for bodies and digging graves. A huge ditch was dug across the white cemetery and a big ditch was opened across the black grave-yard" (314). Told "they makin' coffins fuh all de white folks" and that he must be careful to separate corpses by race, Tea Cake asserts, "Look lak dey think God don't know nothin' 'bout de Jim Crow law" (314). Tea Cake's cosmic conservatism (conserving the basilectal critical voice and the soul repertoires of subalternized humanity) signifies on the blasphemous hypocrisies of a Jim Crow conservatism that guards uninterrupted access to goods and power. Tea Cake laughingly adds that this nationalized Jim Crow brand of civility directs blacks without white sponsorship to be "tried and sentenced tuh six months behind de United States privy house at hard smellin'" (315). This hard-to-escape national privy house smells much like our own "Dirty South."

Often noted for refusing to vocalize black rage, Hurston should be reread for her blues laughter and artful cursing in the face of doing time at hard smelling in the nation's southern privy house. For starters, we could turn to the blistering curse attributed to Marie Laveau in *Mules and Men,* delivered in righteous anger since "My home has been disrespected, my children have been cursed and ill-treated. My dear ones have been back-bitten and their virtue questioned" (187). This Laveau/Rain-Bringer curse is of such extended (three-paragraph) virtuosity that it need not be repeated to readers likely to recognize its longstanding effects and its continuing Dirty South vocalizations. Readers focusing on the bright side of Rain-Bringer must also tend to the "mean and impressive" side, the ill-treated bones of Nat Turner, High Walker, and Earth herself.[54] Working to (con)serve the spirits of Afro-creole memory that disrupt universalizing conservatisms, liberalisms, and radical "isms" of Euro-creole hegemony, Rain-Bringer's is a testy prophetic "road" of Oya that reminds us of obligation to the unattended dead, calls all our bloodied bones—caught in the drift together—into oaths of renegotiated relation.

The Wonders of the Forest—Oya's Shape-shifting Ecologies

In "Swamp Sublime: Ecologies and Resistance in the American Plantation Zone," Monique Allewaert argues that "[t]he entanglements that prolifer-ated in the plantation zone disabled taxonomies distinguishing the hu-man from the animal from the vegetable from the atmospheric, revealing an assemblage of interpenetrating forces that I call an ecology."[55] The deep basilectal sources of creolization—African and indigenous—conserve ori-entations to a world of ecosystemic interpenetration. The bodies of knowl-edge surrounding the orisha Oya—whether the orisha appears in human, atmospheric, animal, or botanical form—have long been built upon this interpenetrative awareness. In the swamp or Everglades, much as Allewaert observes, "the possibility of an Anglo-European sublime vanishes" (345). The terra firma of an all-encompassing vantage point or objective (and objectifying) perspective of detachment is hard to find in Hurston's Gulf South. Since Euro-colonials perceived that Africans and natives could navigate the swamp's ecology more adeptly than they themselves could (350), one recourse of white colonial mastery, according to Allewaert, was in "[r]epresentations that bound Africans to swamps" and that "worked to delegitimize ecological knowledge by making it into a sign of primitivism" (353). It is precisely here that Hurston's twentieth-century forays into Florida's swamps and into circum-Caribbean bodies of *konesans* prove most revolutionary and contestatory. For Hurston's embrace of "Rain-Bringer" authority and her southerly compass setting took ecosystemic directive at a time when so many other authors (in the South and the Caribbean) were following an urban, true-north bearing bound up with the old Enlightenment project of producing model citizen-subjects.

Mules and Men moves in another direction. It presents the Gulf South's spiritual foster-daughter of the Haitian Revolution, Marie Laveau, as its authoritative reader of what Hurston later called "the three layers of life" (an eco-semiotics of intermeshed plant, animal, and human life; tied to a divinatory ability to "see and feel the immense past, what is now, and feel inside you something of what is to come").[56] The "Rain-Bringer" initiation narrated in *Mules and Men* depicts Laveau's three-layered altar-work summoning lightning-flashes over Pontchartrain as "the lake heaved like a mighty herd of cattle rolling in the pasture" (185). Buffalo herds (and in the Americas, bison, cattle, or deer) are Oya's animal avatars. Having once crossed paths with an isolate buffalo near the headwaters of the Gambia River, watching it whirl round in rapid decision of flight or fight, I can attest to the dread power Oya repertoires convey of the most dangerous animal in the African bush. Hurston's Rain-Bringer work forces us to re-essay our ecosystemic knowledge of relation—the loss of wetlands, diminishment of a three-layers-of-life vision, the likelihood that the planet's heated energies (from burning a fossil time's photosynthetic energies to fuel our own moment of time-space compression) may birth more destructive storms and droughts.

As rain-bringing manifestation of Atlantic storms, mother of the nine *egungun* who mediate ancestral passages, and finally as shape-shifting buffalo-woman of the bush, Oya's fields of agency are familiar to Hurston's readers: the contact zone of the abject and sublime, maroonings in wilderness, in hunting and fishing, border crossings beyond nature/culture binaries. Oya teaches us a certain courted and learned permeability. Her bellowing *"heyi!"* cry of possession hails us with a difference. As "the only Orisha to arise out of the animal," Gleason writes, only Oya "is willing to assume a mediating position between the living and the dead at funerals, because her animal nature protects her . . . because Death stands somewhere behind it [the animal], or inside it, not out there in a projected future." In Oya's water buffalo avatar, devotees may find a fluid terrain where "animal wisdom and ancestral representation coalesce."[57]

To follow Rain-Bringer's paths into what Barbara Ladd calls the sublime's "proving ground of authority and authorship," we enter Florida's mucks in an act of tracking akin to the hunt.[58] Here, Oya's shape-shifting takes forms that Hurston incorporated, most visibly in an Ifa tale for the sign Osa Ogunda, in which a hunter spies a buffalo cow from his stand. After the buffalo shucks her hide to become a beautiful market woman, the hunter secretly steals the hide, follows the woman to market, and wins her submission to marriage with an oath to never reveal her identity. Within a few years, Buffalo-woman's "bush" fertility arouses the jealousy of the hunter's co-wives, and her husband drunkenly breaks his oath to her, revealing the secret of her origin to his wives. Remorseful for this betrayal, he soon comes to his wilderness wife's defense against the mockeries of her human co-wives, demanding, "What do you skinny women know / Of the wonders of the forest?"[59] By then, however, Buffalo-woman has slipped into her rehydrated old skin to begin acts of deadly revenge against her hounding tormentors before returning to the wilderness. Just before her disappearance, she breaks off one of her horns to give to her now orphaned children and abandoned husband as a means of communication with her bush powers. Oya returns to the wilderness, leaving husband to hunt new wives in town and otherly companionship elsewhere, and leaving her initiate children orphaned yet with sustenance and communications from beyond.[60] Readers of Rain-Bringer can see that she felt drawn to both Buffalo-woman and hunterly roles. A single letter gets at this most playfully. Writing of fishing from her houseboat and her fondness for hushpuppies and softshell turtle, Hurston shared a postscript on the wonders of the forest with her "three layers of life" Florida "sister," Marjorie Kinnan Rawlings: "Literary secret: I am getting fat where a cow does under the tail."[61]

Hurston's earliest manuscript of traditional Gulf-South narrative performance contains a tale of the forest's carnal wonders, "The Orphan Boy and Girl and the Witches," with precedent in an Ifa Irete Ose narrative of hunting dogs saving a treed master from being eaten by witches (usually a shape-shifting bush seductress and her herd).[62] The Ifa tale of a hunter's encounter with a forest-spirit foresees the finding of a breathtaking spouse "who will be with our soul," but who might also "carry our soul away."[63] Hurston knew the shape-shifter to be a breath-taking hunter herself, one who could—much like a Caribbean soucouyant—"git out her skin and go ride people."[64] Marooning as she did, outside of bourgeois social convention, Hurston has been criticized for what Homi Bhabha dismisses as a strategy of "representing authority in terms of the artifice of the archaic." It was not, however, obsession with the archaic that kept Hurston afield tracking shape-shifting traces of orisha-presence. She tracked what inhabits the in-between spaces of repressed alterity and hybridity, entanglements wherein, as Bhabha proclaims, "we may elude the politics of polarity and emerge as the others of ourselves."[65]

Hurston's frontier-savvy elasticity of consciousness emerges from both basilectal Afro-creole modernity and from modernism's return to the primal and its ecosystemic entanglements. Her ritual crowning as Rain-Bringer revealed the skin-shedding other of herself to be the snake, yet Oya's herds move familiarly through her work and take us into a "preservative ethos" as Gleason remarks of the hunt's sacrificial economy, "which goes back as far as the mind can imagine a distinction ever having been made between ourselves and the other species."[66] With the opening storm of *Jonah's Gourd Vine* comes Oya's emblematic presence: the mother "took the cow-horn that hung on the wall and placed it to her lips" to call her sons (3). Out-of-control libidinal energy (an oath-breaking or erotic indiscretion) leads the novel's protagonist, John, to the Yoruba hunter's trouble divined in the Ifa tale. John "was really searching for a lost self and crying like the old witch with her shed skin shrunken by red pepper and salt" (153). Carnal intimacies of hunting and fishing often script Hurston's scenes of mutually satisfying, marooning romance, as in John's marriage proposal to Sally in *Jonah's Gourd Vine*: "Less go git married and den got [*sic*] set on de fish pond and ketch us uh mess uh speckled perches fuh supper" (159). In *Their Eyes Were Watching God*, Tea Cake Woods shows his desire to share a life outside the domesticating confines of bourgeois conventions by insisting on taking Janie fishing. And after listening to Mrs. Woods tell of love on the muck, Pheoby is converted, swearing, "Lawd! . . . Ah means tuh make Sam take me fishin' wid him after this" (332). When the book ends, Janie's life has been "broomed out" by Oya, and the textual cast-net of her memory catches "[s]o much of life in its meshes!" (333). That Hurston found deep peace in fishing from her Florida houseboat should surprise no close reader.

The hunt in *Their Eyes Were Watching God* centers on Janie's initiation as rabbit-and-gator-hunting Mrs. Woods, who quickly "got to be a better shot than Tea Cake" (281). Her transformation marks an utterly transformed "Alphabet" (Janie's earliest name), one who—after being saved from hurricane floodwaters by a swimming cow—can, weeks later, have the self-possession to kill her snarling, rabies-stricken husband with one shot. Following Tea Cake's beating of Janie and his sentimentally narrated claims to paternalistic control, the novel's narrative logic ultimately demands the monstropolous bestiality of the storm and rabid dog to take Tea Cake's life and blood. Tea Cake teaches Janie how to handle a gun only to enable her to become woman enough to shoot him and stand trial for the killing. Mimetic desire (to be like Tea Cake Woods) drives the novel toward violence: "Real gods require blood." Janie becomes "her sacrificing self with Tea Cake's head in her lap," and she "thanked him wordlessly for giving her the chance for loving service."[67] The story of Janie Woods's gender marooning, her refusal to be the hunter's game, her insistence on being a gun-toting player, her mature rapport with the bush, may have found some of its own initiation just months before the writing of *Their Eyes*, in Jamaica where Hurston accompanied maroons on a five-day wild boar hunt that ended in flavorful jerk pork.[68]

Hurston seems to have recognized the Jamaican maroons' counterparts in the hunters of the Everglades of her native Florida. There she encountered Seminoles (from Spanish *cimarrón*)—the Florida maroons who had welcomed black maroons and assimilated "all who spoke their language."[69] Hurston recognized Florida (and really the entire Gulf South) as a prime marooning space, a location for originating identities and orientations unbound by "domestic" Anglo-nationalist readings of America (or African America). She knew that Cuban, Bahamian, Haitian, West Indian, and Seminole bodies of knowledge had been circulating in Florida in ever-creolizing ways.[70] Her Florida was aflow with "the boiled-down juice of human living," which she saw as "still emerging from the lush glades" with a peculiarly "Florida flavor . . . accumulated in this sort of culture delta."[71] She glimpsed too that the entanglements of postplantation cultures in Florida pointed to dynamic narrative arts unified by an Afro-creole/indigenous core that could substantiate a more holistic consciousness of relation:

> Also in Florida are the Cuban-African and the Bahaman-African folk tales. It is interesting to note that the same Brer Rabbit tales of the American Negro are told by these islanders. One also finds the identical tales in Haiti and the British West Indies. Since it is not possible for these same stories to have arisen in America and become so widely distributed through the western world wherever the Negro exists, the wide distribution denotes a common origin in West Africa. It has been noted by Carita Doggett Corse that these same tales are told by Florida Indians. But this does not mean that they are purely Indian tales . . . On the contrary, it merely accentuates the amount of contact which the Negroes have had with Southeastern Indians in the past. Since it is well known that runaway slaves fled to the Indian communities of southern Georgia and Florida in great numbers, the explanation of the Brer Rabbit tales among Indians is obvious.[72]

These tales link the trickster cycles and divination rites of Nigeria and Mali, Cuba and Brazil and the West Indies with the fabulous encounters narrated by Joel Chandler Harris, recorded by ethnographers among the Creeks and Seminoles, and performed by Hurston herself. Rain-Bringer's Florida was a fluid state of convergence where new ritual families shared old tales to refamiliarize new ground.

In relation to national norms, Florida is certainly a marginal frontier or liminoid time-space devoid of "real" trees, real seasons, and even real culture or history. In relation to most of the rest of the hemisphere and to the black Atlantic, however, Florida can offer the closest thing in North America to the normative ecologies and cultural affiliations of home. In *Jonah's Gourd Vine*, when Lucy moves from Alabama to Florida, an atavistic or soul sense of ecological homecoming is conveyed, from which her prior life had been orphaned: "Lucy sniffed sweet air laden with night-blooming jasmine and wished that she had been born in this climate. She seemed to herself to be coming home. This was where she was meant to be. The warmth, the foliage, the fruits all seemed right and as God meant her to be surrounded. The smell of ripe guavas was new and alluring but somehow did not feel strange" (93).

As with the muck of *Their Eyes Were Watching God* where the domesticated goes marooning—"big beans, big cane, big weeds . . . [g]round so rich that everything went wild" (280), or the "creaming" blossom of Janie's pear tree, or the Haitian Mambo's revelation in *Tell My Horse* that "[t]here is no mystery beyond the mysterious source of life" (376)—this is landscape in which nature is neither exterior to humanity nor a mirror of the self but immanent: a familiar strangeness.

Whether in the Everglades or on the St. Johns River aboard the sprawling *City of Jacksonville*, Hurston wrote as a native to the mysterious source of life:

> The boat trip was thrilling on the side-wheeler *City of Jacksonville*. The water life, the smothering foliage that draped the river banks, the miles of purple hyacinths, all thrilled me anew. The wild thing was back in the jungle.
> . . . Wild hogs appearing now and then along the shore. 'Gators, disturbed by the wash, slipping off of palm logs into the stream. Schools of mullet breaking water now and then. Flocks of water fowl disturbed at the approach of the steamer, then settling back again to feed. Catfish as long as a man pacing the boat like porpoises for kitchen scraps.[73]

This marooning return to native land shares the hunter's desire to slip past domestic frontiers to enter a zone of intercourse with the other. We should also note, however, that her reentry into subtropic "jungle" points our attention to the nonnativeness of much of the "smothering foliage." There had been no "miles of purple hyacinths" on the St. Johns River or anywhere else in North America prior to the Louisiana cotton exposition of 1884–85. The "Wild hogs" came to Florida with the Spanish. From Hurston's Floridian vantage point, we see an aqueous terrain of marooning, creolizing systems. Here, native, invasive, and acclimated creole systems interact in a shape-shifting manner that aligned the West African Oya with the Mayan deity Hurakan and brought "the wild thing" (Rain-Bringer/Zora) to write from her hyacinth-lined, native, jungle waters.

Winds of Orisha—Between-beat Dance Possibility

In her Oya-inspired poem, "Winds of Orisha," Audre Lorde channeled something of Rain-Bringer's mean and impressive side:

> instead of an answer to their search for rain they will read me
> the dark cloud
> meaning something entire
> and different[74]

We may indeed read "something entire and different" in Rain-Bringer's "dark cloud." What has been least understood is the conservative, trauma-tested ethos at work in Rain-Bringer's authority, preserving and transforming "something entire and different." Rain-Bringer's work as conservator of an ethos at the core of Afro-Atlantic religion truly "brings it" to textuality: a different kind of conservatism, working from basilectal agency and nevertheless wholly modern.

Hurston's identification as Rain-Bringer and her invocation of Oya have rarely been taken seriously and could be dismissed as whimsical self-fashioning by an artist who built a career inventorying exotic and potentially remunerative traditions of the folk. Of her entry into the spirits' hermeneutic circles she wrote, "I did not find them any more invalid than any other religion."[75] "People need religion," she insisted, "because the great masses fear life and its consequences," and added, "I do not pray" because "I accept the means at my disposal for working out my destiny."[76] Still, it is hard to see the spirited rites of Afro-creole practice as the avoidance of life that Hurston recognized in scriptural religions which have repressed both the body and female power itself. Perhaps she did not pray to the "Man-God" addressed in *Mules and Men* (187), but her writing suggests other means at her disposal.[77] I insist, along with Edward Pavlić and Teresa Washington, that Hurston's Rain-Bringer/Oya initiation and visionary intuition (crowned on an Afro-Baptist base) presented her with more substantial authorial and personal grounding than has been recognized. But I also agree with John Lowe that her belief system was protean, moving between idiosyncratic "syncretic beliefs" and the "skepticism that kept them in a shape-shifting boil."[78] She consistently gave herself to what Karen McCarthy Brown calls the "inseparably mind-and-body" rites of Afro-Atlantic religion to reach her own between-beat attenuating response.[79] As Hurston explained in a letter to Franz Boas, "I mean by attenuation, the listener to the drum will feel the space between beats and will think up devices to fill those spaces. The between-beat becomes more and more complicated untill [*sic*] the music is all between-beat and the consciousness of the dependence upon the drum id [*sic*] lost."[80] Moving to the between-beat, Hurston is the model of the insider/outsider described by Trinh T. Minh-ha: "She stands in that undetermined threshold place where she constantly drifts in and out . . . the Inappropriate Other/Same who moves about with always at least two/four gestures."[81]

Pitched "headfirst into the Baptist Church when I was born," Hurston acknowledged in her autobiography that Afro-Baptist rites "were a part of me" (713). Although she contended with the theology and patriarchal heft of scripture, she remained a child of Baptist performance traditions. Insisting that "Negro-made church music is dance possible," she calls the Sanctified Church "a revitalizing element in Negro music and religion."[82] From her work on Baptist and Pentecostal churches to her New Orleans study in Mother Catherine's Spiritualist Temple, and from within Jamaican balmyards, Kumina, Voudou, Vodou, and elements of Afro-Cuban tradition, Hurston sought to revitalize circulation of an Afro-Atlantic Gulf Stream of spirituality. Rain-Bringer's "sanctified" attenuation of scriptural authority was simultaneously culturally conservative (of Afro-creole roots) and modern—as exemplified in the jazz-backed preaching of Mother Catherine Seals: "Don't teach what the apostles and the prophets say. Go to the tree and get the pure sap and find out whether they were right."[83] In *Their Eyes Were Watching God,* a maturely authorized Rain-Bringer went to the tree, to the truth and its mystery, and transformed Mother Catherine's injunction for her own novel ministry.

Since Hurston herself has become a much-invoked godmother of many branches of disciplinary and popular attention, we would do well to attend to the politics of her enshrinement as saint. She was, of course, no saint in the Christian sense. Her great leaps of faith and fearlessness could be followed by fear and faithlessness, fed by the difficulties of her insider/outsider position in the Caribbean, the Polk County jooks, at Columbia University or Barnard, or the daily trials of life in the Jim Crow South. She often emphasized the sensational and exotic in writing on "Voodoo," and her words of support for military occupation of Haiti are hard to stomach.[84] But as much heat as Hurston has taken for her conservatism (which could at times be naïve, self-protective, and/or born of creolized ties to Euro-conservative southern values), the grounding of her Afro-conservationist southern ethos lay elsewhere, outside the policings of nation, closer to the performative zone of loving ones that Paul Gilroy has described as a "politics of transfiguration" and that Cornel West envisioned as a "politics of conversion."[85]

Although Hazel Carby argued influentially that Hurston fostered "a discourse of nostalgia" for black folklife in the rural South, allegedly rewriting the representational boundaries of black southerners "in relation to the Caribbean rather than to the northern states," critics from Daphne Lamothe to Edward Pavlić, Teresa Washington, and Martyn Bone have situated Hurston's boundary-crossing work within the ongoing concerns and migrations of the black Atlantic.[86] Going beyond an aesthetic mining of folklore and rural nostalgia, Rain-Bringer's immersion in Afro-creole repertory locates its authority within hermeneutic circles that have navigated New World (and new World) contact situations and wrought much that made the modern ethos possible. Finding ensoulment in Oya rites, Hurston created new openings for congregation across nations and regions, catching wind of hurricane forces that are no respecters of frontiers, of ancestors to whom we are all variously indebted, and of shape-shifting zones that call us to the gaps between beats in attenuation of forces that would own and consume our lives.

CHAPTER SIX

"Vamonos pa'l Monte"
Into Florida's Repeating Bush

. . . anyone who dares set out
For *el monte*, heedless of pagans,
If he returns alive, will have a heart
Full of arrows and heartlessness.
—Father Alonso Gregorio de Escobedo,
   La Florida (fortress St. Augustine, 1605)

American history shall be viewed as factual, not as constructed, shall be viewed
as knowable, teachable, and testable, and shall be defined as the creation of a
new nation based largely on the universal principles stated in the Declaration
of Independence.
—from Act Relating to Education, signed by Governor Jeb Bush (Tallahassee, 2006)

There are occurrences that are not included in written history, they escape people's
knowledge for one reason or another, because they were intentionally erased, or
they were not contemplated or understood, or they occurred in a time outside of
time itself, and the true reality, in all its un-reality, disappears after closer and more
obvious realities.
—Lydia Cabrera, *Cuentos para adultos niños y retrasados mentales*, 1983

It makes sense that Yemaya was the first orisha with whom I had sustained
ritual contact within *Regla de Ocha* (Santería). The mother of waters, oceans,
terrestrial life, she is the genius of first contacts and aqueous beginnings. Her
beach offerings grew increasingly familiar: fruit, flowers, and candles left at
surf's edge, fried pork rinds and plantains surrounding seven pennies. Her
public face—the Virgin of Regla—confronted me daily in neighborhood bo-
degas that double as *botánicas* (spiritual supply shops) where her image on
rows of candles found constantly marketed display. Through a life of travels (hers tied up with my own), something of her multiple manifestations
managed to wash past the breakwaters that my scriptural enculturations had
erected to thwart her free movement. Yemaya's spirit kin in Senegal first took
possession of me through abject fluidities: the traveler's swampings of diar-
rhea, vomiting, fever, linguistic disability, and imaginative inflexibility. After a year of drinking river water daily, my belly finally became a calm host

of the water djinn of the Senegal (Maam Kumba Bang). Having something of a spiritual cousin of Yemaya cultured deep in my gut (if not consecrated fully in my head) helped orient me to the Spirit(s) attending ocean baptisms I've witnessed in the Bahamas, Grenada, and on Sapelo Island in Georgia. Yemaya and Maam Kumba opened my eyes to the offerings of ritual economy I've seen on the beaches of Far Rockaway and Copacabana. Yemaya, Maam Kumba, and the orisha Oshun seem always aflow in the tidal pulsings of Atlantic musics, and manifest their orisha/djinn agency (ashé or genius) through the shape-shiftings and soundings of what English speakers have called "labor" and from within *its* source: what we call "the small death."

My first ritually organized entry into the sacred gro(o)ves of Afro-Cuban Santería came at a drumming or *bembe* in honor of Yemaya, led musically by one of Miami's most celebrated praise singers. The altar to Yemaya was a sumptuous assemblage. Layer upon layer of blue cloth—silk and satin—accented by translucent chiffon, backed and draped her altar with a most dramatic effect. Offerings of fruits and sweets and floral bouquets filled a straw mat on the floor in front of the altar, which centered on a cloth-draped and bead-encased container of the orisha's fundaments (the secretions of her power): a set of consecrated stones (*otanes*), divination cowries, and nautical-themed miniature tools (*herramientas*) concealed in a ceramic soup tureen draped for display on Yemaya's "throne." The space took on a splendor well conveyed in Judith Gleason's description of the multilayered cloth of African masquerades, dramatizing "the surfaces in order to stress the depth of what is thereby concealed."[1] This was the visible stage and analogue for the multi-layered rhythms the bata drummers soon generated.

The profound spiritual embodiment that would heat up the house later in dance was preceded by a solemn initial drum ceremony: the unaccompanied drum salute to Yemaya's throne. The sequence of drum salutes that the drummers played facing the throne is called the *oru de igbodu*, an invocation that transformed a rented upstairs public reception hall on a busy urban street into a true *igbodu* or sacred grove. In this space initiates who had cultivated an ability to be mounted by the spirit were the carriers of the necessary sacrificial labor of honor. Here, the spirit doing the mounting was recognized as female—the cosmic Mother of *las aguas* and *el monte*. This sacred grove of Yemaya hospitality accrued a sweat-drenched charge from the call-and-response chants in Lukumi (Cuban renderings of Yoruba) and the drums' polyrhythms, bringing nigh everyone present to dance, with many of the elder initiates moved to the point of possession by the end of a seven- or eight-hour ceremony. At the end, a ritual container of water, swirled and poured out into the street, moved the ceremonial dregs and "washwater" outside of the collective body. The cleansed congregation concluded with a ritual meal of chicken and plantains, black beans and rice. The ceremony, attended by

Cubans, Latin Americans from across the hemisphere, white Anglos, black Americans, and West Indians, gave its celebrants a sense that other weddings to social and spiritual reality remain possible.

Over time, such ceremonies have a way of imbuing the streets and walls that surround them with an affective patina of ashé grown from the ritual economy's repetition and duration within the heart of the contact zone. In *The Repeating Island*, Antonio Benítez-Rojo observes how one of the defining features of the Hispano-Caribbean is its citizens' moorings in enduring architectures of conquistadorial empire, for "there is no city in the Spanish Caribbean that does not hold a kind of cult worship of its castles and fortresses, its walls and cannons, and by extension the 'old' sections of the city, as with Old San Juan and Old Havana." He is well aware that the Caribbean's fortified cities bear witness to what historical narrative hides. *The Repeating Island* uses a trope both domestic and religious to convey how the fortress walls and colonial buildings of Old Havana and Old San Juan, Old Veracruz or St. Augustine, "have an almost occult prestige, which comes from what lies behind them, something like what's aroused in children by grandmother's huge wardrobe [*el gran escaparate de la abuela*]."[2] It is no accident that Benítez-Rojo uses the grandmother's armoire as trope for the "cult worship" of Spanish Caribbean colonial structures and the "occult prestige" linked to their walls of fossil stone. Within the fortress walls of cities built to guard the Spanish fleet lies a secret history of the contact zone. Herein something of the infidel's sacred bush (*el monte*) found reassertion in creole courtyard gardens and in armoires and china cabinets concealing the fundaments of the orishas.

Benítez-Rojo's linkage of Old Havana's stone walls and a grandmother's armoire (as objects of "cult worship") points knowing readers to the secret stones and divination sacra strategically swallowed, as tradition has it, by African initiates in the bellies of transatlantic slave ships. Such enshrining consumption and "passage" on the part of the subaltern continued in the Americas, allowing the blood-and-herb-fed sacra of the sacred bush to penetrate fortress walls and enter the wardrobes of saint veneration via the colonial city's domestic help, the lovers, guides, translators, and herbalists who dwelled within or along its fortress walls. Thus, in Afro-Cuban Santería the Yoruba initiate's *igbodu*—and something of the sacred groves of other African peoples as well as those of the indigenous Taino and Ciboney—found creolizing forms of agency within the very ramparts meant to exclude and intimidate the infidel. What was thought to be excluded from the fortress city shows up internally within its gated domestic space.

Residents, vendors, and initiates of Old Havana and Old San Juan can carry this chronotopic knowledge in the very movement of their bodies, as Benítez-Rojo observed in Havana during the missile crisis of 1962. Right then and there, as the aspiring writer faced the progressive march of apocalypse-bound time from his Havana balcony, "two old black women passed 'in a certain kind of way' beneath." He admits, "I cannot describe this 'certain kind of way'; I will say only that there was a kind of ancient and golden powder between their gnarled legs, a scent of basil and mint in their dress, a symbolic, ritual wisdom in their gesture and their gay chatter" that thrust him suddenly into an initiate "age of reason": "I knew then at once that there would be no apocalypse."[3] Although white men have a long history of projecting the most bizarre things upon the bodies of black elders, we must recognize the likelihood that something in the behaviors of these two women—restored "in a certain kind of way" as they moved past the colonial city's old stone walls—bears witness from beyond the time of History, the State, and the exam marked in #2 pencil.

The walk of the two women in Old Havana, pointedly not just one as Valérie Loichot has observed, asserts a *conocimiento* (knowledge, or *konesans*) that always leaves something to be imagined and performed since it does not move toward full disclosure.[4] Benítez-Rojo describes this "certain kind of way" in terms of "performance and rhythm," coupled with "something remote that reproduces itself and that carries the desire to sublimate apocalypse and violence: something obscure that comes from the performance" and "takes away the space that separates the onlooker from the participant."[5] What we have described as intent to swing, ethics of antiphony, polyrhythmic balancing, the limbo gateway, Benítez-Rojo presents as an affective know-how that may remove the gulf that blocks movement. It takes standardized time and space away and models its own *conocimiento* from an improvisational sense for what "unfolds irregularly and resists being captured by the cycles of clock and calendar . . . [a] realm of marine currents, of waves, of folds and double folds, of fluidity and sinuosity."[6]

Benítez-Rojo's steady invocation (in both *The Repeating Island* and his novel *Sea of Lintels*) of St. Augustine, Florida, as Spanish Caribbean space works to remind us that North America was a marginal frontier of Spain's transatlantic "Grandest Machine on Earth," built to extract the wealth of Mexico and Peru via the Indies.[7] As Benítez-Rojo points out, the "perfected model" of this machine "was set in motion in 1565" when "[Pedro] Menendez de Aviles, after slaughtering, with indifferent calm, nearly five hundred Huguenots who had settled in Florida, finished his network of fortified cities with the founding of St. Augustine, today the oldest city in the United States."[8] A fortified Florida frontier secured for Spain the homeward Gulf Stream return valve for its fleet system of intake (conquistadorial booty) and supply distribution, assuring Spain's control of transatlantic capital flows. Benítez-Rojo explains that "Menendez de Aviles's machine was complex in the extreme," a "huge assemblage of machines," with the fleet system itself being "a machine of ports, anchorages, sea walls, lookouts, fortresses, garrisons, militias, shipyards, storehouses, depots, offices, workshops, hospitals, inns, taverns, plazas, churches, palaces, streets, and roads," all "geared to be able to take greatest advantage of the energy of the Gulf Stream and the region's trade winds."[9] This is the global system into which Florida was fitted (and administered through Cuba) for a longer period of time than it has been under British and U.S. jurisdiction combined.

The two-county area along the coast of northeast Florida between the old French Huguenot Fort Caroline in Jacksonville (1564) and North America's oldest creole city, St. Augustine (1565), constitutes the oldest enduring contact zone between Europeans, Africans, and indigenous peoples in the United States. It is indeed a "First Coast" of the gated communities and ghettos of our transculturating experience. A certain staying power remains in judgments like those formed in the epic *La Florida* (1605) by Father Alonso Gregorio de Escobedo. Escobedo wrote of the cynic heartlessness instilled in soldiers who left the fortified Castillo de San Marcos and set out for the deep bush of *el monte* to support the evangelization of its indigenous pagans. Escobedo's epic poem observes with brutal clarity what sustains the conversion of Christendom's new subjects in Florida:

> Gunpowder, rendering the treacherous prudent
> Breaks their resolve.
> Powder, when it lands on the head
> Of the bravest, most spirited man
> Gives him virtue if he is insolent
> And obedience to the inobedient man.[10]

Escobedo's epic, completed by the fortieth anniversary of the Spanish founding of St. Augustine and before the English settled Jamestown, receives scant attention in a contemporary Florida that marginalizes its own long witness in favor of narratives guarding the legitimacy of Anglo founding fathers: the nonconstructed, knowable, teachable, and testable chronology of the Massachusetts City on a Hill, the Philadelphia of 1776, a new machinery of obedience answering the Liberty Bell's cracked hailing.

Whether in Old South Jacksonville or St. Augustine, or south of that South in Miami's creolizing space, Florida repeats itself as an "un-American" frontier of the nation, a multi-ethnic borderland, a point of contested migration and immigration, a location of repeating racialized violence, and a divinatory contact space. In contemporary Florida we may set out for *el monte* even by heading to town, where an aesthetics of the earth has been reassembled in miniaturized sacred groves, gardens, and household altars where orisha stones reside within soup tureen–packed armoires. The orishas depend on this cultivation of *el monte* inside urban space to remain circulating in human affairs. Their fundaments (stones, ritual tools, and divination shells) "are 'born' by being washed in the herbal liquid called osain and 'fed' with animal blood," as Michael Mason explains.[11] The ritual economy or ecology of the reproduction and feeding of orisha fundaments may well be necessary to the maintenance of unalienated human rapport with *el monte*.

Literature may also house a nonalienated rapport with the bush and foster a means of neutralizing violence or deferring the march of apocalyptic (progressive, eschatological) time. If Wai Chee Dimock is right in asserting that "[l]iterature is the home of nonstandard space and time," then we may come to read the literature of Florida's ecologies and fortress spaces more richly—for the ways this literature may avoid containment within nationally accredited maps and periodicities.[12] Lydia Cabrera's *El monte* (1954) provides a grand model for such reading. Cabrera's many collections of Afro-Cuban folktales, coupled with the Muskogee Creek tales penned by Earnest Gouge in *New Fire* (1915, 2004), restore much of the older occult patina that has been scoured from Florida's (and the Gulf South's) collective imagination. The Miami-executed performance art of Ana Mendieta and the work of Miami-based poet Adrian Castro also host enduring creolizing linkages routed through Florida. In contemporary Miami it is easy enough to find a spirit house (*ilé*) of Regla de Ocha or one of a number of other Caribbean faiths, along with the more visible botanicas that serve as herbal and religious supply shops. All this takes on an Internet presence too, with sites maintained by established ritual leaders such as Willie Ramos and Ernesto Pichardo. A remarkable ethnobotanical/ecosystemic knowledge of Florida's *montes* and cross-cultural frontiers has been circulating in print from the era of Escobedo's epic *La Florida* and El Inca Garcilaso de la Vega's *Historia de la Florida* (1605) to our own moment's south Florida textual herbariums cultivated by Edwidge Danticat, Adrian Castro, Betty Mae Jumper, Robert Antoni, and many others.

Fundamentos—From Menendez's Machine to the Miami Sound Machine

A circum-Caribbean botanical pharmacy activates the collection *Cantos to Blood and Honey* (1997) by Miami-based performance poet and Ifa herbalist/priest Adrian Castro. Castro's bush-medicated, *osain*-steeped collection is bookended by its opening and closing doubled poem(s): "In the Beginning (I)" and "In the Beginning (II)." In these, Castro revises the biblical word of Genesis in favor of a language imbued with the affect or ashé of ritual performance. "In the Beginning (I)" summons the birth sounds of forced labor, the marks of a people's reassembly and emergence from the sugar plantation:

There were wails echoing
from riverbanks
mining for gold
fertility hidden in shells & stones
cascades made everyone
quietly deaf
In the beginning there were chains
entwined on legs like serpents on sugar cane
the bleeding syrup made the steel stick
many horses were bitten with machetes
There were processions of scars & piercing
tattoos talkin' bout tribe y history
bits of flesh flew from whips
& landed on island soil
(giving birth to a new people)

Crio-o-o-o-o-ollo!13

In the beginning, chain-entwined and formed out of mutilating reorientations, is the word *criollo*, announcing—as we have seen in El Inca Garcilaso de la Vega's *History of Florida*—a new identity: "the Negroes designate all persons criollos who have been born in the Indies of either pure Spanish or pure Negro parents."14 This new orientation recognized by the enslaved in their children born in the Americas points to the first self-conscious native Americanness, a recognition of being *native* to *this* contact zone. In the decade in which the word *criollo* finds definition in Garcilaso's *History of Florida* (1605) we also find the first appearance of *criollo* in Cuban literature in the poem *Espejo de paciencia* by Silvestre de Balboa, used to identify the locally born black hero of a 1604 smugglers' rebellion.15 As Benítez-Rojo observes, this is also the time when "the supersyncretic cult of the Virgen de la Caridad del Cobre appears . . . [in el Cobre, outside of Santiago de Cuba] a fusion of the cults of Atabey (Taino), Oshun (Yoruba), and Our Lady" in the aftermath of the Virgin's appearance to a stormswept trio in their open boat: "Juan Criollo, Juan Indio, and Juan Esclavo."16 This is the new people of Castro's "In the Beginning (I)." A new drink of communion, rum, also enters our pharmacies within a decade or so of the concept of the *criollo*, both produced as byproducts of the machineries of sugar and conquest, their "bleeding syrup."

The *criollo* voice of *Cantos to Blood and Honey*, however, keeps recalling how African "national" congregations of "Yoruba, Arará / Kongo, Carabalí" (the primary African nations remembered in Cuba) faced the daunting work of social reassembly. Castro offers an herbal medicine-gourd of restored behaviors:

talkin' 'bout tribe y history
who they be where
they come from
Ifé, Guinea, Oyo, Dahomey,
Takua, Iyesha
They gathered among the breeze
In tribal organizations
that is
cabildos
the wise the ancestral were remembered
gourds of memory spilled
to refresh the present quench
the future
Tales of animals & flora going through shit
delivering messages that
everything is alive
todo tiene ashé[17]

These gourd-libations of *osains* from a mosaic past remind us of Afro-creole sacred traditions' passage through shit and abjection. The "gourds of memory" do their work now in a Miami patois "talkin' 'bout tribe y history" beneath "un coco hovering above / waiting to crack open & / say something deep" (15). Castro's poem of ethnogenesis turns to divination sacra and herbal mnemonics with a wariness for how the written word has treated living language's fluidity, its multiple performance modes:

there were no books around
& what would a victim do with the murder weapon
anyway—
memory was survival
Tales in song in dance in music[18]

With the opening "canto" of his book deferring to "Tales in song in dance in music," Adrian Castro shows what the victim's descendants can do with the murder weapon, using it as a tool to reconfigure what Benítez-Rojo describes as "creole culture's most important signs . . . found in popular music and dance."[19]

Even when the rule of canonized scripture seems to have done its work as murder weapon, we are reminded that the Spaniards who carried the Christian gospel to the New World had themselves been subject to Moorish occupation and Arabic scripture: "The wedding between Spain & Africa / happened long before."[20] In this recounting of African (Almouravid) marriage to the Iberian peninsula, we get a repeating wedding dance with a dizzying refrain of saints and orishas:

Dios God Olofin
Olofin & Dios God
Saint Barbara y Shangó
Shangó & Santa Barbara
La Caridad Del Cobre & Oshun
Oshun y La Caridad
Our Lady of Mercy Mercedes y Obatalá
Obatalá & Las Mercedes
San Francisco of Assisi y Orula/Ifa
Ifa & San Francisco
Our Virgin of Regla y Yemayá
Yemayá & La Virgen de Regal
Ceramic faces were often even
black
though often even
cracked
when a drum spoke
gun-ki-lak gun
ka-ki-li-ki-lak
ka-ki-li-ki-lak
gun-ki-lak gun (16)

The drums' cracking of Christian iconographies and dancing subjects asserts a cultural sublime that cultivates the cracking moment of possession when the subject is free to incorporate otherness. What results are calling-responsive, polyrhythmic "marriages" (whether in Spain, Cuba, or Florida) of self and other that serve the sonic cracking of language and ego in new becomings.

Castro's "In the Beginning (I)" concludes in a paying of respects to ritual elders' transmissions of divination rites from the "egg" or fruit of an originary fractal *monte:*

Un coco tumbled & split
into four pieces
everything was OK
their pulp pointed skyward
todo está bien
the story continues . . . (17)

That this cracking apart is "OK" marks an attitude toward diaspora and creolization that is at least as oriented toward the story's ongoing narrative as it is toward any desire for a singular backward grasp on a legitimizing root.

The Yoruba sign rendered from this cracking open of the fallen coco (Alafia or "health," four pieces white side up) marks a blessed path and a stunning resilience in the face of gulf transitions. We come to see that there can be no growth, no sustainable vitality, without the cultivation of capacity for cracking apart and reassembling.

There were, of course, many who received the four pieces pulp-downward sign—the poxed and gunpowder-blast sign of devastation, the apocalyptic sign that dominates Western and contemporary global thinking of futurity. Along the shores of the Timucuan Preserve in Jacksonville, one can find enduring traces of a disappeared people: shards of pottery that held the Timucuan black drink of vomiting purgation and sacral vision. This cassine drink, made from parching and brewing the leaves of the yaupon holly, is the purgative medicine of entry into Florida's *monte*. It was served in whelk or conch shells carved with designs of a native mythic bestiary: feathered serpents, rattlesnake phoenixes, creatures through whom one must pass to cleanse oneself of fear—or who rise up from inside the body of the host. We find Florida's "CACINE" illustrated on folio 28 of *Histoire Naturelle des Indes* (circa 1580), a text which is itself a New World bestiary and botanica produced by anonymous Huguenots who found passage somehow with Francis Drake.[21] René Goulaine de Laudonnière wrote of the French paying visit to Timucuan groups near the mouth of the St. Johns River and partaking of "their drink *Cassine*" in 1564 when the Huguenot Fort Caroline was settled by the French under Laudonnière's command.[22] The Spanish creole priest Father Alonso de Leturiondo reported to Madrid (circa 1700) that "*Cacina*" is "a very healthful and medicinal drink," "introduced among the Spaniards."[23] Although many of the First Coast's Timucuan natives must have merged into Creek and Seminole communities that used the black drink ritually, the last Timucuans in the historical record were Christian converts who departed Florida with the Spanish for Cuba at the end of Florida's first Spanish period in 1763. They disappeared into a Cuban population that keeps returning to a Florida to which it is more native than alien. In this shard-strewn, tide-washed space, we must be ready to vomit up much of what we think we know.

Spain's first Florida forays are steeped in conquistadorial treks for gold (De Soto, Narváez, Ayllón, Ponce de León) twinned to medieval alchemies and pilgrimages (toward fountainheads of Viagra, accompanied by apparitions of the Virgin). Here, administration of the necessary cup of communion delineated flows of knowledge, power, and legitimacy along the colonial frontier and called for the planting of vineyards at every new colonial location. The French Huguenots' settlement of Fort Caroline under Jean Ribault and Laudonnière forced the Spanish to commit to Florida's permanent settlement, and set Menendez's fortified fleet-machinery into perfected motion. Father Escobedo's *La Florida* reports on all this in extended poetic form—from slave revolts in Cuba to Menendez's founding of St. Augustine, ending in a fate-changing hurricane and the slit throats of the surrendered French heretics at Matanzas Inlet. Escobedo's epic guards a single lineage of obedience via a sacrificial line drawn in the sand under the Spaniards' order to take no Huguenot prisoner:

> Because obedience is an honor, Vicente executed the mandate by plunging a dagger into the chest; the blood stained the beach, and Ribault fell dead near the sea where the line had been drawn. The other Castilians did the same to the other Frenchmen and their end was indeed bitter and painful. The men of Spain were victorious and the French were left without armada or even life. This event which I have narrated will remain as a glory to God. Thanks to the hurricane, a strong wind from the East which helped our man, the West was cleansed.[24]

This cleansing line of obedience drawn at Matanzas Inlet finds its orientation in authority from the East, a line that runs westward—with God-sent hurricane force—into a futurity of programmatic apocalypse (ethnic and religious cleansings, ecological catastrophe, the end-times toward which we progress in a manner that is already written). Such lines in sand and sediment, curving with westward expansion across the globe, end up marking the loss of the very legitimacy and chain-of-command they would signify. Perceptions of the loss of legitimacy—the single line between fixed points—tend to increase the turn toward violent blood cleansings. We may, however, come to embrace legitimacy's loss (and the loss of progressive time-space). Old contact zones between Western mission and the sacral bush harbor the tropic curvatures where we may vomit up our apocalyptic fixations.

The split coconut's Alafia/Health sign, the "all OK" coupled with an *osain* of cascarilla (crushed-and-powdered eggshell) may help us navigate the egg-crushing paternalism of the Western mission. Consider Washington Irving's depiction of Florida governor William Duval's assertion to the Seminole leader Neamathla: "You are in the palm of the hand of your Great Father at Washington, who can crush you like an egg-shell."[25] Going back to Father Escobedo's epic *La Florida* (with its obedience-bestowing gunpowder praised in royal octaves), we see that the priests' literary conversion mission makes scripture not simply a tool of historical witness but also a murder weapon. Father Francisco Pareja's *Confessional in the Castilian and Timucuan Languages* (1613) enabled Florida-based priests to ask their new communicants questions such as the following: "Have you consented that in your village someone bringing herbs pray words to the Devil with them?" "To this end, have you made a new fire or did you make it during your menses?" "Have you gone around with desire for someone?" "Has someone that has had your younger sister had a duet with you?" And a question for chiefs: "Have you some black slave or servant as your mistress?"[26] We cannot hear the responses. We may read, however, from Pareja's colleague, Father Escobedo, of revolts and martyred priests in the Florida missions, of Spanish pacification by slaughter and crop-burning. We can read the missions' legacy of obedience: a Timucuan population of 150,000 reduced by disease, war, and starvation to fewer than a hundred converts living in two ghettos outside the walls of the gated community of St. Augustine until their resettlement in Cuba.[27]

Even when scripture seems to have done its dispossessing work as murder weapon, the staple concerns of the subalternized find a way to remain in circulation. For example, as one Seminole ritual elder recounts, "*Fishakikome-chi*, the Creator, made the world . . . made a man he called Adam . . . made a woman and called her Eve." Later, when "there was too much drinking and too many wives . . . Noah built a boat and took animals and people away with him." Storms swamped the earth. Jesus came to preach and was killed, but arose and "had a feast with wine." Subsequently, "Jesus said that since people had killed him, he was not going to live on the earth anymore, but first he taught people how to grow corn, and that is how the people came to have corn."[28] If in this beginning is the Word that begat cornbread nation, we can understand Father Escobedo's epic resistance to this bread of the pagan *monte*: "our Spanish people consider the corn bread to be rather noxious" since it "may cause such pressure on the blood as to cause death to our nationals."[29] It would seem, however, that a century of communion within the contact zone can acclimatize the colonizer to a widely differentiated body of Christ. A St. Augustine creole priest, Alonso de Leturiondo, wrote to King Philip V (1700) in praise of the wonderful quality and diversity of local breads made by the Indians.[30] In Florida, as throughout the Caribbean, each group finds its corpus penetrated by the other.

One key site of Florida's transcultural interpenetrations may be found in the first free black incorporated settlement in Euro-colonial North America, Fort Mose (constructed in 1738 to protect St. Augustine's northern approach). From the early eighteenth century, creole and African maroons from the Carolina colony found refuge in Spanish Florida as free Catholic subjects. Blacks were welcomed, armed, and garrisoned at Mose. The captain of the fort's black militia, the Mandinka Francisco Menendez, provided valiant military service against Oglethorpe's Georgians and authored a subsequent letter to the Spanish king (1740) to assert the value of African subjects' service in the far outposts of Florida. When the Spanish ceded Florida to the British in 1763, the fort's forty-eight black families found resettlement in San Agustín de la Nueva Florida (now Ceiba Mocha) in Cuba's Matanzas province, a space that—with its booming sugar economy—was more racially hierarchical and restrictive than the frontier world of Florida had been. Most of the

Fort Mose and St. Augustine black refugees (including creolized Mandinka, Arara, Congo, Carabali, and Yoruba individuals) eventually left the village of Nueva Florida for the cities of Matanzas or Havana.[31] There, they would have had opportunity to reconnect with African countrymen through Cuba's church-sanctioned *cabildos de nación* devoted to mutual aid and the preservation of the social memory of African nations. Fort Mose's soldiers and historical narratives disappear into those of Nueva Florida and into the Afrocreole cultural histories and *osains* of a Cuba in constant patterns of flow with Florida.

With the end of the American Revolution in 1783, Loyalist Florida once again became a Spanish frontier and a ward of Cuba. Only a dozen years into this second Spanish period (1784–1821), the colony's militia received a spectacular addition. Jorge Biassou, a founding leader (and Spanish-commissioned "Vodou" general) of the Haitian Revolution, was exiled to St. Augustine in 1796 with his family and at least twenty-five retainers, many of whom resettled in Cuba with Florida's second Spanish exodus of 1821.[32] Of course, no historical marker in contemporary St. Augustine mentions General Biassou's revolutionary life or points out the impressive two-story coquina-block structure that housed his family. A few Spanish surnames survive in black neighborhoods of St. Augustine, Jacksonville, and Fernandina, but there is almost nothing printed in the tourist-marketings or state-mandated student testing of this "First Coast" to lay claim to Biassou: a revolutionary hero who appears in novels by Victor Hugo and Madison Smartt Bell but hardly at all in the public memory of America's oldest city.[33]

If we were to locate a single continuous nexus of life in Florida's contact zones, we can look to the Seminole, who emerged in ethnogenesis from the region's intense state of flux. The word "Seminole," probably derived from Spanish *Cimarrón* ("wild one"—a source of "maroon"—incorporated into Muskogee Creek as *Simanoli*), came to refer to a Florida coalition of Creeks and Yuchis (along with the peninsula's remnant indigenous peoples) that had absorbed as many black slaves and maroon affiliates as had the Spanish.[34] Bartram's description of their trade patterns (based on his travels in the 1770s) is most instructive:

> In these large canoes they descend the river on trading and hunting expeditions to the sea coast, neighboring islands and keys, quite to the point of Florida, and sometimes cross the gulph, extending their navigations to the Bahama islands and even to Cuba: a crew of these adventurers had just arrived, having returned from Cuba but a few days before our arrival, with a cargo of spirituous liquors, Coffee, Sugar, and Tobacco. One of them politely presented me with a choice piece of Tobacco, which he told me he had received from the governor of Cuba. They deal in the way of barter, carrying with them deer-skins, furs, dry fish,

bees-wax, honey, bear oil, and some other articles. They say the Spaniards receive them very friendlily, and treat them with the best spirituous liquors. The Spaniards of Cuba likewise trade here or at St. Mark's and other sea ports on the west coast of the isthmus.[35]

Seminole, Creek, and allied Geechee bodies of narrative provide unparalleled gateways to a circum-Caribbean orature as complex as the trade and migration patterns of the region. Spanish (and even British) rule facilitated these matrices of exchange in ways that oriented many peoples of the Gulf South to their trading partners to the south.

Although it would be naïve to idealize Spanish rule, Florida's change of possession to U.S. ownership was disastrous for peoples that Spain had been forced to engage in relations of relative mutuality. Indian removal and the Jacksonian-era extension of the plantation system across the Gulf South meant the parceling out of wilderness into individual allotments clear-cut for cotton plantations under white ownership. Writing from this shock of changing subjectivities following Florida's transfer from Spanish rule, the Jacksonville-area plantation owner and slavetrader Zephaniah Kingsley— deeply attached to his Cuba-purchased Wolof wife, Anta Majigeen Ndiaye, and their freed children—published four editions (between 1828 and 1832) of his *Treatise on the Patriarchal or Co-operative System of Society as It Exists in Some Governments and Colonies in America, and in the United States, under the Name of Slavery, with Its Necessity and Advantages*, to protest the new Anglo-American laws restricting (and aimed at eliminating) the agency, civil status, and property rights of Florida's free people of color.[36] Kingsley's Caribbean-patterned life in Spanish Florida, his freeing of his African wife and children, and his pro-slavery advocacy of more racially fluid patterns of stratification (modeled for him in Brazil and the Spanish and Dutch Caribbean) demands our attentiveness to local and intercolonial historical conditions.

In the year Kingsley first published his *Treatise* (1828), Ralph Waldo Emerson was convalescing in St. Augustine, where he could envision the republic's destiny manifesting almost monstrously, across deep time: "The old land of America / I find in this nook of sand / The first footprints of that giant grown."[37] From the coquina-walled plaza of St. Augustine, Emerson observed in his journal that "almost without changing our position we might aid in sending the scriptures into Africa or bid for 'four children without the mother who had been kidnapped therefrom.'"[38] This orphaning/infanticidal economy gave us the racial fundaments entrenched in the Southern Baptist Convention: the nation's largest institutional bastion of Protestant Christianity. Antebellum Baptist denials of the sanctity of slave marriage (coupled with insistence on overseas missions to the heathen) suggest a fortress heartlessness behind the SBC's modern "family values" politics and their congregations' history of opposition to black Baptists' civil rights.[39]

The old walled city of the First Coast reasserted its symbolic value in the twentieth-century civil rights movement. Responding to local organizers, Martin Luther King Jr. targeted St. Augustine the year before its celebration of its four hundredth year of civic history, and used this symbolic stage to push the nation toward passage of the Civil Rights Act. The Southern Christian Leadership Conference's June 1964 *Newsletter* speaks of SCLC's foray into "this rock-bound bastion of segregation" and "ancient stronghold of slave trading" where its demonstrators "suffered the most violent assaults to date at the hands of Ku Klux Klansmen, openly endorsed by law enforcement officials."[40] Another article from the SCLC newsletter speaks of our First Coast's counterlesson to the progressive myth of time—the fact that despite our tendencies to believe that "age and experiences generate wisdom," we face challenges of regression: "for 399 (and one half) years . . . St. Augustine has trapped, preserved and perpetuated all of the prejudice, bigotry and hate against the American Negro ever known to mankind."[41] What a more nuanced approach to First Coast history reveals, however, is a more troubling history of regression than what SCLC writers could recognize: the fact that Florida's black population enjoyed rights held under Spanish law in the 1700s that were withheld in the apartheid Florida of 1964. It was Anglo-American control of Florida that fed many of the crudest forms of our racial gulfs. Nevertheless, the title of King's own contribution to the newsletter, "400 Years of Bigotry and Hate," shows a pointed understanding of the symbolic value of "the nation's oldest city" and how it could be leveraged to dispossess us of our progressivist illusions.[42]

The opening poem of Adrian Castro's *Cantos to Blood and Honey*, "In the Beginning (I)," provides a powerful gateway into Florida's deep time. It may speak as much to colonial beginnings in Florida as it does to those in Cuba or the Spanish Caribbean. When we look at the poem that closes Castro's *Cantos*, we see that it utilizes the exact same structural and narrative frame to reposition contemporary south Florida as a locus of postplantation creolization. "In the Beginning (II)" speaks to North America's current Hispano-Caribbean contact zones, marking divinations with purificatory powdered eggshell for "wails echoing / from that side of the gulf" crossing over in transnational ethnogenesis:

Landed on this soil
(giving birth to a new people)

Crioooooollos!
Those with one foot strutting Cubano, Dominicano
Chicano, Boricua (150)

Miami's contemporary *criollos* have built new ritual families in "poems that dangled on brass chain / all delivering messages que / todo tiene ashé / el café mango calabaza y maiz / have their consciousness," and we recall how "none of this was written in book / tale keeps changing / memory is survival" (151). In this Miami of intense heteroglossia, language and narrative keep changing and making "home with certain hierbas / (herbs that alter the invisible)" (152). Ongoing weddings " 'tween Afro y America" keep finding precedent in what "happened long before" in "migration" and "mix of peoples / you with kalalú" across the Florida Straits—where marriages of "Dios with God con Olofin" have drummers and dancers "summoning heads of nature & spirit" (152).

"In the Beginning (II)" partakes of Kamau Brathwaite's description of creolization as "a cultural action—material, psychological, and spiritual."[43] Castro insists,

> There is no god but in this ground
> this monte we mow we tap
> with machetes of sound y steel
> this cotton reflecting the sun (152–53)

The poem may close Castro's first book, but it does not close the creolizing cultural actions it divines:

> In the beginning
> un coco tumbled & split
> into four pieces
> their pulp pointed skyward
> todo está bien
> the story continues . . .(153)

Castro's coconut reading—"todo está bien"—speaks from sacred groves of *el monte* and from a long *duración*. The split coconut points (in this simplest of Afro-Cuban divination forms) to the health of fractal division, its four pieces with their white pulp facing skyward: Alafia, the good sign of open roads and perfect health.

Entering Osain's Pharmacy—From Primal Bush to *el Monte* in Miniature

Our highlighting of the literary history of Florida's First Coast—writings by priests, explorers, naturalists, slaveholders, soldiers, tourists, and convalescents—suggests that authors have been very slow to apprentice themselves to the basilectal sacred cultures of the bush, which they seem invariably obsessed with representing. From Zora Neale Hurston's ethnographic *Mules and Men* (1935) to her medicine-novel *Their Eyes Were Watching God* (1937), and from

Lydia Cabrera's *Cuentos negros de Cuba* (1940) to her remarkable compilation of Afro-Cuban sacred knowledge in *El monte* (1954), the stuff of ethnography and the stuff of fiction in Florida and the Caribbean finally began to coalesce in works of environmental, creolizing interpenetration. We have examined how Zora Neale Hurston's Rain-Bringer authority found crowning birth in a Voudou initiation in New Orleans in late 1927 or early 1928. The Cuban and Miami author Lydia Cabrera underwent similar authorial reaffiliation in Cuba at about the same time.

The scholar Isabel Castellanos points us to the moment when "the storyteller and ethnographer Lydia Cabrera was truly born": the evening of June 6, 1930, in the Havana home of Calixta Morales (Oddeddei), who was celebrating (on the Catholic feast day of Saint Norbert) the day dedicated to Ochosi, the hunter/tracker of the bush. A notebook entry Cabrera made that day describes the Ochosi throne assembled by Oddeddei: "At night the altar's set up already. Two wildcat skins embroidered with shells. On the ground, a large pot of rice and beans with popcorn. Two burning candles. By touching the ground and kissing the tips of their fingers, they bow to the altar . . . The smell of guava fills the room."[44] This altar finds careful reassembly, Castellanos notes, six years later in the opening story ("Bregantino, Bregantin") of Cabrera's first book, *Afro-Cuban Tales*. In the short story, Cabrera's pregnant fictional avatar Sanune escapes the infanticidal Bull-King's rule by crossing "to the other side of the river" at "the edge of the fearsome forest, guided by the spirit of her mother who . . . was a faithful servant of . . . Ogun and Ochosi."[45] While Sanune arrives at an Ochosi altar by journeying deep into the bush, Cabrera traveled to Ochosi's altar by accompanying her family seamstress, the orisha priestess Teresa Muñoz, straight into the walled colonial city of Havana.

The story of her fictional avatar's transformation into "*Monte Firme*" opened the way for Cabrera's most important work: the massive ethnographic botanica, *El monte* (1954). This is a book that redirects readers to an earth-centered, locally grounded hermeneutics: "The Saints dwell more in *el Monte* than in heaven."[46] As the opening page of the first chapter of *El monte* insists, the earth's living soil and vegetation provide "*contacto directo*" with the divine: "'We are children of *el Monte* because life began there; the Saints are born of *el Monte* and our religion is also born of *el Monte*,' says my old herbalist Sandoval" (13). Pronouns prove especially entangled in the perspectives of Cabrera's *El monte*. The narrative "I," the subject "he/she/they," and first-person plural "we" make possessive claims ("my," "his/her," "their," "our") that reveal an increasingly porous sovereignty as the text progresses and the authorial first-person singular elides into a transculturally possessed "we," "us," and "our."[47] The result is a net gain for Afro-creole initiate authority and for textual orisha agency. The full text of *El monte: Igbo, finda,*

ewe orisha, vititi nfinda: Notas sobre las religiones, la magia, las supersticio-
nes, y el folklore de los negros criollos y el pueblo de Cuba elides any separation between the subtitled *"negros criollos"* and *"pueblo de Cuba"* (Cuban
"folk" or "people") since the book's reterritorializing authority stems from
"our blacks, and here we must say our people, one that in its majority is physi-
cally and spiritually mestizo" (17). The title's use of three languages (Spanish,
Lukumi or Cuban Yoruba, and Congo) casts speakers of Afro-Cuban languages as specialist-authorities holding "a great knowledge," much as scien-
tists, priests, and doctors have drawn an air of expertise from their handling
of Latin names, liturgies, and prescriptive formulae. In sum, the positioning
of authority in *El monte* suggests that attempts to narrate a cultural or natural
history of Cuba must be fostered by Afro-creole expertise and come from the
ground up.

The text of *El monte* defers to its initiate informants as *"los verdaderos
autores"* (the true authors) of the book that bears Lydia Cabrera's name (10).
As Edna Rodriguez-Mangual observes, Cabrera fills the text with quotations,
dialogues, and narratives of others in a book "made up of the cited discourse
of other voices, a book in which the narrative voice, when it does not disappear altogether, is diluted by direct and indirect citations."[48] From the moment when Gabino Sandoval insists, "we blacks go to el Monte like we were
going to church because it is filled with Saints and the dead" (15), readers are
launched into ecologies and economies of Afro-creole initiation. Since *"el
Monte* has its law," one must defer to its pharmacists, "solicit permission respectfully, and above all pay religiously with brandy, tobacco, money, and on
certain occasions with the blood of a chicken or rooster the '*derecho*'" (14–
15). The ritual "courtesy" that acknowledges indebtedness in taking resources
from the land respects the agency of wilderness. Plants "can cure because
they themselves are shamans" (17), and call us to more conscious enmesh-
ment in nature's botanica.

As in the Seminole creation story culminating in the gospel of Christ's
gift of corn to the world, Cabrera presents the Afro-Cubans of *El monte* as
creolizing converters of the Christian gospel: "Wasn't Jesus born in *el monte*
upon a pile of grass . . . [and] didn't he die in a *monte, el Monte* Calvary? He
always walked in the path of the *montes*. He was an herbalist!" (17). Cabrera
writes of a national culture shaped by "[a] religious syncretism that does not
always withdraw from the white, [and] faithfully reflects a social syncretism
that does not astonish anyone who knows Cuba" (19). A polyrhythmic logic
comes into play when her key informant, Oddeddei (Calixta Morales), "one
of the most honored Iyalochas in Havana," speaks to the matter of Cuba's
spiritual transculturation: "The Saints are the same here and in Africa. The
same with different names. The only difference is that ours eat a lot and
have to dance, and yours are satisfied with incense and oil, and don't dance"

(19). Through a language addressing essential sameness, Oddeddei accentuates key difference between "our" and "your" practice. She may as well have said the only difference is that *our* practice is real since our saints partake of life's economies of desire. Still, Oddeddei presents a complex space of *"here"* where what could be the same (both "ours" and "yours") is penetrated by a seeming elsewhere—an Africa full of medicines that are secreted in Caribbean nature as "a concealed botanica . . . all alive." The sacred bush manages to be both *here* (Cuba or even Florida) and Africa, both opaquely "ours" and openly "yours" too . . . if you can apprentice yourself to "our" *conocimiento* enough to feed its saints and dance them in a certain kind of way.

One thing Cabrera's spiritual elders make clear is that the sacral wilderness does not reside on some wholly other side of any binarism. Cabrera insists that "the reader must not think that with this word '*Monte*' . . . is meant exclusively an expanse of uncultivated ground inhabited by trees. In Havana '*un monte*' or savannah—may be any abandoned lot covered with weeds (and a single avocado tree or laurel may also be called a grove!)."[49] Even from within the old walled core of Havana, one "is not obligated to walk much in order to encounter a 'monte'" since any "space in which vegetation grows and spreads is a place for leaving a '*rogación*,' an *ebbo*, the communal offering that in Regla de Ocha is destined for the Saint" (68). This perspective suggests that Western urbanites obsessed with preserving wild space—as national park where "real" wilderness is demarcated—may be among those most alienated from it. On the whole, Cabrera's book serves as a spiritual field guide or "herbarium."[50] In Miami, San Juan, and the Bronx, this herbarium-text has been marketed in botanicas serving Santería and Spiritist clienteles. *El monte* reminds readers that sacral bush may be cultivated anywhere. Atop Havana's *solares* (urban tenements) where the most commonly used herbs are cultivated in containers, "these *montes* in miniature, so accessible," are given "no less dignity and respect" than "the *montes* of more distant and inaccessible forested spaces" (68).

Cabrera describes one of these urban "montes in miniature": the home of "the deceased Miguel Adyái, 'el lucumi,' a creole who spoke admirably in 'Aku,' possessed all the herbs of *curandería* [healing], all the herbs of *Ocha*, *ewe-orisha*, in the patio, rendering his fragrant tenement room totally verdant, on a street as busy and commercial as that of San Rafael" (68). In the densely populated multistory tenements of Havana, hemmed in by concrete, brick, stucco, and asphalt, Cabrera introduces readers to contact zones by which Yoruba spirituality found dialogue with Taino botanical repertoires as well as with Spanish, Chinese, and various African pharmacopeia. From green rooftops in Havana's urban core, Cabrera invokes a greener, truly cosmopolitan aesthetics: "Without a doubt the cement, that condemns a living surface of the earth to death and silence, is the worst enemy of the rustic

African divinities. Urbanism, without urbanity or faith, distances the Orishas from the essence of Osain, of Oggun or Ochosi, who need the warmth and sap of the earth" (68–69). As Chamoiseau's *Texaco* and Osbey's *All Saints* have conveyed from Franco-creole spaces, carefully gardened "montes in miniature" provide vital countermodels to an "urbanism without urbanity or faith."

Chapter 3 of *El monte* explicitly identifies the one-eyed, one-armed, one-legged ventriloquizing orisha Osain as "lord of the leaves of el Monte" (70). The maimed initiatory herbalist of transformation, Osain works through the entire system of initiation, remaining particularly close to the warrior orishas (Eleggua, Ogun, Ochosi) and the dead. A number of stories account for Osain's origins, including one explaining that "Osain was born from the head of the Turtle" (102). Turtle or Tortoise remains deeply associated with Osain (and with the pharmacological powers of the bush).

Chapter 4, "The Tribute to the Lord of el Monte," attends to the ritual economy operating around this "incarnation of *el monte* that is the deity Osain" (113). Whenever a Regla de Ocha practitioner gathers herbal medicines (*ewe*), "the first thing that must be done, upon entering the *monte* is to hail and pay respects to the Lord of *Ewe*, the vegetation, the Egun" (113), via praisesongs to Osain, followed by clear statements of purpose and payments in liquor, tobacco, corn, and/or coin (115). The rest of the book's chapters attend primarily to the herbal medicine and spiritual practices of Palo Mayombe, a.k.a. Regla Congo, and to the lore of particularly powerful trees. The book closes with a massive encyclopedic appendix of plants listed from A to Z, consisting of 257 pages and 549 plant descriptions, offering Latin name, Spanish common name, Lukumi or Congo name, the "saint" who "rules" each plant's agency, and its medicinal or ritual use. This is followed by 23 pages of photographs (most by Cabrera's friend Josefina Tarafa) and a pair of indexes, all of which combine to make *El monte* a stunningly heterodox ethnobotanica.

El monte conveys a sense for the demands of cultural memory, preservation, and synthesis that faced the enslaved inheritors of African cultural systems. Yoruba-based religion in the Americas underwent significant change due to its extreme uprootings from specific communities, lineages, and environments of memory in Africa. What got reconstituted (in Havana and Matanzas, Bahia and Rio de Janeiro, Grenada and Trinidad) were "house"-specific practices from widely different Yoruba lineages, towns, and states—in processes of synthesis with other African and non-African practices. David Brown notes the resultant "'concentration' of regional Yoruba cosmologies accompanied by a radical condensation of ritual space and ritual time in miniaturized New World shrine arrangements, [and] in the compressed sequences of sung invocation" of the orishas.[51] As with the "miniaturized" monte that

Cabrera reveals in Old Havana, Brown describes how Cuban orishas became organized into "pantheons [that] have been confined to small single rooms, the cuarto sagrado or igbodun (sacred room) or multishelved cabinets called canastilleros."[52] We come to see how architecture, furniture, consumer goods, and classical pantheons of the gods can provide imaginative scaffolding of interaction with sacred groves rendered most dense at the urban cores of the contact zone. Helping us to understand Benítez-Rojo's trope of the grandmother's armoire as figure of the "occult prestige" of the buildings of Old Havana, one of the Josefina Tarafa photographs in El monte reveals the soup tureen–encased orisha stones housed within the initiate's armoire. Cabrera's texts are the first to open the doors of the armoire's sacred grove (in photographs, herbal encyclopedia, and text) and to record the voices of "the true authors" who draw their authority from relations with the saints and spirits of the bush. Provided that one's life is not entirely paved in cement, one may access Osain's almost abandoned bridge to cross to "the other side" like orphan Sanune of Cabrera's very first short story. There, entering el monte "thick with the smell of warm foliage and guavas," we may find "several soup tureens with their lids on, a horseshoe, two huge pots of rice, some red beans, and popcorn," and "an old woman with her head wrapped in a veil" holding twenty-one cowries for the orishas' oracular speech.[53]

Between Cuba and the Creek—Turtle's Vision Quest

From the first published turtle stories of Afro-Cuban Tales (1936) to her work in Miami dedicated to him in Ayapá: Cuentos de Jicotea (1971), Cabrera accorded the Yoruba trickster an emblematic medicine-agency, a powerful conocimiento of limbolike dances of resurrection from conditions of violent shattering and fragmentation. In "One-Legged-Osain" from Cuentos negros de Cuba, Cabrera introduces readers to the one-legged, one-armed, one-eyed Lord of el Monte, Osain, and his help-mate Jicotea or Ayapá (Turtle's Lukumi appellation). In "One-Legged Osain," Turtle has lodged himself comfortably under a yam-pile beneath the house of a newly married couple. When the wife goes beneath the house to fetch yams to cook fufu for her husband, she is met with Turtle's proprietary cry that seems to come from the yam-pile itself. The husband also encounters this talking yam and—much like the Yoruba talking skull tale and Hurston's "High Walker and the Bloody Bones"—reports the talking food staple to his king, who sends his own best representatives to face this ultimate subaltern: "Under no condition can we allow yams the privilege of speaking."[54] After many other failed attempts to restore order, it is finally one-legged Osain who is called in and has the wherewithal to expose Jicotea/Turtle as the voice in the yam-pile. Osain gives Jicotea a thorough beating with his stick, satisfying the king and the newly married couple who (with yams silenced) may eat their fufu. Later that evening Jicotea does a familiar limbo dance of recovery: "One small, round, intense eye appeared above a pebble. And then another one, on a cactus nearby. A severed hand about the size of a romerillo leaf was moving the stagnant silence among the grasses. Tiny sounds began to multiply, the sounds of body parts that had been mutilated, killed, and spread far and wide beginning to seek each other out, to piece themselves back together and come back to life!" (148). This is the music by which Turtle/Jicotea pulls his fragmented shell and severed parts together to join the disfigured, ventriloquial Osain for a good Cuban cigar with coffee around a fire deep in the bush. "'Oh, Brother Jicotea,' said One-Legged-Osain. 'It was just a joke'" (149). Indeed for this lord of herbal rebirthings, what Turtle underwent was just another initiatory pulling together of herbs and orisha stones (a "romerillo leaf," "a pebble"). In the multiplied sounds of Turtle's body parts seeking each other out and coming to life, we get a model of the limbo work of black Atlantic ritual and music—or rather, we begin to step to the sounds of our spiritually creolized majority, piecing itself together.

In "Arere Marekén," also from Cabrera's first collection, Turtle falls instantly in love with the king's wife—"the sounds of gold bracelets and of the waves of skirts and petticoats"—as she comes singing and dancing down the dirt road (119). Turtle asks only, "Let my eyes enjoy you Arere" (119). But what is it that his eyes enjoy? What secret fundament is revealed and from what position of gaze? Arere explains herself to the King: "Today the road was full of puddles. I held up my train for fear of soiling it" (120). The direction, object, and secret of puddle-dwelling Turtle's gaze becomes clear. For the affront of penetrating the king's wife with his eyes' enjoyment, turtle gets clubbed to death, while Queen Arere, grinding her corn and coffee in mortar and pestle, grieves. After nightfall, Turtle's many pieces come back to life, reassembling his perpetual Body without Organs, his shell marked and lined with "So many scars for Arere's love" (121). Turtle has a knack for discovering erotic secrets, though he often takes a beating for it. Turtle's carnal quest, however, is also clearly sacral, about desire and knowledge, vision of the true.

Turtle's vision-quest to move beneath "the sounds of gold bracelets and . . . the waves of skirts and petticoats" in order to feast his eyes on Arere certainly takes us back to the ritual question answered by the Vodou Mambo in Hurston's *Tell My Horse,* in which she bore witness that "[t]here is no mystery beyond the mysterious source of life."[55] Turtle, his shell cracked all to hell, keeps coming back for a second and third vision of the truth. "Let my eyes enjoy you, Arere," he says, even at the cost of becoming turtle soup. And here we should recall not only Leah Chase's Eastertime recipes for turtle soup but also the Louisiana Creole lullaby mothers sang to daughters, insisting on the need to sweep the streets of turtles who inhabit roadside puddles and "know how to talk."

A whole mosaic body of circum-Atlantic literature, myth, and history has been covered up, kept from our sight, so that smaller or more partial national and ethnic signs may be held up as wonders. Lydia Cabrera was conscious of this when she wrote from Miami exile of the erasures and uncontemplated (or disappeared) time-spaces of a "true reality" that may appear utterly unreal when glimpsed from our habitually constructed and consumed brandings of "closer and more obvious realities."[56] Turtle can help us reenter the true mysteries and true reality of *el monte*. But we will have to loosen our habits and boundaries and be ready to step across puddles, prepare to become Turtle's *iyawo* or initiate "bride," and learn Turtle's medicine-songs and language (which is usually not English but Yoruba, Spanish, Lukumi, French Creole, and Muskogee). We should keep in mind the likelihood that Turtle may well be a mother or daughter herself, that (s)he at least carries a womanly gnosis of blood loss and limbo-reintegration.

The turtle corpus from *Cuentos negros de Cuba* to Cabrera's Miami volume, *Ayapá: Cuentos de Jicotea*, points repeatedly to Turtle's talents for crossing boundaries as well as to his capacity for reassembly of broken parts (the ultimate emblem of the creole). Given the visibility of Turtle's scars and the enduring nature of his quest, we know Turtle is drawn to time-spaces of life's repeating, procreative music: Arere's ankle bracelets and skirts, Arere's pounding of corn and coffee in mortar and pestle, the Yoruba market of an Ifa tale, the yam-pile of a wedding fufu.[57] From Miami, Cabrera wrote of Turtle as "a mysterious being who knows how to handle secret forces of nature, one whom we may classify perhaps in the category of genie or duende."[58] With visible scars and a close relationship to "One-legged-Osain," Turtle bears witness to the sublime encounter and its maiming as well as to a "potent vitality" derived from "the miracle of a resurrection," as Cabrera affirms.[59] We find Turtle's tales in Miami and Nigeria—and in Afro-Cuban, Afro-Brazilian, and Puerto Rican texts—but hardly at all in African American canons of literature and folklore.[60] Turtle's quest for the naked truth has been walled out of America's classrooms and Sunday schools. One step outside into the bush, however, leads to turtles whose removals and absences speak.

In the continental United States, Cabrera's tales of Turtle circulate mostly in southeastern Indian narratives and in the shell-shaking traditions of sacred Muscogee stomp grounds. In addressing Turtle's tales of reassembly, we should keep in mind both Jane Landers's insistence that Africans operated as culture brokers between groups in Spanish Florida, and recall that the Muskogee- and Mikasuki-speaking Seminole (or Creek/Seminole) emerged from Florida's eighteenth- and early-nineteenth-century cultural brokerage as the best single group of witnesses to the space's long duration as contact zone. Turtle's quest of looking up women's dresses, his courting vision of a sexed sublime, and his subsequent mutilation and reassembly appear in a collection of tales by Earnest Gouge, written in Muskogee Creek in Oklahoma in 1915. Gouge's stunning narrative collection (apparently written at the instigation of the ethnographer John Swanton) only recently found publication when Jack Martin, Margaret McKane Mauldin, and Juanita McGirt (via the University of Oklahoma Press) presented it translated in the dual-language edition *Totkv Mocvse/New Fire* (2004). Gouge's Muskogee tales and written language, much like the performance of Hurston's *Mules and Men* or Cabrera's *Cuentos negros de Cuba*, insist on sovereignty of imagination, language, and authority—no small matter. Anyone familiar with West African tales, however, will find this Creek-language text to be a treasure trove of African diaspora narrative. Gouge presents many of the Brer Rabbit tales popularized by Joel Chandler Harris, but he also offers two Turtle tales that I have found in no collection of African American lore, only in the Lukumi world of Cabrera's Cuba reassembled in Miami—or in trace form in Creole Louisiana.

Earnest Gouge's Muskogee-scripted "Turtle Tries to Look up Women's Dresses" presents Turtle hunkering familiarly low, trying to gain vision of women's private parts, getting beaten to a pulp by them as a result, having his shell shattered, his own bloody parts scattered. He manages, however, with a shell-shaking stomp song ("I come-come together / I shake-shake together") to sing and shake himself back together.[61] Caught on his vision-quest yet again (hiding down low beneath the mortar and pestle where he knows the women will pound corn), Turtle begs the women—no matter what mode of death they choose—to please, please not wrap his neck in a necklace made of their pubic hair and sling him into the river. Born and bred in that briar patch, Turtle gets his initiatory medicine necklace and his swim in their waters. "When they do that to me, I just die!" Turtle says, "creating a wake" over the water.[62] The Muscogee turtle's vision-quest offers a powerful perspective for rereading Janie Crawford beneath the creaming pear tree, Caddy Compson muddy-drawered in a Yoknapatawpha pear tree, the stomp grounds of LeAnne Howe's Choctaw novel *Shell Shaker*, and even the shimmy dancing *Fe Chauffe* rites of Creole New Orleans. When we read Gouge's tale "Turtle Is Beaten by Three Mothers" (in which Turtle brags of his having "skunked around" with the Skunk clan mother, "cooned around" with the Raccoon clan mother, and "possumed around" with the Opossum clan mother), we get a feel for why the Louisiana lullaby (of chapter 4) sings of sweeping the road free of turtles since "Turtle knows how to talk."[63] Through this shared body of Cuban, Franco-creole, and Muskogee narrative, Turtle keeps managing to shake back together in what may be the Gulf South's most compelling opening to the limbo gateway. Nothing in American literature is richer than these Afro-creole and Amerindian narratives of mythopoetic vision. Why we do not study this material more often and more carefully than we do is a key question.

Gouge's tales convey what Creek literary critic Craig Womack calls a "capacity to take in new realities." They are, as Womack insists, thoroughly Creek, and Womack rightly asserts that "Gouge is an author, not an ethnographic responder," since something of Creek linguistic and imaginative sovereignty is at stake in escaping the clutches of ethnography.[64] This tale of Turtle (Creek *Loca*) is, in fact, so crucial to Creek medicinal and narrative hermeneutic (stomp) circles that Womack uses a kinswoman's telling of "Turtle Tries to Look up Women's Dresses" to give traditional performative orientation to his remarkable monograph, *Red on Red: Native American Literary Separatism*, which presents and engages a specifically Creek literary tradition of profound power. Womack suggests that Turtle's quest may in fact be directed at acquisition of the mothers' menstrual knowledge/power, a reading that gets to the heart of Turtle's shell-shaking medicine-song and powers of reassembly.[65]

As thoroughly Creek as Turtle's tale appears to be, it also draws from matrices of performance across the black Atlantic. Earnest Gouge's stunning collection dips into a hybrid Afro-Creek fabulosity so packed with African diaspora narrative that any study of Native souths must include Africans, and any holistic approach to Black Atlantic culture must look to Native repertory. The study of Afro-Indian contacts forces us to rethink the contact zone more locally and also beyond national and ethnic boundaries. This body of narrative speaks truth *and* power—from a capacity to take in new realities and from a living *monte*. In the Florida waters, mucks, and low terrain where the Creek have met Cubans, Bahamians, and Seminoles, Turtle may well be our most evocative mosaic emblem of a poetics of relation, a limbo gateway. How much time and collective will we have for nourishing such environments of memory is a most pressing question.

Earth-body Work—From Polyrhythm to Cosmovision

As Barry Estabrook reveals in *Tomatoland: How Modern Industrial Agriculture Destroyed Our Most Alluring Fruit* (2011), the region of Zora Neale Hurston's south Florida muck is a microcosm of much that ails us.[66] Debt enslavement of migrant workers, exposure of the agricultural workforce to pesticidal and herbicidal toxicity, the poisoning of the soil and waterways—all in the production of a tasteless tomato that reddens when gassed and travels well to winter supermarkets—point to a divorce from ecologies of relation and from a carnal erotics of taste. Earth and body meet with profound disrespect. The normative practice, as Estabrook describes it, is to "create the rows in the sand, and then they inject methyl bromide, which is a fumigant which kills every living organism in the soil—every germ, every bug, every bacteria," after which the row is covered in plastic, and then "[a]fter a couple of weeks, when the soil is sterile—dead—they poke holes in the plastic and put seedlings in."[67] The living orisha-filled soil of *el Monte* is fumigated and sterilized. As a result of this kind of industrial relation to Florida's soil, the Lake Apopka where Hurston often fished for speckled perch (crappie) has been so poisoned by agricultural runoff as to be toxic to birds and to cause extreme reproductive mutations in alligators. Of course, the migrant workforce most at risk is also the group politically scapegoated for our system's ailments.

Orientations toward culture do not fall far from the tree of agriculture and culinary practice. The very guardians of trauma-tested creole repertory often refuse to convey the basilectal (most *country*) restorative behaviors, lore, and language to the young. Heirloom creole gardening hardly seems to advance anyone along the road to progress. It doesn't pay for (or produce) goods at Walmart. Not turtle soup. Not breadfruit or even cornbread. The franchised market determines value and is stocked with branded consumer items shipped from elsewhere. A resultant internal censorship and devaluing of local cultural production is not just the threat faced in Florida or the Sea Islands but in postplantation spaces across the globe. Writing of death rites and wakes in Guyana, Gentian Miller observes that "reluctance to value and share traditional knowledge is widespread and almost automatic" and "has played a major role in the non-transmission of African cultural traditions." Al Creighton concurs, asserting that shame (over "obeah" or old-fashioned "bush" practice) suppresses much of the cultural basilect, "severely reducing its passage down to succeeding generations," and he notes that this has a very real social cost since the culture's lack of internal valorization increases levels of violence in a society that provides its youth with no rituals by which they may be integrated and initiated into a sustainable community.[68] Nevertheless, movements legitimizing the practice of black Atlantic religion and Atlantic Creole languages have been pursued with something of the resiliency of Turtle's assembly from every form of death thrown his way. A new creole literature has been piecing itself together through tested gateways—even as English departments and colleges of the humanities in postplantation spaces reproduce what has been branded and anthologized from the metropolitan centers that determine value, taste, and accreditation. A true poetics of relation must go beyond globally and nationally franchised marketings to draw from a localized aesthetics of the earth.

With his shell blasted apart and shards scattered in Miami at one corner and among Oklahoma's Indian nations at another, Turtle's shell-shaking efforts at reassembly of the Gulf's sacred gro(o)ves offer what may be the most endangered and most vital hope we have for movement—in a certain kind of way—toward a cure for apocalyptic consumer fixations. Adrian Castro's long poem sequence "The Cantos" (lodged between his bookended "In the Beginning" poems) does its part in presenting a poetic analogue to Santería *oru* (praisesongs sung in sequence to the orishas, including orisha Osain and his Turtle-companion Ayapá). Castro leads us out of fortress America's cynical heartlessness and into a polyrhythmic, multilingual consciousness geared toward spiritual, cultural, and ecosystemic diversity:

> In order to find the cure
> we had to
> enter el monte—
> Oba ewe o awa ni ye ti wi ti wi
> yo busca palo pa' curá christiano
>
> Don Masayá spilled handfuls of toasted corn
> showered certain trees with aguardiente
> There was a shadow
> whistling
> which caused many a goosebumps
> The figure wasn't
> clear
> but
> with its one arm
> pointed out leaves & roots
> needed for the solution
> Occasionally he spoke with a nasal song
> staccato rhythm like
> walking on
> one leg
> He had a small army of turtles following him[69]

Osain, the one-armed, one-legged initiating spirit of the bush, may have navigated so many initiatory gulfs that the hobbled, healing orisha appears as just a shadow or ventriloquial "whistling," not quite "clear," at times just "a nasal song," a "staccato rhythm." But the "small army of turtles following" Osain helps point the way to living solutions and cures. Whoever would follow must follow at turtle's speed. Like the slow food movement, with its embrace of local, organic, heirloom, and consistently fresh cuisine (or perhaps a slow idea, slow epistemology movement), Turtle's deceptively supple way of moving models a way of being in the world—an enduring vision of the long haul that is unimpressed with tales and practices of end-times.

As Joseph Murphy makes clear in *Working the Spirit*, entry into the sacred gro(o)ve indeed requires work: "The generalized term for any 'work' for the orishas is *ebo*, which is usually translated as 'sacrifice.'"[70] The result is a work ethic quite different from Max Weber's Protestant work ethic. Just as people "make" the orisha or saint through sacrifice and initiation in the sacred room of the *igbodu*, drum parties for the saints make a certain kind of love find crowning in rhythmic labor as "the orishas allow the community to show this love that can only 'descend' or emerge from the hard work of the dance."[71] Our readings of Orphan Kumba, Paule Marshall, Marie Laveau, Brenda Marie Osbey, Zora Neale Hurston, and Lydia Cabrera suggest that women are generally the ones most open to this labor of love and its sacrifice of the ego (and body) to being mounted by the saint. But the work of becoming bride of the orishas remains open to whoever is willing and able to take it up. The "reconstruction of the igbodu in urban America," condensed and miniaturized, as Murphy points out, fosters a three-layered immersion in "vegetable, mineral, and animal worlds" manifested in polyrhythmic and sacrificial ritual labor.[72]

This urban *igbodu* gets reconfigured in the tonalities of jazz's Spanish-tinged swing—in the Cuban *son* music that insists on combining "the animal-skin tones of the bongos" with "the vegetal sound" of the clave (polished hardwood sticks struck together) or guiro, coupled with the metallic flare of cowbell and horns.[73] From old contradances to modern recordings like Arsenio Rodríguez's "Bruca Maniguá," Eddie Palmieri's "Vamonos pa'l Monte," Dizzy Gillespie's "Manteca," Carlos Santana's "Soul Sacrifice," and the Miami Sound Machine's "The Rhythm Is Gonna Get You," Caribbean musics have kept bush ecologies of relation active inside the city gates. The Haiti-informed styles of Cuba's Oriente province and of New Orleans *Fe Chauffe* brought polyrhythm, swing, call-and-response, improvisational aesthetics, and a certain beat-driven trance orientation to the flux of global dancefloors that have also swung the art world (most famously via cubism's multiplicity of perspective) toward what art critic Gerardo Mosquero calls a "cosmovisual" agency capable of opening up "the long road of a possible de-Eurocentralization" of knowledge, art, and culture.[74] A cosmovisual orientation to earth and the arts moves us in divergent directions from the short-term profit motives of Euro-centralized mastery—whether that mastery be found in plantation monoculture, conquistadorial missions, or university certification of knowledge.

This holistic artistic practice is exemplified in the "earth-body works" of Ana Mendieta, who was airlifted from Cuba to the United States at the age of thirteen via Operation Pedro Pan in 1961.[75] Moved to a boarding school and foster families in Iowa, Mendieta experienced a difficult virtual orphaning. Her memory of Cuban landscape, cultural history, and the spiritual practices of her family's domestic help (a semiotics familiar to white southerners of a certain privilege) pulled her steadily southward from her art education at Iowa (MFA in painting in 1972 and mixed media in 1976) to undertake work in Mexico, Miami, and Cuba. As a graduate student transitioning from painting to "mixed media" and performance, Mendieta observed "*that my paintings were not real enough for what I wanted the image to convey—and by real I mean I wanted my images to have power . . . [so] I had to work directly with nature . . . to go to the source of life, to mother earth.*"[76] For Mendieta, "not real enough" meant going to the mysterious source of life—the "truth" flashed by the Haitian mambo for Zora Neale Hurston (and by the pear tree in *Their Eyes Were Watching God*). Works like *Tree of Life* (1976, in which Mendieta's otherwise naked, mud-and-grass encrusted body is photographed against a huge tree) and titles like *Ñáñigo Burial* (1976), *Fundamento Palo* (1981) and *Figura con Nganga* (1984) bear witness to Turtle's vision quest and to the growing mentorship of Cabrera's *El monte* upon Mendieta's "earth-body" work.[77] We may take a cue from Mendieta's 1984 vision statement: "My art is grounded on the primordial accumulations, the unconscious urges that animate the world, not in an attempt to redeem the past but rather in confrontation with the void, the orphanhood, the unbaptized earth of the beginning, the time that from within the earth looks upon us."[78]

Photographs of Mendieta's Taino- and Ciboney-inspired inscriptions in Cuba's Jaruco National Park in 1981 document her attempt at creating contemporary petroglyphs honoring indigenous deities like *Itiba Cuhababa* (Old Mother Blood), *Guacar* (Our Menstruation), *Atabey* (Mother of the Waters), *Maroya* (Moon), and *Guabancex* (Goddess of the Wind).[79] Her meetings with Lukumi priests in Havana and her work undertaken in Miami during the same year continued the process of earth-body reclamations via attentiveness to fluvial and marine flows. Mendieta executed a beach-body-work on Key Biscayne subtitled "Ochún" for a group exhibition in Miami. Named after Cuba's patron orisha-saint, the "Ochún-body" (silhouetted around the form of Mendieta's body in the beach's tidal wash by two slightly raised serpentine contours of sand) becomes a trough or gulf channeling the surf's waters in ways that—in the documentary photograph reprinted on my book's cover— illuminate the moving waters' reflected sunlight—a sparkling flow (almost like a thousand minnows or gulls) gesturing toward the ephemeral, the body's absence, the elemental, and toward gravitational pulls from heavenly bodies.[80]

Mendieta's *Ceiba Fetish* (1981), a more public and communally interactive work, was executed on the buttressed trunk of a huge ceiba tree in Miami's Cuban Memorial Park. Glueing hair collected from a neighborhood barbershop into her own "lover's mix" incorporated into the tree, Mendieta gave this particular *Ceiba* a visible face of receptivity to sacrificial *derechos*.[81] Here Mendieta's art met with the Little Havana community's response: "*The last time I saw the tree, the people had added coconuts, chicken wings, all kinds of offerings. For a while they put a figure of Santa Barbara underneath it, cut an opening in what would be the face and stuck a shell in the mouth. They have really activated the image and claimed it as their own.*"[82] If this variety of work executed in Miami—from *Ceiba Fetish* to the *Tallus Mater* (Stem Mother) sculptural series—goes to the root of umbilical ties to *el monte*, Mendieta's habit, initiated in Miami, of drawing miniaturized body-silhouettes on individual tree leaves (especially "copey" or balsam apple leaves referred to as "autograph" leaves in the Caribbean) testifies to the deciduating aspects of her art. Outlines of the body etched onto these green leaves take on a luminescent patina as these bio-parchments grow brown and brittle over time.[83]

Ana Mendieta's combinatory performance art—along with the poetry of Miami's Adrian Castro and the music and rites of a whole syndicate of Regla de Ocha, Regla Congo, and Vodou affiliates in Miami—call us to interpenetrating creole/native ritual economies that sustain simultaneously primal and cosmopolitan countercultures of modernity. There is nothing really exotic about this, especially for acclimated Floridians. As Jane Landers writes, the state's past has been steadily "bleached and homogenized" to render it "less disturbingly Caribbean and more comfortably southern." Landers points out that currents of immigration, however, have "once again made Florida a part of the Afro-Hispanic Caribbean," making for a "reblending of peoples" that constitutes "both a return to a more historically 'normal' state of affairs, and a move toward the future."[84] This move toward the future carries with it the "everything OK" sign, the nonapocalyptic healthy sign of Alafia: "the story continues." This is Turtle's sign and is what Benítez-Rojo intuited that October day in Havana, on the brink of nuclear war, as two *santeras* processed in a certain kind of way. With such models and mentors, we may learn to imagine, perform, and swing a futurity that is not apocalypse, not doom or monstrosity . . . but a future of repeating and recongregating musication.

"White Women Have Never Known What to Do with Their Blood"

Gulf Carriers and Sanguine Knowledge

It done soaked clean through onto you.
—Dilsey to Caddy, *The Sound and the Fury*

When Governor George Wallace took his infamous doorway stand to block a descendant of enslaved Africans from admission to the University of Alabama, he doubtless felt he was serving the intent of the state's and nation's founding fathers. He was not wrong in that conviction. Even America's most liberal colleges of humanistic studies have yet to grapple meaningfully with what happens when gateways to the cross-cultural imagination and its repertory are opened. Canons change or crumble. Bodies of knowledge shift shape, and terrain we think we know or possess reveals baffling relations, unthought enfranchisements and interpenetrations calling for epistemological shape-shifting. We should pause, therefore, before naming any single politician or electorate a scapegoat for burdens and becomings more widely shirked.

The great gulf-crossings registerable in deep southern time and creole space constitute more than a multicultural addendum, just as Wallace's stand constituted more than a blockage of access to the halls of Western knowledge. The South's peculiar institutions of higher learning would have to change not just what they taught and whom they served but also how knowledge gets made, vetted, disciplined, and pressed into political and economic service. Wallace intuited these kinds of revolutionary change as surely as did Edgar Allan Poe in his pre–Civil War/post-Haitian encounter with "The Raven": gulfs of knowledge would be exposed, and neither "the pallid bust of Pallas" nor the library "volume[s] of forgotten lore" would regain their sure hold in the face of shadows "lifted—nevermore!"[1]

The Deep South is an old territory of *créolité* that entered the American Union only through the most violent upheavals and prolonged colonial contestation. Back in 1839 when the poet and historian Alexander Meek gave a talk on "The Southwest: Its History, Character and Prospects" at the newly christened University of Alabama, he spoke of a frontier brought from chaos to cosmos, a space "wrought and consecrated through a bitter sacrament of blood."[2] The university itself, of course, was similarly wrought and consecrated. The states of Alabama and Mississippi had been opened up to a massive expansion of plantation economy that wrought irrevocable shifts in the Republic (the rise of Jacksonian democracy), setting and deferring a bloody stage for civil war and—over a century later—the confrontations of the civil rights movement. What may have seemed self-evident to Alexander Meek's (or George Wallace's) Tuscaloosa audience—because of their proximity to so much of the frontier's bloody-mindedness—begs questioning. Whose blood wrought and consecrated this space? Who partakes of the bitter state sacrament? Whose blood spilled and keeps spilling to make it? And who cleans up the mess? What are the workings by which blood-spill may constitute an uncontainable contagion even as it hails into being a fortress community and imagined cultural homogeneity? How is knowledge itself wrought and consecrated in blood?

Attentiveness to the blood-consecrated time-space that Meek conjured from the University of Alabama in 1839 may return us to a more holistic understanding of the sacred, rooted—as René Girard emphasized—in "the Latin *sacer*, which is sometimes translated 'sacred,' sometimes 'accursed,' for it encompasses the maleficent as well as the beneficent."[3] The sacred remains a repeatable time-space of sublime encounter with potentially apocalyptic violence. No space in America invokes the sacred more resolutely than does the Gulf South. In this Bible Belt space of hurricanes and oil rigs, penitentiaries and high cotton, a coming to terms with the sacrificial gulfs we inhabit may force us into multiple gro(o)ves of perspective, putting our narratives of affiliation at risk.

LeAnne Howe's 2001 novel *Shell Shaker* affirms a vital counterpoint to Alexander Meek's University of Alabama lecture. *Shell Shaker* treats its readers to a lecture on Native history by Auda Billy, a Choctaw professor from Southeastern Oklahoma State. Things quickly go south in Professor Billy's interaction with the women attending an event sponsored by the Oklahoma Historical Society. We hear about Choctaw women in pre-Removal Mississippi going into battle with bullet-proofing menstrual blood smeared on their breasts. The speaker's sister, a New Orleans "Wall Street Shaman," hears the white audience's aggressive exasperation in "an audible gasp." She thinks to herself, "Auda should have stopped long before the menstrual blood story. White women have never known what to do with their blood."[4] Well, where Auda Billy should have stopped is where I start this conclusion: in repeating sacraments and consecrations of blood.

"Taste My Bull's Blood, Master"—Shell Shakers and Blossoming Pears

Nothing in American literature is richer than the Deep South's narratives of fabulous, mythopoetic vision. These tales (inscribed by authors as varied as Joel Chandler Harris, Zora Neale Hurston, Lydia Cabrera, Alfred Mercier, and Earnest Gouge) essay ethics, violence, and the sacred from a shared repertory in Gulf contact zones. Why we do not study this literature more often and more carefully than we do remains a key question. Once the fables are put to paper, however, their fabulosity can lose medicinal power and become, in fact, poisonous. The tales may be treated condescendingly as child's play or dismissed for their apparent folk nostalgia, their primitivism or perversions of good moral code. When Betty Mae Jumper offered the first full text of Seminole tales in 1994, for instance, she had difficulty finding a Seminole illustrator because the originally desired illustrator, Paul Billie, insisted they should not be put to paper in English. It would be "bad medicine," an exposure of private parts that could facilitate shameful mutilations of the sacred.[5] Alice Walker has described how the white power structure of the hometown she shared with Joel Chandler Harris (Eatonton, Georgia) appropriated the trickster classics in a manner that shamed black southerners: via an Uncle Remus "dummy in the window" of a local café, a lawn-jockey-like Brer Rabbit sculpture on the courthouse square, and showings of Disney's *Song of the South* in the Jim Crow theaters of Walker's youth.[6] Our most profound pharmacopoeic narrative traditions present this dilemma. No wonder, really, that we no longer read and teach this corpus of medicine-tales that can so quickly become "bad medicine."

As we saw in the previous chapter from Lydia Cabrera's and Earnest Gouge's tales of Turtle's quest for the Truth (vision/gnosis of women's private parts and women's life-carrying temporalities), Turtle gets beaten to a bloody pulp, then manages to "shake-shake-together" a medicine song/dance of reassemblage. We may need, however, to do more to consider Turtle's blood consecrations from the perspective of the mothers. The best literary source for such a consideration may be Howe's *Shell Shaker*, which begins with a chapter titled "Blood Sacrifice" set in Choctaw country during the autumnal equinox of 1738. Shakbatina, a Choctaw peacemaker, recalls her grandmother, "the first Shell Shaker of our people," on the eve of the war-chief Tuscalusa's battle-contact with Hernando de Soto. Preparing for the loss of her husband in battle with the Spanish conquistador—"a very different kind of *Osano*, bloodsucker, he always hungers for more"—Shakbatina's grandmother took novel action: "She built a fire and she strapped the empty shells of turtles round each ankle" and sang and danced without stop for four days until her "ankles were swollen and bloody where the shells and leather twine had cut into them."[7] This blood sacrifice wins favor with the spirit of the autumnal equinox, who gives her a song with equinoctial power to "*make things even*" (2). Shakbatina recounts her grandmother's balancing action as she prepares to give her own life to the Chickasaw (as sacrificial scapegoat for her daughter's alleged crime), recalling how "Grandmother shed blood for her people's survival," an act the novel's contemporary Choctaw "women continue to honor . . . by shaking shells" (4). Interestingly, the novel presents the innovation of shell-shaking as a kind of *Fe Chauffe* balancing act born on the eve of Tuscalusa's disastrous encounter with Europeans (and Africans). That contact moment (with its new turtle-shell rites) corresponds with what René Girard terms "the sacrificial crisis," when the efficacy of traditional sacrament falters and "[t]he sacrificial rites . . . [are] no longer able to accomplish their task," resulting in a "surging tide of impure violence instead of channeling it." Instead of small-scale ritual warfare's balancings between peoples, what arises is "a superabundance of violence of a particularly virulent kind."[8]

From Howe's narrative of counterclockwise stomp-dances created in response to De Soto's contact with Southeastern Indians, the novel moves to connect events surrounding the autumnal equinox of 1991 to historical narratives of the warrior Red Shoes (and Choctaw engagements with the French, English, and Chickasaw) from 1738. In 1991 in Durant, Oklahoma, a "spirit woman with turtle shells strapped to her ankles" appears to a matrilineal descendant of Shakbatina, Auda Billy, who knows this shell-shaking dance "still spiritually reconnects the earth and Indian people during Green Corn time" (18). The autumnal equinox brings Professor Auda Billy to her own moment of sacrificial crisis. We see her tell her Oklahoma Historical Society audience how, in the midst of civil war and pestilence in 1738, Choctaw women "pulled red water and fire from their menstruating bodies and smeared it across their chests," causing the enemy English soldiers to break ranks and run (44). Against the audience's shocked gasps, Auda's sister Adair's unvoiced thoughts of response take on a powerful textual resonance: "White women have never known what to do with their blood" (44).

Shell Shaker addresses a systemic miseducation and removal of integral knowledge. One of the novel's contemporary characters, Delores Love, speaks of attending an Indian boarding school, and of how when she had her first menstrual period after attending a funeral, she thought she was dying. After Delores and her sister escaped the school, "[a] few days later the cook at the 101 Ranch, where they had taken refuge, told them it was natural for a girl to bleed when she got her period. No one at school had bothered to educate them on becoming women" (155). The teachers can't teach it, but Ranch 101 and exposure to the fabulous animal world does. Perhaps we could refer the Love sisters to Deleuze and Guattari on becoming women: how all becomings start with becoming women, becoming egg of intense energies. In *Shell Shaker,* women "create life and, during Green Corn, we shake shells to reconnect with all living things" (152). Turtle's medicine-tale and the women's shell-shaking dance constitute a single calling-responsive gateway of sacrificial recongregation.

In getting his bones picked to make the Gulf Coast's sherry-splashed Easter soup, Turtle plays an indispensable role. We see something of this too in the funeral rites performed on the shell-shaker Shakbatina by her husband, Koi Chitto. He consumes tobacco and black drink, and enters the visionary possession-state's "something white," an antiphonal "indulgence in the sublime" attentive to "the internal drumming of the plant world" (104, 105). Koi Chitto becomes horse of something other: "I am the Bone Picker . . . the one who brings sex, the one who brings rebirth" (106), "the ecstasy of life and rebirth" (107), to his rending of Shakbatina's spinal column. Women signify upon this act in the music they make (much like High Walker and the Bloody Bones) from their stomp-dancing shell-strapped legs. Almost nowhere in Tuscaloosa or Baton Rouge, Jackson or Jacksonville, can we find this blood-and-bone knowledge in the curricula. It is a removed knowledge—aside from what *Shell Shaker* and other Gulf narratives manage to reassemble.

As much as I do love and admire Howe's *Shell Shaker*, I am not altogether convinced that the text knows what to do with its blood. For in spite of the fact that Turtle's repertoire in the Indian country of the Deep South was powerfully impacted by Afro-creole contributions, and in spite of the substantial contribution of Africans to Native lore and life, there isn't a single reference to Africans, black Indians, maroons, or chattel slavery in this historical novel superabundant with English, French, Choctaw, Chickasaw, Alibamu, Spanish, and even Irish and Italian reference. Blacks get removed from the historical narrative of *Shell Shaker* in a manner similar to their erasure from the Dawes Rolls' Degree of Indian blood records. LeAnne Howe's powerful novel does not know what to do with its African blood.[9] This marks a repression doubly unfortunate: for the richness of Afro-Indian contacts that could be explored and for the disingenuousness of Choctaw, Creek, and Chickasaw claims to sovereignty that utilize an Africanized traditional culture to buttress Native cultural capital. We recognize, of course, a pattern replicating the white South's (and white America's) dismissive appropriations of Afro-creole cultural agency.

What gets erased is the fact that Africans and black creoles were key go-betweens and translators in the Gulf South's contact zones. Jane Landers speaks of blacks as "culture brokers" in colonial Florida, and Gwendolyn Midlo Hall discusses African-Indian networks that culminated in "an underground railway involving the Western Choctaw" (led by Red Shoes, *Shell Shaker*'s historic warlord), who were seeking black warriors ready to assist them and their Chickasaw and English allies against the French and Eastern Choctaw during the period Howe's novel chronicles.[10] As with African contact with Europeans, what often gets left out of discussion is the reciprocal agency of Afro-Indian contact: the Afro-creole medicine-agency carried to the stomp grounds, where—as with the ring shouts and orisha dances—the dance moves counterclockwise around the fire.[11]

New Fire, Earnest Gouge's collection of Creek folktales, certainly attests to the reciprocal enculturation of Afro-Indian contacts. Almost half the tales in his collection have clear African precedents. If bodies of Creek narrative (such as Gouge's rich collection of rabbit, turtle, and other tales) have been thrown away from what might constitute a holistic body of Gulf South literature, the Afro-Creek remains utterly abandoned and simultaneously crucial. The earliest-known Creek author, George Stiggins, gave black Red Stick Creeks their due, insisting that they "would not cease" in the crucial moments of the attack on Fort Mims and were invaluable to the Red Stick triumph there at the onset of the Creek War.[12] However, Kinnie Hadjo, a Red Stick war veteran, told historians that his people "had compromised the dignity of their nation in stooping so low as to call to their aid the services of such a servile and degraded race as negroes to assist them in fighting the battles of their country."[13] In Oklahoma, the Dawes Commission's completion by 1903 of racially segregated lists of "Indians" by degree of "blood" and of "freedmen" by phenotypic evidence of black "race" helped to orphan Afro-Indians from claims to Indian citizenship at a time when blacks were being disenfranchised across the United States and when Indians were again removed from sovereignty and land by (Oklahoma) statehood. The study of Afro-Indian contacts forces systemic rethinking of our contact zones— well beyond habitual Euro-colonial and current Choctaw or Creek national boundaries.

When reading Earnest Gouge's and Lydia Cabrera's Creek and Cuban turtle narratives, we may ask, What do we do with our gulfs' challenging shell-shaking blood consecrations? For pointers we can turn to Zora Neale Hurston, who came, like Turtle, "face to face with the truth" while studying the Vodou mysteries and while writing *Their Eyes Were Watching God*.[14] A Caribbean/ Gulf sanguine knowledge also suffuses Hurston's first novel (rather darkly), in the pages in which Baptist preacher John Pearson gets told that his second wife has been working "all kinds uh roots and conjure"; most specifically, "She been feedin' you outa her body fuh years."[15] Something of this *konesans* appears in the Dominica of Marie-Elena John's *Unburnable* as a character is instructed how to "tie" her man with rice "[t]hat have to cook on coal pot, because you have to stand over it for your blood to mix in good, straight from inside your body."[16] We may recall too the knowledge Christophine drops on Rochester (and our reading of *Jane Eyre*) in the Dominica of Jean Rhys's *Wide Sargasso Sea*: "Taste my bull's blood, master."[17] Several of my students at the University of North Florida have recognized this power of the blood in their own region's hoodoo pharmacology, attesting to the need for young men to eat red spaghetti sauce prepared only by trusted kin . . . because Jacksonville women can still do a thing or two with their blood. These manifestations of Gulf/Caribbean sanguine knowledge are not merely a matter of sensational mystification. Rather, they signify an attitude toward embodiment and desires. These are women who will not be shamed by their blood-stained calabash or punch bowl—women who will instead draw power from their sacral journeys.

A strong undercurrent of matrifocality and women's agency shaped the basilect of creolization in New World plantation societies. Neither the Choctaw women of *Shell Shaker*, nor the Haitian *femme-jardin*, nor the women of Hurston's jooks and spirit-houses need a man to legitimize them or their "blood." Women of power and knowledge have, nevertheless, had to face steady, nigh-hegemonic ideological currents that work to shame the very matrices of their (and their children's) hold on corporeal, intergenerational, and ritual *konesans*. These modes of shaming have had a heavy hand in the disappearance of narrative bodies of knowledge at the contact zone. For instance, nowhere in African American bodies of folk narrative do we find "Turtle Looks up Women's Dresses." We encounter the tale in Creek, Yuchi, and Cuban narrative, along with traces of it from Louisiana, and strong prototypes in contemporary Nigeria. Afro-creoles (and Nigerians) may very well have deselected and disappeared Turtle's quest for vision of women's private parts out of the same cultural shame and focus on racial uplift that led to the disappearance of the ring shout, initiatory "seeking," saraka, junkanoo, and service to the *lwa* and orisha across much of North America: a self-censorship of access to the limbo gateway (encouraged by black elites via ideologies of racial uplift or radical/nationalist politics).

Most often, all we find of Turtle or Kumba are traces of the wake of Gulf or riverine submersion. The *hippikat* vision of Langston Hughes's "Jazzonia," however, refuses to be shamed, and moves steadily low and into the waters of its brazen Harlem cabaret vision-quest:

A dancing girl whose eyes are bold
Lifts high a dress of silken gold.

Oh singing tree!
Oh shining rivers of the soul![18]

Drawn through a *Fe Chauffe* swing-space into deep time, all eyes gaze upon the sacred here—as the poem and dancer move us from the reassembled souths of jazz-age Manhattan back to Egypt (Cleopatra), Eden (Eve), and the tree of an African *monte* blooming with life's mystery. In the shining rivers of "Jazzonia" and the embodied rhythms of its dancer's flows, we may find access to what Dana Medoro describes as a pharmacy of remediation for "patriarchal monotheisms" and their "repudiation of all that menstruation and menstrual blood signified." Medoro helps us see that Kumba's and Turtle's sanguine knowledge "did not disappear; it went underground, so to speak, and it continues to inform our cultural narratives and myths"—giving a poem like "Jazzonia" its perspective on the sacred, and giving even a novel like Faulkner's *The Sound and the Fury* its curative initiatory project.[19] Moving steadily through the breakages of phallic and racialized legitimacy, *The Sound and the Fury* forces author, plot, and comprehensibility to lie low and submit to Turtle's quest around a single, multiply observed image: "Caddy Compson climbing the pear tree to look in the window at her grandmother's funeral while Quentin and Jason and Benjy and the negroes looked up at the muddy seat of her drawers."[20]

Turtle's entire re-assembled body of tales and texts (in Gouge, Cabrera, Howe, Hurston, et al.), along with a body of *hippikat* criticism (Dana Medoro, Ruth Salvaggio, Minrose Gwin, Valérie Loichot, Monique Allewaert, Édouard Glissant) prepares us to reread a text like *The Sound and the Fury* for the ways its blood-periodicities course through the wetlands of the Yoknapatawpha County it constructs. In its swamping displacement of the ego and persona of the author, *The Sound and the Fury* serves as a sacral retreat of becoming-Turtle and becoming-Caddy. This is how Faulkner recalled the time-space of the text's remaking of self and imagination: "One day I seemed to shut a door between me and all publishers' addresses and book lists. I said to myself, Now I can write . . . So I, who never had a sister and was fated to lose my daughter in infancy, set out to make myself a beautiful and tragic little girl."[21] In *The Sound and the Fury*, Faulkner *makes* girl akin to the way followers of Santería *make* saint by becoming-bride (*iyawo*) in initiation. This becoming-girl/woman must always be *made*, and is never given. Not for Hurston who had to make it, not for Cabrera or Mendieta, not for Kumba or Oya's children. What was once a widespread practice of initiation has gone underground and made the modern novel an uncanny refuge. Strangely enough, as both Glissant and Harris have insisted, it was a man of Mississippi's patriarchal planter class who did as much as anyone to reopen and transfigure this limbo gateway to initiatory knowledge of the blood.[22]

"Blood en de Ricklickshun"—Moaning Deciduations, Sanguine Knowledge

Western modernity's awakening to perspective—what we might call the parallax effect—meant that any effort to write responsibly from a gulf of contact zones must emerge from multiplicity, contrapuntal awareness, basilectal as well as acrolectal renderings. It is not too much to speak of Faulkner's performance in *The Sound and the Fury* as constituting, according to Wendy Belcher, a form of discursive possession hailing from modes of "reciprocal enculturation" whereby the discursive or performative agency of Afro-creole genius may "penetrate, we might even say animate or possess, European identities and literatures."[23] Yoknapatawpha presents such a transcultural space that it fills with the seepage of all that plantation rule had excluded. For Faulkner, this text marked the death and birthing of another kind of author(ity), recognized less by filiation than by carriage of—or possession by—what had been called contagion. Faulkner acknowledged this in his multiple attempts to narrate perspective upon what he recognized as the novel's catalytic image: "the muddy bottom of a little doomed girl climbing a blooming pear tree in April to look in the window at the funeral."[24]

Dana Medoro has attended most powerfully to how *The Sound and the Fury* adopts what she calls a "menstrual economy," pushing it "to fathom the extensive conceptual alignment of menstrual blood with other forms of flowing blood—from the blood of wounds to the sacrificial blood of Christ."[25] She observes that the writing allies itself with a rhythmic/periodic bleeding that is "a poison and remedy at once" and ultimately "pharmacopoeic."[26] I follow Medoro (and LeAnne Howe and the orphan Kumba/Cinderella tale) in examining what Faulkner's initiatory novel reveals about *why* white (wo)men of the Gulf South have never known what to do with their blood, and *how* folk pay for this lack of sanguine knowledge. In Faulkner's Jefferson, Mississippi, when white girls reach the age of the Senegalese Kumba (with her dirty calabash) or the St. Kittitian Cinderella (with her blood-daubed punch bowl), they have no process to guide them in becoming-woman. This lack of a journey into the bush to be swallowed under the guidance of a wise and wounded crone marks the first erasure of gulf *konesans*.

Since no time-space of initiation exists for Jefferson's "ladies," the hegemonic cultural space faces an underdeveloped rapport with periodic, repeating time and the ethics and erotics of antiphony. The suppression of women's periodic time diminishes the possibilities of stepping outside the steady march to a universal standard time geared toward apocalypse. With the suppression of periodic time comes an accompanying suppression of (wo)men's shape-shifting, becoming-animal, becoming-sorcerer, linked to the menstrual cycle, pregnancy and childbearing, menopause. For white women, as for good colonial subjects, there would be no more becoming-porcupine-spirit (as in *Shell Shaker*), no more becoming-buffalo (as in Ifa tales and in Cabrera), no more becoming-vulture (as with Kumba's initiating crone), no more becoming-river siren or Fury or Turtle. Deleuze and Guattari argue that "[a]ll so-called initiatory journeys include these thresholds and doors where becoming itself becomes."[27] It is for this reason that *The Sound and the Fury* has readers approach Caddy first through the autistic, rather alien Benjy, whose narrative moaning makes for a threshold of rapport with the animal and vegetal worlds, and with alterity itself.

In the advent of a neoplatonic Christianity geared for transcendence and ticking toward apocalypse, the pharmacological value of menstruation and the carnal knowledge attached to Eve's curse came to be displaced by a questionable cure: Christ's sacrificial blood-spill. All subsequent blood spillage (other than the apocalyptic) would be meaningless. Nevertheless, specters of older and other periodicities find their way into the Christian calendars and evangelized colonial spaces. Beyond Christian patriarchal reroutings of sacral time-space, the determinative block to white (wo)men's blood-gnosis was the advent of the racializing modifier itself. Whiteness, as (non)marker of ethnicity, positioned whites as a people who could not possibly know what to do with their blood (save keep it consanguine, i.e., "in the family") since to spill or mix blood was to enter into the denaturing stain of color and impurity. Certainly since the Enlightenment and the making of lucrative plantation economies out of transatlantic chattel slavery, "Whites" could not know what to do with so much impure blood on their hands. Nor could whites know what to do with the rhythmic blood-spill from those fragile vessels of whiteness: the women whose purity carried the white man's burdens, *his* powers of legitimization. We see that the burdens of (im)purity took on their most explosive form at the threatened margins of the Western colonial system—in the contact zones of plantation southlands inhabited by bloodsucking hags, soucouyants, bluegum sorcerers—where whiteness gets backed into impossible corners of sacrificial crisis, leading demographically and symbolically to choices of incest and/or miscegenation. Every text and ledger of Yoknapatawpha County reveals this "impossibility of being able to assume a stable identity," an impasse, according to Benítez-Rojo, that "can only be made right through the possibility of existing 'in a certain kind of way' in the midst of the sound and fury of chaos."[28] The character of the black matriarch Dilsey models the possibility of being fully and enduringly present "in a certain kind of way" amidst the chaos of *The Sound and the Fury*. However, as the narrative of the failed or "spoiled" sister Kumba acknowledges, African women do not necessarily know what to do with their blood either. *Konesans* is no given. It must be courted and fetched in seekerly rites of adoptive reaffiliation.

From the novel's opening page, when Benjy is told to "Shut up that moaning" after the golfer's call, "Here, caddie," Faulkner scripts Caddy Compson in the role of carrier of the burdens (white balls) of Compson and Bascomb blood. Caddy's mother, Caroline, admits, "I am not one of those women who can stand things" (6), and insists that Caddy not carry her little brother: "All of our women have prided themselves on their carriage. Do you want to look like a washerwoman" (40). Caddy must paradoxically carry the burden of Compson/Bascomb blood by not carrying anything, anyone, any stain at all. We meet Caddy, a little girl squatting in the branch (the creek that signifies tree) "all wet and muddy behind" (12). When the black servant-child Frony asks if the funeral (for Caddy's grandmother) has begun yet, and then defines the word for little Jason Compson—"Where they moans"—Caddy is right to insist, "Oh . . . That's niggers. White folks don't have funerals" (21), meaning white folks (other than "idiots" like Benjy) don't moan. They don't know what to do with life or death and fear making a show of their fear—their lack of containment, lack of *konesans*. So Caddy climbs up into the pear tree to see for herself: "We watched the muddy bottom of her drawers . . . We could hear the tree thrashing" (25). It is finally the black surrogate mother (Dilsey), charged with raising all the Compson children, who points to Caddy's carriage of sanguine knowledge, a gnosis that white Mississippians view only as curse or shameful contagion. Dilsey tells Caddy, "It done soaked clean through onto you . . . But you won't get no bath this night" (48). Caddy can't know what to do with this muddy, abject "it" that has soaked clean through onto her. And despite Caddy's carriage of a transcultural osmosis, her racialized relationship with Dilsey does not foster the respect that would allow her to receive Dilsey's mentoring. So Caddy ultimately carries the text into its doom and unladylike hope, described via her brothers' projections. She does "*like nigger women do in the pastures the ditches the dark woods*" (59). Caddy moans from sacred gulfs.

The text's initial avatar, the autistic Benjy, also carries the burden of moaning in *The Sound and the Fury*. His perspective launches the novel's plunge into becomings-animal, sorcerer, syncopator of a moaning word-flow. Benjy is constantly rendered in a quasi-animal state—"He just runs along the fence" (34); "*Has he got to keep that old dirty slipper on the table*" (45); "*It's like eating with a pig*" (45); "*He must learn to mind*" (41). His narrative, aligned with what Dilsey calls "*the Lawd's own time*" (16), forces readers to unmind much of their learning—pushing us into a deeper, more periodic time than anything registerable on Jefferson's or Harvard's clocks and calendars. The older, castrated Benjy also shares a certain ball-lessness with his young black "keeper" Luster, who tells him, "That white man hard to get along with . . . You see him take my ball," even as Luster threatens Benjy: "They going to send you to Jackson" to be "with the rest of the looneys and slobber" (35). Faulkner throws readers—sink or swim—into a zone where legitimacy (based on having [white] balls) falls apart, where names change and a hoodoo contagion asserts authority: "*Versh said, Your name Benjamin now. You know how come your name Benjamin now. They making a bluegum out of you. Mammy say in old time your granpaw changed nigger's name, and he turn preacher, and when they look at him, he bluegum too. Didn't use to be bluegum, neither. And when family woman look him in the eye in the full of the moon, chile born bluegum*" (44). In this first great novel of Gulf modernity, strange conversions take place, including this tale of becoming bluegum preacher (attributed to Dilsey's authority) with a vampirelike bite.[29]

Blood, however, remains the ultimate pharmaceutical here, and the novel's viral "bluegum" subnarrative thickens Dana Medoro's argument—that this is "a story obsessed with blood, purity, and Caddy's torn hymen," tied to an "inability to keep women and black servants in their place."[30] Quentin Compson, the eldest son obsessed with the relentless march of clock-time, is heir to his region's and blood's racialized ideology of gender: the notion "that there is no halfway ground that a woman is either a lady or not" (66). Quentin finds himself continually called to restore unvarying plantation patterns of racialized behavior since "a nigger is not a person so much as a form of behavior; a sort of obverse reflection of the white people he lives among" (55). The novel, however, moves in contrapuntal loops of behavior since Caddy ends up behaving "like nigger women do in the pasture the ditches the dark woods" (59), and Quentin's obsession with becoming-Caddy brings him to obsess over his obverse reflection—"my shadow leaning flat upon the water"—as transculturally defined for him: "Niggers say a drowned man's shadow was watching for him in the water all the time" (57). Driven finally to lynch the incestuous nigger he has obversely become, Quentin first ponders the possibility of genital mutilation that was performed upon his brother Benjy: "Versh told me about a man who mutilated himself . . . did it with a razor . . . flinging them backward over his shoulder the same motion complete the jerked skein of blood backward not looping" (73). Despite Versh's exemplary tale, Quentin finds that he cannot fling the stain backward in time. Caddy and her daughter must serve as the carriers (and scapegoats) of otherwise shorn Compson balls.

An incestuous and suicidal white logic drives Quentin's obsession over "Oh her blood or my blood Oh" (85), as he yearns to be the defender of his sister's (and blood's) honor. In an attempt to fight one of Caddy's lovers, however, he "just passed out like a girl" (103). As Medoro points out, Quentin bleeds like a girl after a fight with a fellow southerner at Harvard, and is told he "lost caste . . . by not holding your blood better" (105). Quentin almost becomes Caddy in the way this fight stains his vest with his blood: "You can't get that off . . . You'll have to send it to the cleaner's" (104). A culturally cultivated lack of *konesans* leads to his Charles River death-plunge (obversely—for readers—a baptismal immersion) in a narrative colored by Quentin's "Father said" perspective on women's time and transcultural space: "Delicate equilibrium of periodical filth between two moons balanced," "Liquid putrefaction like drowned things floating like pale rubber flabbily filled getting the odor of honeysuckle all mixed up" (81). In this postplantation space, everything's being "all mixed up" and out of metronome time drives the white need for sacrificial differentiation, spatial and temporal control.

Dana Medoro has thus far been the best reader of the menstrual economy of Faulkner's initiatory novel. Medoro is especially insightful in illuminating how it is left to Caddy's illegitimate daughter, "Miss Quentin," to follow her mother's path and escape the Compson/Bascom entombment of life via an Easter-morning descent of her mother's old pear tree: "on the floor lay a soiled undergarment of cheap silk a little too pink . . . The window was open. A pear tree grew there, close against the house. It was in bloom and the branches scraped and rasped against the house and the myriad air, driving in the window, brought into the room the forlorn scent of blossoms" (176). Jason, Dilsey, and Mrs. Compson stare together here at an absence and at the Truth of resurrection: the pear tree's scrape and rasp, the sexed "myriad air" pungent with blossoms. Caddy's illegitimate daughter (here, no female can legitimate anything) follows her mother's path, moving down a pear tree in Easter bloom, to the carnival man in the red tie, some Tea Cake who can impart something like the moaning and shiver of Dilsey's church.

It takes Benjy, in Dilsey's care, to get the narrative perspective of the novel inside Dilsey's black congregation on Easter Sunday. Through Benjy the text can bring readers to moan with Rev. Shegog's Easter sermon and its rites of spirit possession: "the voice consumed him, until he was nothing and they were nothing and there was not even a voice but instead their hearts were speaking to one another in chanting measures beyond the need for words" (183). A blood-consecrated gnosis gets summoned by the Reverend's initiate call: "I got de ricklickshun en de blood of de Lamb!" "Is you got de ricklickshun en de Blood of e Lamb?" (184). The erotic response of a congregation come aflow knows what to do with its blood's recollection: " 'Mmmmmmmmmmmmmm!' . . . 'Yes, Jesus! Jesus!' " (184). In its seemingly apocalyptic call to all the "arisen dead whut got de blood en de ricklickshun of de Lamb!" (185), Rev. Shegog's sermon invites us to see our way through apartheid zombifications—to kiss the truth and moan what we know not save in our moaning. In spite of the church's theology (its base in apocalyptic scripture), the congregation's behavioral performance is hardly concerned with the alpha and omega of the book of Revelation. Rather, it awakens a durational balance across time, exemplified in Dilsey's moaning: "I've seed de first en de last . . . Never you mind me" (185). What Dilsey speaks of from a repeating performance knowledge of the blood is not a matter of apocalyptic doom but a more limited damnation—that of whoever cannot endure whelming flows of change. Shegog's Easter sermon and Dilsey's response co-create a repeating, periodic wash of blood for which one name, as Édouard Glissant tells us, is " 'creolization,' the unstoppable conjunction . . . (like a tumultuous Mississippi)" that brings the drowning or "the damnation of those who fight it."[31]

Faulkner's figure for a cultivated ignorance of symbolic and ritual wisdom is Caroline Compson, the text's real and symbolic white mother. She speaks for all white women who have never known what to do with their own or their wayward daughters' blood: "Fiddle sticks . . . It's in the blood . . . It can't be simply to flout and hurt me. Whoever God is, He would not permit that. I'm a lady" (186). A lady, of course, neither sweats nor bleeds. God would not permit her moaning (though she may whine and complain like hell) since God is a gentleman. A lady remains the altar built in God's honor—on the backs, sweat, tears, and blood of others—and drained of life's every abject fluidity by a host of help. Of course, neither Caddy Compson nor Janie Crawford Woods nor the shell-shaking mothers of Turtle's quest will turn out to be ladies. Medoro's menstrual rubric for reading *The Sound and the Fury* is most apt in positioning menstrual blood as the *pharmakon*'s paradigmatic fluid element, and in insisting that "[as] *pharmakon* or abjection, the contamination Caddy and Miss Quentin represent is also the cure of an ideology that divides women into 'ladies' and 'bitches.' "[32]

Faulkner's Yoknapatawpha itself, when read "in a certain kind of way" as Benítez-Rojo advocates, provides a potent bush-pharmacy. All of Yoknapatawpha becomes a sacred grove for new genealogies of affiliation. From the Yoknapatawpha River's often engulfing waters and tributaries, to Frenchman's Bend (and its links to ports in Haiti and Martinique), to the initiatory frozen creek of *Intruder in the Dust* (into which the young Charles Mallison falls and is rescued by Lucas Beauchamp's hospitality), to the "branch" in which Caddy muddies her drawers, to Quentin's final plunge into Boston waters, Yoknapatawpha's fluvial sacraments conjoin abject and sublime experience.

In public appearances, Faulkner often occluded the sacrifices his texts obsessively unearth. His discussion of a single story, "Red Leaves," is most telling on this point. When asked in Virginia of his choice of title for the story (which chronicles the ritual-funerary chase and sacrifice of a dead Chickasaw chief's African slave by Chickasaw clan members), Faulkner described the blood on those leaves in naturalistic terms: "The red leaves referred to the Indian. It was the deciduation of Nature which no one could stop that had suffocated and destroyed the Negro . . . it was normal deciduation which the red leaves, whether they regretted it or not, had nothing more to say in."[33] Faulkner's explanation of the Darwinian sacrifice of "the Negro" by Indians, attributed to the "normal deciduation" of Nature itself, uses a menstrual/periodic trope (the decidua of the vaginal lining . . . or of autumn leaves) to try to slip free from white responsibility for genocide against deciduated "red leaves" (the entire process of Indian removal) and from white supremacy's daily racial suffocations at home in Mississippi. But those of us who enter Yoknapatawpha's woods know that its texts always say more, that this has less to do with Indians or the periodicities of unstoppable Nature than with white southerners' perceptions of their own deciduations.

Doubly uncanny for its transcultural intertextuality is the way Faulkner's scripting of human sacrifice in "Red Leaves" parallels the Yoruba sacrificial rite that structures Wole Soyinka's play *Death and the King's Horseman* (1975). Engaging historical incidents in the Nigerian Yoruba Kingdom of Oyo in 1946, Soyinka's drama also presents a funerary ceremony at a moment of sacrificial crisis. The play features the king's "Horseman," Elesin, as he watches for the new moon in order to fulfill his role of committing ritual suicide at the appropriate lunar period following the death of the king. In both Faulkner's and Soyinka's narratives, the funeral of a leader is delayed for the sacrifice of a retainer who will accompany the dead leader's horse and dog to serve him in the afterlife. Both funerary texts find resolution (a carrier of their ills or traumas) in human sacrifice at a moment of contagious cultural crisis, and both seek to open encounter with inadequately mourned losses by invoking the judiciary Dead (the *egungun* society for Soyinka and the clan/ Klan of "Red Leaves"). Faulkner's feel for the temporal-spatial-cultural interpenetrations of Yoknapatawpha's sacrificial crises and blood consecrations moves readers into unfathomably creolizing swamps. A single scene from "Red Leaves" plunges rereadings of *The Sound and the Fury* into Yoknapatawpha's deep, repeating time—into fluid periodicities that link the creeks and branches feeding the Mississippi and Niger deltas.

We enter this swamp in "Red Leaves" as the parricidal Moketubbe is goaded to lead the hunt for his dead father's runaway slave so that burial may be completed and he may hold the chiefly title "the Man" and claim a pair of fetishized red slippers. Only until Moketubbe can open "the door to the earth" by saying to his dead father, "Here is thy dog, thy horse, thy Negro . . . [B]egin the journey," can he legitimately wear the ill-fitting Cinderella shoes that mark his status as the Man (327).

As with Soyinka's rhythmic backing for Elesin's moon-appointed death-passage, the African creek bottom rites of "Red Leaves" take on a polyrhythmic intensity in the Afro-Chickasaw funeral rhythms for their own man's passage: "let the drums talk . . . let the drums tell it" (328). These drum rhythms of sacrificial blood-spill across deep time constitute something of the deciduation that Caddy Compson steps into when she muddies her drawers in a creek on the Compson property on the eve of her grandmother's funeral. The creek branch of *The Sound and the Fury* is really the same fluvial body as the one in "Red Leaves," "where at certain phases of the moon the Negroes would . . . [go] to the creek bottom, where they kept their drums" (314–15). Moon-phase ceremonies held in the creek bottom with drums normally "buried in the mud on the bank of a slough" (328) attune our readings of *The Sound and the Fury* to feminine gulfs and to circum-Atlantic time-space. When we read Caddy in antiphonal dialogue with the pre-Removal time-space of "Red Leaves" (wherein "Tomorrow is just another name for today"

[337]), we see that she also becomes the object of a narrative hunt and a carrier of others' deciduations—her slippers a fetish, her blood-rhythm mixed with honeysuckle and leaves. The old creek bottom from which her muddy-drawered image emerges up into a pear tree turns out to be a locus harboring transcultural genius . . . along with a certain unmourned grief.

The death rites of "Red Leaves" reveal Yoknapatawpha's creek bottoms to be sites of moon-phase ceremonies for otherwise mud-buried Afro-Chickasaw drums. The Compsons do not know how to respond to those waters and rhythms—though Faulkner's art (rather than the author's public statements of Nature's deciduations) does. We can understand the bottom's mud—what's "done washed clean onto you"—as sign of sacral flow, initiatory blood. According to René Girard, spilt blood's "very fluidity gives form to the contagious nature of violence" since "Blood stains everything it touches the color of violence and death."[34] In considering how the flow and stains of menstrual blood may find equation with blood spilled (and vengeance demanded) by violence—which the Greek symbology of the Furies acknowledges—Girard would have us "inquire whether this process of symbolization does not respond to some half-suppressed desire to place the blame for all forms of violence on women."[35] Yoknapatawpha's deciduations do place a heavy sacrificial load upon the Indians, Africans, and bitches scripted to carry white ladies' and gentlemen's unthought blood-gnosis. "Red Leaves," however, like *The Sound and the Fury* and Faulkner's subsequent work, points to the profound dysfunction of these old scapegoating displacements, a doom served in channeling this repeating violence . . . in not knowing what to do with our blood.

"Red Leaves" and *The Sound and the Fury* present readers with a degeneration of relations to sacral bush, a surge of dispiriting violence, and a yearning for something simultaneously old and new in what's left of Yoknapatawpha's sacred swamps and branches. Glissant positions Faulkner as a circum-Caribbean creole whose texts ceaselessly plumb the breakup of Western legitimacy (the single root), offering in Yoknapatawpha a composite "new type of origin," a rhizomatic "open frontier" entered "only through initiation into the wilderness of the unnamed," a time-space in which "Thought rides from one person to another, the way the loas . . . ride those they have chosen to possess."[36] The West African novelist Tierno Monénembo writes similarly of his first encounters with *The Sound and the Fury*, calling it a virtual sacred grove: "to read Faulkner is to be initiated."[37] It is to learn how to read in such a way as to be ridden by thought and restored behaviors of the gulf.

The deciduating pharmacy of "Red Leaves" helps us learn to hear Caddy's voice, resense Benjy's moaning, and recollect ourselves in Dilsey's calling-responsive Easter rites. As text, *The Sound and the Fury* swamps and possesses us, moves us into a limbo gateway. Faulkner's malleably wrought sentences, Wilson Harris insists, serve as carriers of premises and intuitions that "are reluctant to be raised to consciousness," sending writer/reader across "a prickly regionalism or fortress homogeneity" in a "demanding art in which . . . a transformed mosaic of community comes into play."[38] Following Harris, Glissant, Monénembo, and Medoro in acknowledging so much that has done soaked clean through onto us, I'm inclined to take my final pointerly directive for entering *The Sound and the Fury*'s initiatory groves from Minrose Gwin, who in calling for a kind of hyperattentiveness to Caddy's voice in the novel, uses a language aligned with spirit possession's ritual displacements of ego: "Our willingness to relinquish mastery, to admit that we do not know, frees us to seek out what it *is* we do not know," and she asserts that "by relinquishing our (imagined) mastery over it, our attempts to *fix* it, we may find ourselves being engulfed by it (much, I think, as Faulkner allowed himself to be) and losing ourselves in it and to it. We may believe ourselves in danger."[39] Faulkner's first *great* novel of Gulf-modernity takes away the space that would separate the reader from the co-writing participant, who must also bleed, not mind, drink the black drink, and vomit up poisons to endure Yoknapatawpha's most trying cure—immersion in its tannin-stained waters.

In the beginning of *The Sound and the Fury*, the Man that was Faulkner let his writing lose its balls. In the end this is the only way to get us all inside Dilsey's church. We have to open ourselves to periodic lunacy and a bleeding from our private parts, maybe even be sent to Jackson (to the looney bin and/or to the "Great White Father with a sword" [203]) just to get a glimpse of it up there in the pear tree. The Truth . . . the great mystery. Think of Turtle, beaten to bloody pulps—doing that wicked shell-shake thing of recollection. Turtle stays after a vision of it. You can wrap those necklaces round his neck, throw him in the deepest river. Shake his bones till you bleed. But Turtle keeps going low for an immersion in it. Caddy and daughter keep climbing and descending the pear tree for a vision of death and resurrection in the blood. We may also recall Kate Chopin's women's immersion in gulfs and bayous. Or we return to Hurston, our eyes watching "it" become God rolling in stunning waves over our heads. We have to be ready to read across these waters for guidance: Jean Rhys's Antoinette having her third eye opened with a rock upside the forehead by Tia in *Wide Sargasso Sea*, or the "divine window women still have on life" that serves as a reading lens in Patrick Chamoiseau's *Texaco*. Turtle and the mothers point to a writing that relinquishes mastery in its bleeding, that moves like Quentin's Harvard friend (Spoade) "in the middle of them like a terrapin in a street of dead leaves" (50), seeking what, all mixed up, smells like leaves, like honeysuckle, like Truth's ricklickshun of the blood.

The Way of the Saints—Welty's Worn Path

I want to take a parting look at initiatory travel narratives to test a circum-Atlantic reading of Eudora Welty's and Phoenix Jackson's "A Worn Path." Welty's "A Worn Path" has been one of the most widely read stories in introductory literature classes in America. It has not, however, been read with adequate enough orientation to the Gulf's commonplace experience and *konesans*. It makes poetic sense that "A Worn Path" first appeared in *The Atlantic* (1941) and found book publication as the final "travel" of Welty's first book, *A Curtain of Green* (1941). Engaging periodic ritual time, referencing festival figures, and depicting its fabulous central avatar as a bird-woman (Phoenix) on a mythic errand for a "peeping" grandchick, "A Worn Path" carried Welty into the gulf authority that the tale essayed and affirmed from behind the initiate's veiled *Curtain of Green*.

I step into Welty's "Worn Path" in the tradition of Baptist praise-house travelers by acknowledging key "pointers" or guides along the way. Dawn Trouard has charged us with reading "the fiercest secrets" of orphaning in Welty. Trouard takes the following exclamation from the character Nina Carmichael in Welty's "Moon Lake" as a rubric for our journey into the wilderness to be swallowed: "The orphan! She thought exultantly. The other way to live . . . It's only interesting, only worthy, to try for the fiercest secrets. To slip into them all—to change for a moment into Gertrude, into Mrs. Gruenwald, into Twosie—into a boy. To have been an orphan."[40] To speak from the position of *having been* an orphan is to bear witness from the reaffiliated position of a blood-consecrated initiate. Barbara Ladd also points us (with an emphasis slightly different from my own) on our path by calling attention to Welty's assertive handling of an editor's demand for a preamble to be added to "A Pageant of Birds" (1943) recounting a black Baptist performance from Mississippi. The cheeky sanguinity of Welty's *New Republic*–decreed opening to "Pageant" bears its own cosmopolitan witness to gulf authority: "I have been told that this little account needs a generality of some kind made in the first paragraph to Northern readers. I do not think it does, since any generality could only be the commonplace belief I have that magic-making is often the strange compound of humbleness and pride, or in the other direction, out of pride to humbleness, the way the saints, for instance, achieved it."[41] Welty refuses to exoticize or provincialize a church pageant that she clearly finds most common to human experience across time and space on the planet. The provincial is the one who cannot recognize this. She would move her reader "out of [Yankee or white and male] pride to humbleness" in the path of the saints (what Cubans call "Santería"). This includes a wresting of normative, accrediting authority from the metropole, laying claim to an authority of "the other direction," from Jackson, Mississippi, in what is truly a commonplace performance of belief, "a strange compound of humbleness and pride."

Keeping mindful of the useful potentialities of plagiarism, I should also note how a student's appropriation of Alfred Appel's now-dated but strangely apt praise of "A Worn Path" via enotes.com helped hasten my travel down a path that, as Appel and enotes present it, "passes far beyond its regionalism because of its remarkable fusion of various elements of myth and legend, which invest the story with a religious meaning that can be universally felt."[42] Welty's story of Phoenix Jackson's saintly journey seems to me to draw its subtle power directly *from* its deep temporal/mythic foray *into* its region. This is a region where elements of myth and legend have come to us already remarkably fused and invested with religious meaning. We recognize this commonplace practice as creolization. But we may also recognize in Appel's commonplace statement from 1965 the claims to universal appeal found on so many of the era's back-cover blurbs, replete with assertions that although the author writes of Southside Chicago, a Nigerian village, Haiti's revolution, or Mississippi, the text nevertheless speaks from a human world. We are only beginning to see how Welty's or Hurston's Gulf regionalism emerged out of a remarkable and violent fusion shaping, as Glissant would have it, Whole World relation. Welty's "commonplace belief"—like the lines of Phoenix Jackson's face—exerts "a fierce and different radiation" revealing the Gulf region's worn paths to be, as Barbara Ladd sees it, no mere backwater but a common space of cross-cultural history and destiny.[43]

Whatever else it may be, "A Worn Path" is an initiatory travel narrative emergent from Gulf contact zones. All the New World texts I have treated here come at us from spaces of a generalized and profligate creole "contagion" capable of baffling any literary or canonical genealogy of placement. If, as Derrida argued in *Dissemination*, writing always is orphan, in the terms of Phoenix's pharmaceutical travel both soothing medicine and poisonous lye, then all writing needs the godparentage that Phoenix Jackson brings to her readers, moving us all from habits of reading grounded in Euro-colonial hubris into new compounds of humbleness and pride.

Gulf-matrix models for walking and reading "A Worn Path" have, however, long been available. The Senegalese orphan tale of Kumba had fostered extensions of ritual family throughout the black Atlantic. Additional paths to commonplace belief (braided out of diverse practices) may be found in Geechee praise-house practices of "seeking" religion. In the Gullah/Geechee path to praise society membership, as we have seen, pointers (or spiritual parents) guide their mourning "travelers" in prayer, in dream interpretation, and in composition of their travel narratives delivered to the congregation for examination. With Phoenix Jackson as both its traveling avatar and spiritual parent, "A Worn Path" moves readers to the medicinal vision of the "seeking religion" narratives collected in Lorenzo Turner's *Africanisms in the Gullah Dialect*. In the initiatory narratives collected by Turner, the seeker might travel to a multi-storied house to meet a welcoming white-bearded man (God), or she might envision being given a baby, as with Rosina Cohen, who recalled her pointer's clear instruction: "Don't let nobody fool you; the baby is your soul."[44] From the Sea Islands to Grenada, St. Vincent, and Trinidad, praise-house novitiates have undertaken "travels" to receive spiritual gifts. Their heads are banded to seek "an authoritative energy" that emerges in the Holy Ghost's "sacred wind," bestowing medicines, newborn songs, and a feeling "like a baby coming out of the womb."[45] The travel *schools* "mourners" for the authoritative spirit possession called "adoption." This spirited authority and tradition reached Mississippi from rhizomatic pathways—through New Orleans, through Chickasaw and Choctaw Afro-enculturations, and from the Gullah lowcountry, as we find with Faulkner's revered "Mammy" Caroline Barr.[46]

Scripted according to ritual protocol, Phoenix Jackson steps into "A Worn Path's" second sentence as "an old Negro woman with her head tied in a red rag."[47] The color of this head-tie signals an initiate elder who has long known what to do within the pathways of her (and others') blood. Beginning in the Christmas season of the journey of the Magi, "A Worn Path" sends Phoenix on her errand in ritual time. "She makes these trips just as regular as clockwork," a nurse notes, in the only measure of time available to this clinic's school-trained observers. Phoenix carries herself with a certain sense of swing—"from side to side in her steps with the balanced heaviness and lightness of a pendulum in a grandfather clock" (142). Head bound, stepping to *balance* latent energies, she taps the ground with a cane, making "a grave and persistent noise in the still air, that seemed meditative like the chirping of a solitary little bird" (142). Not only an Egyptian bird of repeating rebirth, Phoenix Jackson becomes a whole pageant of birds: mourning dove of Holy Spirit, hunted quail, bone-picking buzzard, and Yoruba bird-of-the-spirit's-head. The sugar-sack apron that she wears bears its ties to economies of slavery as do the cotton and cornfields through which she moves. Even Phoenix's skin, which "had a pattern all its own of numberless branching wrinkles . . . as though a whole little tree stood in the middle of her forehead" (142) bears scarified witness to that performative "certain kind of way" embodied in the banter and carriage of Havana orisha initiates.

Performing Orphan Kumba's and Creole Cinderella's test of animal empathy, Phoenix wields her cane with care, driving beetles, rabbits, and bobwhites out of harm's way while protecting herself from harmful critters. The path presents her with its familiar repeated challenges: "chains about my feet" in facing a hill, "the thorny bush" greeted, "the trial" of crossing a creek by log as Phoenix shuts her eyes and levels her cane to march "like a festival figure in some parade" (143). This festival crossing shows Phoenix that her own limber/limbo access remains viable. In deep trance then, beneath "a tree in a pearly cloud of mistletoe," she is kissed by the vision of a boy offering "a plate with a slice of marble-cake," which summons her lovely response: "That would be acceptable" (143). Phoenix's and Welty's acceptance of a most-marbled reality speaks to what Fredric Jameson calls the "marbled structure" of heterogeneous novelistic narratives, carrying with it a certain openness to what is really global creolization itself.[48] When Phoenix's path gets blocked later by barbed wire, she limbos down "to creep and crawl, spreading her knees and stretching her fingers like a baby trying to climb the steps" (143). She faces yet again the infancy of her soul's initiatory travel even as she ponders being (becoming again) the initiating wilderness crone (Osain's double) who has sacrificed many parts of herself to the barbed wire blocking the path: "she could not let her dress be torn now . . . and she could not pay for having her arm or leg sawed off if she got caught fast where she was" (143). Finally limboing free from the fence, and gazing at "dead trees, like black men with one arm, standing in the purple stalks of the withered cotton field," Phoenix meets the gaze of a buzzard perched over the old field. She faces the amputating costs of plantation endurance, hails the buzzard unflinchingly ("Who you watching?"), and sticks to her groove: "In the furrow she made her way along" (144).

When Phoenix leaves the cotton field and steps into "dead corn," she enters "the maze" where no path is marked. In this dead maize, she greets a dancing ghost matter-of-factly before recognizing it as a scarecrow. Given Phoenix's identification with birds, her response, "Dance, old scarecrow . . . while I dancing with you," marks another triumph against fears, and she morphs into a raffia-clad festival figure: "She kicked her foot over the furrow, and with mouth drawn down, shook her head once or twice in a little strutting way. Some husks blew down and whirled streamers about her skirts" (144). After her "adoption" of death and its *egungun* strut, she goes lower into a swamp-mire, a deeper green underworld beneath a dense live-oak canopy. The hunter who encounters her upended by a dog there, and who "gave her a swing in the air, and sat her down" (145), is familiar to initiates of Afro-Atlantic divination lore. But he is no Ogun adept and brings real arrogance to the ritual economy of the encounter, assuming "I get something for my trouble" (the sacrificial quail in his bag) while Phoenix could not be getting anything for the trouble of her own journey. She replies in terms of binding commitment (*religio*): "I bound to go to town, mister," since "The time come around" (145).

In her red head-tie and deep into postmenopausal life, Phoenix remains bound to an engrained periodicity and to an enduring reproductivity. "A Worn Path" turns out to be an initiating narrative of authority from below and beyond. The young white man with the gun (emblematic of the ruling ideological structures of the state and the literati) assumes that he carries the authority in the encounter: "I know you old colored people! Wouldn't miss going to town to see Santa Claus!" (145). But his *naïve* assumption only renders *him* a clownish Santa taxed by Phoenix's gaze when—after a nickel falls from his pocket—the wrinkle-lines of the tree on Phoenix's forehead coalesce "into a fierce and different radiation" (145). Her hands move slyly to pocket the gift-sign of Afro-creole initiation tales: "with the grace and care they would have in lifting an egg from under a setting hen" (146). Placing this magic egg (or nickel) in her sugar-sack apron as a witnessing bird soars overhead, Phoenix Jackson practices the ritual theft common to Santería initiations and to writerly authority. As we consider Welty's appropriation of Afro-creole authority (via the avatar of Phoenix) in the face of a patriarchal authority that reads the fierce and different radiation of powerful women's writing condescendingly, we can trace something of Welty's travel in the hunter's words to a woman unintimidated by his pointed gun: "Well, Granny . . . you must be a hundred years old, and scared of nothing. I'd give you a dime if I had any money with me. But you take my advice and stay home and nothing will happen to you" (146). Ms. Jackson, like Ms. Welty, however, is set on getting her dime and adamant about her ritual commitments: "I bound to go on my way, mister," she says, and "inclined her head in the red rag," departing into "shadows [that] hung from the oak trees to the road like curtains" (146) with her first egg in her apron.

Any fear of violent threat that Phoenix may feel is trumped by transgenerational need and by the wisdom of her mindful body. Phoenix's feet "know where to take her" in the paved city of Natchez (146), and she climbs one particular building's steps "until her feet knew to stop" (147). What she arrives upon there attests to her travel narrative's intent: "she saw nailed up on the wall the document that had been stamped with the gold seal and framed in the gold frame, which matched the dream that was hung up in her head" (147). It is Phoenix Jackson's dream (packed with very marbled ideological formations) that hails her. And when she announces "Here I be" with "a fixed and ceremonial stiffness over her body," the medical office staff identify her as "[a] charity case" (147). Phoenix's charity case, however, certainly marks an excess of charity's Latin or Anglo-Christian meaning and is supplemented with Afro-creole notions of *saraka* (rooted in Arabic *sadaqa*—alms, charity, sacrifice, practiced in West Africa and the Caribbean as we examined in chapter 1's focus on saraka rites in Georgia, Trinidad, St. Vincent, Grenada, and Carriacou).[49] Saraka rites allow the living to receive the blessings of ancestors whose grace and protections are activated in festive offerings to their freshest representatives on earth: children. Such an energy industry sustains a nonapocalyptic worldview that counters the hegemonic consumer individualism surrounding us. Saraka's attentiveness to the cooperative recycling of resources and energies places an enduring value on performance. Behavior trumps theological credo since it may be more important to make saraka and to feed the children than to profess any sort of fundamentalist belief in the reincarnation or agency of the dead. It may be most important to *behave* as if we inherit the earth and belong here intergenerationally since performed ritual behaviors actualize belief. Saraka rites feed the children with a vision apart from savage capitalism and its ruthless competition, apart from nihilism and apocalypse, and offer the only salvation or "charity" we need.

The economy of the text insists that Phoenix Jackson is an energy generator whose journey to a Natchez health clinic does not reduce her to submission to clinical authority. The attendants who call Phoenix to "Speak up," insisting "We must have your history, you know" (147), are incapable of inscribing such a history's fusions. What they would write would be in the terms of an authority that cannot read Phoenix Jackson's worn path. Incapable of understanding Phoenix's saraka-work, they hold themselves to be paternalistic dispensers of "charity" to her. Their school-taught understanding of history (its chronological periods and parades of eras) would differ markedly from the restored behaviors of Phoenix's mindfully embodied periodicity itself. The clinic and the systems that certify it cannot possibly "have" Phoenix's history, at least not without a system-altering apprenticeship to it.

We begin to get at this when a nurse more familiar with Phoenix announces: "She doesn't come for herself—she has a little grandson" (147). The nurse's question concerning the grandson, "He isn't dead, is he?" (148), gives an apt sign for reading "A Worn Path." As a praise-house elder would point out, "the baby is your soul." The question of the grandson's death thus becomes a question of spiritual sustenance and rebirth for Phoenix—and for all readers whom she carries with her as medicine-seeking textual avatar. The endurance of a people, the soul-survival of our whole species (and even species in vulnerable relation to us), may be at stake in this moment. The nurse now plays the role of pointer, reminding Phoenix why she made the trip: to restore breath and voice to the grandson. Phoenix apologizes for her memory lapse, explaining that she "was too old at the Surrender" to attend school and receive the kind of certification of authority sealed in gold that she so admires. But she immediately conveys another, unsurrendered though submerged Afrocreole authority. The orphaned grandson's throat and voice have been damaged (perhaps in his inevitable subject formation within Jim Crow schooling): "[t]hroat never heals" from having "[s]wallowed lye" and "[h]e not able to swallow . . . get his breath," thus the periodic travel for "the soothing medicine" for this "obstinate case"(148). Against swallowed lies of history, the school curricula, white supremacy, patriarchal religion, and Jacksonian democracy, an unsurrendered Phoenix Jackson travels for medicine for her own soul and for all the fostered (and fosterable) grandchildren for whom she may serve as medicine-fetching avatar. It may be an obstinate case, but the grandson "going to last" as he waits, bound in "a little patch quilt" and peeping, "his mouth open like a little bird" (148). This little bird of Phoenix's spirit-head won't be forgotten again "the whole enduring time" (148). And Phoenix's apocalypse-deferring travel narrative is validated with the awarding of the medicine, marked "Charity" in a notebook.[50] Any adequate readerly performance of "A Worn Path" must tend to this "whole enduring time" of Phoenix's travels through deep time, and to her unsurrendered saraka-patchwork supporting a grandson's ability to last.

As Welty's avatar, Phoenix went on an errand on behalf of a spiritual child for medicine to speak and publish. Phoenix journeys to treat and initiate a peeping author's voice, a southern young "lady" who had inevitably swallowed much lye. Traveling through Phoenix to voice and authority, Welty placed "A Worn Path" as final testimonial to the author's ritual death and rebirth behind A Curtain of Green (1941), her first published collection. In Welty's South—like Faulkner's, Hurston's, Cabrera's, Chamoiseau's—any quest for authority emergent from deep time-space has had to travel across gulfs of dispossession to fetch medicinal spirits for the toddy that cuts through the lye-blocked throat, soothes and gives voice. This is a regionalism of the contact zone's remarkable fusions. To write or read powerfully from this zone may require a surrender of a certain kind of authority, an orphaning of the "I" of the story in order to travel and seek reaffiliation. Something (of blood and ego) must be surrendered to voice something unsurrendered and submerged of a repeating, nonapocalyptic vision. It may take an orphan text with a dead or gone mamma and a sacrifice of blood-pride to step into our fiercest secrets and radiations, into wildernesses of transcultural intertext wherein we recognize built-in gulfs in our fabric—and find binding in the repair work of saraka.

The remarkable fusions of "A Worn Path" lead to a common place of knowledge that we still—like Governor Wallace or the hunter of Welty's story—too often block. In this particular story the white Protestant lady that was Eudora Welty had to die to become orphaned grandson of the strangely grooved text. Herein our avatar keeps (us) always on the verge of becoming spirit bird. Requesting and receiving a final gift egg—the "[f]ive pennies is a nickel" that completes her dime—Phoenix "stared at her palm closely, with her head on one side" (149). The nickels nesting in her palm like eggs radiate a rebirthing power and serve as currency for the text's gift-sign—the wonder of a paper windmill for her grandchild: "He going to find it hard to believe there such a thing in the world" (149). Let's make no mistake about it, Phoenix's march home is a crowned procession of commonplace belief down a worn Gulf South path. What we are left with at story's end is the sound of her slow step "on the stairs, going down" (149). Soothing medicine for the voice presumably in her sugar-sack apron, left hand holding Oya's (and the Holy Spirit's) paper windmill high, right hand with cane tapping out the ground home—this is the way Phoenix Jackson makes her way down, back to, out of a limbo gateway opened somewhere between Natchez and Jackson, Mississippi, routed through Kumba's Sea of Ndayaan, Cinderella's Johnson River, and a Haitian manbo's gombo patch.

Phoenix Jackson carries an unsurrendered, nonapocalyptic knowledge on behalf of a grandson who has swallowed lye. Her sacrificial journey along the grooves of a worn path can remediate the lies we have swallowed and allow us to receive our gift-eggs. Phoenix, Caddy Compson, Janie Woods, Auda Billy, Kumba, and Turtle take us into spaces of our real and potential breakup and reassembly. As avatars, they move us to an all-okay sign more focused on the dance of reassembly than on the dread of facing a heap of broken images of ourselves. Through them, we may learn not to be paralyzed by the fluidity (or seeming impasses) of gulf spaces or by the moment when we recognize that the Gulf's mires and blood consecrations have always done soaked clean through onto us.

Knowledge of relation to sacral gro(o)ves is something we "make" repeatedly in ritual reassembly. It comes simultaneously in porousness to the time-space that precedes and exceeds us. My backyard patio in Jacksonville has been a space of my own cultivation of fraught relations to the wild and to a creole city that misrecognizes itself. For me, the planting of little *montes* (citrus, figs, herbs, flowering plants, lemongrass, pomegranate, palms, sugarcane, avocado, loquat, and jujube); the tending of plants in containers (mango, guava, baobab, cocoa, star fruit, and tamarind); the nurturance of animal relations (wormpiles and treefrogs, birds, fish, turtle, the family dog), amidst a skyline of huge live oaks (holding Spanish moss and resurrection fern, raccoons and owls) has made for an utterly necessary spirit-sustaining space of parties and grilling, libations and fish-cleaning, reading and writing, through the cumulative draftings of *Sacral Grooves, Limbo Gateways*. Each year I have freed up a little more of what had been a mostly paved-over backyard by taking a sledge-hammer to a bit more concrete, building up soil in the sand beneath for planting. Only in this way am I able to read and write—and especially to assign and grade essays—in response to the obligations of a profession that seems to have more to do with the pouring of concrete, the maintenance of disciplinary boundaries and national fortifications, than with relations of give-and-take hospitality to each and every other. My work remains an apprenticeship to submerged authorities and relations, an ongoing saraka-cycle.

I received my orisha warriors (*los guerreros:* Eleggua, Ogun, Ochosi, Osun) in a time and place of intense national refortification. Shortly after the events of 9/11, at the very beginning of the nation's War on Terror, I traveled to complete some tasks necessary for receiving the warrior initiation in an *ilé* (spirit house) in our nation's capital. Even now, some nine years later, this night stays washed in surreal memory. The blood sacrifices central to Santería rites have been much sensationalized. Still, there is no getting away from the fact that there is a power in the blood: ritual sacrifice creates thresholds of sacral time and space. Spilled blood calls the living into larger circles of relation and makes us acknowledge the momentariness of our lives together. On this night we had to dispose of carcasses from a family member's "making" of Olokun: a number of dove, rooster, and duck carcasses were to be received at the end by this spirit of salt- and freshwater comminglings, down by the Potomac River. The only one attending with a pickup truck, I volunteered, helped load my truckbed with the sacrificed birds, and headed to the Potomac with an Afro-Cuban elder—an Eleggua initiate—as my guide to the side streets of D.C. It was a strange world out there. For with a truck-bed full of bloody carcasses, and the two of us bound to be on our way (dressed in skullcaps or berets and ritual white), we needed to avoid the numerous crossroads blocked off and monitored by soldiers. With the military manning nigh every key cross-road in heavy armor, my ritual elder's knowledge of the back-routes and the military's guard assignments was crucial to avoiding what might otherwise have been a most trying detainment. Taking direction from this Cuban-American Eleggua, dodging the sandbag-fortified crossways, and moving in labyrinthine detours toward the Potomac—with the Washington Monument and Lincoln Memorial looming in the background—I was driving my old hand-me-down truck in a space that was strikingly unfamiliar and quite truly and strangely home. We came to a park on the river not far from the National Mall, and my Eleggua guide-and-elder took a slug of rum, passed the pint flask my way. When we stopped the truck at the Potomac's banks and successfully slipped the birds into its waters for crabs and turtles to feast upon, I felt an overwhelming sense of peace. The moonlit river rolled through *el monte* to the Atlantic with the Washington Monument's white obelisk like a hard-to-believe wonder behind us. Never had I felt so simultaneously at home and estranged in the nation's capital, nor have I ever been so sure of the wild and cultivated heterogeneity inside the fortress gates.

Notes

Introduction

1. I generally use "voodoo" to refer to Hollywood/Western (mis)representations of Afro-creole religion. I use Vodou (uppercase) to refer to Haitian practice, and I use Voudou to refer to Louisiana practice. Also, I adhere to the various renderings of the authors whom I cite (Vaudou, Vodoun, voodoo, etc.).

2. National Geographic Society, *Fast Facts Book* (2009), 233.

3. I take the term *hippikat* from the West African Wolof language, signifying an "open-eyed" person, a seer. See my first book, *Reading Africa into American Literature*, for a *hippikat* perspective into a countercultural tradition of hipcats, hippies, and hip-hoppers (1–22).

4. I refer to Quentin Compson's statement to his Harvard roommate Shreve, who has been usurping or co-creating Quentin's Mississippi narrative in William Faulkner's *Absalom, Absalom!*, 289. My point is that Shreve *becomes* born there—in the narrative performance, at least well enough to co-narrate the story, though he is no more enlightened than is Quentin. I reference the famous "My mother is a fish" chapter from Faulkner's *As I Lay Dying* (84) to suggest an initiatory baptismal demand that all of Faulkner's fluid Yoknapatawpha County texts place upon characters and readers.

5. W. Faulkner, *Absalom, Absalom!*, 289.

6. W. Faulkner, *The Sound and the Fury*, 57. I treat Yoknapatawpha holistically, as a singular "space" of immersion.

7. Christophe, "Rainbow over Water," 88.

8. Hurston, *Their Eyes Were Watching God*, 332. Hurston wrote *Their Eyes Were Watching God* in Haiti in 1936 and published the novel in 1937. Faulkner's Haiti-possessed *Absalom, Absalom!* appeared in 1936, shortly after the U.S. Marines were withdrawn.

9. Kristeva, *The Powers of Horror*, 2, 4.

10. See J. Smith, "Postcolonial, Black, and Nobody's Margin: The U.S. South and New World Studies," 144–61, 144; Paravisini-Gebert and Olmos, introduction to *Sacred Possessions: Vodou, Santería, Obeah, and the Caribbean*, 1–12.

11. There is little in all this that was not predicated by the mosaic view and parallax effect essayed over a century ago by W. E. B. Du Bois in his articulation of double consciousness from folk figurations of second sight. *The Souls of Black Folk* (1903) indeed sought to have its readers born(e) *there*—wrapped in the veil's amniotic sac—within a plantation Black Belt that was also a transposed Egypt and always anywhere south of the color line.

12. I use lowercase "creole" when speaking in general terms but uppercase "Creole" when speaking of a specific language or identity (Louisiana Creole).

13. Weaver, *That the People Might Live*, 38.

14. Dimock, *Through Other Continents*, 2–4.

15. Girard, *Violence and the Sacred*, 257.

16. D. Brown, *Santería Enthroned*, 77.

17. Patterson, *Slavery and Social Death*, 7, 38.

18. Gilroy, *The Black Atlantic*, 36, 198, 200.

19. Gilroy, *The Black Atlantic*, 37.

20. Harris, "History, Fable and Myth in the Caribbean and Guianas," in *Selected Essays of Wilson Harris*, 159, 152–66. For recent invocations of Harris's limbo gateway, see Dimock, *Through Other Continents*, 162–63; and Russell, *Legba's Crossing*, 7–10, 32.

21. Harris, "History, Fable and Myth in the Caribbean and Guianas," 157. M. M. Bakhtin introduced the term "chronotope" in *The Dialogic Imagination*, defining it as "[a] unit of analysis for studying texts according to the ratio and nature of the temporal and spatial categories represented . . ." (426).

22. Harris, "History, Fable and Myth," 158, 164.

23. Margaret Thompson Drewal, *Yoruba Ritual*, 24, xiii; Daniel, *Dancing Wisdom*, 253.

24. Julien, *Travels with Mae*, 2. I come to the idea of "restored behavior" via Roach's presentation of it in *Cities of the Dead*, 3.

25. Julien, *Travels with Mae*, 2.

26. Twain, *The Adventures of Huckleberry Finn*, 2. Lafcadio Hearn offered early linguistic/culinary pointers in his *Gombo Zhèbes* (1885), which addressed "[t]he literature of 'gombo'" (199) from a perspective attendant to the culinary and linguistic range of Creole Louisiana's emblematic dish and its most profoundly vernacular style of speech.

27. Loichot, *Orphan Narratives*, 29. See also 12, 29–30.

28. See Allewaert, "Swamp Sublime."

29. Quoted in Creel, "Gullah Attitudes toward Life and Death," 79.

30. Cable, *The Creoles of Louisiana*, 316.

31. Nwankwo, *Black Cosmopolitanism*, 14.

32. Soyinka, *Myth, Literature, and the African World*, 158.

33. Soyinka, *Myth, Literature, and the African World*, 145, 149.

34. Soyinka, *Myth, Literature, and the African World*, 142, 143.

35. Soyinka, *Myth, Literature, and the African World*, 150.

36. Glissant, *Poetics of Relation*, 1.

37. Glissant, *Poétique de la relation*, 18. I translate *"le gouffre"* as "gulf" rather than "abyss" (as Betsy Wing renders it). "Gulf" seems to me to be the best translation, and "gulf" also sets up a set of charged relations with the maritime (the Gulf of Mexico, the Gulf Stream) while conveying a sense of a space-between territories, a chasm, an abyssal expanse or no-man's space of transition.

38. Glissant, *Poetics of Relation*, 6; *Poétique de la relation*, 18.

39. Glissant, *Poétique de la relation*, 20.

40. K. Brown, *Mama Lola*, 349.

41. K. Brown, *Mama Lola*, 356.

42. Gilroy, *The Black Atlantic*, 37; for Gilroy's discussion of "the slave sublime," see 131, 187–223.

43. Kant, *The Critique of Judgement*, 91.

44. See Allewaert, "Swamp Sublime," 345.

45. Budick, *The Western Theory of Tradition*.

46. Pease, "Authority," 107.

47. Madrazo, Medina, and Alleyne, "Semantic Diversity in the Caribbean: Interrogating the 'Creole' Concept," 14.

48. Vega, *The Florida of the Inca*, 106.

49. Pratt, *Imperial Eyes*. Pratt's *Imperial Eyes: Travel Writing and Transculturation* (1992) drew directly from Fernando Ortiz's *Cuban Counterpoint* (1940) in which Ortiz coined his term for the reciprocal enculturations facing each Cuban ethnic group as each responded to "the problem of disadjustment and readjustment, of deculturation and acculturation—in a word, of transculturation" (98).

50. Rodwick, "Mobile Citizens, Media States," 15; Chambers, "Citizenship, Language, and Modernity," 25.

51. Glissant, *Poetics of Relation*, 149, 151.

52. Harris, *Selected Essays of Wilson Harris*, 166.

53. Pratt, "Arts of the Contact Zone," 531.

54. Barthes, *Image-Music-Text*, 142.

55. Barthes, *Image-Music-Text*, 142; Barthes, "La mort de l'auteur," 491.

56. Somé, *Of Water and the Spirit*, 9.

57. On Faulkner's indebtedness to Dilsey and to her life-model, Caroline Barr, see Sensibar, *Faulkner and Love*, 25–125.

58. N'Dour, *Rokku Mi Rokka*.

59. Somé, *Of Water and the Spirit*, 308, 309; Ellison, *Invisible Man*, 16.

60. Meicholas, *More Talking Bahamian*, 24.

61. Cartwright, *Reading Africa into American Literature*, 97–98.

62. Kesteloot and Mbodj, *Contes et mythes Wolof*, 24–31.

63. See Thompson, *Flash of the Spirit*, 42–51.

64. The orphan initiate is also named Kumba in Magel's *Folktales from the Gambia*, 90–95. Equilbecq also collected this tale in Hausa in 1911, 384–86, and presented a Wolof version featuring the initiation of an orphan boy, 276–82.

65. See M. Diouf, "The French Colonial Policy of Assimilation," 671–96.

66. M. Drewal, *Yoruba Ritual*, 72.

67. M. Drewal, *Yoruba Ritual*, 180–83.

68. M. Drewal, *Yoruba Ritual*, 183.

69. Owusu-Sarpong, foreword, "The Poor Orphan: A Folktale by Nana Yaa Tiakaa," 347.

70. Deleuze and Guattari, *A Thousand Plateaus*, 276, 277.

71. Equilbecq, *Contes Populaires d'Afrique Occidentale*, 278.

72. For the Bahamas, see Parsons, *Folk-Tales of Andros Island, Bahamas*, 5–6; and Glinton, *An Evening in Guanima*, 39–49. From South Carolina, see Parsons, *Folk-*

Lore of the Sea Islands, South Carolina, 137–38. From St. Kitts, see Parsons, *Folk-Lore of the Antilles, French and English*, 367–69. For versions of the tale in franco-creole languages, see Parsons, *Folk-Lore of the Antilles*, 1: 87–88, 124–44, 422–25, and 2: 159–60, 277–78, 569–70, and also Fortier, *Louisiana Folk-Tales*, 117–19. From Haiti via Florida, see Louis, *When Night Falls, Kric! Krac!*, 71–73.

73. Fortier, *Louisiana Folk-Tales*, 117. In *Of Water and Spirit*, Malidoma Somé writes, "The Dagara refrains from asking questions when faced with a riddle because questioning and being answered destroys one's chance to learn for oneself" (264).

74. Deleuze and Guattari, *A Thousand Plateaus*, 164.

75. Deleuze and Guattari, *A Thousand Plateaus*, 164.

76. Harris, *Nights with Uncle Remus*, 232.

77. Harris, *Nights with Uncle Remus*, 232.

78. W. Johnson, *Black Savannah 1788–1864*, 93.

79. L. Turner, *Africanisms in the Gullah Dialect*, 117.

80. P. Morgan, *Slave Counterpoint*, 448.

81. Koger, *Black Slaveowners*, 115, 113. John Holman Sr. willed Cumbah to his son John Holmam Jr. The son had previously possessed a woman named Cumba when father and son were in business together on the coast of West Africa (113).

82. Parsons, *Folk-Lore of the Sea Islands, South Carolina*, 137–38.

83. Bailey, *God, Dr. Buzzard, and the Bolito Man*, 278.

84. Bailey, *God*, 211–12.

85. See W. Wylly, *A Short Account of the Bahama Islands*, 5–6; McKinnen, *A Tour through the British West Indies in the Years 1802 and 1803*, 216–17; Craton and Saunders, *Islanders in the Stream*; Slave Registries of Former British Colonial Dependencies, ancestry.co.uk, Sept. 17, 2009.

86. Craton and Saunders, *Islanders in the Stream*, 338.

87. Parsons, *Folk-Tales of Andros Island, Bahamas*, 19–23; Glinton, *An Evening in Guanima*, 39–49.

88. Weiss, *The Merikens*, 42, 41, 45.

89. Slave Registries of Former British Colonial Dependencies, ancestry.co.uk, Sept. 17, 2009.

90. Merle Collins, "Emancipation," www.bigdrumnation.org/notes/emancipation .htm, Sept. 16, 2009.

91. Parsons, *Folk-Lore of the Antilles, French and English*, 2: 367–69.

92. Bell, *Major Butler's Legacy*, 230, 552.

93. Bell, *Major Butler's Legacy*, 182.

94. Bell, *Major Butler's Legacy*, 229.

95. K. Brathwaite, *Ancestors*, 16.

96. McPherson, "No Natural Disaster," 331–35.

97. Hall, *Africans in Colonial Louisiana*, 409.

98. Hall, *Africans in Colonial Louisiana*, 411, 382–97, 58–72.

99. For franco-creole versions of the tale from Grenada, St. Lucia, and Dominica, see Parsons, *Folk-lore of the Antilles, French and English*, 1: 87–88, 142–44, 422–25. For versions from Guadeloupe, Marie-Galante, and Haiti, see Parsons, *Folk-lore of the Antilles, French and English*, 2: 159–60, 277–78, 569–70. For another version from

Haiti, see Louis, *When Night Falls, Kric! Krac!*, 71–73. For Louisiana, see Fortier, *Louisiana Folk-Tales*, 117–19.

100. Sansay, *Secret History*, 70.

101. See Roach, *Cities of the Dead*, 124–25, on circum-Atlantic superabundance, the colonial/enslaved female body, and performance.

102. Fortier, *Louisiana Folk-Tales*, 117–19.

103. Louis, *When Night Falls*, 71–73.

104. Figures for Saint-Domingue migration to New Orleans are given by Lachance, "The Foreign French," 105.

105. Césaire, *The Collected Poetry*, 35. I riff off of Donald Cosentino's observation that Vodou altars reveal the triumph of "a myth broad enough and . . . a ritual complex enough to encompass all this disparate stuff," "Imagine Heaven," 27.

106. Schafer, *Anna Madgigine Jai Kingsley*, 28, 23, 30, 57, 59. See Landers, *Black Society in Spanish Florida* on the border-frontier conditions of Florida.

107. Bateman, "Naming Patterns," 233–34.

108. Alabama Creek Nation Court Cases, www.afrigeneas.com/forum-states/index .cgi?mid=read;id, Sept. 16, 2009.

109. Itawamba County, Mississippi history and genealogy, Itawamba Historical Society, Deed Book 1, page 36, www.itawambahistory.org/deed1.htm, Sept. 16, 2009.

110. Murphy, *Working the Spirit*, 81. On the *cabildos de nación*, see D. Brown, *Santería Enthroned*, 49, 34–35, 51–55.

111. See Murphy, "Yéyé Cachita: Ochun in a Cuban Mirror," 88–90.

112. See Ortiz, *Poesía y canto de los negros afrocubanos*, 86, for discussion of Senegambian Muslim greetings in Afro-Cuban rites.

113. Benítez-Rojo, *The Repeating Island*, 13, 16.

114. Bishop Felipe de Jesús Estévez, www.kofc.org/un/en/columbia/detail/458998 .html, accessed Sept. 8, 2009. The emblem of the Virgin found enshrinement not only in Cobre but throughout Cuba, including a reproduction smuggled out of Cuba in 1961 and used to found the sanctuary Ermita de la Caridad del Cobre in Miami.

115. Estévez, www.kofc.org.

116. The black Virgin enshrined in the Spanish seaport of Regla in the mid-fourteenth century became the Havana harbor's patron saint, creolized by Afro-Cuban recognition of her as an icon of Yemaya, the oceanic orisha mother. The Canary Islands' black Virgin of Candelaria ("La Morenita" enshrined in a Tenerife cave around 1392) found rerouting through Cuban Yoruba consumptions of her as Oya, deity of whirlwinds, passages to ancestors, animal shape-shifting, and the market.

117. That Cabrera's work was published first in translation in French (1936) and thus certified for publication in Spanish, and not translated into English until 2004, speaks to economies of authority.

118. Cabrera, *Afro-Cuban Tales*, 1.

119. Rodriguez-Mangual, *Lydia Cabrera*, 130.

120. Cabrera's story reminds us that Ochosi, an orphan "protector of women," married Yemaya (maternal ocean orisha) after Orumbila's (Ifa's) dismissal of her upon her discovery of Ifa's divinatory secrets. If Ifa, "the Seer of all . . . gave Yemaya to Ochosi because he wanted nothing to do with a woman who knew more than he,"

then in Ochosi's openness to his wife's power, we have a tale that enters *el monte* from a woman-empowering (ocha-centric rather than male Ifa-centric) direction.

121. Wedel, *Santeria Healing*, 76, 85; Thompson, *Flash of the Spirit*, 44–47.

122. Gleason, *Oya*, 197. Gleason summarizes Dieterlen's tale of encounter between a refugee woman with her newborn and the two hunters. When the woman withholds the water rations she is carrying through the desert, the hunters seize the calabash. She curses them. They kill her child. Their two dogs fight over the infant corpse, one dog killing the other, and soon only the woman is left alive from uncontained reciprocal violence. Testifying to the hunters' knowledge of violence committed against the mother, Sanene-Kontron's altar found witness in Cabrera's Sanune and the bull-child Monte Firme.

123. Gleason, *Oya*, 197.

124. See Yaeger, *Dirt and Desire*, 15, 61–87, on southern women's writing and the "throw-away body."

Chapter 1. Down to the Mire

1. Toomer, *Cane*, 26.

2. Wilson Harris, "History, Fable, and Myth in the Caribbean and Guianas," 166.

3. *Webster's Eleventh New College Dictionary*, 699.

4. Georgia Writers' Project, *Drums and Shadows*, 141; Austin, *African Muslims in Antebellum America: A Sourcebook*, 400; Du Bois, *The Souls of Black Folk*, 182. For another example of restored memory in relation to the Pulaar *maayo* (more specifically the Senegal River), listen to Baaba Maal's "Kowoni mayo (mi yeewnii)" on *Missing You (Mi yeewnii)* PALMCD 2067-2. In *Drums and Shadows*, Alec Anderson of Possum Point (McIntosh County, Georgia) describes "Come Down tuh duh Myuh," 141.

5. Quoted in Murphy, *Working the Spirit*, 116, 117–18.

6. Parrish, *Slave Songs of the Georgia Sea Islands*, 71.

7. Mason, *Living Santeria*, 38, 39.

8. See Derrida, *Acts of Religion*, 72–75, on the binding ties of *religare* and Daniel, *Dancing Wisdom*, 2, 253, on Yoruba *awo*. In *Yoruba Ritual*, Margaret Thompson Drewal writes that "The generic term in Yoruba for ritual specialist is alawo or simply awo, that is, one who possesses specialized, esoteric knowledge and wisdom (awo)."

9. See Belcher, "Consuming Subjects," for what she calls "the reciprocal enculturation model" (213).

10. See Alleyne and Fraser, *The Barbados-Carolina Connection*, 10–13.

11. For Loyalist migration to the Bahamas, see Craton and Saunders, *Islanders in the Stream*, 179–212. For the narratives of black Loyalist ministers who fled the Sea Islands to establish Baptist congregations in Jamaica, Nova Scotia, and Sierra Leone, see the writings by and of George Liele, David George, and Boston King in Carretta, *Unchained Voices*, 325–68.

12. See Weiss, *The Merikens*.

13. Deleuze and Guattari, *A Thousand Plateaus*, 7.

14. Pierre Nora, "Between Memory and History," 12. National Park Service, *Low Country Gullah/Geechee Culture Special Resource Study and Final Environmental*

Impact Statement, www.nps.gov/sero/planning/gg_srs/ggsrsindex.htm, 2006, accessed Sept. 16, 2009.

15. Quoted in Epstein, *Sinful Tunes and Spirituals*, 201.

16. Quoted in Creel, "Gullah Attitudes toward Life and Death," 79.

17. Quoted in Murphy, *Working the Spirit*, 123.

18. Quoted in Craton and Saunders, *Islanders in the Stream*, 334.

19. See Frey and Wood, *Come Shouting to Zion*, 116–17, 131. The charismatic ministry of George Liele may have launched the independent Afro-Baptist movement in Georgia as Liele organized congregations near Augusta and in Savannah before leaving with the Loyalist evacuation of Savannah to found the Baptist Church in Jamaica in 1784. David George continued Liele's ministry in establishing the South's first black Baptist congregation in Silver Bluff, South Carolina (across from Augusta), between 1773 and 1775 and then fled with his Tory master to Nova Scotia before moving on to Sierra Leone to establish the first black Baptist church in Africa in 1792 (Lum 32–33). Andrew Bryan, after being baptized by Liele, ministered the Savannah congregation that separated into today's Bryan Street African Baptist Church and First African Baptist Church in 1788 (J. F. Smith 143–49). Samuel Scriven and Prince Williams departed with the 1784 Loyalist evacuation from St. Augustine and founded the first black Baptist congregations in the Bahamas: Bethel Baptist, erected in 1801, following some fifteen years of holding meetings in private homes and open air, and St. John's Baptist (Craton and Saunders 330–31). William Hamilton of St. Simons Island, Georgia, is credited with establishing the Baptist Church in Trinidad in 1815 as reported by Stapleton, *The Birth and Growth of the Spiritual Baptist Church in Trinidad and Tobago*, 13.

20. West, *Race Matters*, 19; Gilroy, *The Black Atlantic*, 37.

21. Frey and Wood, *Come Shouting to Zion*, 116–17, 131.

22. Sobel, *The World They Made Together*, 79–98.

23. J. F. Smith, *Slavery and Rice Culture in Low Country Georgia*, 95.

24. Frey and Wood, *Come Shouting to Zion*, 118.

25. Creel, "*A Peculiar People*," 281.

26. See Creel, "*A Peculiar People*," 276–302.

27. Creel and Bailey both give excellent accounts of seeking: Creel as historian and Cornelia Bailey as initiate member. In line with West African and other Afro-creole notions of the componential nature of the person, Bailey describes her training on Sapelo Island: "We didn't believe just in the body and the soul. We believed in the body, the soul *and* the spirit, just like the people in Africa had believed. The way it worked was that when a person died, the body went to the grave and the soul rested in peace, and the spirit remained on earth. So the spirit was *always* here" (31).

28. Turner, *Africanisms in the Gullah Dialect*, 275.

29. See Creel, "*A Peculiar People*," 167–210; and Heyrman, *Southern Cross*, 78, 20–21.

30. Morgan, "Lowcountry Georgia and the Early Modern Atlantic World," 27.

31. Creel, "Gullah Attitudes toward Life and Death," 78.

32. Creel, "Gullah Attitudes," 77.

33. Quoted in Creel, "*A Peculiar People*," 286.

34. Creel, *"A Peculiar People,"* 286.

35. Parrish, *Slave Songs of the Georgia Sea Islands,* 131.

36. Georgia Writers' Project, *Drums and Shadows,* 113.

37. Quoted in Epstein, *Sinful Tunes and Spirituals,* 284–85.

38. Gomez, *Exchanging Our Country Marks,* 267.

39. Parrish, *Slave Songs of the Georgia Sea Islands,* 81, 46, 46.

40. J. F. Smith, *Slavery and Rice Culture in Low Country Georgia,* 162.

41. Quoted in Rosenbaum, *Shout Because You're Free,* 76.

42. Ex-slaves interviewed by the Georgia Writers' Project (1940) testified to the ring shout being used as a key part of antebellum Geechee funerals.

43. Turner, *Africanisms in the Gullah Dialect,* 256; Parrish, *Slave Songs,* 46–48; Georgia Writers' Project, *Drums and Shadows,* 54; Morrison, *Song of Solomon,* 303.

44. *Florida Times Union,* February 24, 1997, A-1, A-17.

45. Parrish, *Slave Songs of the Georgia Sea Islands,* 46.

46. See Grosvenor, *Vertamae Cooks in the Americas' Family Kitchen,* "In Memoriam" on "rescue."

47. George was a stunningly well-traveled man who was born in slavery to African parents in Virginia, escaped to the Creek Nation, and finally appeared in Georgia (where Liele converted him) before moving with the Loyalist exodus to Nova Scotia, visiting England, and settling in Sierra Leone.

48. Roach, *Cities of the Dead,* xi–xii, xiii, xi.

49. Bailey, *God, Dr. Buzzard, and the Bolito Man,* 237.

50. Quoted in Berlin, *Generations of Captivity,* 270.

51. S. Diouf, "African Muslims in Bondage," 78–79.

52. Georgia Writers' Project, *Drums and Shadows,* 162. See McFeely, *Sapelo's People,* on the foundations of the island's First African Baptist Church. I had occasion to observe saraka rites as a sacrificial thanksgiving to the ancestors (via feeding the children from tables of sweets and abundance) when I served as a Peace Corps volunteer in Senegal from 1983 to 1985.

53. Georgia Writers' Project, *Drums and Shadows,* 167. Shadwick Rudolph of Camden County, Georgia, also recalled the sweetened rice cakes generally identified as saraka cakes.

54. M. G. Smith, *Dark Puritan,* 18, 32–33, 74–75. See also Lum, *Praising His Name in the Dance,* 16, 136–37; and Glazier, *Marchin' the Children Home,* 68. Saraka appears to have been among the rites and repertoires carried to Trinidad by Georgia refugees. The islands where saraca tables continue to be set (especially Trinidad, Grenada, and Carriacou) most likely developed their saraca traditions from local African populations as well as from interisland migrations.

55. Lomax, *Caribbean Voyage: Saraca, Funerary Music of Carriacou.*

56. See Carretta, *Unchained Voices,* 325–32; Murphy, *Working the Spirit,* 122–27; Frey and Wood, *Come Shouting to Zion;* Stewart, *Three Eyes for the Journey.*

57. Craton and Saunders, *Islanders in the Stream,* 179–82.

58. Pascoe, *Two Hundred Years of the S. P. G.,* 223; See Craton and Saunders, *Islanders in the Stream,* on lowcountry Loyalist migration to the Bahamas from East Florida, 182, 188–95. See also Cartwright, "Loyalists, Geechees, and Africans" for

how Bahamian slave registries reveal a number of Senegambian Muslim names (Mahomet, Moosa, Boucarry, Sambo, Fatima, Cumba, Janaba, Penda, Silla) on the rolls of islands populated largely by lowcountry Loyalists, 53–54.

59. Craton and Saunders, *Islanders in the Stream*, 330.

60. Holm, "On the Relationship of Gullah and Bahamian," 303–18, 310.

61. Weiss, *The Merikens*. The 781 black American refugees resettled as free black yeoman farmers in Trinidad from 1812 to 1821 came to be known as "the Merikans" and played an important foundational role in the development of an Anglo-creole culture in Trinidad. The six Company Villages were settled according to company enlistment with companies 1–3 coming from the Chesapeake and companies 5–6 coming from Camden and Glynn Counties of Georgia. The 4th Company consisted of a mixture of Georgia and Chesapeake settlers. The Georgia companies represent a mass transplantation of Sea Island culture. St. Simons Island, Ga., alone is represented by twenty-one people escaped from John Couper's plantation, nine from Alexander Wyley's, eight from Pierce Butler's, eight from James Hamilton's, five from John Frazier's, and four from John Floyd's plantations (36–47). Other black refugees siding with the British and resettling in Trinidad included eighty-eight largely Franco-creole settlers from New Orleans arriving in May 1815, fifty-eight settlers from West Florida arriving in July 1815, and sixty-five settlers from East Florida "Indian Country" (many of them maroons, and Seminole captives) arriving in November 1815 (54–61).

62. Weiss, *The Merikens*, 40–47. Archbishop Ashram Stapleton notes that Trinidad's first black Baptist church was established by William Hamilton in 1816 and was located on the site where the Fifth Company Baptist Church now stands (13). Malcolm Bell Jr., *Major Butler's Legacy*, documents Major Pierce Butler's contract to free a St. Simons Island slave by the name of William S. Hamilton after a period of ten-year indenture provided that he "Keep all his Master's secrets, and obey his lawful commands and shall not absent himself from such service without leave, and generally during the term aforesaid shall behave himself in all respects as a faithful, honest and diligent servant ought to do" (137).

63. Stapleton, *The Birth and Growth of the Spiritual Baptist Church*, 13.

64. Lum, *Praising His Name*, 72–78.

65. See Glazier, *Marchin' the Children Home*; and Keeney, *Shakers of St. Vincent*, 17.

66. McDaniel, "Memory Spirituals," 119–43.

67. Glazier, *Marchin' the Children Home*, 29.

68. Glazier, *Marchin' the Children Home*, 64.

69. Glazier, *Marchin' the Children Home*, 64. As Glazier notes, the Spiritual Baptist faith's incorporations of other rites and religions reveals a position that is both heterodox and conservative (64).

70. M. G. Smith, *Dark Puritan*, 75. See 74–78 on Paul's table-setting vision of Oshun, and for his discussions of saraca offerings, see 18, 32–33.

71. See Henry, *Reclaiming African Religions in Trinidad* for an account of (and tribute to) the life of Samuel Ebenezer Elliott.

72. Walker, *In Search of Our Mother's Gardens*, 232.

73. Harris, *Selected Essays of Wilson Harris*, 160.

74. Loichot, *Orphan Narratives*, 29, 12.

75. McNeil, "The Gullah Seeker's Journey," 185–209.

76. Hayden, *Collected Poems*, 59–61.

77. Marshall, *Praisesong for the Widow*, 12.

78. Rosenbaum, liner notes, *The McIntosh County Shouters*, 4.

79. See Bell, *Major Butler's Legacy*, 132.

80. See Georgia Writers' Project, *Drums and Shadows*, for the Ibo Landing tale, 185; Chernoff, *African Rhythm and African Sensibility*, 156.

81. Chernoff, *African Rhythm and African Sensibility*, 158.

82. Even Avatara's novel text is componental and the work of no single individual author since *Praisesong* adopts much of its power from its intertextual fostering. Gwendolyn Brooks's "Children of the Poor" is the poem (along with Hayden's "Runagate Runagate") that is most central to activating *Praisesong*'s saraka economy.

83. Keeney, *Shakers of St. Vincent*, 160.

84. See McNeil, "The Gullah Seeker's Journey"; Cosentino, "Envoi: The Gedes and Bawon Samdi," 399–414; Deren, *Divine Horsemen*, 102–3.

85. For starters, see Christian, "Ritualistic Process"; Benjamin, "Weaving the Web of Reintegration"; Thorsson, "Dancing up a Nation"; and McKoy, "The Limbo Contest."

86. Lorde, "Uses of the Erotic: The Erotic as Power," 56.

87. Keeney, *Shakers of St. Vincent*, 97.

88. Keeney, *Shakers of St. Vincent*, 164.

89. Keeney, *Shakers of St. Vincent*, 74.

90. Keeney, *Shakers of St. Vincent*, 65.

91. Keeney, *Shakers of St. Vincent*, 74.

92. Keeney, *Shakers of St. Vincent*, 74.

93. On Santería initiation and *omiero* as emetic, see Hagedorn, *Divine Utterances*, 214–19.

94. Wilentz, *Binding Culture*, 100.

95. Keeney, *Shakers of St. Vincent*, 151.

96. Métraux, *Voodoo in Haiti*, 200.

97. Murphy, *Santería*, 132.

98. Drewal and Drewal, *Gelede*, 38–65.

99. Drewal and Drewal, *Gelede*, 65.

100. See Drewal and Drewal on women's access to the head, 74; and Thompson, *Flash of the Spirit*, on "the bird of the head," 11.

101. West, *Race Matters*, 29, 30, xvi.

102. West, *Race Matters*, 29.

103. McClure, *Partial Faiths*, 193.

104. McClure, *Partial Faiths*, 100.

105. McClure, *Partial Faiths*, 106.

106. Holloway, "On Morrison and Black Female Memory," 162.

107. Dianne M. Stewart, *Three Eyes for the Journey*, 69, 9.

108. See Carby, "The Politics of Fiction, Anthropology, and the Folk"; and Dubey, *Signs and Cities*, 144–85; for critiques of the southern folk turn in African American

writing. In support of a womanist approach to Sea Island folk culture, see Brondum, "'The Persistance of Tradition'"; Metting, "The Possibilities of Flight"; and Alao, "Islands of Memory." As Dianne Stewart points out, the term "folk" itself most often betrays a position of paternalistic condescension toward the carriers of *hippikat* knowledge: "the knowledge such seers inherit is customarily characterized as folk culture and folk religion" (ix) and thereby dismissed "as a credible epistemological source" (xii).

109. On Morrison's use of Geechee folk material, especially the narratives in the WPA text *Drums and Shadows*, see Cartwright, *Reading Africa into American Literature*, 80–89.

110. Morrison, *Song of Solomon*, 183.

111. For a glimpse at Morrison's likely use of northeast Florida sources, see Rymer, *American Beach*.

112. Bambara, *The Salt Eaters*, 170, 171.

113. Naylor, *Mama Day*, 285, 295, 295.

114. Brodber, *Myal*, 4, 2.

115. Brodber has admitted that her challenging novel has not fully reached the communities it would catalyze and represent. She has, therefore, created a local assemblage space of community education, outreach, and "educo-tourism" known as Blackspace, grounding diasporic discussions and educational performance outside of academic spaces and publishing houses. See Nixon, "'We Have Something to Teach the World.'" On Myalism in Jamaica, see Murphy, *Working the Spirit*, 114–27; and especially Stewart, *Three Eyes for the Journey*.

116. Lovelace, *The Wine of Astonishment*, 3.

117. Kaplan, "Souls at the Crossroads, Africans on the Water," 515.

118. Dash, *Daughters of the Dust*, 143.

119. Dash, *Daughters of the Dust*, 159.

120. Kaplan, "Souls at the Crossroads," 519.

121. Quoted in Joyner, *Remember Me*, 39–40. In *Dancing Wisdom*, Yvonne Daniel writes of dance as "social medicine" (55).

Chapter 2. Lift Every Voice and Swing

1. J. W. Johnson, "Lift Every Voice and Sing," 875.

2. See Bruce, *Black American Writing from the Nadir*, 232–51, 194, 195.

3. Edwards, "The Seemingly Eclipsed Window of Form," 580–601.

4. Dimock, in *Through Other Continents*, makes much of "un-American" handlings of deep time and nonstandard time-space.

5. J. W. Johnson, *The Autobiography of an Ex-Colored Man*, 114.

6. Johnson, *Autobiography*, 3. Johnson wrote the preface.

7. Edwards, *The Practice of Diaspora*, 41.

8. Edwards, *The Practice of Diaspora*, 41.

9. Russell, *Legba's Crossing*, 29, 29, 30, 32.

10. J. W. Johnson, preface to *The Book of American Negro Poetry*, 713. His respect for Afro-creole syntax and sensibility led him to disavow (prematurely) efforts to use "dialect" as a literary medium, acknowledging, "This is no indictment against the

dialect as dialect, but against the mould of convention in which Negro dialect in the United States has been set" (714).

11. See Hargrove, "Mapping the 'Social Field of Whiteness,'" 94, 103.

12. Hurston, *Dust Tracks on a Road*, 775.

13. The best accounts of Johnson's life are the somewhat dated biography by Levy, *James Weldon Johnson*; and Johnson's autobiography, *Along This Way*.

14. www.stantoncollegeprep.org, January 4, 2010; www.jwjohnson.org, January 4, 2010. Johnson, whose family home in Jacksonville was demolished in the 1980s without a single public marker commemorating the man's memory, is remembered only within some of Jacksonville's black communities, primarily the Lavilla community that was his home.

15. Rymer, *American Beach*, 113–14.

16. Johnson, *Autobiography*, 115, 127, 117.

17. Johnson, *Along This Way*, 184, 185.

18. Quoted in Levy, *James Weldon Johnson*, 8; quoted in Rymer, *American Beach*, 115.

19. Johnson, *Along This Way*, 135.

20. Johnson, *Along This Way*, 139.

21. Johnson, *Along This Way*, 148–49.

22. Johnson, preface to *The Book of American Negro Poetry*, 713.

23. Arrighi, *The Long Twentieth Century*, 82; Benítez-Rojo, *The Repeating Island*, 441–45.

24. J. W. Johnson, *God's Trombones*, 847.

25. My readings here are informed by my Sewanee undergraduate introduction to the Agrarian essayist and novelist Andrew Lytle and readings of his essays collected in *From Eden to Babylon*, by my simultaneous introduction to Bob Marley's music during his "Babylon by Bus" tour, and by the substantial reorientations of thinking forged by a white southerner's subsequent Peace Corps service in Senegal. Investigations begun in Nassau suggest family ties of my own to the Bahamas, as Thomas Cartwright, a Loyalist founder of Long Island in the Bahamas, arrived from the Virginia coast with several enslaved "retainers" following the American Revolution. His father, Robert Cartwright, emigrated with the rest of the family from Virginia to pioneer Nashville, Tennessee, my own ancestral home. A trip to the settlement of Cartwrights on Long Island (Bahamas) with my father and our spirited reception there as kin has expanded my sense for what Johnson's seeking "symbols from within" might entail.

26. Craton and Saunders, *Islanders in the Stream*, 182.

27. Eneas, *Bain Town*, 54; Holm, "On the Relationship of Gullah and Bahamian," 310, 303.

28. Johnson, *Along This Way*, 169–70.

29. Johnson, *Along This Way*, 194.

30. Tate, *Essays of Four Decades*, 526.

31. Johnson, preface to *The Book of American Negro Poetry*, 691.

32. See Egerton, *Speak Now Against the Day*, 68.

33. Johnson, preface to *The Book of American Negro Poetry*, 689.

34. Johnson, preface to *The Book of American Negro Poetry*, 689. See also the

Jacksonville section of *The Autobiography of an Ex-Colored Man*, 54; and *Along This Way*, 495

35. Johnson, preface to *The Book of American Negro Poetry*, 697.

36. Johnson, preface to *The Book of American Negro Poetry*, 697, 713.

37. E. C. Bethel, "Music in the Bahamas,"91.

38. Parrish, "Records of Some Southern Loyalists," 174–75.

39. Georgia Writers' Project, *Drums and Shadows*, 76, 167, 113, 192, 194, 107, 67.

40. Strachan, "The Power of the Dead," 62–71, 66.

41. Johnson, *Along This Way*, 197. Born in a region of long commerce with the Bahamas and to an extended family that migrated from Nassau, Johnson also studied under a Bahamian principal at Jacksonville's Stanton School, was tutored by another Jacksonville West Indian, and learned Spanish from a Cuban boarder in his home in a late-nineteenth century Jacksonville that had a large population of Cubans mixed into its Bahamian, West Indian, and Geechee Afro-Atlantic matrix.

42. Johnson, preface to *The Book of American Negro Spirituals*, 33.

43. Johnson, preface to *The Book of American Negro Spirituals*, 33.

44. Johnson, *Along This Way*, 157, 158.

45. Johnson, *Along This Way*, 521.

46. Johnson, preface to *The Book of American Negro Spirituals*, 34.

47. See MacMillan, "John Kuners," 53–57. MacMillan writes that John Kuners "is remembered by various persons in Wilmington as late as the eighteen eighties" and "that the preachers finally succeeded by their influence in abolishing the custom as, in their opinion, it tended to degrade the negroes in the eyes of the white people in the community" (57).

48. Jacobs, *Incidents in the Life of a Slave Girl*, 572. See also E. Clement Bethel, *Junkanoo*, 10–24, for a comparative history of junkanoo in the Americas.

49. See Allewaert, "Swamp Sublime."

50. Strachan, *Paradise and Plantation*, 129.

51. Strachan, "The Power of the Dead," 66–67. On junkanoo and tourism, see Saunders, "The Impact of Tourism on Bahamian Society and Culture," 83; and Strachan, *Paradise and Plantation*, 129–30.

52. Johnson, preface to *The Book of American Negro Spirituals*, 21.

53. Edwards, "The Seemingly Eclipsed Window of Form," 590.

54. Johnson, preface to *The Book of American Negro Spirituals*, 28–30.

55. Edwards, "The Seemingly Eclipsed Window of Form," 590–92.

56. Deleuze and Guattari, *A Thousand Plateaus*, 154, 159.

57. Deleuze and Guattari, *A Thousand Plateaus*, 161.

58. J. W. Johnson, "O Black and Unknown Bards," in *Writings*, 817.

59. Johnson, *Autobiography*, 108.

60. Johnson, *Autobiography*, 109, 110.

61. Hagedorn, *Divine Utterances*, 130.

62. Johnson, *Autobiography*, 108.

63. Hagedorn, *Divine Utterances*, 131.

64. Hagedorn, *Divine Utterances*, 131

65. Johnson, preface to *The Book of American Negro Spirituals*, 28.

66. Hagedorn, *Divine Utterances*, 131–32.

67. Hagedorn, *Divine Utterances*, 131, 132.

68. Johnson, *Autobiography*, 83, 81, 83, 83.

69. Johnson, preface to *The Book of American Negro Spirituals*, 30.

70. Johnson, preface to *The Book of American Negro Spirituals*, 42–43.

71. Johnson, preface to *The Book of American Negro Spirituals*, 22–23. Johnson mentions his childhood appreciation of both Singing Johnson and Ma White as song leaders.

72. Johnson, preface to *The Book of American Negro Spirituals*, 22.

73. Johnson, preface to *The Book of American Negro Spirituals*, 31.

74. Johnson, preface to *The Book of American Negro Spirituals*, 31

75. Johnson, preface to *The Book of American Negro Spirituals*, 31.

76. Johnson, preface to *The Book of American Negro Spirituals*, 50.

77. Johnson, *Along This Way*, 162.

78. Johnson, *Along This Way*, 162.

79. Johnson, *Along This Way*, 164.

80. Johnson, *Along This Way*, 167.

81. Johnson, *Along This Way*, 167.

82. Johnson, preface to *God's Trombones*, 835.

83. Johnson, preface to *God's Trombones*, 835, 836.

84. Johnson, preface to *God's Trombones*, 836, 839, 839, 840, 840.

85. Johnson, preface to *God's Trombones*, 837.

86. Johnson, preface to *God's Trombones*, 848.

87. Johnson, preface to *God's Trombones*, 848.

88. Johnson, preface to *God's Trombones*, 850, 851.

89. From *The Autobiography of an Ex-Colored Man* (1912) to *The Book of American Negro Poetry* (1922) to *Along This Way* (1933), Johnson repeatedly referred to "the Uncle Remus stories" (meaning a whole body of "Aframerican" narratives beyond Joel Chandler Harris's specific rendering) as one of the four most vital cultural gifts of America to the world. The other three realms of vital agency were, for him, the spirituals, ragtime (black secular music), and the cakewalk (dance).

90. Parsons, *Folk-Tales of Andros Island, Bahamas*, 19–23.

91. C. S. Wylly recounts the "Marriage to the Devil" story as "Mary Bell" in *The Seed That Was Sown in the Colony of Georgia*, 153, as he recalled hearing it from his nurse, Baba. Wylly, a native of St. Simons Island, Georgia, was the grandson of Alexander Wylly, a Georgia Loyalist who emigrated to Nassau along with his better-known older brother, William Wylly (author of *A Short Account of the Bahama Islands*, 1789), and eventually returned to Georgia. Charles Spaulding Wylly's other grandfather, Thomas Spalding of Sapelo Island, Georgia, was also a Loyalist who emigrated to the Bahamas and later returned to Georgia. We know that Spalding brought several Senegambian slaves with him from the Bahamas, including the Pulaar-speaking headman of his Sapelo Island plantation, Bilali Muhammad. Another St. Simons Island Loyalist, John Couper, purchased another well-documented Senegambian Muslim in the Bahamas, Salih Bilali. See James Hamilton Couper's letter, in Curtin, *Africa Remembered*, 145–51. For a Bahamian telling of the "Marriage to the Devil" story,

see Glinton. Parsons records the story in both South Carolina and the Bahamas as "Mary Bell."

92. Rosenbaum, *Shout Because You're Free*, 57–58.

93. See Handley, *Postslavery Literatures in the Americas*, 6, 41–74.

94. Johnson, "The Dilemma of the Negro Author," in *Writings*, 748.

95. See Crook, Bailey, Harris, and Smith, *Sapelo Voices; Grovner*, Bailey, and Doc. Bill, *The Foods of Georgia's Barrier Islands;* and Bailey, *God, Dr. Buzzard, and the Bolito Man.*

96. Bailey, *God, Dr. Buzzard, and the Bolito Man*, 187.

97. See Gullah/Geechee Nation website, www.ihraam.org/Gullahproject.html, accessed July 2, 2012.

98. Goodwine, *The Legacy of Ibo Landing: Gullah Roots of African American Culture*, 6.

99. See Hargrove, "Mapping the 'Social Field of Whiteness,'" 94, 103.

100. Poitier, *This Life.*

101. Strachan, *Paradise and Plantation*, 96.

102. Johnson, *Autobiography*, 3.

103. J. Cartwright, "Everything Babylon," 39.

104. Thomas Cartwright and the Boys have been recorded on *The Bahamas: Islands of Song;* see Cindy Cartwright Armbrister, *Runnin' Sheep: A Collection of Stories from Long Island* (Nassau: Guanima Press, 1995), 81.

105. Glinton-Meicholas, *More Talkin' Bahamian*, 81, 82.

106. Bethel, *Guanahani, Mi Amor y otros Poemas*, 8.

107. Bethel, *Guanahani*, 42.

108. Glinton, *An Evening in Guanima*, 45.

109. See Kernghan, "Mickey Mouse in Port-au-Prince," 126–27.

Chapter 3. *Fe Chauffe, Balanse,* Swing

1. Trouillot, *Silencing the Past*, 73.

2. Long, *A New Orleans Voudou Priestess*, 88.

3. Dash, "Haïti Chimère," 10.

4. Buck-Morss, "Hegel and Haiti," 837. See also Fischer, *Modernity Disavowed.*

5. See Allewaert, "Swamp Sublime."

6. Tesh, "The Jambalaya Spirit," 47–48.

7. In Ken Burns's PBS jazz documentary, Giddins had this to say about Louis Armstrong: "Armstrong invented what for lack of a more specific phrase we call swing. He created modern time."

8. Donaldson, "Visibility, Haitian Hauntings, and Southern Borders," 716.

9. Hunt, *Haiti's Influence on Antebellum America*, 111.

10. Reed, *Mumbo Jumbo*, 6. On Haiti and the Louisiana Purchase, see Dessens, *From Saint-Domingue to New Orleans*, 18–19; see also Douglass Egerton, *Gabriel's Rebellion*, 47. On Biassou, see Landers, *Black Society in Spanish Florida*, 209–17. An assessment of President Jefferson's debts to the Haitian revolutionaries for making the Louisiana Purchase possible is offered in Ellis, *American Sphynx*, 246–47.

11. Gioia, *The History of Jazz*, 7.

12. K. Brown, "Afro-Caribbean Spirituality," 8–9.

13. Deren, *Divine Horsemen*, 49; Métraux, *Voodoo in Haiti*, 257–63.

14. K. Brown, "Afro-Caribbean Spirituality," 9. See also Métraux, *Voodoo in Haiti*, 257–63.

15. Roach, *Cities of the Dead*, xiii.

16. Armstrong, *Swing That Music*, 53.

17. Cable, *The Creoles of Louisiana*, 138.

18. The foundational role played by Senegambian slaves in the formation of Louisiana Creole culture has been assessed by Hall, *Africans in Colonial Louisiana*. Figures for Saint-Domingue migration to New Orleans are given by Lachance, "The Foreign French," 105.

19. Lachance, "The Foreign French," 111–12. See also Bell, *Revolution, Romanticism, and the Afro-Creole Protest Tradition in Louisiana*, 37–38.

20. Lachance, "The Foreign French," 117.

21. Dessens, *From Saint-Domingue to New Orleans*.

22. Lachance, "Were Saint-Domingue Refugees a Distinctive Cultural Group in Antebellum New Orleans?" 191.

23. Lachance, "The Foreign French," 117.

24. Dessens, *From Saint-Domingue to New Orleans*, 125–26, 152. Charles and Roudanez founded *L'Union* in the Civil War, which became *La Tribune de la Nouvelle Orleans* in 1864. Desdunes founded the *Union Louisianaise* in 1887 and contributed to the *New Orleans Crusader*, eventually becoming associate editor of the bilingual *Crusader*. Desdunes was key to the struggle against segregation on railcars that led to Homer Plessy's Supreme Court test case. See Rodolphe Lucien Desdunes, *Nos Hommes et Notre Histoire*.

25. Cosentino, "Imagine Heaven," 27.

26. Cosentino, "Imagine Heaven," 28; Cosentino, "It's All for You, Sen Jak!" 255.

27. A. Faulkner, "Does Jazz Put the Sin in Syncopation?" 40; Bechet, *Treat It Gentle*, 10.

28. For a discussion of "mindful body" and ritual embodiment in the practice of Vodou, see K. Brown, "The Ritual Economy of Haitian Vodou", 205, 220–23.

29. Séjour, "The Mulatto," 290.

30. On Valmour and Testut, see C. Bell, *Revolution, Romanticism, and the Afro-Creole Protest Tradition in Louisiana 1718–1868*, 205–7.

31. Testut, *Le Vieux Saloman*, 96.

32. Mercier, *L'habitation Saint-Ybars*, 87.

33. Dessens, *From Saint-Domingue to New Orleans*, 155–57.

34. Augustin, *Le Macandal*, 2; www.centenary.edu/french/macandal1.html, accessed Nov. 10, 2003.

35. Augustin, *Le Macandal*, 14, 39.

36. Cable, *The Grandissimes*, 131.

37. Cable, *The Grandissimes*, 40, 306.

38. K. Brown, "The Ritual Economy of Haitian Vodou," 217.

39. Cable, *The Grandissimes*, 96.

40. Cable, *The Grandissimes*, 184.

41. K. Cartwright, *Reading Africa into American Literature*, 97–98.

42. Fortier, *Louisiana Folk-Tales in French Dialect with English Translations*, 5, 110, 13. Roach, *Cities of the Dead*, 252.

43. By "deep play" I refer to Clifford Geertz, *The Interpretation of Cultures*. See especially the essay " 'Deep Play': Notes on the Balinese Cockfight."

44. Bakhtin, *The Dialogic Imagination*, 82; Cable, *The Creoles of Louisiana*, 315–16.

45. Mintz and Trouillot, "The Social History of Haitian Vodou," 127.

46. Asbury, *The French Quarter*, and Tallant, *Voodoo in New Orleans*, give popular accounts of Sanité Dédé's leadership of Voudou rites in New Orleans. Mulira's "The Case of Voodoo in New Orleans" offers a synthesizing account of New Orleans Voudou and speaks to Sanité Dédé's foundational role.

47. Asbury, *The French Quarter*, 264, 261. I am informed as well by Long, *A New Orleans Voodoo Priestess*, 98–100, which discusses the earlier publishing of this narrative account by Marie B. Williams, "A Night with the Voudous," *Appleton's Journal*, March 27, 1875, published as the narrative of "Professor D_____ of New Orleans," whom Long identifies as Alexander Dimitry (1805–13).

48. Asbury, *The French Quarter*, 264–65.

49. Long, *A New Orleans Voudou Priestess*, 102.

50. See Dayan, *Haiti, History, and the Gods*, 72.

51. Ward, *Voodoo Queen*, 191; Long, *A New Orleans Voudou Priestess*, 22.

52. See Long, *A New Orleans Voudou Priestess*, on Glapion, 51–53. Ward, *Voodoo Queen*, presents Glapion as a free man of color from Saint-Domingue, 88–92.

53. Long, *A New Orleans Voudou Priestess*, 108.

54. "The Rites of Voudou," *Daily Crescent*, July 31, 1850, p.3, c1., quoted in Long, *A New Orleans Voudou Priestess*, 105.

55. Ward, *Voodoo Queen*, 135.

56. "The Virgin of the Voudous," *Daily Delta*, August 10, 1850, p.1, c4; "Local Intelligence—Recorder Long's Court," *Daily Crescent*, July 12, 1859, p.1, c7; quoted in Long, *A New Orleans Voudou Priestess*, 106, 107, 108.

57. See Long, *A New Orleans Voudou Priestess*, on Marie II, 190–205. Long convincingly argues that we cannot know the identity of this second Marie Laveau but that she was probably someone who lived in the Laveau-Glapion household on St. Ann Street for a period of time.

58. Tallant, *Voodoo in New Orleans*, 90.

59. Tallant, *Voodoo in New Orleans*, 103.

60. Cosentino, "Imagine Heaven," 48, 49. See Ward, *Voodoo Queen*, 143, for ritual use of ash from St. John's Eve bonfires in New Orleans.

61. K. Brown, *Mama Lola*, 362.

62. Ward, *Voodoo Queen*, 140.

63. Ward, *Voodoo Queen*, 143.

64. Tallant, *Voodoo in New Orleans*, 89. See also Ward, *Voodoo Queen*, 144.

65. Ward, *Voodoo Queen*, 144.

66. Moreau de Saint-Méry, *A Civilization That Perished*, 321.

67. Saint-Méry, *A Civilization That Perished*, 322.

68. Ward, *Voodoo Queen*, 115.

69. Ward, *Voodoo Queen*, 8.

70. Tallant, *Voodoo in New Orleans*, 67.

71. Tallant, *Voodoo in New Orleans*, 75–76.

72. Tallant, *Voodoo in New Orleans*, 111.

73. Hearn, "The Last of the Voudoos," *Harper's Weekly;* reprinted in Frederick S. Starr, ed., *Inventing New Orleans*, 77–82.

74. "A Visit to a Professor of the Black Art," *Daily Crescent*, December 24, 1866, p.2, c2; quoted in Long, *A New Orleans Voudou Priestess*, 137, 138. Long also makes the point about the similarities here to Afro-Cuban divination.

75. Tallant, *Voodoo in New Orleans*, 145–46. See Ward, *Voodoo Queen*, 147–48, for discussion of Eliza.

76. Long, *A New Orleans Voudou Priestess*, 40.

77. Asbury, *The French Quarter*, 278. Similar ritual or altar designs may be found in photographs in Brown, *Mama Lola*, 42; and in Delgado, "From the Sacred Wild to the City," 102, 104, 112–13, and especially 118.

78. Long, *A New Orleans Voudou Priestess*, 110–11.

79. Quoted in Tallant, *Voodoo*, 42, 40. See also Long, *A New Orleans Voudou Priestess*, 111–13.

80. Tallant, *Voodoo*, 40, 42.

81. Long, *A New Orleans Voudou Priestess*, 129.

82. See Chapman, *Bananas*, and Crowther, *The Romance and Rise of the American Tropics*, on New Orleans, United Fruit, and American imperialism.

83. Long, *A New Orleans Voudou Priestess*, 132.

84. M. P. Smith, *Mardi Gras Indians*, 97. R. Turner, *Jazz Religion*, asserts that "[i]n 1883 Chief Becate Batiste . . . began 'masking Indian' on Mardi Gras day with his downtown Seventh ward Creole Wild West Indian gang" (53).

85. Turner, *Jazz Religion*, 58, 33, 39–68.

86. On jazz and Mardi Gras Indian families, see Turner, *Jazz Religion*, 49–50; and Berry, Foose, and Jons, *Up from the Cradle of Jazz*, 9–13.

87. Long, *A New Orleans Voudou Priestess*, 67, 34–36.

88. Kodat, "Conversing with Ourselves," 2.

89. Bechet, *Treat It Gentle*, 6.

90. Quoted in Long, *A New Orleans Voudou Priestess*, 10

91. Quoted in Epstein, *Sinful Tunes and Spirituals*, 97.

92. Quoted in Epstein, *Sinful Tunes and Spirituals*, 97.

93. Asbury, *The French Quarter*, 242.

94. Creecy, *Scenes in the South*, 20–23, quoted in Long, *A New Orleans Voudou Priestess*, 43.

95. Long, *A New Orleans Voudou Priestess*, 43; Epstein, *Sinful Tunes and Spirituals*, 134.

96. On Congo Square's role in the ongoing story of jazz stagings and commmodifications, see Kodat, "Conversing with Ourselves."

97. See Long, *A New Orleans Voudou Priestess*, 85; and Turner, *Jazz Religion*, 29.

98. K. Brown, *Mama Lola*, 134.

99. K. Brown, "The Ritual Economy of Haitian Vodou," 222.

100. Armstrong, *Swing That Music*, 30, 31, 42, 31, 73, 33, 31–32.

101. Gara, *The Baby Dodds Story*, 12.

102. R. Turner, *Jazz Religion*, 108, 101–102, 102.

103. Lomax, *Mister Jelly Roll*, 62. For discussion of the search for Morton's family name, see Pastras, *Dead Man Blues*, 13.

104. Lomax, *Mister Jelly Roll*, 62.

105. Pastras, *Dead Man Blues*, 70–71. Long, *A New Orleans Voudou Priestess*, (78), reports Christophe Glapion selling thirty-two-year-old Eliza to Pierre Monette for $600 on April 26, 1854.

106. See Pastras, *Dead Man Blues*, 53–58; and Lomax, *Mister Jelly Roll*, 9–10.

107. Lomax, *Mister Jelly Roll*, 9.

108. Lomax, *Mister Jelly Roll*, 46. Jelly Roll mentions that he did not pay Papa Sona: "I have lived to regret this ungrateful action" (47).

109. Reich and Gaines, *Jelly's Blues*, 37–38, 152; Roach, *Cities of the Dead*, 231. See Roach (224–33) on the Storyville of Morton's adolescence.

110. Reich and Gaines, *Jelly's Blues*, 86.

111. Ward, *Voodoo Queen*, 147.

112. Tallant, *Voodoo in New Orleans*, 146.

113. Ward, *Voodoo Queen*, 147–48.

114. Brown, *Mama Lola*, 374, 362.

115. Métraux, in *Voodoo in Haiti*, introduced the notion of "danced religions" (29) in speaking of the importance of music and dance to West African (and particularly Dahomean) religion. In *Dancing Wisdom*, Yvonne Daniel writes of dance as "social medicine" (55).

116. Mignolo, *Local Histories / Global Designs*, feeds my understanding of how "undisciplined forms of knowledge . . . were reduced to subaltern knowledge by colonial disciplined knowing practices" (10).

117. Chernoff, *African Rhythm and African Sensibility*, 155, 156, 158.

118. Mackey, "Sound and Sentiment, Sound and Symbol," 613–14.

119. Ellison, *Invisible Man*, 8.

120. Ellison, *Shadow and Act*, 200–201, 205–6, 206.

121. Ellison, *Shadow and Act*, 216, 214.

122. Ellison, *Shadow and Act*, 219. I point here to Pavlić's *Crossroads Modernism*.

123. Reed, *Mumbo Jumbo*, 6.

124. Métraux, *Voodoo in Haiti*, 29; Daniel, *Dancing Wisdom*, 55.

125. Dayan, *Haiti, History, and the Gods*, 74.

126. Hurbon, "American Fantasy and Haitian Vodou," 197.

127. Curtius, *Symbioses d'une mémoire*, 10.

128. Komunyakaa, *Blue Notes*, 4.

129. Komunyakaa, *Blue Notes*, 4.

130. Carpentier, prologue to *The Kingdom of This World*, 87.

131. Komunyakaa, *Blue Notes*, 7.

132. Komunyakaa, *Blue Notes*, 8.

133. Dayan, *Haiti, History, and the Gods*, 138; Cosentino, "Imagine Heaven," 35.

134. Komunyakaa, *Blue Notes*, 8.

135. See Pavlić, *Crossroads Modernism*, and "Open the Unusual Door," 780–96, for discussion of a Legba-ruled modernity, Komunyakaa's poetics, and *durée*.

136. Coleridge, "Kubla Khan," 431. Komunyakaa may have been informed by Roach's *Cities of the Dead* and its account of the St. Charles Hotel as "a kind of homosocial pleasure dome" (214), its discussion of Storyville as "reconstituting the homosocial pleasure dome" (225), and discussion of New Orleans (including the Louisiana Superdome) as "a ludic space, the behavioral vortex, for the rest of the nation" (231).

137. Komunyakaa, *Pleasure Dome*, 354.

138. See Depestre, *A Rainbow for the Christian West*.

139. Girard, *Violence and the Sacred*, 39–67.

140. Girard, *Violence and the Sacred*, 37.

141. Komunyakaa, *Blue Notes*, 14, 15.

142. See Enloe, *Maneuvers*, 67. Komunyakaa also spoke to me of American soldiers' wonderment over the presence of women of African descent in Vietnam, with many of these women (daughters of Senegalese soldiers) working as prostitutes (Komunyakaa, personal communication, Feb. 21, 2001, Salem, Virginia).

143. Komunyakaa, *Blue Notes*, 94, 78.

144. Komunyakaa, *Blue Notes*, 55.

145. Komunyakaa, *Blue Notes*, 15

146. Robeson, *Paul Robeson Speaks*, 377; Duiker, *Ho Chi Minh*; Long, *A New Orleans Voudou Priestess*.

147. Komunyakaa, *Blue Notes*, 81.

148. Komunyakaa, *Blue Notes*, 115.

149. Rowell, "Kim Dung Nguyen," 1085.

Chapter 4. Making Faces at the Sublime

1. I take the line in Louisiana Creole from Sybil Kein's poem "Mo Oulé Mourrir Dans Lac-la" in Kein's *Gumbo People*, 29. It is most famously present in Luke Turner's tale of Laveau's death in Zora Neale Hurston's *Mules and Men*. "I want to die in New Orleans," Brenda Marie Osbey insists in a recent essay on her home city's long history of attentiveness to "the greatest and grandest of Journeys" (245, 251).

2. The "m'o" of "M'o get me a mojo hand," is a southernism, a contraction of "I am going to" that differs from the Louisiana Creole first-person pronoun *mo* but that also shares a space with it in its sound and contracting/convergent logic, even its animating or swinging launch into futurity.

3. Roach, *Cities of the Dead*, 28.

4. See Hall, *Africans in Colonial Louisiana*, on foundational ties between St. Louis and New Orleans, both supplied under a charter held by the French Company of the Indies.

5. Salvaggio, "Hearing Sappho in New Orleans," 308.

6. Salvaggio, "Hearing Sappho in New Orleans," 294, 294–95, 299.

7. Fossett, "Sold Down River," 327.

8. McPherson, "No Natural Disaster," 331.

9. Salvaggio, "Hearing Sappho in New Orleans," 299; McPherson, "No Natural Disaster," 334.

10. Quoted in Petersen and Rutherford, "Fossil and Psyche," 185.

11. McPherson, "No Natural Disaster," 334, 332.

12. Fossett, "Sold Down River," 327.

13. I come to Nora's ideas through Roach's *Cities of the Dead*, 26.

14. Jackson, "Love, Loss, and the 'Art' of Making Gumbo: An Interview with Eileen Julien," 102.

15. Jackson, "Interview with Eileen Julien," 103.

16. Codrescu, "Love Note to New Orleans," 1112.

17. Rowell, "My Byzantium," 1028, 1029. If we were to look for a time and place for the emergence of a New Southern critical vision appreciative of this Gulf energy, food, and vision thing, the journal *Callaloo*, founded by Charles Rowell, Tom Dent, and Jerry Ward in Louisiana in 1976, could lay claim to being a primary generator.

18. Walcott, *Collected Poems*, 104, 107.

19. See Degiglio-Bellemare, "Vodou Hybridity and 'Voodoo Economics,' " 196.

20. Quoted in Dyson, *Come Hell or High Water*, 180. While McKissic is a black pastor within a white-dominated Southern Baptist Convention, the number of black pastors who responded to the catastrophe by blaming the victims suggests that Princeton professor Eddie Glaude had good reason to title a 2010 Jeremiad "The Black Church Is Dead."

21. Brooks, *New York Times*, Jan. 15, 2010.

22. Will, "Leviathan in Louisiana," 88.

23. O'Driscoll, " 'The Looters, They're like Cockroaches,' " *USA Today*, 2 September 2005, 3A.

24. K. Brown, "Serving the Spirits," 207, 209.

25. Glissant, *Poetics of Relation*, 63, 64.

26. Rowell, "Carol Bebelle," 1214.

27. Glissant, *Poetics of Relation*, 145, 176.

28. See Westhoff, *Dirty South*, and Richardson, *From Uncle Tom to Gangsta*, 197–227. Rick Koster's *Louisiana Music* describes the evolution of contemporary "bounce" music from uptown housing projects, citing in particular a moment "in the St. Thomas project in 1989 when a young DJ, Kevin Tucker—a.k.a. MCT—improvised a series of street slogans in the fashion of Mardi Gras Indian call-and-response chants, and an immediate crowd gathered," resulting in "a local scene that spawned dozens of 'bounce' songs, all infectiously danceable, rap-pop fusions that glistened with summery possibility" (293).

29. Juvenile, "Get Ya Hustle On," *Reality Check*.

30. Glissant, *Poetics of Relation*, 197.

31. Richardson, *From Uncle Tom to Gangsta*, 221, 236.

32. DJ Drama and Lil Wayne, *Dedication 2 Gangsta Grillz*.

33. McPherson, "No Natural Disaster," 334.

34. New Orleans bounce artists have carried themselves like avatars of the "foul-

mouthed" *lwa* Gédé, "master of the two absolutes: fucking and dying," the all-consuming spirit of cosmic Dynaflow who cannot lie, at least as Cosentino describes the Gédés, "Envoi," 413.

35. I am not in position to offer anything close to an adequate assessment of grass-roots hip-hop in New Orleans. Let me simply acknowledge here that a close examination of the best grassroots artists in New Orleans (as in my own home of Jacksonville) would find a wonderful variety of work exploring the space's poetics of relation.

36. Derrida, *Of Hospitality*.

37. Chamoiseau, *Texaco*, trans. Réjouis and Vinokurov, 21. For the fullest flavor of how Marie-Sophie uses an old/aged rum (*rhum vieux*) to bring this *urbaniste* through a *cirque créole* to face *la parole d'une femme-matador*, readers must turn to the original: Chamoiseau, *Texaco* (Paris: Gallimard, 1992), 43, 17.

38. Lowe, "An Interview with Brenda Marie Osbey," 106.

39. Lowe, "Interview with Brenda Marie Osbey," 100, 102.

40. Osbey, *All Saints*, 37.

41. Osbey, *All Saints*, 39. See Funny Papa Smith's "Seven Sisters Blues" parts 1 and 2, on Funny Papa Smith, *The Original Howling Wolf, 1930–1931* (Shanachie, 2005).

42. Osbey, *All Saints*, 39, 40.

43. Lowe, "Interview with Brenda Marie Osbey," 100.

44. Osbey, *All Saints*, 45.

45. Deren, *Divine Horsemen*, 144, 138.

46. Dayan, *Haiti, History, and the Gods*, 63, 64.

47. Osbey, *All Saints*, 46.

48. This chant-centered poem, however, probably emerges from Osbey's re-creative Erzulie encodings since the traditional Mardi-Gras Indian chant is "Shallow Water, Oh Mama" rather than "Shallow Water Loa-Mama." The first recording of this song appeared on an album by Big Chief Monk Boudreaux and the Golden Eagles, *Lightning and Thunder* (1988). See also Bo Dollis and the Wild Magnolias, *I'm Back at Carnival Time!* The HBO hit series *Treme* titled its sixth episode "Shallow Water" and featured a bare-bones performance of the song.

49. R. Turner, *Jazz Religion*, 33, 39, 45–48, 54–58, 68.

50. Osbey, *All Saints*, 51.

51. Chamoiseau, *Texaco*, 286, 287, 288.

52. The creature of Osbey's "Suicide City" seems to share much with the Caribbean *loup-garou* or *soucouyant*.

53. Chamoiseau, *Texaco*, 165, 263.

54. Julien, *Travels with Mae*, 1.

55. On the skeleton krewes or skull-and-bones gangs, see R. Lewis, *The House of Dance and Feathers*, 185–90.

56. Julien, *Travels with Mae*, 21.

57. The placement of Sy's *Signares* on the cover bespeaks profound mourning hardly mentioned directly in this book. Kalidou Sy died suddenly in Senegal, shortly after Katrina struck New Orleans: "He was to come back in two months. When I spoke with him after the city flooded, he said I should not worry, he would soon be

there and we would clean up Havana Street together. I would never see him again" (124). Tending to Havana Street thereafter becomes a most stunningly charged act of remembrance.

58. Chancy, *Framing Silence*, 14.

59. Lipsitz, *Dangerous Crossroads*, 16.

60. Rowell, "Jason Berry," 1251.

61. Rowell, "Donald Harrison, Jr.," 1297.

62. Ellis Marsalis quoted in M. P. Smith, *Mardi Gras Indians*, 5.

63. Wynton Marsalis quoted in Logsdon and Elie, *Faubourg Tremé*.

64. Rowell, "Carol Bebelle," 1212.

65. Salvaggio, "Hearing Sappho in New Orleans," 306.

66. Salvaggio, "Hearing Sappho in New Orleans," 306. Salvaggio's source for the Creole song of Ti Cowan is Monroe, *Bayou Ballads* (1921), 6.

67. For Turtle's tale, look to Cabrera, *Afro-Cuba Tales*; Cabrera, *Ayapá: Cuentos de Jicotea*; and a Creek variant in Gouge, *New Fire*. A tale told recounted in Chinua Achebe's *Things Fall Apart* offers precedent (96–99), some of which we find too in narratives from William Bascom, *Ifa Divination*; Oyekan Owomoyela, *Yoruba Trickster Tales*; and Julia Cristina Ortiz Lugo, *De Arañas, Conejos y Tortugas: Presencia de Africa en la Cuentística de Tradición Oral en Puerto Rico*.

68. Saloy, *Red Beans and Ricely Yours*, 4.

69. See Cabrera, *El Monte*, 102; Castro, *Cantos*, 72–73.

70. Saloy, *Red Beans and Ricely Yours*, 45.

71. Chase, *The Dooky Chase Cookbook*, 36.

72. Osbey, *In These Houses*, 51.

Chapter 5. "Come and Gaze on a Mystery"

1. Hurston, *Tell My Horse*, 376.

2. Hurston, *Their Eyes Were Watching God*, 183.

3. Hurston, *Mules and Men*, 191. For Hurston's descriptions of this Rain-Bringer initiation, see her "Hoodoo in America," *Journal of American Folklore* 44 (October– December 1931): 317–418; *Mules and Men*, 182–95; and *Dust Tracks on a Road*, 699–700.

4. Hurston, *Their Eyes Were Watching God*, 332.

5. Duck, *The Nation's Region*, 116, 121.

6. Lowenthal, "'Marriage is 20, Children are 21,'" 74; quoted in Dayan, *Haiti, History, and the Gods*, 134.

7. Hurston, *Their Eyes Were Watching God*, 183.

8. Hurston, *Their Eyes Were Watching God*, 183; Hurston, *Tell My Horse*, 376; Hurston, *Their Eyes Were Watching God*, 314.

9. Kristeva, *The Powers of Horror*, 2, 4.

10. Carby, "The Politics of Fiction, Anthropology, and the Folk," 131.

11. Hurston, "Communication," 664–67.

12. See Landers, *Black Society in Spanish Florida*, 29–60, on Fort Mose.

13. Bone, "The (Extended) South of Black Folk," 753–79, see especially 767–69.

14. Gibbs, "An American Tragedy," 46.

15. Hurston, *Dust Tracks on a Road*, 699.

16. Hurston, *Jonah's Gourd Vine*, 3.

17. Hurston, *Their Eyes Were Watching God*, 305.

18. Hurston, *Moses, Man of the Mountain*, 595.

19. Hurston, *Seraph on the Suwanee*, 623.

20. Southerland, "The Influence of Voodoo on the Fiction of Zora Neale Hurston," 182.

21. Pavlić, *Crossroads Modernism*, 193.

22. Washington, *Our Mothers, Our Powers, Our Texts*, 101.

23. See Washington, *Our Mothers, Our Powers, Our Texts*, on *ajé*. Henry John Drewal and Margaret Thompson Drewal in *Gelede* have this to say about *ajé*: "Ajé— a generally pejorative term—is used rarely and with caution. No one would address a woman suspected of possessing such power as *ajé*, not just out of fear but because such women also work positive wonders. Therefore they are called 'our mothers' (*awon iya wa*) and are addressed personally with 'my mother' (*ìyámi*)" (9).

24. Gleason, *Oya*, 32.

25. Ramos, "Afro-Cuban Orisha Worship," 65, 67.

26. Gleason, *Oya*, 40, 41.

27. Gleason, *Oya*, 33, 290, 290. On Oya's rites and repertoires in Brazilian candomblé (as orixa Iansa), see Guilhermino (Guilherme D'Ogum), *Iansâ do Balé*.

28. Gleason, *Oya*, 253, 46.

29. Hagedorn, *Divine Utterances*, 54.

30. See "Questions and Answers about Lightning," National Severe Storms Laboratory, www.nssl.noaa.gov/edu/ltg (24 June 2006).

31. Hurston, "How It Feels to Be Colored Me," 828. See also Harry M. Hyatt, *Hoodoo-Conjuration-Witchcraft-Rootwork*. Hemenway first exposed Hurston's plagiarism in his *Zora Neale Hurston*, 96–99.

32. See M. Mason, *Living Santería*, 64–65; and D. Brown, *Santería Enthroned*, 134.

33. D. Brown, *Santería Enthroned*, 71.

34. Wall, "Mules and Men and Women," 53–70.

35. Gleason, *Oya*, 40, 44, 43, 39.

36. Hurston, *Seraph on the Suwanee*, 627, 628.

37. Gleason, *Oya*, 248.

38. See Hagedorn, *Divine Utterances*, 71.

39. Hagedorn, *Divine Utterances*, 54.

40. Quoted in Gleason, *Oya*, 247.

41. I am indebted to prior readings of this jook scene offered by Pavlić, *Crossroads Modernism*, 189; and by Gussow, *Seems Like Murder Here*, 233–71.

42. Gleason, *Oya*, 43. See also Drewal and Drewal, *Gelede*, on Yoruba "cooling" or propitiatory rites (etutu), especially as used in sacrificial cooling spectacle for the mothers, 14.

43. Gleason, *Oya*, 31.

44. Gleason, *Oya*, 61.

45. See C. Tate, *Psychoanalysis and Black Novels;* and Duck, *The Nation's Region,* 132–45.

46. See Gleason, *Oya,* 78.

47. Gleason, *Oya,* 247, 250.

48. C. Tate, *Psychoanalysis and Black Novels,* 160.

49. I think Leigh Anne Duck is right to equate this private space with the formal difference the novel itself makes as a protected (or "liminoid") time-space (as Duck deploys the anthropological work of Victor Turner), a "grove" of folkloric or ritual preservation, innovation, and re-creative mourning and travel (141–42). I also refer here to Glissant's call for "an aesthetics of the earth."

50. Bascom, *Ifa Divination,* 429, 431, 431, 433.

51. I borrow the term "diasporic modernism" from Pavlić, *Crossroads Modernism.*

52. See Walker, "In Search of Zora Neale Hurston," 74–79, 85–87; and Boyd, *Wrapped in Rainbows,* 436–38.

53. Hurston to W. E. B. Du Bois, 11 June 1945, in *Zora Neale Hurston: A life in Letters,* 518, 519, 520.

54. I refer here to Hurston's now well-circulated response to a couple of photographs of her that Carl Van Vechten shot and mailed her: "I love myself when I'm laughing . . . and then again when I'm looking mean and impressive," which is also the title given to a popular Alice Walker–edited selection of Hurston's work.

55. Allewaert, "Swamp Sublime," 341.

56. Hurston to Marjorie Kinnan Rawlings, 16 May 1943, in *Zora Neale Hurston: A Life in Letters,* 486.

57. Gleason, *Oya,* 249, 250, 250.

58. Ladd, *Resisting History,* 10, 9; see Gleason, *Oya,* 152–221, on Oya and the hunt.

59. Gleason, *Oya,* 187.

60. Gleason, *Oya,* 183–89; see also Bascom, *Ifa Divination,* 375–85.

61. Hurston to Rawlings, 16 May 1943, 486, 488.

62. Hurston, *Every Tongue Got to Confess,* 63; Bascom, *Ifa Divination,* 423; see also Bascom, *African Folktales in the New World.*

63. Bascom, *Ifa Divination,* 423.

64. Hurston, *Every Tongue Got to Confess,* 63.

65. Bhabha, *The Location of Culture,* 35, 39.

66. Gleason, *Oya,* 159, 160.

67. Gleason, *Oya,* 326.

68. See Hurston, *Tell My Horse,* 301–8.

69. Hurston, *Dust Tracks in a Road,* 562.

70. See Hurston, "Folklore and Music," 891–92.

71. Hurston, "Folklore and Music," 875.

72. Hurston, "Folklore and Music," 891–92.

73. Hurston, *Dust Tracks.* 631.

74. Lorde, "Winds of Orisha," 2205–6.

75. Hurston, *Dust Tracks on a Road,* 711.

76. Hurston, *Dust Tracks on a Road,* 763.

77. Hurston's young husband, Albert Price III, took her prayers seriously, complaining in their divorce papers that he was "in fear of his life" due to the "black magic" and "'voodooism'" she allegedly worked on him; see Kaplan, *Life in Letters*, 131, 230, 457; and also Boyd, *Wrapped in Rainbows*, 338. The primary Voodoo Hurston seems to have worked on Price was that of passing for twenty-nine on the marriage license when she was forty-eight years old; see Boyd, *Wrapped in Rainbows*, 325.

78. Lowe, "Seeing beyond Seeing," 85.

79. K. Brown, "The Ritual Economy of Haitian Vodou," 217.

80. Hurston to Franz Boas, 21 April 1929, In *Zora Neale Hurston: A Life in Letters*, 138.

81. Minh-ha, *When the Moon Waxes Red*, 74.

82. Hurston, "The Sanctified Church," 901, 903.

83. Hurston, "Mother Catherine," 857.

84. See J. W. Johnson, "Self-Determining Haiti," 660–87.

85. Gilroy, *The Black Atlantic*, 37; West, *Race Matters*, 19.

86. Carby, "The Politics of Fiction, Anthropology, and the Folk." See Lamothe, Pavlić, Washington, Bone.

Chapter 6. "Vamonos pa'l Monte"

1. Quoted in D. Brown, *Santería Enthroned*, 245.

2. Benítez-Rojo, *The Repeating Island*, 33, 33–34, 34.

3. Benítez-Rojo, *The Repeating Island,* 10.

4. Loichot, *Orphan Narratives*, 10.

5. Benítez-Rojo, *The Repeating Island*, 16.

6. Benítez-Rojo, *The Repeating Island*, 11.

7. Benítez-Rojo, *The Repeating Island*, 6

8. Benítez-Rojo, *The Repeating Island*, 6, 7, 8.

9. Benítez-Rojo, *The Repeating Island*, 7–8.

10. Escobedo, *La Florida*, 20.

11. M. Mason, *Living Santeria*, 68–76

12. Dimock, *Through Other Continents*, 4.

13. Castro, *Cantos of Blood and Honey*, 14.

14. Vega, *The Florida of the Inca*, 106.

15. Benítez-Rojo, *The Repeating Island*, 52.

16. Benítez-Rojo, *The Repeating Island*, 52.

17. Castro, *Cantos of Blood and Honey*, 15.

18. Castro, *Cantos of Blood and Honey*, 15.

19. Benítez-Rojo, *The Repeating Island*, 53.

20. Castro, *Cantos of Blood and Honey*, 16.

21. *Histoire Naturelle des Indes: The Drake Manuscript*, 257.

22. Laudonnière, *A Notable Historie*, 235.

23. Hann, "Translation of Alonso de Leturiondo's Memorial," 202.

24. Escobedo, *Pirates, Indians, and Spaniards*, 164.

25. Irving, "The Conspiracy of Neamathla," 100.

26. Milanich and Sturtevant. *Francisco Pareja's 1613 Confessionario*, 34, 28, 37, 39, 34.

27. See Hann, "The Missions of Spanish Florida," 94.

28. Garbarino, *The Seminole*, 63.

29. Escobedo, *Pirates, Indians, and Spaniards.*

30. Hann, "Translation of Alonso de Leturiondo's Memorial," 168–70, 201–2.

31. Landers, *Black Society in Spanish Florida*, 61–64. See also Deagan and Mac-Mahon, *Fort Mose.*

32. Landers, *Black Society in Spanish Florida*, 209–17, 242, 246–48.

33. See Victor Hugo, *Bug Jargal*, and Madison Smartt Bell's *All Souls Rising* as well as his *Master of the Crossroads.*

34. See R. Howard, *Black Seminoles in the Bahamas*, 12–13. Sturtevant and Littlefield both concur that Seminole first referred to the Alachua band of Lower Creeks (in the 1770s) and came to be the ethnonym for all Florida Indians by the 1820s. See Sturtevant, "Creek into Seminole"; and Littlefield, *Africans and Seminoles from Removal to Emancipation.*

35. Bartram, *Travels*, 195–96.

36. Kingsley, *Balancing Evils Judiciously*, 10.

37. Emerson, "An Unfinished Poem on St. Augustine," 63.

38. Emerson, "From Journals (1827–28)," 62.

39. Jacksonville First Baptist is a megachurch long-pastored by a two-time SBC president memorable for labeling the Prophet Mohammad as a "demon-possessed pedophile." This is the space of fortress heartlessness and circum-Caribbean response to it: the site that taught Zora Neale Hurston (in chapter 5) her place as a "little colored girl" and led her to the muck, the site of James Weldon Johnson's own near lynching.

40. "Demonstrators Assaulted by Police, Ku Klux Klan," 1.

41. "Why St. Augustine?" 12.

42. M. L. King Jr. "400 Years of Bigotry and Hate," 7.

43. E. Brathwaite, *The Development of Creole Society in Jamaica*, 296.

44. Castellanos, "Introduction," vii.

45. Cabrera, *Afro-Cuban Tales*, 10.

46. Cabrera, *El monte*, 13.

47. See Rodriguez-Mangual, *Lydia Cabrera and the Construction of an Afro-Cuban Cultural Identity*, 74.

48. Rodriguez-Mangual, *Lydia Cabrera*, 82.

49. Cabrera, *El monte*, 67.

50. Rodriguez-Mangual, *Lydia Cabrera*, 67.

51. D. Brown, *Santería Enthroned*, 117.

52. Brown, *Santería Enthroned*, 117.

53. Cabrera, *Afro-Cuban Tales*, 13.

54. Cabrera, *Afro-Cuban Tales*, 146.

55. Hurston, *Tell My Horse*, 370.

56. Cabrera, *Cuentos adultos niños y retrasados mentales.*

57. See Bascom, *Ifa Divination*, 398–405.

58. Cabrera, *Ayapá*, 9.

59. Cabrera, *Ayapá*, 11, 12.

60. Bascom's *African Folktales in the New World* catalogs a range of tales that find rearticulation in three different narrative motifs spread throughout the Americas: "The Talking Skull Refuses to Talk," "The Talking Animal Refuses to Talk," and "Singing Tortoise Refuses to Sing." Hurston's "High Walker and the Bloody Bones" and a number of stories about a talking or singing terrapin from Alabama, Mississippi, Arkansas, Oklahoma, and Texas all carry some version of the message "Nigger . . . you talk too much" and "Don't tell all you see" (31, 33).

61. Gouge, *Totkv Mocvse / New Fire*, 114.

62. Gouge, *Totkv Mocvse / New Fire*, 115.

63. Gouge, *Totkv Mocvse / New Fire*, 33–36; see Salvaggio on the Creole lullaby.

64. Womack, foreword to *Totkv Mocvse / New Fire*, xii.

65. Womack, *Red on Red*, 97, 75–101.

66. Estabrook, *Tomatoland*.

67. Peck, "Strange Fruit," 13.

68. G. Miller, "African Religious Survivals in Death Rituals," 205; Creighton, quoted in Miller 205–6.

69. Castro, *Cantos to Blood and Honey*, 72–73.

70. Murphy, *Working the Spirit*, 111.

71. Murphy, *Working the Spirit*, 113.

72. Murphy, *Working the Spirit*, 111.

73. Fernandez, *From Afro-Cuban Rhythms to Latin Jazz*, 27, 29.

74. Mosquero, "Eleggua at the (Post?)Modern Crossroads," 232, 244.

75. Viso, *Ana Mendieta*, 22; Roulet, "Ana Mendieta: A Life in Context," 226–27. Fearing that the Cuban state would assume guardianship over Cuba's children, Mendieta's parents—like thousands of other Cuban parents—turned to Operation Pedro Pan, which was sponsored by the Catholic Church and U.S. State Department, to airlift and relocate their children, placing them in foster homes in the United States and thereby ostensibly guarding the children's Catholic faith and innocence from Marxist-Leninist reorientation.

76. Quoted in Roulet, "Ana Mendieta," 230.

77. Viso, *Ana Mendieta*, 177, 58–59, 65, 64.

78. Quoted in Viso, *Ana Mendieta*, 32

79. Viso, *Ana Mendieta*, 89, 80–93. Viso notes that these names and translations were probably drawn from Juan Arrom's *Mythology and Arts of the Prehispanic Antilles* (1975).

80. Viso, *Ana Mendieta*, 92–93. On Mendieta's travels in Miami and meetings with Lukumi diviners, see Viso 80.

81. Viso, *Ana Mendieta*, 95.

82. Quoted in Roulet, "Ana Mendieta," 236; see also Viso, *Ana Mendieta*, 95.

83. See Viso, *Ana Mendieta*, 106–8, 112, 114–15. These leaf *siluetas* were given to friends and sent as gallery representations of her work from 1982–84.

84. Landers, *Black Society in Spanish Florida*, 253.

1. Poe, *The Complete Tales and Poems,* 946, 943, 946.

2. Quoted in Rothman, *Slave Country,* 219. In speaking of the movement from "chaos to cosmos," I invoke Éliade in *The Myth of the Eternal Return,* 87.

3. Girard, *Violence and the Sacred,* 257.

4. Howe, *Shell Shaker,* 44.

5. Jumper, *Legends of the Seminoles,* 18.

6. Walker, "The Dummy in the Window," in *Living By the Word,* 25–32.

7. Howe, *Shell Shaker,* 1, 2.

8. Girard, *Violence and the Sacred,* 40.

9. As Eric Anderson pointed out to me, Howe makes up for this in her second novel.

10. Landers, *Black Society in Spanish Florida,* 167; Hall, *Africans in Colonial Louisiana,* 118, 114–18.

11. See Redmond, "A Harbor of Sense: An Interview with Joy Harjo," for Harjo's assertion, "The movement of our stomp dances is around the fire, counterclockwise. I understand that is the direction of dances in some of the West African tribes who were forced here" (29).

12. Quoted in Rothman, *Slave Country.* 127.

13. Quoted in Rothman, *Slave Country,* 132.

14. Hurston, *Tell My Horse,* 376.

15. Hurston, *Jonah's Gourd Vine,* 135.

16. John, *Unburnable,* 165.

17. Rhys, *Wide Sargasso Sea,* 50.

18. Hughes, "Jazzonia," 226.

19. Medoro, *The Bleeding of America,* 9.

20. Medoro, *The Bleeding of America,* 227.

21. Medoro, *The Bleeding of America,* 227–28.

22. See Édouard Glissant, *Faulkner, Mississippi,* and Wilson Harris, *The Womb of Space.*

23. Belcher, "Consuming Subjects," 228.

24. Faulkner, introduction to *The Sound and the Fury,* 232.

25. Medoro, *The Bleeding of America,* 80.

26. Medoro, *The Bleeding of America,* 74.

27. Deleuze and Guattari, *A Thousand Plateaus,* 277, 249.

28. Antonio Benítez-Rojo, *The Repeating Island,* 27.

29. The HBO vampire series *Trueblood* is set in Louisiana and markets racialized and eroticized Gulf-becomings familiar to readers of Faulkner, Howe, and Afrocreole folk narrative.

30. Medoro, *The Bleeding of America,* 7, 4.

31. Glissant, *Faulkner, Mississippi,* 30.

32. Medoro, *The Bleeding of America,* 79.

33. Gwynn and Blotner, eds., *Faulkner in the University,* 39. For a fuller treatment of "Red Leaves" and Wole Soyinka's *Death and the King's Horseman,* see my "Blood on the Leaves, Blood at the Root: Ritual Carriers and Sacrificial Crises of Transition in

Yoknapatawpha and Oyo," in *Global Faulkner*, edited by Annette Trefzer and Ann J. Abadie, 78–98 (Jackson: University Press of Mississippi, 2009).

34. Girard, *Violence and the Sacred*, 34.

35. Girard, *Violence and the Sacred*, 36

36. Glissant, *Faulkner, Mississippi*, 195, 218, 137, 176.

37. Monénembo, "Faulkner and Me," 177.

38. Harris, *The Womb of Space*, 5.

39. Gwin, *The Feminine and Faulkner*, 35.

40. Trouard, "Landing in Akron," ix.

41. Quoted in Ladd, " 'Writing against Death,' " 167.

42. Alfred Appel, quoted in enotes.com, www.enotes.com/worn-path-criticism /worn-path-eudora-welty/introduction, accessed Aug. 20, 2012.

43. Ladd, " 'Writing against Death,' " 162.

44. L. Turner, *Africanisms in the Gullah Dialect*, 275.

45. Keeney, *Shakers of St. Vincent*, 164, 151, 163.

46. Caroline Barr appears to have been a Gullah speaker from the South Carolina coast. See Judith Sensibar, *Faulkner and Love*, 34–43.

47. Welty, "A Worn Path," 142.

48. Jameson, *The Political Unconscious*, 144.

49. S. Diouf, "African Muslims in Bondage," 78–79.

50. Welty does not come out and say this, but she seemed exasperated with certain kinds of realist plot speculations concerning the grandson. In *The Eye of the Story*, Welty insisted "it is the journey, the going of the errand, that is the story, and the question is not whether the grandchild is in reality alive or dead" (160). And in reply to that most commonplace of questions, "Is the grandson really dead?" Welty offers her emphatic "best answer": "*Phoenix* is alive" (160). The lasting travel is alive, and so is its initiating authority, too old at the Surrender to fully surrender to subalternizing codes.

Bibliography

Achebe, Chinua. *Things Fall Apart*. 1959. New York: Random House, 1994.

Agamben, Giorgio. *The Sacrament of Language: An Archaeology of the Oath*. Translated by Adam Kotsko. Stanford: Stanford University Press, 2010.

Alabama Creek Nation Court Cases, www.afrigeneas.com/forum-states, September 16, 2009.

Alao, Folashadé. "Islands of Memory: The Sea Islands, Black Women Artists, and the Promise of Home." PhD diss., Emory University, 2009.

Allewaert, M. "Swamp Sublime: Ecologies of Resistance in the American Plantation Zone." *PMLA* 123, no. 2 (2008): 340–57.

Alleyne, Warren, and Henry Fraser. *The Barbados–Carolina Connection*. London: Macmillan, 1988.

Appel, Alfred, Jr. *A Season of Dreams: The Fiction of Eudora Welty*. Baton Rouge: Louisiana State University Press, 1965.

Armbrister, Cindy Cartwright. *Runnin' Sheep: A Collection of Stories from Long Island, Bahamas*. Nassau: Guanima Press, 1995.

Armstrong, Louis. *Swing That Music*. 1936. New York: Da Capo Press, 1993.

Arrighi, Giovanni. *The Long Twentieth Century: Money, Power, and the Origins of Our Times*. London: Verso, 1994.

Asbury, Herbert. *The French Quarter: An Informal History of the New Orleans Underworld*. New York: Knopf, 1936.

Augustin, Marie. *La Macandal: Episode de l'insurrection des noirs à St. Domingue*. New Orleans: Imprimerie Geo. Muller, 50 rue Bienville, 1892.

Austin, Allan. *African Muslims in Antebellum America: A Sourcebook*. New York: Garland, 1984.

Bailey, Cornelia, with Christena Bledsoe. *God, Dr. Buzzard, and the Bolito Man: A Saltwater Geechee Talks About Life on Sapelo Island*. New York: Doubleday, 2000.

Bakhtin, Mikhail M. *The Dialogic Imagination*. Translated by Caryl Emerson and Michael Holquist. Austin: University of Texas Press, 1981.

Bambara, Toni Cade. *The Salt Eaters*. New York: Random House, 1980.

Barnes, Sandra T. "Introduction: The Many Faces of Ogun." In *Africa's Ogun: Old World and New*, edited by Sandra T. Barnes, 1–26. Bloomington: Indiana University Press, 1989.

Barthes, Roland. *Image–Music–Text*. Translated by Stephen Heath. New York: Hill & Wang, 1978.

———. "La mort de l'auteur." In *Œuvres complètes*. Paris: Éditions du Seuil, 1993.

Bartram, William. *Travels through North and South Carolina, Georgia, and East and West Florida*. 1791. New York: Library of America, 1996.

Bascom, William. *African Folktales in the New World*. Bloomington: Indiana University Press, 1992.

———. *Ifa Divination: Communication between Gods and Men in West Africa*. Bloomington: Indiana University Press, 1991.

Bateman, Rebecca. "Naming Patterns in Black Seminole Ethnogenesis." *Ethnohistory* 49, no. 2 (2002): 227–57.

Bauman, Margaret. *Ajapa the Tortoise: A Book of Nigerian Folk Tales*. Mineola, N.Y.: Dover, 2002.

Bechet, Sidney. *Treat It Gentle*. New York: Hill & Wang, 1960.

Belcher, Wendy Laura. "Consuming Subjects: Theorizing New Models of Agency for Literary Criticism in African Studies." *Comparative Literature Studies* 46.2 (2009): 213–32.

Bell, Caryn Cossé. *Revolution, Romanticism, and the Afro-Creole Protest Tradition in Louisiana, 1718–1868*. Baton Rouge: Louisiana State University Press, 1997.

Bell, Malcolm, Jr. *Major Butler's Legacy: Five Generations of a Slaveholding Family*. Athens: University of Georgia Press, 1987.

Bellegarde-Smith, Patrick, and Claudine Michel, eds. *Haitian Vodou: Spirit, Myth, and Reality*. Bloomington: Indiana University Press, 2006.

Benítez-Rojo, Antonio. *The Repeating Island: The Caribbean and the Postmodern Perspective*. 1989. Translated by James E. Maraniss. Durham: Duke University Press, 1996.

Benjamin, Shanna Greene. "Weaving the Web of Reintegration: Locating Aunt Nancy in *Praisesong for the Widow*." *MELUS* 30, no. 1 (2005): 49–68.

Berlin, Ira. *Generations of Captivity: A History of African-American Slaves*. Cambridge: Harvard University Press, 2003.

Bernabé, Jean, Patrick Chamoiseau, and Raphaël Confiant. *Éloge de la Créolité / In Praise of Creoleness*. Paris: Gallimard, 1993.

Berry, Jason, Jonathan Foose, and Tad Jones. *Up from the Cradle of Jazz: New Orleans Music Since World War II*. New York: Da Capo, 1992.

Bethel, E. Clement. *Junkanoo: Festival of the Bahamas*. Edited and expanded by Nicolette Bethel, with paintings by Brent Malone. London: Macmillan, 1991.

———. "Music in the Bahamas: Its Roots, Development, and Personality." MA thesis, University of California at Los Angeles, 1978.

Bethel, Marion, *Guanahani, Mi Amor y otros Poemas*. Havana: Casa de las Américas, 1993.

Bhabha, Homi K. *The Location of Culture*. London: Routledge, 1994.

Bone, Martyn. "The (Extended) South of Black Folk: Intraregional and Transnational Migrant Labor in *Jonah's Gourd Vine* and *Their Eyes Were Watching God*." *American Literature* 79, no. 4 (2007): 753–79.

Boyd, Valerie. *Wrapped in Rainbows: The Life of Zora Neale Hurston*. New York: Scribner, 2003.

Brathwaite, Edward. *The Development of Creole Society in Jamaica*. Oxford: Oxford University Press, 1971.

Brathwaite, Kamau. *Ancestors*. New York: New Directions, 2001.

Breunlin, Rachel, ed. *The House of Dance and Feathers: A Museum by Ronald W. Lewis*. New Orleans: University of New Orleans Press, 2009.

Brodber, Erna. *Myal*. London: Beacon Books, 1998.

Brondum, Lene. "'The Persistence of Tradition': The Retelling of Sea Islands Culture in Works by Julie Dash, Gloria Naylor, and Paule Marshall." In *Black Imagination and Middle Passage*, edited by Maria Diedrich and Henry Louis Gates, 153–63. New York: Oxford University Press, 1999.

Brooks, David. *New York Times*, Jan. 15, 2010.

Brown, David. *Santería Enthroned: Art, Ritual, and Innovation in an Afro-Cuban Religion*. Chicago: University of Chicago Press, 2003.

Brown, Karen McCarthy. "Afro-Caribbean Spirituality: A Haitian Case Study." In *Vodou in Haitian Life and Culture: Invisible Powers*, edited by Claudine Michel and Patrick Bellegarde-Smith, 1–26. New York: Palgrave, 2006.

———. *Mama Lola: A Vodou Priestess in Brooklyn*. Berkeley: University of California Press, 2001.

———. "Serving the Spirits: The Ritual Economy of Haitian Vodou." In *Sacred Arts of Haitian Vodou*, edited by Donald Cosentino, 205–23. Los Angeles: UCLA Fowler Museum of Cultural History, 1995.

———. "Systematic Remembering, Systematic Forgetting: Ogou in Haiti." In *Africa's Ogun: Old World and New*, edited by Sandra Barnes, 65–89. Bloomington: Indiana University Press, 1989.

Bruce, Dickson D., Jr. *Black American Writing from the Nadir: The Evolution of a Literary Tradition, 1877–1915*. Baton Rouge: Louisiana State University Press, 1992.

Buck-Morss, Susan. "Hegel and Haiti." *Critical Inquiry* 26, no. 4 (2000): 821–65.

Budick, Sanford. *The Western Theory of Tradition: Terms and Paradigms of the Cultural Sublime*. New Haven: Yale University Press, 2000.

Cable, George W. *The Creoles of Louisiana*. New York: Scribner's, 1884.

———. *The Grandissimes*. 1880. New York: Hill & Wang, 1968.

Cabrera, Lydia. *Afro-Cuban Tales*. Translated by Alberto Hernandez-Chiroldes and Lauren Yoder. Lincoln: University of Nebraska Press, 2004.

———. *Ayapá: Cuentos de Jicotea*. 1971. Miami: Ediciones Universal, 2006.

———. *Cuentos para adultos niños y retrasados mentales*. Miami: Colección del Chicherekú en el exilio, 1983.

———. *El Monte: Igbo-finda, ewe orisha-vititi nfinda*. 1954. Miami: Colección Chicherekú, 1983.

Carby, Hazel. "The Politics of Fiction, Anthropology, and the Folk: Zora Neale Hurston." In *Their Eyes Were Watching God: A Casebook*, edited by Cheryl A. Wall, 117–36. New York: Oxford University Press, 2000.

Carpentier, Alejo. "On the Marvelous Real in America." In *Magical Realism: Theory, History, Community*, edited by Lois Parkinson Zamora and Wendy Faris, 76–88. Durham: Duke University Press, 1995.

Carretta, Vincent, ed. *Unchained Voices: An Anthology of Black Authors in the English-Speaking World of the Eighteenth Century*. Lexington: University Press of Kentucky.

Cartwright, Jerome. "Everything Babylon." In *From the Shallow Seas: Bahamian Creative Writing Today*, edited by Ileana Sanz Cabrera, 39. Havana: Casa de las Américas, 1993.

Cartwright, Keith. "Loyalists, Geechees, and Africans: North American Roots of Afro-Bahamian Culture." *Yinna: The Journal of the Bahamas Association for Cultural Studies* 1 (2000): 49–61.

———. *Reading Africa into American Literature*. Lexington: University Press of Kentucky, 2002.

Castellanos, Isabel. "Introduction to the English Edition." *Afro-Cuban Tales*, by Lydia Cabrera. Lincoln: University of Nebraska Press, 2004.

Castro, Adrian. *Cantos to Blood and Honey*. Minneapolis: Coffee House Press, 1997.

Césaire, Aimé. *The Collected Poetry*. Translated by Clayton Eshleman and Annette Smith. Berkeley: University of California Press, 1983.

Chambers, Ian. "Citizenship, Language, and Modernity." *PMLA* 117, no. 1 (2002): 24–31.

Chamoiseau, Patrick. *Texaco*. Translated by Rose Myriam Rejouis and Val Vinokurov. New York: Vintage, 1997.

———. *Texaco*. Paris: Gallimard, 1992.

Chancy, Myriam J. A. *Framing Silence: Revolutionary Novels by Haitian Women*. New Brunswick, N.J.: Rutgers University Press, 1997.

Chapman, Peter. *Bananas: How the United Fruit Company Shaped the World*. New York: Canongate, 2007.

Chase, Leah. *The Dooky Chase Cookbook*. Gretna, La.: Pelican, 2004.

Chernoff, John Miller. *African Rhythm and African Sensibility: Aesthetics and Social Action in African Musical Idioms*. Chicago: University of Chicago Press, 1979.

Christian, Barbara. "Ritualistic Process and the Structure of Paule Marshall's *Praisesong for the Widow*." *Callaloo* 6, no. 2 (1983): 74–84.

Christophe, Marc A. "Rainbow over Water: Haitian Art, Vodou Aestheticism, and Philosophy." In *Haitian Vodou: Spirit, Myth, Reality*, edited by Patrick Bellegarde-Smith and Claudine Michel, 85–102. Bloomington: Indiana University Press, 2006.

Clarke, Erskine. *Wrestlin' Jacob: A Portrait of Religion in Antebellum Georgia and the Carolina Low Country*. 1979. Tuscaloosa: University of Alabama Press, 2000.

Codrescu, Andrei. "Love Note to New Orleans." *Callaloo* 29, no. 4 (2006): 1112–13.

Coleridge, Samuel Taylor. "Kubla Khan; or, a Vision in a Dream" In *English Romantic Writers*, edited by David Perkins, 430–31. New York: Harcourt Brace Jovanovich, 1967.

Collins, Merle. "Emancipation." *Big Drum Nation*. www.bigdrumnation.org/notes /emancipation.htm, last modified Sept. 16, 2009.

Cosentino, Donald J. "Envoi: The Gedes and Bawon Samdi." In *Sacred Arts of Haitian Vodou*, edited by Donald Cosentino, 399–414.

———. "Imagine Heaven." In *Sacred Arts of Haitian Vodou*, edited by Donald Cosentino, 25–55.

———. "It's All for You, Sen Jak!" In *Sacred Arts of Haitian Vodou*, edited by Donald Cosentino, 242–63.

———, ed. *Sacred Arts of Haitian Vodou*. Los Angeles: UCLA Fowler Museum of Cultural History, 1995.

Craton, Michael, and Gail Saunders. *From Aboriginal Times to Slavery*. Vol. 1 of *Islanders in the Stream: A History of the Bahamian People*. Athens: University of Georgia Press, 1992.

Creel, Margaret Washington. "Gullah Attitudes toward Life and Death." In *Africanisms in American Culture*, edited by Joseph Holloway, 69–97. Bloomington: Indiana University Press, 1990.

———. *"A Peculiar People": Slave Religion and Community-Culture among the Gullahs*. New York: New York University Press, 1988.

Crook, Ray, and Cornelia Bailey, Norma Harris, and Karen Smith. *Sapelo Voices: Historical Anthropology and the Oral Traditions of Gullah-Geechee Communities on Sapelo Island, Georgia*. Carrolton, Georgia: State University of West Georgia, 2003.

Crowther, Samuel. *The Romance and Rise of the American Tropics*. Garden City, N.Y.: Doubleday, 1929.

Curtin, Philip D. *Africa Remembered: Narratives by West Africans from the Era of the Slave Trade*. Madison: University of Wisconsin Press, 1967.

Curtius, Anny Dominique. *Symbioses d'une mémoire: Manifestations religieuses et littératures de la Caraïbe*. Paris: L'Harmattan, 2006.

Daniel, Yvonne. *Dancing Wisdom: Embodied Knowledge in Haitian Vodou, Cuban Yoruba, and Bahian Candomblé*. Urbana: University of Illinois Press, 2005.

Daniels, Lorna. "Memory Spirituals of the Ex-Slave American Soldiers in Trinidad's 'Company Villages.'" *Black Music Research Journal* 14, no. 2 (1994): 119–43.

Danticat, Edwidge. *Brother, I'm Dying*. New York: Vintage, 2007.

Dash, J. Michael. "Haïti Chimère: Revolutionary Universalism and Its Caribbean Context." In *Reinterpreting the Haitian Revolution and its Cultural Aftershocks*, edited by Martin Munro and Elizabeth Walcott-Hackshaw, 9–19. Kingston: University of the West Indies Press, 2006.

Dash, Julie. *Daughters of the Dust: The Making of an African American Woman's Film*. New York: New Press, 1992.

Davis, Thadious M. *Southscapes: Geographies of Race, Region, and Literature*. Chapel Hill: University of North Carolina Press, 2011.

Dayan, Joan. *Haiti, History and the Gods*. Berkeley: University of California Press, 1995.

Deagan, Kathleen, and Darcie MacMahon. *Fort Mose: Colonial America's Black Fortress of Freedom*. Gainesville: University Press of Florida, 1995.

Degiglio-Bellemare, Mario. "Vodou Hybridity and 'Voodoo Economics': Crossroads Theology at the Intersection of the Local and the Global." In *Talitha Cum: The Grace of Solidarity in a Globalized World*, edited by Gabriela Miranda Garcia and Mario Degiglio-Bellemare, 190–222. Geneva: WSCF Publications, 2004.

Deleuze, Gilles, and Felix Guattari. *A Thousand Plateaus: Capitalism and Schizophrenia*. 1980. Translated by Brian Massumi. Minneapolis: University of Minnesota Press, 1987.

Delgado, Hector. "From the Sacred Wild to the City: Santería in Cuba Today." In *Sacred Possessions: Vodou, Santería, Obeah, and the Caribbean*, edited by Margarite Fernandez Olmos and Lizabeth Paravisini-Gebert, 101–21. New Brunswick, N.J.: Rutgers University Press, 1997.

Depestre, René. *A Rainbow for the Christian West*. Translated by Joan Dayan. Amherst, Mass.: University of Massachusetts Press, 1977.

Deren, Maya. *Divine Horsemen: The Living Gods of Haiti*. New York: McPherson, 1970.

Derrida, Jacques. *Acts of Religion*. Edited and translated by Gil Anidjar. New York: Routledge, 2002.

———. *Dissemination*. Translated by Barbara Johnson. Chicago: University of Chicago Press, 1983.

———. *The Gift of Death*. Translated by David Willis. Chicago: University of Chicago Press, 1995.

———. *Of Hospitality (Cultural Memory in the Present)*. Translated by Rachel Bowlby. Stanford: Stanford University Press, 2000.

———. *Specters of Marx: The State of the Debt, the Work of Mourning, and the New International*. Translated by Peggy Kamuf. New York: Routledge, 1994.

Desdunes, Rodolphe Lucien. *Nos Hommes et Notre Histoire*. Montreal: Arbour & Dupont, 1911.

Dessens, Nathalie. *From Saint-Domingue to New Orleans: Migration and Influence*. Gainesville: University Press of Florida, 2007.

Dimock, Wai Chee. *Through Other Continents: American Literature Across Deep Time*. Princeton: Princeton University Press, 2006.

Diouf, Mamadou. "The French Colonial Policy of Assimilation and the Civility of the Originaires of the Four Communes (Senegal): A Nineteenth Century Globalization Project." *Development and Change* 29, no. 4 (1998): 671–96.

Diouf, Sylviane. "African Muslims in Bondage: Realities, Memories, Legacies." In *Monuments of the Black Atlantic: Slavery and Memory*, edited by Joanne M. Braxton and Maria I. Diedrich, 77–90. Piscataway, N.J.: Transaction Publishers, 2004.

DJ Drama and Lil Wayne. *Dedication 2, Gangsta Grillz*. 2006 mixtape.

D'Ogum, Guilherme. *Iansa do Balé: Senhora dos Eguns (Oya Igbale)*. Rio de Janeiro: Pallas, 2002.

Donaldson, Susan V. "Visibility, Haitian Hauntings, and Southern Borders." *American Literature* 78, no. 4 (2007): 714–16.

Drewal, John Henry, and Margaret Thompson Drewal. *Gelede: Art and Female Power among the Yoruba*. Bloomington: Indiana University Press, 1990.

Drewal, Margaret Thompson. *Yoruba Ritual: Performers, Play, Agency*. Bloomington: Indiana University Press, 1992.

Dubey, Madhu. *Signs and Cities: Black Literary Postmodernism*. Chicago: University of Chicago Press, 2003.

Du Bois, W. E. B. *The Souls of Black Folk*. 1903. New York: Bantam, 1989.

Duck, Leigh Anne. *The Nation's Region: Southern Modernism, Segregation, and U.S. Nationalism*. Athens: University of Georgia Press, 2006.

———. "'Rebirth of a Nation': Hurston in Haiti." *Journal of American Folklore* 117, no. 464 (2004): 127–46.

Duiker, William J. *Ho Chi Minh.* New York: Hyperion, 2002.

Dyson, Michael Eric. *Come Hell or High Water: Hurricane Katrina and the Color of Disaster.* New York: Civitas, 2006.

Edwards, Brent Hayes. *The Practice of Diaspora: Literature, Translation, and the Rise of Black Internationalism.* Cambridge: Harvard University Press, 2003.

———. "The Seemingly Eclipsed Window of Form: James Weldon Johnson's Prefaces." In *The Jazz Cadence of American Culture,* edited by Robert O'Meally, 580–601. New York: Columbia University Press, 1998.

Egerton, Douglass R. *Gabriel's Rebellion: The Virginia Slave Conspiracies of 1800 and 1802.* Chapel Hill: University of North Carolina Press, 1993.

Egerton, John. *Speak Now Against the Day: The Generation before the Civil Rights Movement in the South.* Chapel Hill: University of North Carolina Press, 1995.

Éliade, Mircea. *The Myth of the Eternal Return: Or, Cosmos and History.* Translated by Willard Trask. New York: Bollingen, 1971.

Ellis, Joseph J. *American Sphynx: The Character of Thomas Jefferson.* New York: Vintage, 1998.

Ellison, Ralph. *Invisible Man.* 1952. New York: Vintage, 1972.

———. *Shadow and Act.* New York: Signet, 1966.

Emerson, Ralph Waldo. "From *Journals* (1827–28)." In *The Florida Reader,* edited by Maurice O'Sullivan and Jack C. Lane, 61–63. Sarasota: Pineapple Press, 1991.

———. "An Unfinished Poem on St. Augustine." In *The Florida Reader,* edited by Maurice O'Sullivan and Jack C. Lane, 63. Sarasota: Pineapple Press, 1991.

Eneas, Cleveland. *Bain Town.* Nassau: Timpaul, 1976.

Enloe, Cynthia H. *Maneuvers: The International Politics of Militarizing Women's Lives.* Berkeley: University of California Press, 2000.

Epstein, Dena J. *Sinful Tunes and Spirituals: Black Folk Music to the Civil War.* Urbana: University of Illinois Press, 1977.

Equilbecq, François-Victor. *Contes populaires d'Afrique Occidentale.* Paris: Editions G. P. Maisonneuve et Larose, 1972.

Erskine, Noel Lee. *From Garvey to Marley: Rastafarian Theology.* Gainesville: University Press of Florida, 2005.

Escobedo, Alonso Gregorio de. "From *La Florida.*" In *Florida in Poetry,* edited by Jane Anderson Jones and Maurice O'Sullivan, 20. Sarasota: Pineapple Press, 1995.

———. *Pirates, Indians, and Spaniards (Father Escobedo's "La Florida").* Translated by A. F. Falcones and edited by James W. Covington. St. Petersburg: Great Outdoors, 1963.

Estabrook, Barry. *Tomatoland: How Modern Industrial Agriculture Destroyed Our Most Alluring Fruit.* Kansas City: Andrews McMeel, 2011.

Estévez, Bishop Felipe de Jesús. Quoted in "Our Lady of Charity," by María Ruiz Scaperlanda, September 1, 2007. www.kofc.org/un/en/columbia/detail/458998 .html, September 8, 2009.

Faristzaddi, Millard. *Itations of Jamaica and I Rastafari.* Miami: Judah Anbesa Ihntahnahshinahl, 1987.

Faulkner, Anne Shaw. "Does Jazz Put the Sin in Syncopation?" 1921. In *Riffs and Choruses: A New Jazz Anthology*, edited by Andrew Clark, 38–40. London: Continuum, 2001.

Faulkner, William. *Absalom, Absalom!* 1936. New York: Vintage, 1990.

———. *As I Lay Dying*. 1930. New York: Vintage, 1990.

———. *Collected Stories*. New York: Random House, 1950.

———. "An Introduction to *The Sound and the Fury*." 1933. In *The Sound and the Fury*. New York: Norton, 1994. 228–32.

———. *The Sound and the Fury*. 1929. New York: Norton, 1994.

Fernandez, Raul A. *From Afro-Cuban Rhythms to Latin Jazz*. Berkeley: University of California Press, 2006.

Fischer, Sibylle. *Modernity Disavowed: Haiti and the Cultures of Slavery in the Age of Revolution*. Durham: Duke University Press, 2004.

Florida Times Union. "Song of Sierra Leone Calls Georgia Woman," Monday, February 24, 1997, sec. A.

Fontenot, Wonda L. *Secret Doctors: Ethnomedicine of African Americans*. Westport, Conn.: Bergin and Garvey, 1994.

Fortier, Alcée. *Louisiana Folk-Tales in French Dialect and English Translation*. New York: American Folklore Society, 1895.

Fossett, Judith Jackson. "Sold Down River." *PMLA* 122, no. 1 (2007): 325–30.

Frazier, E. Franklin. *The Negro Church in America*. 1964. New York: Schocken Books, 1971.

Frey, Sylvia R., and Betty Wood. *Come Shouting to Zion: African American Protestantism in the American South and British Caribbean to 1830*. Chapel Hill: University of North Carolina Press, 1998.

Gannon, Michael, ed. *The New History of Florida*. Gainesville: University Press of Florida, 1996.

Gara, Larry. *The Baby Dodds Story: As Told to Larry Gara*. 1959. Baton Rouge: Louisiana University Press, 1992.

Garbarino, Merwyn S. *The Seminole*. New York: Chelsea House, 1989.

Geertz, Clifford. *The Interpretation of Cultures*. New York: Perseus, 1973.

Georgia Writers' Project. *Drums and Shadows: Survival Stories among the Georgia Coastal Negroes*. 1940. Athens: University of Georgia Press, 1986.

Gibbs, Nancy. "An American Tragedy." *Time*, September 12, 2005, 46.

Gilroy, Paul. *The Black Atlantic: Modernity and Double Consciousness*. Cambridge, Mass.: Harvard University Press, 1993.

Gioia, Ted. *The History of Jazz*. New York: Oxford University Press, 1997.

Girard, René. *Violence and the Sacred*. 1972. Translated by Patrick Gregory. Baltimore: Johns Hopkins University Press, 1977.

Glazier, Stephen. *Marchin' the Pilgrims Home: Leadership and Decision-Making in an Afro-Caribbean Faith*. Westport, Conn.: Greenwood, 1983.

Gleason, Judith. *Oya: In Praise of an African Goddess*. San Francisco: HarperCollins, 1992.

Glinton, Patricia. *An Evening in Guanima: A Treasury of Folktales from the Bahamas*. Nassau: Guanima Press, 1994.

Glinton-Meicholas, Patricia. *More Talkin' Bahamian*. Nassau: Guanima Press, 1995.

Glissant, Édouard. *Caribbean Discourse*. Translated by J. Michael Dash. Charlottesville: University of Virginia Press, 1996.

———. *Faulkner, Mississippi*. Translated by Barbara Lewis and Thomas C. Spear. New York: Farrar, Straus and Giroux, 1999.

———. *The Poetics of Relation*. Translated by Betsy Wing. Ann Arbor: University of Michigan Press, 1997.

———. *Poétique de la relation*. Paris: Gallimard, 1990.

Gomez, Michael. *Exchanging Our Country Marks: The Transformation of African Identity in the Colonial and Antebellum South*. Chapel Hill: University of North Carolina Press, 1998.

Goodwine, Marquetta L., and the Clarity Press Gullah Project, eds. *The Legacy of Ibo Landing: Gullah Roots of African American Culture*. Atlanta: Clarity Press, 1998.

Gouge, Earnest. *Totkv Mocvse / New Fire: Creek Folktales by Earnest Gouge*. Edited and translated by Jack B. Martin, Margaret McKane Mauldin, and Juanita McGirt. Norman: University of Oklahoma Press, 2004.

Griaule, Marcel, and Germaine Dieterlen. *The Pale Fox*. 1965. Translated by Stephen C. Infantino. Baltimore: Afrikan World Books, 1986.

Grosvenor, Vertamae. *Vertamae Cooks in the Americas' Family Kitchen*. San Francisco: KQED Books, 1996.

Grovner, Yvonne J., Cornelia Walker Bailey, and Doc Bill (William Thomas). *The Foods of Georgia's Barrier Islands*. Gainesville, Ga.: Baris Savas, 2004.

Gunn, Giles. "Introduction: Globalizing Literary Studies." *PMLA* 116, no. 1 (2001): 16–31.

Gussow, Adam. *Seems Like Murder Here: Southern Violence and the Blues Tradition*. Chicago: University of Chicago Press, 2002.

Gwin, Minrose C. *The Feminine and Faulkner: Reading (Beyond) Sexual Difference*. Knoxville: University of Tennessee Press, 1990.

Gwynn, Frederick L., and Joseph L. Blotner, ed. *Faulkner and the University*. Charlottesville: University Press of Virginia, 1995.

Hagedorn, Katherine J. *Divine Utterances: The Performance of Afro-Cuban Santeria*. Washington, D.C.: Smithsonian Institution, 2001.

Hall, Gwendolyn Midlo. *Africans in Colonial Louisiana: The Development of Afro-Creole Culture in the Eighteenth Century*. Baton Rouge: Louisiana University Press, 1992.

Handley, George. *Postslavery Literatures in the Americas: Family Portraits in Black and White*. Charlottesville: University of Virginia Press, 2000.

Hann, John H. "The Missions of Spanish Florida." In *New History of Florida*, edited by Michael Gannon, 78–99. Gainesville: University Press of Florida, 1996.

———. "Translation of Alonso de Leturiondo's Memorial to the King of Spain." *Florida Archaeology* 2 (1986): 165–225.

Hargrove, Melissa. "Mapping the 'Social Field of Whiteness': White Racism as Habitus in the City Where History Lives." *Transforming Anthropology* 17, no. 2 (2009): 93–104.

Harris, Joel Chandler. *Nights with Uncle Remus: Myths and Legends of the Old Plantation.* 1883. New York: Penguin, 2003.

Harris, Wilson. "The Complexity of Freedom." In *Perspectives on Wole Soyinka: Freedom and Complexity,* ed. Biodun Jeyifo. Jackson: University Press of Mississippi, 2001.

———. "History, Fable and Myth in the Caribbean and Guianas." In *Selected Essays of Wilson Harris: The Unfinished Genesis of the Imagination,* edited by Andrew Bundy, 152–66. New York: Routledge, 1999.

———. *Jonestown.* London: Faber & Faber, 1996.

———. *The Womb of Space: The Cross-Cultural Imagination.* Westport, Conn.: Greenwood Press, 1983.

Harvey, David. *The Condition of Postmodernity.* Cambridge, Mass.: Blackwell, 1989.

Hayden, Robert. "Runagate." In *Selected Poems of Robert Hayden,* 59–61. New York: Liveright, 1985.

Hearn, Lafcadio. "Gombo Zhèbes." In *Inventing New Orleans: Writing of Lafcadio Hearn,* edited by Frederick S. Starr, 199–224. Jackson: University Press of Mississippi, 2001.

———. "The Last of the Voodoos." In *Inventing New Orleans: Writing of Lafcadio Hearn,* edited by Frederick S. Starr, 77–82. Jackson: University Press of Mississippi, 2001.

Hemenway, Robert E. *Zora Neale Hurston: A Literary Biography.* Urbana: University of Illinois Press, 1977.

Henry, Frances. *Reclaiming African Religions in Trinidad: The Socio-Political Legitimation of the Orisha and Spiritual Baptist Faiths.* Kingston: University of West Indies Press, 2003.

Heyrman, Christine Leigh. *Southern Cross: The Beginnings of the Bible Belt.* New York: Knopf, 1997.

Histoire Naturelle des Indes: The Drake Manuscript in the Pierpont Morgan Library. Foreword by Patrick O'Brian. New York: Norton, 1996.

Hitt, Christopher. "Toward an Ecological Sublime." *New Literary History: Ecocriticism* 30, no. 3 (1999): 603–23.

Holloway, Karla. "On Morrison and Black Female Memory." In *New Dimensions of Spirituality: A Biracial and Bicultural Reading of the Novels of Toni Morrison,* edited by Karla Holloway and Stephanie Demetrakopoulos, 149–56. New York: Greenwood, 1987.

———. *Passed On: African American Mourning Stories.* Durham: Duke University Press, 2003.

Holm, John A. "On the Relationship of Gullah and Bahamian." *American Speech* 58, no. 4 (1983): 303–18.

Houk, James. *Spirits, Blood and Drums: The Orisha Religion in Trinidad.* Philadelphia: Temple University Press, 1995.

Howard, Rosalyn. *Black Seminoles in the Bahamas.* Gainesville: University Press of Florida, 2002.

Howe, LeAnne. *Shell Shaker.* San Francisco: Aunt Lute Books, 2001.

Hughes, Langston. "Jazzonia." In *The New Negro*, edited by Alain Locke, 226. New York: Atheneum, 1969.

Hunt, Alfred. *Haiti's Influence on Antebellum America: Slumbering Volcano in the Caribbean*. Baton Rouge: Louisiana University Press, 1988.

Hurbon, Laënnec. "American Fantasy and Haitian Vodou." In *Sacred Arts of Haitian Vodou*, edited by Donald Cosentino, 181–97.

Hurston, Zora Neale. "Communication." *Journal of Negro History* 12 (Oct. 1927): 664–67.

———. *Dust Tracks on a Road*. In *Folklore, Memoirs, and Other Writings*, 557–808. New York: Library of America, 1995.

———. *Every Tongue Got to Confess: Negro Folk-Tales from the Gulf States*. Edited by Carla Kaplan. New York: Harper Collins, 2001.

———. "Folklore and Music." In *Folklore, Memoirs, and Other Writings*, 875–94. New York: Library of America, 1995.

———. "Hoodoo in America." *Journal of American Folklore* 44 (Oct.–Dec. 1931): 317–418.

———. "How It Feels to Be Colored Me." In *Folklore, Memoirs, and Other Writings*, 826–29. New York: Library of America, 1995.

———. *Jonah's Gourd Vine*. In *Novels and Stories*, 1–171. New York: Library of America, 1995.

———. *Moses, Man of the Mountain*. In *Novels and Stories*, 335–595. New York: Library of America, 1995.

———. "Mother Catherine." In *Folklore, Memoirs, and Other Writings*, 854–60. New York: Library of America, 1995.

———. *Mules and Men*. In *Folklore, Memoirs, and Other Writings*, 1–267. New York: Library of America, 1995.

———. "The Sanctified Church." In *Folklore, Memoirs, and Other Writings*, 901–5. New York: Library of America, 1995.

———. *Seraph on the Suwanee*. In *Novels and Stories*, 597–920. New York: Library of America, 1995.

———. *Tell My Horse*. In *Folklore, Memoirs, and Other Writings*, 269–555. New York: Library of America, 1995.

———. *Their Eyes Were Watching God*. In *Novels and Stories*, 173–333. New York: Library of America, 1995.

———. *Zora Neale Hurston: A Life in Letters*. Edited by Carla Kaplan. New York: Doubleday, 2002.

Hyatt, Harry M. *Hoodoo–Conjuration–Witchcraft–Rootwork: Beliefs Accepted by Many Negroes and White Persons*. Hannibal, Mo.: Western, 1970.

Irving, Washington. "The Conspiracy of Neamathla: An Authentic Sketch." In *The Florida Reader: Visions of Paradise from 1530 to Present*, edited by Maurice O'Sullivan Jr. and Jack C. Lane, 98–102. Sarasota: Pineapple Press, 1991.

Itawamba Historical Society, Itawamba County, Mississippi History and Genealogy. www.itawambahistory.org/deed1.htm, September 16, 2009.

Jackson, Michael. *Allegories of the Wilderness: Ethics and Ambiguity in Kuranko Narratives*. Bloomington: Indiana University Press, 1982.

Jackson, Shona. "Love, Loss, and the 'Art' of Making Gumbo: An Interview with Eileen Julien." *Callaloo* 30, no. 1 (2007): 95–109.

Jacobs, Harriet. *Incidents in the Life of a Slave Girl*. 1861. In *The Classic Slave Narratives*, edited by Henry Louis Gates Jr., 333–515. New York: Mentor, 1987.

Jameson, Fredric. *The Political Unconscious*. Ithaca: Cornell University Press, 1981.

John, Marie-Elena. *Unburnable*. New York: Amistad, 2006.

Johnson, James Weldon. *Along This Way*. 1933. In *James Weldon Johnson: Writings*, 129–604. New York: Library of America, 2004.

———. *The Autobiography of an Ex-Colored Man*. 1912. In *James Weldon Johnson: Writings*, 1–127. New York: Library of America, 2004.

———. *Black Manhattan*. 1930. New York: Da Capo Press, 1991.

———. "The Dilemma of the Negro Author." 1928. In *James Weldon Johnson: Writings*, 744–52. New York: Library of America, 2004.

———. *God's Trombones: Seven Negro Sermons in Verse*. 1927. In *James Weldon Johnson: Writings*, 834–67. New York: Library of America, 2004.

———. "Lift Every Voice and Sing." In *James Weldon Johnson: Writings*, 874–75. New York: Library of America, 2004.

———. "O Black and Unknown Bards." In *James Weldon Johnson: Writings*, 817–18. New York: Library of America, 2004.

———. Preface to *The Book of American Negro Poetry*, edited by James Weldon Johnson. 1921. In *James Weldon Johnson: Writings*, 688–719. New York: Library of America, 2004.

———. Preface to *The Books of American Negro Spirituals*. Vol. 1, 1925; Vol. 2, 1926. Edited by James Weldon Johnson and J. Rosamund Johnson. New York: Da Capo, 1977.

———. "Self-Determining Haiti." 1920. In *James Weldon Johnson: Writings*, 660–87. New York: Library of America, 2004.

Johnson, Whitington B. *Black Savannah, 1788–1864*. Fayetteville: University of Arkansas Press, 1996.

Joyner, Charles. *Down by the Riverside: A South Carolina Slave Community*. Urbana: University of Illinois Press, 1984.

———. *Remember Me: Slave Life in Coastal Georgia*. Athens: University of Georgia Press, 2011.

Julien, Eileen. "Excerpts from a Journal." *Callaloo* 29, no. 4 (2006): 1400–1403.

———. *Travels with Mae: Scenes from a New Orleans Girlhood*. Bloomington: Indiana University Press, 2009.

Jumper, Betty Mae. *Legends of the Seminoles*. Sarasota: Pineapple Press, 1994.

Juvenile. *Reality Check*. March 7, 2006, Atlantic/Wea B00009FXIZK.

Kant, Immanuel. *The Critique of Judgement*. Translated by James Creed Meredith. Oxford: Clarendon, 1973.

Kaplan, Carla, ed. *Zora Neale Hurston: A Life in Letters*. New York: Doubleday, 2002.

Kaplan, Sara Clarke. "Souls at the Crossroads, Africans on the Water: The Politics of Diasporic Melancholia." *Callaloo* 30, no. 2 (2007): 511–26.

Keeney, Bradford, ed. *Shakers of St. Vincent*. Philadelphia: Ringing Rocks Press, 2002.

Kein, Sybil. *Gumbo People*. 1981. New Orleans: Margaret Media, 1999.

Kennedy, Al. *Big Chief Harrison and the Mardi Gras Indians*. Gretna, La.: Pelican, 2010.

Kernghan, Charles. "Mickey Mouse in Port-au-Prince" In *Libète: A Haiti Anthology*, edited by Charles Arthur and Michael Dash, 126–27. Princeton, N.J.: Markus Wiener, 1999.

Kesteloot, Lilyan, and Cherif Mbodj. *Contes et mythes Wolof*. Dakar: Les Nouvelles Éditions Africaines, 1983.

Kimball, A. Samuel. *The Infanticidal Logic of Evolution and Culture*. Newark: University of Delaware Press, 2007.

King, Martin Luther, Jr. "400 Years of Bigotry and Hate." *SCLC Newsletter Special St. Augustine Issue* 2, no. 7 (June 1964): 7.

Kingsley, Zephaniah. *Balancing Evils Judiciously: The Proslavery Writings of Zephaniah Kingsley*. Edited by Daniel W. Stowell. Gainesville: University Press of Florida, 2000.

Kodat, Catherine Gunther. "Conversing with Ourselves: Canon, Freedom, Jazz." *American Quarterly* 55, no. 1 (2003): 1–28.

Koger, Larry. *Black Slaveowners: Free Black Masters in South Carolina, 1790–1860*. Columbia: University of South Carolina Press, 1995.

Komunyakaa, Yusef. *Blue Notes: Essays, Interviews, and Commentaries*. Edited by Radiciani Clytus. Ann Arbor: University of Michigan Press, 2000.

———. *Pleasure Dome: New and Collected Poems*. Middletown, Conn.: Wesleyan University Press, 2001.

Koster, Rick. *Louisiana Music: A Journey from R&B to Zydeco, Jazz to Country, Blues to Gospel, Cajun Music to Swamp Pop to Carnival Music and Beyond*. Cambridge, Mass.: Da Capo Press, 2002.

Kristeva, Julia. *The Powers of Horror: An Essay on Abjection*. Translated by Leon S. Roudiez. New York: Columbia University Press, 1982.

Lachance, Paul F. "The Foreign French." In *Creole New Orleans: Race and Americanization*. Edited by Arnold R. Hirsch and Joseph Logsdon. Baton Rouge: Louisiana University Press, 1992.

———. "Were Saint-Domingue Refugees a Distinctive Cultural Group in Antebellum New Orleans? Evidence from Patterns and Strategies of Property Holding." *Revista/Review Interamericana* 29, no. 1–4 (1999): 171–92.

Ladd, Barbara. *Resisting History: Gender, Modernity, and Authority in William Faulkner, Zora Neale Hurston, and Eudora Welty*. Baton Rouge: Louisiana State University Press, 2007.

———. "Writing Against Death: Totalitarianism and the Nonfiction of Eudora Welty at Midcentury." In *Eudora Welty and Politics*, edited by Harriet Pollack and Suzanne Marrs, 155–77. Baton Rouge: Louisiana State University Press, 2001.

Lamothe, Daphne. "Vodou Imagery, African American Tradition, and Cultural Transformation in Zora Neale Hurston's *Their Eyes Were Watching God*." In *"Their Eyes Were Watching God": A Casebook*, edited by Cheryl A. Wall, 165–87. New York: Oxford University Press, 2000.

Landers, Jane. *Black Society in Spanish Florida*. Urbana: University of Illinois Press, 1999.

Laudonnière, René Goulaine de. "From *A Notable Historie Containing Foure Voyages Made by Certaine French Captaines unto Florida.*" Translated by Richard Hakluyt, 1587. In *The Heath Anthology of American Literature.* Vol. A, *Beginnings to 1800*, edited by Paul Lauter, 234–36. Boston: Wadsworth, 2009.

Levy, Eugene. *James Weldon Johnson: Black Leader, Black Voice.* Chicago: University of Chicago Press, 1973.

Lewis, Ronald W., Rachel Breunlin, and Helen Regis. *The House of Dance and Feathers: A Museum by Ronald W. Lewis.* New Orleans: University of New Orleans Press / Neighborhood Story Project, 2009.

Lindsay, Arturo, ed. *Santeria Aesthetics in Contemporary Latin American Art.* Washington, D.C.: Smithsonian Institution Press, 1996.

Lipsitz, George. *Dangerous Crossroads: Popular Music, Postmodernism, and the Poetics of Place.* New York: Verso, 1994.

Littlefield, Daniel. *Africans and Seminoles from Removal to Emancipation.* Westport, Conn.: Greenwood Press, 1977.

Loichot, Valérie. *Orphan Narratives: The Postplantation Literature of Faulkner, Glissant, Morrison, and Saint-John Perse.* Charlottesville: University Press of Virginia, 2007.

Lomax, Alan. *Caribbean Voyage: Saraca, Funerary Music of Carriacou.* 1962. Rounder B0012JJP18, Sept. 19, 2000.

———. *Mister Jelly Roll: The Fortunes of Jelly Roll Morton, New Orleans Creole and "Inventor of Jazz."* Berkeley: University of California Press, 1973.

Long, Carolyn Morrow. *A New Orleans Voudou Priestess: The Legend and Reality of Marie Laveau.* Gainesville: University Press of Florida, 2006.

Lorde, Audre. *Sister Outsider.* Trumansburg, N.Y.: Crossing Press, 1984.

———. "Winds of Orisha." In *The Norton Anthology of African American Literature*, edited by Henry Louis Gates and Nellie McKay, 2205–06. New York: Norton, 1997.

Louis, Lilliane Nérette. *When Night Falls, Kric! Krac! Haitian Folktales.* Edited by Fred J. Hay. Englewood, Colo.: Libraries Unlimited, 1999.

Lovelace, Earl. *The Wine of Astonishment.* New York: Aventura, 1984.

Lowe, John. "An Interview with Brenda Marie Osbey." In *The Future of Southern Letters*, edited by Jefferson Humphries and John Lowe, 93–118. New York: Oxford University Press, 1996.

———. "Seeing Beyond Seeing: Zora Neale Hurston's Religion(s)." *Southern Quarterly* 36, no. 3 (1998): 77–87.

Lowenthal, Ira P. "'Marriage Is 20, Children Are 1': The Cultural Construction of Conjugality and the Family in Rural Haiti." PhD diss., Johns Hopkins University, 1987.

Lugo, Julia Cristina Ortiz. *De Arañas, Conejos y Tortugas: Presencia de Africa en la Cuentística de Tradición Oral en Puerto Rico.* San Juan: Centro de Estudios Avanzados de Puerto Rico y el Caribe, 2004.

Lum, Kenneth Anthony. *Praising His Name in the Dance: Spirit Possession in the Spiritual Baptist Faith and Orisha Work in Trinidad, West Indies.* Melbourne: Harwood Academic Publishers, 2000.

Maal, Baaba. *Missing You (Mi Yeewnii).* PALMCD 2067-2.

Mackey, Nathaniel. "Sound and Sentiment, Sound and Symbol." In *The Jazz Cadence of American Culture*, edited by Robert O'Meally, 602–28. New York: Columbia University Press, 1998.

MacMillan, Douald. "John Kuners." *Journal of American Folklore*, Jan. 1926, 53–57.

Madrazo, Ilia Aixa, Migdalia Medina, and Mervyn Alleyne. "Semantic Diversity in the Caribbean: Interrogating the 'Creole' Concept." In *In a Sea of Heteroglossia: Pluri-Lingualism, Pluri-Culturalism, and Pluri-Identification in the Caribbean*, edited by Nicholas Faraclas et al., 13–35. Willemstad, Curaçao: Fundashon pa Planifikashon di Idioma and University of the Netherlands Antilles, 2010.

Magel, Emil. *Folktales from the Gambia: Wolof Fictional Narratives.* Pueblo, Colo.: Passeggiata Press, 1984.

Mahon, John K., and Brent R. Weisman. "Florida's Seminole and Miccosukee Peoples." In *The New History of Florida*, edited by Michael Gannon, 183–206. Gainesville: University Press of Florida, 1996.

Marshall, Paule. *Praisesong for the Widow.* New York: Dutton, 1983.

Mason, Michael Atwood. *Living Santería: Rituals and Experiences in an Afro-Cuban Religion.* Washington, D.C.: Smithsonian Institute, 2002.

Matory, J. Lorand. *Black Atlantic Religion: Tradition, Transnationalism, and Matriarchy in the Afro-Brazilian Candomblé.* Princeton: Princeton University Press, 2005.

McClure, John A. *Partial Faiths: Postsecular Fiction in the Age of Pynchon and Morrison.* Athens: University of Georgia Press, 2007.

McDaniel, Lorna. "Memory Spirituals of the Liberated American Soldiers in Trinidad's 'Company Villages.'" *Black Music Research Journal* 14, no. 2 (1994): 119–43.

McFeely, William S. *Sapelo's People.* New York: Norton, 1994.

McKinnen, Daniel. *Tour through the British West Indies in the Years 1802 and 1803, Giving a Particular Account of the Bahama Islands.* London, 1804.

McKoy, Sheila Smith. "The Limbo Contest: Diaspora Temporality and Its Reflection in *Praisesong for the Widow* and *Daughters of the Dust.*" *Callaloo* 22, no. 1 (1999): 208–22.

McNeil, Elizabeth. "The Gullah Seeker's Journey in Paule Marshall's *Praisesong for the Widow.*" *MELUS* 34, no. 1 (2009): 185–209.

McPherson, Tara. "No Natural Disaster: New Orleans, Katrina, and War." *PMLA* 122, no. 1 (2007): 331–35.

Medley, Keith Weldon. *We as Freemen: Plessy v. Ferguson.* Gretna, La.: Pelican, 2003.

Medoro, Dana. *The Bleeding of America: Menstruation as Symbolic Economy in Pynchon, Faulkner, and Morrison.* Santa Barbara, Calif.: Praeger, 2002.

Meicholas, Patricia Glinton. *More Talking Bahamian.* Nassau: Guanima Press, 1995.

Mercier, Alfred. *L'habitation Saint-Ybars ou maîtres et esclaves en Louisiane.* 1881. Montreal: Guérin littérature, 1989.

Métraux, Alfred. *Voodoo in Haiti.* 1959. Translated by Hugo Charteris. New York: Schocken, 1972.

Metting, Fred. "The Possibilities of Flight: The Celebration of Our Wings in *Song of Solomon, Praisesong for the Widow*, and *Mama Day.*" *Southern Folklore* 55, no. 2 (1998): 145–68.

Mignolo, Walter. *Local Histories / Global Designs: Coloniality, Subaltern Knowledges, and Border Thinking.* Princeton: Princeton University Press, 2000.

Milanich, Jerald T., and William C. Sturtevant. *Francisco Pareja's 1613 Confessionario: A Documentary Source for Timucuan Ethnography.* Translated by Emilio F. Moran. Tallahassee: Florida Division of Archives, History, and Records Management, 1972.

Miller, Gentian. "African Religious Survivals in Death Rituals." In *In a Sea of Heteroglossia: Pluri-Lingualism, Pluri-Culturalism, and Pluri-Identification in the Caribbean*, edited by Nicholas Faraclas et al., 201–8. Willemstad, Curaçao: Fundashon pa Planifikashon di Idioma and University of the Netherlands Antilles, 2010.

Minh-ha, Trinh T. *When the Moon Waxes Red: Representation, Gender and Cultural Politics.* New York: Routledge, 1991.

Mintz, Sidney, and Michel-Rolph Trouillot. "The Social History of Haitian Vodou." In *Sacred Arts of Haitian Vodou*, edited by Donald Cosentino, 123–47.

Monénembo, Tierno. "Faulkner and Me." In *Global Faulkner*, edited by Annette Trefzer and Ann J. Abadie, 174–84. Jackson: University Press of Mississippi, 2009.

Monroe, Mina. *Bayou Ballads: Twelve Folk-Songs from Louisiana.* New York: G. Schirmer, 1921.

Moreau de Saint-Méry, Médéric Louis Élie. "From *A Civilization That Perished: The Last Years of White Colonial Rule.*" In *Libète: A Haiti Anthology*, edited by Charles Arthur and Michael Dash, 34. Princeton: Markus Wiener, 1999.

Morgan, Philip D. *Slave Counterpoint: Black Culture in the Eighteenth-Century Chesapeake and Lowcountry.* Chapel Hill: University of North Carolina Press, 1998.

———, ed. *African American Life in the Georgia Lowcountry: The Atlantic World and the Gullah Geechee.* Athens: University of Georgia Press, 2010.

Morrison, Toni. *Song of Solomon.* New York: Signet, 1977.

Mosquero, Gerardo. "Eleggua at the (Post?)Modern Crossroads: The Presence of Africa in the Visual Art of Cuba." In *Santería Aesthetics in Contemporary Latin American Art*, edited by Arturo Lindsey, 225–58. Washington, D.C.: Smithsonian Institution Press, 1996.

Mulira, Jessie Gaston. "The Case of Voodoo in New Orleans." In *Africanisms in American Culture*, edited by Joseph Holloway, 34–68. Bloomington: Indiana University Press, 1990.

Murphy, Joseph M. *Santería: An African Religion in America.* Boston: Beacon, 1988.

———. *Working the Spirit: Ceremonies of the African Diaspora.* Boston: Beacon, 1994.

———. "Yeye Cachita: Ochun in a Cuban Mirror." In *Osun across the Waters: A Yoruba Goddess in Africa and the Americas*, edited by Joseph M. Murphy and Mei-Mei Sanford, 87–101. Bloomington: Indiana University Press, 2001.

National Geographic Society 2009 Fast Facts Book. Washington, D.C.: National Geographic Society, 2009.

National Park Service. *Low Country Gullah/Geechee Culture Special Resource Study and Final Environmental Impact Statement.* www.nps.gov/sero/planning/gg_srs/ggsrsindex.htm. 2006.

National Severe Storms Laboratory. "Questions and Answers about Lightning." www .nssl.noaa.gov/edu/ltg. 24 June 2006.

Naylor, Gloria. *Mama Day*. New York: Ticknor & Fields, 1988.

N'Dour, Youssou. *Rokku Mi Rokka (Give and Take)*. Nonesuch Records 266044-2, 2007.

Nixon, Angelique V. "'We Have Something to Teach the World': Erna Brodber's Blackspace, Building Community, and Educo-tourism." *MaComère: The Journal of the Association of Caribbean Women Writers and Scholars* 11 (2009): 61–79.

Nora, Pierre. "Between Memory and History: Les Lieux de Mémoire." *Representations* 26 (Spring 1989): 7–25.

Nwankwo, Ifeoma. *Black Cosmopolitanism: Racial Consciousness and Transnational Identity in the Nineteenth-Century Americas*. Philadelphia: University of Pennsylvania Press, 2005.

O'Driscoll, Patrick. "'The Looters, They're like Cockroaches.'" *USA Today*, September 2, 2005, 3A.

Ortiz, Fernando. *Cuban Counterpoint: Tobacco and Sugar*. Translated by Harriet de Onis. Durham: Duke University Press, 1995.

———. *Poesía y canto de los negros afrocubanos*. Habana: Colección Raices, 1994.

Osbey, Brenda Marie. *All Saints: New and Selected Poems*. Baton Rouge: Louisiana State University Press, 1997.

———. *In These Houses*. Middleton, Conn.: Wesleyan University Press, 1988.

O'Sullivan, Maurice, and Jack C. Lane, eds. *The Florida Reader: Visions of Paradise*. Sarasota: Pineapple Press, 1991.

Owomoyela, Oyekan. *Yoruba Trickster Tales*. Lincoln: University of Nebraska Press, 1997.

Owusu-Sarpong, Christiane. Foreword to "The Poor Orphan: a Folktale by Nana Yaa Tiakaa." In *Women Writing Africa*, edited by Esi Sutherland-Addy and Aminata Diaw, 347–48. New York: The Feminist Press, 2005.

Paravisini-Gebert, Lizabeth, and Margarite Fernández Olmos. *Sacred Possessions: Vodou, Santería, Obeah, and the Caribbean*. New Brunswick, N.J.: Rutgers University Press, 1997.

Parrish, Lydia. "Records of Some Southern Loyalists." Department of Archives, Nassau, Bahamas. n.d.

———. *Slave Songs of the Georgia Sea Islands*. 1942. Athens: University of Georgia Press, 1992.

Parsons, Elsie Clews. *Folk-Lore of the Antilles, French and English*, vol. 1. New York: American Folk-Lore Society, 1933.

———. *Folk-Lore of the Antilles, French and English*, vol. 2. New York: American Folklore Society, G. E. Stechert and Co., 1936.

———. *Folk-Lore of the Sea Islands, South Carolina*. New York: Memoirs of the American Folk-lore Society, vol. 16, 1923.

———. *Folk-Tales of Andros Island, Bahamas*. Memoirs of the American Folklore Society, vol. 13, 1918.

Pascoe, C. F. *Two Hundred Years of the S. P. G.: An Historical Account of the Society for the Propagation of the Gospel in Foreign Parts, 1701–1900*. London, 1901.

Pastras, Phil. *Dead Man Blues: Jelly Roll Morton Way Out West*. Berkeley: University of California Press, 2001.

Patterson, Orlando. *Slavery and Social Death: A Comparative Study*. Cambridge, Mass.: Harvard University Press, 1982.

Pavlić, Edward A. *Crossroads Modernism: Descent and Emergence in African American Literary Culture*. Minneapolis: University of Minnesota Press, 2002.

———. "Open the Unusual Door: Visions from the Dark Window in Yusef Komunyakaa's Early Poems." *Callaloo* 28, no. 3 (2005): 780–96.

Pease, Donald. "Author." In *Critical Terms for Literary Study*, edited by Frank Lentricchia and Thomas McLaughlin, 105–17. Chicago: University of Chicago Press, 1990.

Peck, Megan. "Strange Fruit: The Author of 'Tomatoland' Dishes the Dirt on Florida's Agricultural Aberration." *Folio Weekly*, August 16–22, 2011, 13–15.

Petersen, Kirsten Holst, and Anna Rutherford. "Fossil and Psyche." In *The Postcolonial Studies Reader*, edited by Bill Ashcroft, Gareth Griffiths, and Helen Tiffin, 185–89. New York: Routledge, 1995.

Poe, Edgar Allan. *The Complete Tales and Poems*. New York: Random House, 1965.

Poitier, Sidney. *This Life*. New York: Ballantine, 1981.

Pratt, Mary Louise. "Arts of the Contact Zone." In *Ways of Reading*, 4th ed., edited by David Bartholomae and Anthony Petrosky, 527–42. New York: Bedford Books, 1996.

———. *Imperial Eyes: Travel Writing and Transculturation*. London: Routledge, 1992.

Ramos, Miguel. "Willie" and "Afro-Cuban Orisha Worship." In *Santería Aesthetics in Contemporary Latin American Art*, edited by Arturo Lindsay, 51–76. Washington, D.C.: Smithsonian Institution, 1996.

Redmond, Eugene D. "A Harbor of Sense: An Interview with Joy Harjo." In *Crossing Waters, Crossing Worlds: The African Diaspora in Indian Country*, edited by Sharon P. Holland and Tiya Miles, 25–30. Durham: Duke University Press, 2006.

Reed, Ishmael. *Mumbo Jumbo*. 1972. New York: Atheneum, 1988.

Reich, Howard, and William Gaines. *Jelly's Blues: The Life, Music, and Redemption of Jelly Roll Morton*. Cambridge, Mass.: Da Capo Press, 2003.

Rhys, Jean. *Wide Sargasso Sea*. New York: Norton, 1999.

Richardson, Riché. *From Uncle Tom to Gangsta: Black Masculinity and the U.S. South*. Athens: University of Georgia Press, 2007.

Roach, Joseph. *Cities of the Dead: Circum-Atlantic Performance*. New York: Columbia University Press, 1996.

Robeson, Paul. *Paul Robeson Speaks*. Ed. Philip S. Foner. New York: Kensington Press Books, 2002.

Rodowick, D. N. "Mobile Citizens, Media States." *PMLA* 117, no. 1 (2002): 13–23.

Rodriguez-Mangual, Edna. *Lydia Cabrera and the Construction of an Afro-Cuban Cultural Identity*. Chapel Hill: University of North Carolina Press, 2004.

Rosenbaum, Art. Liner notes. *The McIntosh County Shouters*. 1984. The Smithsonian Institution Folkways Cassette Series 04344, 1993.

———. *Shout Because You're Free: The African American Ring Shout Tradition in Coastal Georgia*. Athens: University of Georgia Press, 1998.

Rothman, Adam. *Slave Country: American Expansion and the Origins of the Deep South*. Cambridge, Mass.: Harvard University Press, 2005.

Roulet, Laura. "Ana Mendieta: A Life in Context." In *Ana Mendieta: Earth Body, Sculpture and Performance, 1972–1985*, edited by Olga Viso, 224–39. Washington, D.C.: Hirshhorn Museum, 2004.

Rowell, Charles Henry. Carol Bebelle interview, *Callaloo* 29, no. 4 (2006): 1210–14.

———. Donald Harrison, Jr. interview, *Callaloo* 29, no. 4 (2006): 1295–1300.

———. Herreast Harrison interview, *Callaloo* 29, no. 4 (2006): 1233–37.

———. Jason Berry interview, *Callaloo* 29, no. 4 (2006): 1239–51.

———. Keith Weldon Medley interview, *Callaloo* 29, no. 4 (2006): 1038–48.

———. Kim Dung Nguyen interview, *Callaloo* 29, no. 4 (2006): 1083–87.

———. "My Byzantium: An Editor's Note." *Callaloo* 29, no. 4 (2006): 1028–31.

Russell, Heather. *Legba's Crossing: Narratology in the African Atlantic*. Athens: University of Georgia Press, 2009.

Rymer, Russ. *American Beach: A Saga of Race, Wealth, and Memory*. New York: HarperCollins, 1998.

Saloy, Mona Lisa. *Red Beans and Ricely Yours*. Kirksville, Mo.: Truman State University Press, 2005.

Salvaggio, Ruth. "Hearing Sappho in New Orleans." In *Louisiana Culture from the Colonial Era to Katrina*, edited by John Lowe, 294–310. Baton Rouge: Louisiana University Press, 2008.

———. *Hearing Sappho in New Orleans: The Call of Poetry from Congo Square to the Ninth Ward*. Baton Rouge: Louisiana State University Press, 2012.

Sansay, Leonora. *Secret History; or, The Horrors of St. Domingo and Laura*. Michael P. Drexler, ed. Peterborough, Ontario: Broadview Editions, 2007.

Saunders, Gail. "The Impact of Tourism on Bahamian Culture." *Yinna* 1 (2000): 72–87.

Schafer, Daniel L. *Anna Madgigine Jai Kingsley: African Princess, Florida Slave, Plantation Slaveowner*. Gainesville: University Press of Florida, 2003.

Séjour, Victor. "The Mulatto." In *The Norton Anthology of African American Literature*, edited by Henry Louis Gates and Nellie McKay, 286–99. New York: Norton, 1997.

Sensibar, Judith. *Faulkner and Love: The Women Who Shaped His Art*. New Haven: Yale University Press, 2009.

Slave Registries of Former British Colonial Dependencies. Ancestry.co.uk, Sept. 17, 2009.

Smith, Funny Papa. *The Original Howling Wolf, 1930–1931*. Shanachie, 2005.

Smith, Jon. "Postcolonial, Black, and Nobody's Margin: The U.S. South and New World Studies." *American Literary History* 16, no. 1 (2004): 144–61.

Smith, Julia Floyd. *Slavery and Rice Culture in Low Country Georgia, 1750–1860*. Knoxville: University of Tennessee Press, 1985.

Smith, Michael Garfield. *Dark Puritan*. Kingston: Department of Extra-Mural Studies, University of the West Indies, 1963.

Smith, Michael P. *Mardi Gras Indians*. Gretna, La.: Pelican, 1994.

Sobel, Mechal. *Trabelin' On: The Slave Journey to an Afro-Baptist Faith*. Westport, Conn.: Greenwood Press, 1979.

———. *The World They Made Together: Black and White Values in Eighteenth-Century Virginia*. Princeton: Princeton University Press, 1987.

Somé, Malidoma. *Of Water and the Spirit: Ritual, Magic, and Initiation in the Life of an African Shaman*. New York: Penguin, 1995.

Southerland, Ellease. "The Influence of Voodoo on the Fiction of Zora Neale Hurston." In *Sturdy Black Bridges: Visions of Black Women in Literature*, edited by Roseann P. Bell, Bettye J. Parker, and Beverly Guy-Sheftell, 172–83. Garden City, N.Y.: Anchor, 1979.

Southern Christian Leadership Conference Newsletter. "Demonstrators Assaulted by Police, Ku Klux Klan." Special St. Augustine Issue, vol. 2, no. 7, June 1964, 1.

———. "Why St. Augustine?" Special St. Augustine Issue, vol. 2, no. 7, June 1964, 12.

Soyinka, Wole. *Death and the King's Horseman*. Ed. Simon Gikandi. New York: Norton, 2003.

———. *Myth, Literature, and the African World*. New York: Cambridge University Press, 1995.

Stapleton, Ashram L. *The Birth and Growth of the Spiritual Baptist Church in Trinidad and Tobago and the Caribbean*. Siparia, Trinidad: Sookdai's Printery, 1983.

Stepto, Robert B. *From Behind the Veil: A Study of Afro-American Narrative*. Urbana: University of Illinois Press, 1979.

Stewart, Dianne M. *Three Eyes for the Journey: African Dimensions of the Jamaican Religious Experience*. New York: Oxford University Press, 2005.

Strachan, Ian. *From Paradise to Plantation*. Charlottesville: University of Virginia Press, 2002.

———. "The Power of the Dead: African Beliefs and Rituals in the Bahamas." *Yinna: The Journal of the Bahamas Association of Cultural Studies* 1 (2000): 62–71.

Sturtevant, William. "Creek into Seminole." In *North American Indians in Historical Perspective*, edited by E. B. Leacock and N. O. Lurie. New York: Random House, 1971.

Swanton, John R. *Myths and Tales of the Southeastern Indians*. Norman: University of Oklahoma Press, 1995.

Tallant, Robert. *Voodoo in New Orleans*. 1946. New York: Collier Books, 1965.

Tate, Allen. *Essays of Four Decades*. Chicago: Swallow, 1968.

Tate, Claudia. *Psychoanalysis and Black Novels: Desire and the Protocols of Race*. New York: Oxford University Press, 1998.

Tesh, Chief Luisah. "The Jambalaya Spirit: Words of Wisdom from Ile Orunmila Oshun." *Sage Woman* 78 (Spring 2010): 47–48.

Testut, Charles. *Le Vieux Saloman; ou une Famille d'esclaves au XIXe siècle*. New Orleans: No. 200 Rue Chartres, 1872.

Thompson, Robert Farris. *Flash of the Spirit*. New York: Vintage, 1983.

Thorsson, Courtney. "Dancing up a Nation: Paule Marshall's *Praisesong for the Widow*." *Callaloo* 30, no. 2 (2007): 644–52.

Toomer, Jean. *Cane*. 1923. New York: Liveright, 1975.

Trouard, Dawn. "Landing in Akron: A Introduction." In *Eudora Welty: Eye of the Storyteller*. Ed. Dawn Trouard. London: Kent University Press, 1989.

Trouillot, Michel-Rolph. *Silencing the Past: Power and the Production of History*. Boston: Beacon Press, 1995.

Turner, Lorenzo Dow. *Africanisms in the Gullah Dialect*. 1949. Ann Arbor: University of Michigan Press, 1973.

Turner, Richard Brent. *Jazz Religion, the Second Line, and Black New Orleans*. Bloomington: University Press, 2009.

Twain, Mark. *The Adventures of Huckleberry Finn*. New York: Penguin, 1994.

Vega, El Inca Garcilaso de la. *The Florida of the Inca*. Edited and translated by John Grier Varner and Jeanette Johnson Varner. Austin: University of Texas Press, 1986.

Viso, Olga M. *Ana Mendieta Earth-Body: Sculpture and Performance, 1972–1985*. New York: Hirshhorn Museum and Sculpture Garden Smithsonian Institution/ Hatje Cantz Publishers, 2004.

Walcott, Derek. *Collected Poems, 1948–1984*. New York: Farrar, Straus and Giroux, 1986.

Walker, Alice. *In Search of Our Mothers' Gardens*. New York: Harcourt Brace Jovanovich, 1983.

———. "In Search of Zora Neale Hurston." *Ms.*, March 1975, 74–79, 85–87.

———. "The Dummy in the Window: Joel Chandler Harris and the Invention of Uncle Remus." In *Living by the Word: Selected Writings, 1973–1987*. New York: Harcourt Brace Jovanovich, 1989. 25–32.

———. *Meridian*. Orlando: Harcourt, 2003.

Wall, A. Cheryl. "Mules and Men and Women: Zora Neale Hurston's Strategies of Narration and Visions of Female Empowerment." In *Critical Essays on Zora Neale Hurston*, edited by Gloria L. Cronin, 53–70. New York: G. K. Hall, 1998.

Ward, Martha. *Voodoo Queen: The Spirited Lives of Marie Laveau*. Jackson: University Press of Mississippi, 2004.

Washington, Teresa. *Our Mothers, Our Powers, Our Texts: Manifestations of Àjé in Africana Literature*. Bloomington: Indiana University Press, 2005.

Weaver, Jace. *That the People Might Live: Native American Literatures and Native American Community*. New York: Oxford University Press, 1997.

Wedel, Johan. *Santeria Healing: A Journey into the Afro-Cuban World of Divinities, Spirits, and Sorcery*. Gainesville: University Press of Florida, 2004.

Weiss, John McNish. *The Merikens: Free Black American Settlers in Trinidad, 1815– 16*. London: McNish and Weiss, 2002.

Welty, Eudora. *The Collected Stories of Eudora Welty*. New York: Harcourt Brace Jovanovich, 1980.

———. *The Eye of the Story: Selected Essays and Reviews*. New York: Random House, 1977.

West, Cornel. *Race Matters*. Boston: Beacon Press, 1993.

Westhoff, Ben. *Dirty South: Outkast, Lil Wayne, Soulja Boy, and the Southern Rappers Who Reinvented Hip-Hop*. Chicago: Chicago Review Press, 2011.

Wilentz, Gay. *Binding Cultures: Black Women Writers in Africa and the Diaspora.* Bloomington: Indiana University Press, 1992.

Will, George. "Leviathan in Louisiana." *Newsweek*, September 12, 2005, 88.

Womack, Craig. Foreword to *Totkv Mocvse / New Fire: Creek Folktales by Earnest Gouge*, edited and translated by Jack Martin et al., ix–xiii. Norman: University of Oklahoma Press, 2004.

———. *Red on Red: Native American Literary Separatism.* Minneapolis: University of Minnesota Press, 1999.

Wylly, Charles Spaulding. *The Seed That Was Sewn in the Colony of Georgia, 1740–1870.* New York: Neall, 1910.

Wylly, William. *A Short Account of the Bahama Islands.* London, 1789.

Yaeger, Patricia. *Dirt and Desire: Reconstructing Southern Women's Writing, 1930–1990.* Chicago: University of Chicago Press, 2000.

Index

abjection: and fluid-stains, 224, 227; and Kristeva, 5; and low spaces, 167, 172; in Marshall, 54–55; and microbial possessions, 184; and Middle Passage, 6, 191; and plantation violence, 24; and submersion, 4, 31, 145

acrolect, 8, 98, 102, 139, 221

Adyái, Miguel, 202

Afro-Cuban Tales (Cabrera), 29–31, 200, 204–6, 207

agency: Afro-creole, 5, 8, 25, 181; appropriations of, 218–19; of blacks in Spanish Florida, 27; and carnival, 148; circum-Caribbean and Haitian, 99, 162; congregational, 41, 62, 64; and creolization, 35–36, 39, 44, 50, 186; crossroads or reciprocal, 37, 119, 141; of the dead, 236; and discursive possessions, 222; initiatory, 14–15, 20, 24, 143; jazz modes of, 114, 118; and musical performance, 66, 78–79, 112–13, 131; and orisha/cosmovisual, 185, 200, 211; rhizomatic, 119–20; subaltern, 118; and Vodou/Voudou, 55, 115; wild, 201; women's, 174, 220

Allen, William Francis, 42

Allewaert, Monique, 5, 8, 175–76, 221

All Saints (Osbey), 141–46

Along This Way (Johnson), 71–74, 76, 82–83, 90

Amelia Island, 59, 89

Andros Island, Bahamas, 19, 83–84, 88–89

apocalypse: Afro-creole sublimation of, 28, 187, 189, 213; and contact-zone violence, 193–94; and global consumerism, 209; and progressive standard time, 222; scriptural programmings of, 226; and Walcott's

"The Gulf," 133; Welty's deferral of, 235–37

Appel, Alfred, 232

Armbrister, Cindy Cartwright, 92

Armstrong, Louis: and culinary representations, 126, 147; modern time, 99; and ritual heat, 118, 130; on second line, 119; *Swing That Music*, 116–17

ashé: as agency or affect, 185, 189, 199; in Marshall, 54, 55; in New Orleans, 137, 152; patina of, 186

assemblages: and aesthetics, 103, 118; of deities, 31; Deleuzian, 37; and ecosystemic interpenetration, 175–76; laws against, 115; in Marshall, 54; and New Orleans, 146, 148, 152, 154, 155; and praise houses, 22, 39; and Spanish fleet system, 187–88. *See also* selfhood and subjectivity; swing

Augustin, Marie, 104–5

author, the, 11–13; death of, 12–13, 27, 222, 237; and ethnography, 208; and folk transculturation, 201, 204; submersion of, 221

authority, 11–13; and the archaic, 178; basilectal, 67, 87, 174, 204, 234; black institutions of, 6, 31, 83, 108, 110, 117; and countercultural resistance, 9, 66, 86, 113, 121; cross-cultural, 24, 32, 104, 114, 235; culinary, 143; and energy production, 52; and fictional avatars, 237; of the folk in Hurston, 159–64, 167–69, 174, 176, 200; from gulfs of knowledge, 68, 231–32; hegemonic, 8, 182, 194, 235, 236; and hoodoo contagion, 224; initiate, 200, 233; of J. W. Johnson, 69; and lowcountry texts, 49, 50, 57, 60–62; orphaning of,

authority (*continued*)
16, 18, 22; and reterritorializations, 84, 87–88, 201; ritual, 32, 41, 80, 114, 119; secular-performative, 82; and sovereignty, 207; submerged, 7, 23, 36–37, 58, 62, 81, 120, 167, 171, 237, 238; surrenders of, 237; and Vodou/Voudou, 99, 115. *See also* autoethnography

Autobiography of an Ex-Colored Man, The (Johnson), 66, 68, 70, 71, 79–81

autoethnography, 12; and Cabrera, 200; and Césaire, 26; and Hurston, 162; and Johnson, 31, 79, 84, 85; and Osbey, 142

Bahamas: black Baptist congregations established, 38–39, 40, 45; broughtupsy, 14; cultural-historical connections with the Gullah/Geechee coast, 41, 73, 75–76, 83–84, 87–90, 92–94; and Florida contact zones, 208; government of, 78; Gulf oil spill, 135; and Hurston, 5, 159, 162, 179; and J. W. Johnson, 68, 72, 73–78, 253n41; literature of, 90–94; Loyalist migrations to, 19, 37; and orphan Kumba narrative, 16; Seminole presence in, 28, 88–89, 196; as tourist paradise, 90–91; wakes and funerals, 75–76

Bailey, Cornelia, 18–19, 43, 89, 94, 143; *God, Dr. Buzzard, and the Bolito Man*, 85–87

Balboa, Silvestre de, 190

Bambara, Toni Cade, 31, 39, 58, 60; *The Salt Eaters*, 59

banana trade: and migration, 125, 167; and radical racism, 113

Baptists: and Afro-creole agency, 8, 83, 231; cemeteries, 43; and civil rights, 197–98; in Hurston, 172, 182, 219; and Jamaican Revival Zion, 44, 60; praise houses, 22, 31, 38–41, 52–53, 87, 232; ring shout performance, 42–43; rites of baptism, 42, 86; rites of seeking, mourning, traveling, 40–41, 86, 232–33; the spread of black Atlantic faith, 19, 39–40, 44–46, 185; virtual praise-housings, 62. *See also* Spiritual Baptists

Barbados, 20, 21, 23, 37

Barthes, Roland, 12–13, 70, 87

Bartram, William, 8, 11, 196–97

basilect, 8; and agency, 181; censorship of, 12, 209; in Chamoiseau, 139, 140; and cosmopolitanism, 9, 109, 221; and creole time-space, 69; and debasilectalization, 89; and Florida, 199; as grounding of creole consciousness, 21, 22, 67; in Hurston, 175, 178; and matrifocality, 220; and New Orleans Creole culture, 102–6 *passim*, 133, 152, 156, 221

Bebelle, Carol, 137, 152

Bechet, Sydney, 26, 103, 114, 117

Benítez-Rojo, Antonio, 5, 28, 190, 191; the armoire's occult prestige, 204; and "a certain kind of way," 187, 213, 223, 227; on music and perspective, 72; on the Spanish Caribbean's "Old Towns" as chronotopes, 186–88

Beoku-Betts, Josephine, 89

Berry, Jason, 152

Bethel, E. Clement, 75

Bethel, Marion, 94; *Guanahani, My Love*, 92–93

Bethel, Mary, 72

Betsch, MaVynne, 89

Bhabha, Homi, 177–78

Biassou, Jorge, 99, 196

Bilali, Salih, 36, 254n91

birthing, 5, 15–16, 36, 56; baptism as initiatory rite of, 3–5; in Dash, 63; and midwifery, 85, 93; rebirthing rites, 100, 225, 233, 236, 237

blood, bleeding, 140, 148, 161, 170; and abjection, 172; and menstrual periodicity, 16–17, 20–22, 194, 208, 212, 215–21, 233; as *pharmakon*, 222–31; and sacrifice, 179, 186, 189, 194, 216–17, 219; as sacrificial currency, 32, 237, 239; vampiric/contagious feeding upon, 216, 224–25

blues, 75; and blue devils, 114–15, 118; and Hurston, 168, 169, 175; and New Orleans, 123, 126, 142, 145

Bois Caïman, 98, 105

Bolden, Buddy, 116

Bone, Martyn, 162, 183

Book of American Negro Spirituals, The (Johnson), 76, 78–79, 81–82 botanica, 184, 189, 193, 200–203

BP Deepwater Horizon oil spill, 101, 127, 135

Brathwaite, Kamau, 21–23, 136, 199

Brazil, 72, 165, 179, 197, 203, 206

Brodber, Erna, 31, 39, 58, 251n115; *Myal*, 60–61

Brooks, David, 134–35, 203–4

Brown, Karen McCarthy, 10, 105, 109, 115, 136, 181

Brown, Katie, 41, 44

Brown, Marie, 111

Brown, Michael, 162

Bryan, Ada, 18

Bryan, Andrew, 40, 83

Budick, Sanford, 11

Burt, Hilma, 117

Bush, George H. W., 134

Bush, George W., 138, 162

Butler, Pierce, 21

Cabeza de Vaca, 11

cabildos de nación, 28, 196

Cable, George Washington, 8, 101–2, 105, 106

Cabrera, Lydia, 32, 189, 216, 237; *Afro-Cuban Tales*, 29–31, 200, 204–6, 207; *Ayapá*, 204, 206; *El monte*, 200–204, 212; and feminine openness to the spirits, 211; and Turtle's truth, 219, 221; and women's becomings, 222

call-and-response: aesthetics of, 118, 211; in Afro-Cuban rites, 185; altar calls, 50, 53, 54; and dissolution of the spectator, 28, 36; in Faulkner, 226; in Hurston, 160; in Indian country, 52, 218; and marriage to otherness, 192; readerly responsibilities and dialogic ethics, 6, 8, 47; and the ring shout, 42; as structure of desire, 52, 130; and swing, 78–83, 187

Campbell, Emory, 89

Cantos to Blood and Honey (Castro), 189–92, 198–99, 209–10

Carby, Hazel, 58, 161, 182–83

carnival: circum-Caribbean influence on Mardi Gras Indians, 113; depictions of black religion as, 39; in Faulkner, 226; Haitian rara, 122; in Julien, 148–49, 150; in New Orleans, 8, 23, 26, 106, 122, 154; Trinidadian, 46, 62, 113

Carpentier, Alejo, 121, 136

Carriacou, 20, 44, 46, 235; fictional and documentary representations of Big Drum/saraca ceremony, 53–57, 63–64

Cartwright, Jerome, "Everything Babylon," 91–92

Cartwright, Keith (authorial reflections and experience): on the Bahamas and Sea Islands, 66–68, 70–71, 93–94, 252n25; on Florida and the practice of Santería, 162, 184–86, 238–39; on New Orleans, 128–29

Cartwright, Thomas and the Boys, 92

Cartwright's, Bahamas, 68, 252n25

Cash Money Records, 137–38

Castellanos, Isabel, 200

Castillo de San Marcos, 188

Castro, Adrian, 32, 213; *Cantos to Blood and Honey*, 189–92, 198–99, 209–10

Catholicism: and the Franco-creole world, 103, 110, 127, 133, 143, 149–50; and praise-house traditions, 46, 62, 63; and the Spanish Caribbean, 27–29 passim, 195, 200

Cat Island, Bahamas, 19, 90, 93

Cenelles, Les, 102, 142

Césaire, Aimé, 126; *Notebook of a Return to the Native Land*, 26–27

Chamoiseau, Patrick, 132, 237; *Texaco*, 139–41, 142–43 passim, 146–47, 151, 230

Charles, Louis, 102, 256n24

Charleston, 17, 19, 37, 73; the dance, 82

Chase, Leah (of Dooky Chase Restaurant), 149, 155, 205

Cherokee, 6, 31

Chickasaw, 5, 28, 233; in Faulkner, 227, 228, 229; in Howe, 217–18

Choctaw, 5, 28, 31, 32, 233; in Howe, 207, 215, 216–18; in New Orleans, 104, 113–14, 152, 154

Chopin, Kate, 31, 230

chronotope: the Charleston as, 82; Congo Square as, 114–15; food as, 147, 154; the fortress colonial city as, 186–87, 189; New Orleans as, 119; ring shout and Ibo Landing as, 50; and spirit

embodiment (*continued*)
  of community, 136; and swing, 78–83;
  and unloosing of mind/body splittings,
  116; and women's gnosis, 220
Emerson, Ralph Waldo, 197
En-ba-dlo, 5, 100–101, 127
Eneas, Cleveland, 73, 90
erotic, the: and call-and-response, 222,
  226; and death rites, 218; in Hurston,
  159–60, 169, 178; in Marshall, 51–53,
  58; and Oya, 165; and taste, 208; and
  Turtle, 130, 153, 154, 155, 205
Erzulie, 51, 122, 143–44, 151, 164
Escobedo, Father Alonso Gregorio de, 188,
  194, 195
Estabrook, Barry, 208
Estévez, Bishop Felipe de Jesus, 28
Exuma, 45

Farquharson, Charles, 19
Faulkner, William, 4, 13, 32, 136, 141, 237;
  Absalom, Absalom!, 4, 241n4; *Intruder
  in the Dust*, 227; "Red Leaves," 227–29;
  The Sound and the Fury, 4, 221–30
Fe Chauffe (ritual heat), 109–10, 115–16,
  118, 127, 217, 220
Florida: agricultural toxicity in, 208; and
  Amer-Indian peoples, 27–28, 193–95,
  218; blacks as culture-brokers in, 195–
  96, 206; as circum-Caribbean creole
  space, 8, 16, 199–200, 213; and Cuban
  authors and culture, 29, 32, 193, 196;
  and French/Spanish conflicts, 193–94;
  and Geechee culture, 19, 36, 37; and
  Hurston, 5, 159, 161–64, 166–67, 174–
  80; and the legacy of J. W. Johnson,
  70–72, 74; Santería in, 165, 202; and
  the Spanish Caribbean, 27–28, 187–89;
  as un-American frontier, 188–89, 208
folk narratives, creole, 24, 179, 216, 238;
  Bahamian orphan tale, 83; Cabrera's
  orphan Sanune, 29–31; Cat Island
  orphan Camille, 93; censorships and
  erasures of, 216, 219–21; Coomba and
  password song, 17–18; "The Good
  Child and the Bad" (on St. Kitts),
  20–21; Hunter and the Buffalo-woman,
  177; Lapin (Rabbit), 106, 138, 179,
  207; Louisiana "Rose and Blanche" 25,

105; "Manbo Cia" 25–26; marriage to
  the devil, 83–84, 254–55n91; mermaid
  tale, 18; "Orphan Boy and Girl and the
  Witches," 177–78; Sansay's Euro-creole
  Coomba tale, 24–25, 26; "The Talking
  Skull," 173–74; Turtle/Tortoise, 153,
  204–8, 263n67; "Why the Waves Have
  Whitecaps," 168; Wolof Kumba tale,
  14–17, 19
Fort Caroline, 188, 193
Fortier, Alcée, 105–6
Fort Mims, 219
Fort Mose, 161, 195–96
Fortune, May, 44
Fossett, Judith Jackson, 130–31
fossils and fossil fuels, 131, 133, 141,
  146, 176

Gaitán, Tata, 167
Garner, Margaret, 123
gated communities: in the Bahamas and
  Sea Islands, 37, 88–89, 91, 94; in
  Florida, 186, 188, 195; and voodoo
  economics, 134
Gédé, 50, 138, 261–62n34
Geechee: and Bahamian culture and
  creolization, 19, 45, 83–84, 88–90,
  92–94, 253n41, 254–55n91; Baptist
  faith and Afro-Christian practices,
  39–47, 232–33; foodways, 73–74;
  language, 35–36, 45, 67, 73, 81, 84,
  85, 89; and literary praise houses,
  31, 35, 47, 57–58; memoirists and
  cultural activists, 85–90; missionaries'
  dismissal of religious practices, 38–39;
  oral narratives and authority, 17–19;
  and Seminole, 88–89, 197; struggles
  to hold on to land and community, 89,
  93–94; wakes, 75–76. *See also* Georgia
  lowcountry
genius or genie, 12–13; in Brathwaite, 23;
  and circum-Atlantic orisha, 185, 222,
  229; négritude as, 27; of New Orleans,
  141; of nonstandard time-space, 32,
  229; and Toomer's "Conversion," 35;
  Turtle as, 206; West African djinn,
  12, 15–17, 59, 150, 185
George, David, 40, 43, 247n19, 248n47
Georgia lowcountry: and Bahamian

Haiti: and carnival, 145; in Césaire, 27; commerce with Louisiana, 112, 113, 147, 151; contributions to jazz, 117, 119–20; earthquake of, 2010, 134–35; emigres to Louisiana, 26, 32, 98–99, 101–8, 115–18, 129; in Faulkner, 4–5, 227; and folk narrative, 16, 24–25, 179, 238; and global Franco-creole colonial connections, 126, 127; Hurston in, 5, 159–61, 163, 166, 182, 212; and "the marvelous real," 121; music of, 211; revolution of, 23–24, 26, 71, 97–99, 182, 196; ritual practices in, 3, 77, 109, 113; as trope for post-Katrina New Orleans, 137; U.S. occupation of, 70, 84, 120

Hall, Gwendolyn Midlo, 24, 218
Hall, Shad, 44
Hamilton, William, 45, 46, 247n19, 249n62
Harris, Joel Chandler, 17–18, 83, 179, 207, 216
Harris, Wilson, 5, 160; on Faulkner, 221; and "the limbo gateway," 7, 10, 12, 35–36, 68, 230; and living fossils, 131; on "submerged authority," 12, 36, 58
Harrison, Donald, Jr., 152
Havana, 148, 233; in Benítez-Rojo, 186–87, 233; and Cabrera, 200–203; colonial Floridians' relocation to, 196; home of Congo Circus, 112; in Julien, 167
Haynes, Mother, 52
Hazel, Alexander, 20–21
Hearn, Lafcadio, 111
Hecaud, Eulalie, 117
hermeneutic circles: counterclockwise movements of, 5; in Dash, 62; earth-centered, 200; Geechee/Bahamian, 76; in Hurston, 164, 181, 183; and ring shout, 67; and stomp grounds, 208; and Voudou, 121, 136
hip-hop, 137–38
hippikat, 3, 58, 116, 119, 138–39 passim, 220–21 passim
Histoire Naturelle des Indes, 193
Ho Chi Minh, 126
Holloway, Karla, 58
hospitality: and Derrida, 138–39; ecosystemic, 140–41; in Julien, 149–50, 155; New Orleanian, 131, 132, 137;

135; in Osbey, 143, 144, 146; ritual modes of in Ifa, 168, 170; and spirit possession, 138–39
Howe, LeAnne, 221, 222; Shell Shaker, 31, 207, 215, 216–18, 238
Hughes, Langston, "Jazzonia," 220
Huguenots, 193–94
Hurbon, Laënnec, 121
hurricanes and storms: in Cabrera, 30; in Florida, 194; in Hurston, 159, 162–64, 166–69; Katrina, 126–27, 130, 132–37, 150–51, 152, 162; in Naylor, 59–60; in Osbey, 145; and Oya, 165, 170, 174–75, 176, 178, 183
Hurston, Zora Neale, 4, 32, 47, 120, 151; and Cabrera, 199–200, 204; and death rites, 171–74; Dust Tracks on a Road, 163–64, 166, 180; and eco-systemic shape-shiftings, 175–81; "How It Feels to Be Colored Me," 166; initiation as Rain-Bringer, 159–70; and J. W. Johnson, 69; "John Redding Goes to Sea," 163; Jonah's Gourd Vine, 163, 166, 169, 171–72, 174, 178, 180, 219; legacy of, 181–83; Moses, Man of the Mountain, 163; Mules and Men, 163, 166, 167–68, 169, 171, 172, 173–74, 175, 176, 181, 199, 204, 207; Seraph on the Suwanee, 164, 168; Tell My Horse, 159, 163, 166, 171, 180, 205; Their Eyes Were Watching God, 4, 5, 118–19, 159–63, 164, 168, 169, 171, 172–73, 174–75, 178, 179, 180, 182, 199, 207, 212, 219, 238; and Vodou Truth, 205, 220, 230
Hyatt, Harry, 166

Ibo Landing: in Dash, 62–63; The Legacy of Ibo Landing, 87–89; in Marshall, 49–50, 53, 56, 57; on St. Simons Island, 88, 93
imagination, cross-cultural, 138, 214
incest, racialized logic of, 223, 225
Indian, American: black/Indian contacts and relations, 5–6, 27–28, 113–14, 195, 206–8, 218–19; in Florida, 179, 188, 195–96, 206; and Geechee relations, 41, 42; and New Orleans Creole culture, 106, 113–14, 153; removal, 6, 28, 197,

polyrhythm: in Faulkner, 228; in Hurston, 160; and pluralistic perspective, 49, 72, 118, 201, 210, 211; and praise-house shouting, 39, 42, 46, 67, 77; in Santería rites, 185, 192; and swing, 78–83, 187

Poro society, 41, 62

Port Royal, South Carolina, 42

possession: as "adoption" 22, 46, 53–54, 61–62, 233–34; becoming mount or horse, 13, 15–16, 115–16, 185, 211; and becoming-subject of Creole City, 146; discursive, 221; and dispossession, 50; in Faulkner, 226, 229, 230; in Howe, 218; hosting alterity, 139, 150, 192; and language, 200; movement beyond self, 27, 120–21; in New Orleans Voudou, 107; in the ring shout, 76–77; and swing, 79–80

Praisesong for the Widow (Marshall), 47–57, 60, 62

Pratt, Mary Louise, 11–12; auto-ethnography, 12

Presley, Elvis, 21

Protestantism: and Afro-Atlantic conversions, 35, 37, 40, 41; hymnals and spirituals, 42; and the ring shout, 43, 49; and Welty, 237; work ethic of, 210

Puerto Rico, 84, 206

Pulaar, 36, 41

Quet, Queen, 87–90, 94

Quimbois, 121

ragtime, 80, 116, 117

Ramos, Miguel "Willie," 165, 189

Raphael, Charles, 112, 113

Rastafarianism, 60, 121

Rawlings, Marjorie Kinnan, 177

Reagan, Ronald, 3, 8, 134, 136

reassembly, 7, 37, 61, 193, 204–8, 209, 216–18

Red Beans and Ricely Yours (Saloy), 147, 153–55

"Red Leaves" (Faulkner), 227–29

Red Shoes, 217, 218

Red Stick Creeks, 219

Reed, Ishmael, 141; *Mumbo Jumbo*, 119–21

Regla de Ocha. *See* Santería

Rhys, Jean, 133; *Wide Sargasso Sea*, 219, 230

Ribault, Jean, 193

Richardson, Riché, 138

ring shout: the Buzzard Lope, 86; censorship of, 78, 220; circle dance in Congo Square, 114; circle dance in Voudou, 110; "Down to the Mire," 35–36, 42, 64; in J. W. Johnson, 76–77; in Marshall, 48–50; in Morrison, 58–59; relations to stomp dance, 219; in the Sea Islands and eastern Caribbean, 19, 35–36, 39, 42–43, 67, 86–87

Roach, Joseph, 43, 106, 260n136

Robertson, Pat, 134

Robeson, Paul, 126

Robichaux, John, 116

Rodriguez-Mangual, Edna M., 29, 201

Rogers, James, 43

rootwork: and Dr. Buzzard, 86; and hoodoo, 122, 142, 166, 171; as Jes Grew, 119–20; as mojo, 106; Mystic Keys Botanica, 93; in the Sea Islands, 60, 63

Roudanez, Jean-Baptiste, 102, 256n24

Rowell, Charles, 132

Russell, Heather, 68

Rymer, Russ, 70–71

sacred, the: and abjection or violence, 6, 65–66, 215; and the naked "truth," 220, 221; and *religare*, 37, 234

sacred groves: armoire as, 204; cemeteries as, 173–74; degeneration of relations to, 229; and *el monte* ("the bush"), 29–31, 186, 188–89, 199–204, 209–10; Gullah/Geechee "seeking" within, 40–41; Ibo Landing as consecrated ground, 49–50, 62–63; in initiation narratives, 25, 29; and memory gardens, 172–74; miniaturized *igbodu*, 203–4, 211; musical grooves productive of, 51, 211, 215; New Orleans as, 152; the Sea Islands as, 37, 87; space of initiation, 6, 13–15, 28; urban, 93, 139, 141, 188–89, 202; violated womb as, 62; Yoknapatawpha as, 227, 229 sacrifice: and the ancestors/the unborn, 170; and *balanse*/balance, 124; and crisis, 215, 216–18, 223, 225, 227–29; and *derechos*, 212; and divination, 168, 170, 172, 174; *ebbo* or *ebo*, 202, 210–11; economy of, 178; in fiction, 60; logic of, 124; in lynching or infanticidal violence, 29, 81; as numinous threshold of transition, 171, 239; of the self, 27, 40–41; and warfare purgations, 194

Saint-Domingue. *See* Haiti

Saloppé, Queen Marie, 112

Saloy, Mona Lisa, *Red Beans and Ricely Yours*, 147, 153–55

Salt Eaters, The (Bambara), 58, 59

Salvaggio, Ruth, 130–31, 152–53, 221

Samuel, Mother, 52, 53

San Agustín de la Nueva Florida (Cuba), 195–96

Sanctified Church, 116–17, 182

Sande society, 41, 62

Sandoval, Gabino, 200, 201

Sandy, Mother Superior, 53

Sanene-Kontron, 31, 246n122

sanguine knowledge, 140, 219–21, 222, 224

San Juan, Puerto Rico, 186

Sansay, Leonora, 24

Santería: altars, 112; bembe for Yemaya, 184–85; in Cabrera, 29–31; in Cuba, 6, 28, 200–204, 209–10; and Florida, 32, 189, 213; and fortress cities, 186, 239; and Hurston, 165, 166, 182; making saint, 221; and New Orleans Voudou, 111, 112; and resistance to Western hegemony, 121; ritual theft in, 235; and Welty, 231

Sapelo Island, Georgia: author's experience of, 67, 185; and Cornelia Bailey, 18, 85–87, 143; and praise-house culture, 41, 43–44; and Thomas Spalding, 84, 254n91

saraka: in Brodber, 61; censorship of, 220; in Dash, 63–64; in Georgia and the Eastern Caribbean, 39, 43–44, 46–47, 67, 248nn53–54; Haitian equivalents, 136; in Marshall, 52, 57; in Morrison, 59; in Senegal, 248n52; and Welty, 235–37; Yoruba equivalents, 170

Savannah: Black Baptists in, 39–40, 44, 83; as creole port-city, 17, 19, 37, 67, 73, 85; Koomba Johnson in, 18

Scribben, Dublin, 42

Scriven, Samuel, 45, 247n19

Seals, Mother Catherine, 160, 182

second-line culture: and Armstrong, 116, 119; and carnivalesque resistance, 138, 139, 145; in Julien, 148, 149, 151–52; and New Orleans's mosaic assemblages, 129

Séjour, Victor, 103, 142

selfhood and subjectivity: composite nature of, 40, 85, 100, 128, 247n27; displacement and reassembly of, 67, 160; in Marshall, 50, 53; and the plural creole "we," 140; vacating the self and recongregation, 76–77, 80, 120–21, 150

Seminole: Cumba among, 28; in Florida, 193, 194, 206, 267n34; and Geechee, 85, 88–89; in Hurston, 161, 162, 179; importance to Afro-creole studies, 5, 32; myth, 195, 201; and narrative-medicine, 208, 216; trade with Cuba and Bahamas, 196–97

Senegal: author's experience in, 44, 66, 129, 185; and Franco-colonial routes, 126, 127, 260n142; in Julien, 147, 148, 151; orphan narratives in, 13–16, 25, 222, 232; presence in Florida, 27; source of Geechee culture, 41; source of Louisiana culture, 23, 24, 102, 103, 106, 111

Seventh Ward of New Orleans, 113, 117, 132, 147–48, 154–55

Shango, 23, 54, 125, 163, 165

shapeshifting: and ancestral mothers, 56; and blockage of white women's powers of, 222; and Hurston, 163, 176–78, 183; and natives to the terrain of, 68; and post-Civil Rights demands, 214

Shell Shaker (Howe), 31, 207, 215, 216–18, 238

shell-shaking: Gulf traditions of, 206, 207, 209, 230; and Howe, 216–19; in New Orleans, 115, 154, 156. *See also* Turtle/Tortoise

Sierra Leone, 19, 21, 39, 43, 85–87

Smith, Bessie, 145, 160, 166

The New Southern Studies

The Nation's Region: Southern Modernism, Segregation, and U.S. Nationalism
by Leigh Anne Duck

Black Masculinity and the U.S. South: From Uncle Tom to Gangsta
by Riché Richardson

Grounded Globalism: How the U.S. South Embraces the World
by James L. Peacock

Disturbing Calculations: The Economics of Identity in Postcolonial Southern Literature, 1912–2002
by Melanie R. Benson

American Cinema and the Southern Imaginary
edited by Deborah E. Barker and Kathryn McKee

Southern Civil Religions: Imagining the Good Society in the Post-Reconstruction Era
by Arthur Remillard

Reconstructing the Native South: American Indian Literature and the Lost Cause
by Melanie Benson Taylor

Apples and Ashes: Literature, Nationalism, and the Confederate States of America
by Coleman Hutchison

Reading for the Body: The Recalcitrant Materiality of Southern Fiction, 1893–1985
by Jay Watson

Latining America: Black-Brown Passages and the Coloring of Latino/a Studies
by Claudia Milian

Finding Purple America: The South and the Future of American Cultural Studies
by Jon Smith

The Signifying Eye: Seeing Faulkner's Art
by Candace Waid

Sacral Grooves, Limbo Gateways: Travels in Deep Southern Time, Circum-Caribbean Space, Afro-creole Authority
by Keith Cartwright